THE SANDINISTAS AND NICARAGUA SINCE 1979

THE SANDINISTAS

AND NICARAGUA

SINCE 1979

EDITED BY
David Close
Salvador Martí i Puig
Shelley A. McConnell

LYNNE
RIENNER
PUBLISHERS

BOULDER
LONDON

Published in the United States of America in 2012 by
Lynne Rienner Publishers, Inc.
1800 30th Street, Boulder, Colorado 80301
www.rienner.com

and in the United Kingdom by
Lynne Rienner Publishers, Inc.
3 Henrietta Street, Covent Garden, London WC2E 8LU

Library of Congress Cataloging-in-Publication Data
The Sandinistas and Nicaragua since 1979 / David Close, Salvador Martí i
Puig, and Shelley A. McConnell, editors.
    p.   cm.
Includes bibliographical references and index.
ISBN 978-1-58826-798-6 (hardcover : alk. paper)
1. Frente Sandinista de Liberación Nacional. 2. Nicaragua—Politics and
government—1979–1990. 3. Nicaragua—Politics and government—1990–
I. Close, David, 1945– II. Martí i Puig, Salvador. III. McConnell, Shelley A.
    JL1619.A52S36   2011
    324.27285'075—dc22
                                                          2011011375

British Cataloguing in Publication Data
A Cataloguing in Publication record for this book
is available from the British Library.

Printed and bound in the United States of America

∞   The paper used in this publication meets the requirements
       of the American National Standard for Permanence of
       Paper for Printed Library Materials Z39.48-1992.

5 4 3 2 1

Contents

THE SANDINISTAS AND NICARAGUA SINCE 1979

1

The Sandinistas and Nicaragua Since 1979

David Close and Salvador Martí i Puig

THIS BOOK IS ABOUT THE SANDINISTA NATIONAL LIBERATION Front (Frente Sandinista de Liberación Nacional, or FSLN) and how it has affected Nicaragua since the party's founding in 1961.[1] Although the guerrilla front–turned–political party has governed the country for just over a quarter of its fifty-year existence, from 1979 to 1990 and since January 2007, the Sandinistas have influenced their country's evolution and general well-being far more than their relatively short time in office would suggest. The reasons are manifold.

They start with the determination of the United States throughout the 1980s to destroy the Sandinista Revolution, even if that meant destroying Nicaragua, too. Clearly the FSLN government had no control over US policy toward it, short of saying "uncle" and disbanding. Nevertheless, a revolutionary regime that began promisingly in 1979 ended in 1990 with a mixed record: significant social achievements, the institutionalization of electoral democracy, and a democratized political culture on the one hand; but a polarized and war-torn society, a ravaged economy, and a set of lame-duck laws that tarnished the FSLN's reputation on the other.

During its years out of power (1990–2007), the party repeatedly struck deals with the governments of the day that served the Sandinistas' short-term objectives perhaps more than the longer-term interests of the nation. Obviously, the three administrations with which the Sandinistas dealt— those of Presidents Violeta Chamorro, Arnoldo Alemán, and Enrique Bolaños—shared their opponents' self-interested perspective and thus share the responsibility for Nicaragua's fate since 1990. Presumably, any party that had either governed a country or been the biggest opposition party for over thirty years would have to defend a similar record. However, the FSLN was not just any party, and Nicaragua's history shaped what it is.

1

Nicaraguan History: A Primer

Since independence in 1821, Nicaragua has traveled a troubled political road.[2] Although none of the five Central American republics has had an uneventful past (no nation anywhere has), Nicaragua's has been notably violent and unstable. Its first four decades of independence were marked by nearly continuous civil war between Liberals from León and Conservatives from Granada. That cycle of violence ended only in 1858, after a dictatorship imposed by William Walker, a US mercenary brought in by the Liberals to aid their cause, was defeated by the massed armies of the other Central American states. Then came Nicaragua's golden age, when it was known as the Switzerland of Central America. The *treinteno* (thirty years of Conservative rule) brought stability to the country through a pact among regional elites, but it also carried with it a certain political and economic stasis. As often happens in pacted political systems, the emerging elite of *cafeteleros* (coffee growers from around Managua and from the mountains in the country's center), who wanted a share of political power commensurate with their economic importance, needed a revolution to get it.

José Santos Zelaya was a Liberal caudillo who ruled from 1893 to 1909 and returned Nicaragua to strongman rule. Not only did he dominate national politics, but like his predecessors in other countries, he sought to make himself the suzerain of all Central America. This naturally disquieted Washington, especially when Zelaya, having failed to win the interoceanic canal for Nicaragua, offered German and Japanese interests the rights to develop a competitor to Panama. The result was a US-backed revolution mounted by the Conservatives. Zelaya fell, but Nicaragua entered another cycle of civil warfare that lasted until 1927. Further, from 1910 to 1934, the United States maintained a contingent of marines in Nicaragua, almost continuously. It was to fight this frankly imperial presence that Augusto César Sandino, a Liberal general in the civil war, refused a peace brokered by Washington and took to the hills to wage guerrilla war.[3]

From 1927 until 1934, when the United States withdrew its troops, Sandino fought the marines and the Nicaraguan National Guard, a new national military force that the United States had established in Nicaragua as a way to put an end to party-based civil wars. In 1934, Sandino was invited to Managua to meet with then-president Juan Bautista Sacasa. However, the national guard intercepted the guerrilla leader and executed him, supposedly on the orders of the guard's commander, Anastasio Somoza García. By 1936, Somoza had ousted Sacasa, his wife's uncle, and then succeeded in being elected president. Thus began forty-three years of family dictatorship that ended only when another guerrilla force bearing Sandino's name brought down the Somoza dynasty.

The new Sandinistas, the FSLN, began as a guerrilla organization. Formed by Carlos Fonseca, German Pomares, and Tomás Borge in 1961, the Sandinistas were one of a larger class of revolutionary organizations that drew their inspiration from the success of Fidel Castro's Cuban guerrillas. Like their model, the Sandinistas adopted the *foco* theory that Che Guevara propounded, based on his experience in the Cuban Revolution.[4] *Foquismo* held that armed struggle waged by small groups of committed revolutionary guerrillas, operating in rural areas, would build support among the people and lead to the conquest of power. Although this modified version of Mao Zedong's strategy of people's war had astounding success in Cuba, bringing the *fidelistas* to power in less than three years, it failed elsewhere. Even the Sandinistas, the only other revolutionary guerrilla movement to take power in Latin America, had to move beyond the *foco* theory to ensure their revolution's triumph.

From 1961 to 1979, the Sandinistas fought the Somoza family dictatorship. That the Somozas had created an intergenerational dictatorship (the father and his two sons ruled Nicaragua for forty-three years) demonstrated both the dictators' political skill and the inability of Nicaraguans to displace the family. Although there were attempts to unseat the Somozas, they were repelled.[5] Until 1974, the FSLN had no better luck than its predecessors. However, that year the guerrillas staged a magnificent *coup de théâtre,* raiding a Christmas party at the house of one of Somoza's cousins, netting a bundle of high-profile hostages that just missed including the US ambassador, and setting the scene for negotiations that saw the guerrillas leave unhindered and wealthier.

This high note, however, was soon followed by a very low one. In 1975 the organization split into three factions, or tendencies, as they became known. The oldest, and the one that purged the others, was the Prolonged People's War (GPP), whose members were Bayardo Arce, Tomás Borge, and Henry Ruiz. GPP emphasized the "patient accumulation of forces" and focused on rural guerrilla warfare. The second faction was the Proletarian Tendency (TP, or *proles*), whose members were Luis Carrión, Carlos Nuñez, and Jaime Wheelock. It favored an urban guerrilla strategy and stressed organizing in factories and poor neighborhoods. Last to form were the Insurrectionary Tendency (the Terceristas, or the third group), whose members were Daniel Ortega, Humberto Ortega, and Victor Tirado. They sought a multiclass alliance that would make possible a massive insurrection and rapid overthrow of the dictatorship.

Schisms along ideological and strategic lines are not uncommon among radical movements. Failing to take power or secure important objectives leads to a search for better alternatives that can cause a movement to fracture or even destroy it. However, the Sandinistas were lucky enough to have had Fidel Castro mediate a resolution among the three tendencies that saw each group naming three of its *comandantes guerrilleros* (guerrilla commanders) to a nine-person National Directorate that became the Frente Sandinista's governing body in 1979 and coordinated the guerrillas' efforts, albeit for only a few months before the dictatorship fell.

Despite being divided, the Frente remained very active. The January 1978 assassination of anti-Somoza newspaper publisher Pedro Joaquín Chamorro produced spontaneous rioting and was in many ways the spark that set in motion the insurrectional stage of the Nicaraguan Revolution. In August of that year, the Sandinistas staged a raid on Nicaragua's Congress that netted the revolutionaries tremendous publicity, the release of prisoners, money, the reading of their manifesto over the radio, and unimpeded transport out of the country. June 1979 saw the FSLN declare the beginning of its final offensive, a drive that ended with the flight of the Somozas and the seizure of power by the Sandinistas on July 19, 1979.

The First Sandinista Government, 1979–1990

Revolutionary regimes, whatever the character of their revolution, all have certain traits in common. First, they have vision of what the society they want to build should look like, and they have a road map that they believe will get them there. Second, revolutionaries are not patient. They want to set to work immediately to take apart the old and lay the foundations for the new. Further, their impatience generally inclines them to be intolerant of those who do not share their aspirations, although some revolutionaries seem more disposed than others to persuade and convert rather than coerce. Finally, there are few revolutionaries who want piecemeal changes; the norm, in fact, is to remake humanity or at least cure it of its current depravity.

We acknowledge that the foregoing is rather broad and that every revolution will have its own traits, yet we believe that it captures the essence of what a movement set up to revolutionize society, to alter radically its structure of power and prestige, wants to do. It is in regard to that revolutionizing society that the FSLN found itself in a rather different situation than other revolutionaries. During the last few years of guerrilla struggle, the Frente, especially the Terceristas, recruited all manner of anti-Somocista forces into their insurrectionary coalition. This extended to the radical Christians, inspired by liberation theology, and even to the bourgeoisie. Unconventional behavior for any Marxist-leaning, revolutionary organization, these pacts may have been produced by pragmatic calculation, but they left the revolutionary state with non-Marxist and anti-Marxist allies.

Further, the FSLN promised to deliver greater political pluralism and a mixed economy to Nicaraguans. In the revolution's initial phase, pluralism—the existence of centers of political power that are independent of the state—was limited by the Frente's vanguardist outlook. Revolutionary vanguards normally take control of the state as part of the spoils of victory and then claim to monopolize the right to govern by arguing that only they know how to build the revolution. What results is a tutelary regime of the left that shares with its rightist counterparts a reluctance to let citizens choose their own political futures. The Sandinistas, however, had a more moderate position, accepting that allies could share in governing but could not actually govern. Of course, the revolutionary government abandoned this stand forever before the 1984 elections.

The FSLN's moderation extended to economic policy. Instead of preaching root-and-branch socialism, which eliminates all manifestations of private enterprise, the revolutionaries proposed a mixed economy.[6] To be sure, the public sector would dominate and direct economic development, but even large private firms could keep operating and make money. And the *pulperías,* the mom-and-pop stores that sell almost everything, also kept operating.

Nevertheless, the FSLN set to work quickly to consolidate its hold on power. Within a year, on the Governing Junta of National Reconstruction (JGRN), the official executive and most senior administrative positions (e.g., ministers and directors) were held by Sandinistas. In addition, the composition of the Council of State, a weak, unelected representative body, was changed to give the revolutionaries more seats than a pre-triumph agreement had granted them. Yet this attempt to monopolize state power halted and went into reverse after only three years.

Although the Sandinistas resisted holding elections until 1984, they changed their position on elections dramatically in 1982 with the introduction of a law governing the formation and functions of political parties (see Chapter 6). These laws, found in many countries, set the criteria a party must meet to be recognized as an official party with the right to run in elections, receive state funding for its campaigns, and so on. As introduced into the Council of State, the Sandinistas' law was typically Leninist: it allowed other parties to run for office as long as they did not promote the return of Somocismo. But they would never be allowed to govern. That right was reserved for the vanguard, the FSLN.

However, the version of the law that passed gave any registered party the right to govern if it could win. Because the FSLN controlled the council, we can presume that it was the government's will. What changed the revolutionaries' view of elections was probably a combination of factors. One was pressure from European social democrats, who were important aid donors. Another was the government's need to boost its conventional democratic credentials in the face of an increasingly bloody, US-financed counterrevolutionary war. Finally, the Sandinistas doubtlessly believed that they were unbeatable and could maintain themselves as Nicaragua's natural governors. Naming two JGRN members to head the FSLN's ticket—Comandante Daniel Ortega as the party's presidential candidate and Sergio Ramírez as his running mate—suggested that the Sandinistas were comfortable running on their record.

Deciding to put power at stake in open and what proved to be honestly run elections marked a turning point for the revolutionary regime. Regimes define the bases of a system's legitimacy, and in Nicaragua after 1984 the latter would no longer be based on the revolutionary triumph of the FSLN but on winning elections. In addition, the revolutionaries henceforth would be accountable to an electorate of all citizens, not just to history or the revolutionary classes of workers and peasants. These changes would necessarily alter the operational style of the revolutionary party, which would have to adapt to the exigencies of electoral competition. The party would not, however, have to abandon its vertical, top-down style because there was no reason to open the organization's structures to permit greater participation by the grass roots.

The results of the first elections held under a Sandinista government confirmed their popularity: the party romped home with two-thirds of the vote in both the presidential and National Assembly races.[7] Even better from the revolutionaries' point of view, the electoral system was weighted to benefit small parties; thus the FSLN saw all six parties that ran against it gain seats in the new legislature, presenting a real but manageable opposition.[8] This set the stage for what the Sandinistas called "the institutionalization of the revolution," which meant borrowing much of the machinery of liberal democracy and using it to achieve social transformation. In practice this took the form of a president-centered system that gave Daniel Ortega substantially greater power than the other members of the National Directorate of the FSLN.

In the end, the seemingly endless counterinsurgency campaign Managua had to wage against the counterrevolutionaries (formally called the Nicaraguan Resistance, but more usually just the Contra or contras) took an estimated 30,000 lives on both sides, wrecked the economy, and left Nicaraguans skeptical about the Ortega administration's ability to set things right, mainly because the US government showed no signs that it would cease harassing a reelected Sandinista administration. Thus on election day, February 25, 1990, Daniel Ortega and his Sandinistas saw Nicaraguans hand a 13-point (54 percent to 41 percent) victory to Violeta Chamorro and the National Union of the Opposition (Union Nacional Opositora, or UNO). Although the Sandinistas recognized their defeat, becoming only the second party to do so in Nicaraguan history, Ortega promised to fight on and to "govern from below."

Despite being rejected by the voters, the FSLN made at least four notable contributions to Nicaraguan democracy. To begin with, they overthrew four decades of dictatorship and personal rule. Second, although the Sandinistas' array of social and economic reforms—to agriculture and land tenure, housing, health, and education—did not survive long after the change of governments, they were important first steps toward greater social and economic equality. Harder to measure but plausibly more important in the long run was the revolutionary government's empowerment of ordinary Nicaraguans as it pursued the "logic of the majority." The political culture became less deferential, and men and women of humble origin began taking their places among the governors of their country. Finally, the Sandinistas abided by the constitution they drafted and adopted in 1987 and handed over power when they lost the 1990 elections. Although their successor, Violeta Chamorro, was the president who made the construction of an *estado de derecho* (a political system operating under the rule of law) a central part of her discourse, it was the revolutionaries who first acted in accordance with the rule of law's key principle that no one, not even the state, is above the law.[9]

The Right Regnant, 1990–2006

From the Sandinistas' revolutionary triumph until at least 2006, Nicaraguan politics aligned itself into two blocs: Sandinistas and anti-Sandinistas. Further, during the first few years of the swing to the right after 1990, both groups housed two distinct factions, one accommodationist and the other maximalist. The accommodationists accepted working within the limits that the context placed on them. Among the anti-Sandinistas, this meant acknowledging that the FSLN was a significant political force that was not going to disappear overnight and that attempting to hasten its demise through persecution would produce violence and instability. On the Sandinista side, accommodationists believed that the days of heroic transformational politics had ended for the foreseeable future and that the FSLN should fulfill its duty to Nicaragua's poor majority through institutional changes that protected gains already won.

Maximalists naturally saw things differently. In the anti-Sandinista camp, they were inclined to take their electoral victory as their license to turn all the forces of the state against their antagonists and annihilate them. Politics for maximalists is always a zero-sum game, but in Nicaragua, as in too many other countries in Latin America and the Third World generally, all politics had this winner-take-all quality. As viewed from the opposition's side, maximalism had different qualities. Sandinistas of this persuasion wanted to maintain the FSLN's top-down, Leninist structure, strengthen the hand of the party leader, and ensure that the nation's president remained unfettered by accountability and transparency. In fact, maximalists of both partisan schools shared the last two objectives.

In the end, the maximalists captured both groups. Daniel Ortega and his followers drove from the party ranks the accommodating reformers aligned with Sergio Ramírez in 1994; others have since joined the Sandinista political diaspora. Arnoldo Alemán, president of the republic from 1996 to 2001, applied the same iron grip to his party, the Constitutionalist Liberal Party (Partido Liberal Constitutionalista, PLC), but he did not pursue his one-time jailers with the zeal many expected. Rather he found a way to collaborate with Ortega by forging an agreement (the Pact) between their parties that aimed to give them unshakeable control of the Nicaraguan state.[10] So strong has this Pact proven, even if for reasons unforeseen when it was formed, that it effectively hobbled Alemán's successor, Enrique Bolaños (2001–2006), also of the PLC, and has survived Ortega's return as chief executive. Although the Sandinistas lost three straight electoral battles, they kept fighting the political war and then returned to power.

The Administration of Doña Violeta Chamorro, 1990–1996

Her full name is Doña Violeta Barrios de Chamorro, but she has always been known by her married name, Chamorro, or more commonly simply as Doña Violeta, in keeping with the Nicaraguan custom of referring to presidents by their first name. Before routing the FSLN in 1990 and becoming president, she was not a politician. Her fame derived from the fact that she was the widow of Pedro Joaquín Chamorro, the anti-Somoza newspaper publisher who was murdered by the dictator's thugs in 1978. Mrs. Chamorro served briefly as a member of the first JGRN and then withdrew from public life until she was recruited to head the UNO's ticket. Chamorro won this honor because she was uncontroversial and not abrasive, and thus a figure around whom a majority of Nicaraguans could rally.

Chamorro's administration was marked by managing a triple transition: from a revolutionary to an orthodox democracy; from a statist, transformational political economy to an equally transformational neoliberal one; and from a polarized society to one that was more united. Although she fell short of total success on all counts, Doña Violeta came closer with the first and second than with the third. Perhaps her greatest accomplishment, however, was to show Nicaraguans that it was possible to govern without proposing pharaonic projects or harassing your opponents too much.

The Sandinistas used those six years to shake off the effects of an unexpected electoral drubbing, reassert the party's traditional identity as a revolutionary organization, and develop an oppositional style they would use until they regained power. The essence of that style was to stage contentious, disruptive, extraparliamentary movement politics (protest, at times accompanied by violence) while making deals with the government. This worked with the Chamorro administration because the president did not have majority backing in the National Assembly. When dealing with the Alemán government, it was more a matter of the two leaders—who were both electoral caudillos and thus practitioners of boss-style politics—seeing eye-to-eye on basic issues like the need for extensive, unaccountable presidential power. Only President Bolaños was unable to benefit from deals with the FSLN, though that was mainly the result of Washington discouraging the president from dealing with the White House's historic enemies.

The Administration of Arnoldo Alemán Lacayo, 1996–2001

Arnoldo Alemán was the perfect adaptation of classical Latin American caudillo politics to the demands of electoral democracy. He made the PLC his personal machine, ignored or revised the law when it constrained him, and made a deal with Daniel Ortega in 2000 that has shaped Nicaraguan politics ever since. Alemán grew up in the old Somocista Nationalist Liberal Party (PLN) (Partido Liberal Nacionalista) and was jailed by the Sandinista government in the late 1980s for opposing the government too vigorously. His entry onto the national scene came in 1990, when he was elected mayor of Managua. As the capital's chief executive, Alemán drew national attention for his "can do" attitude, shown mostly in his constant work on the city's roads. He became part of the PLC's rebuilding project and emerged as the party's standard-bearer in 1996. Like Chamorro before him, Alemán comfortably beat Daniel Ortega, who is still the only person to have topped an FSLN ticket, although it took a nearly direct endorsement from Cardinal Miguel Obando y Bravo, archbishop of Managua, to ensure the Liberals' victory.

Although Alemán had been a committed anti-Sandinista, he quickly found ways to work with his old nemesis Daniel Ortega. The first installment in this project involved settling a property law concerning the disposition of land and houses expropriated by the revolutionary government.

But the crowning glory of the Alemán-Ortega/Liberal-Sandinista venture was the Pact.

Begun in 1999 and concluded a year later, the Pact was the latest install-ment in a long-running Nicaraguan political melodrama. In a pact, a govern-ment offers its principal opposition party a deal in which the latter accepts its subordinate status in return for "quotas of power," which in practice has meant access to public sector jobs. The logic behind pacts was always that the op-position knew that the government would win elections by fraud, so the smart thing to do was take the jobs, use them for your supporters, and keep your party alive. However, the advent of a relatively clean electoral process changed the nature of pacting. Now there would be competition during elections, whose outcome would determine not only which party controlled government but also the relative weight of the Sandinistas and Liberals in appointed posts. These two dominant parties would collude to exclude others. Between elections, decisionmaking often would take place outside formal institu-tions, through negotiation between the two caudillos, Ortega and Alemán.

The content of the 2000 Pact included constitutional amendments and changes to ordinary statutes. In both cases, the reforms aimed to strengthen the executive at the expense of other parts of government, reducing presi-dential accountability, turning nonpartisan administrative agencies into party strongholds, and reshaping the electoral system to make the PLC and FSLN Nicaragua's only significant parties in perpetuity. Although the jury is still out on the last count, the Pact achieved its other objectives.

The Administration of Enrique Bolaños Geyer, 2001–2006

President Bolaños began his term on a high note. He charged his predeces-sor with defrauding the Nicaraguan state of over $100 million. Even more, his government was able to secure a conviction that handed former president Alemán a twenty-year sentence. After that, however, things fell apart. By the time he left office, Bolaños faced a political system increasingly respond-ing to the influence of Daniel Ortega, whose official role was limited to the assembly seat he received for again being the presidential runner-up.[11]

Things could have turned out differently. At first, Ortega and the FSLN supported the administration in its pursuit of the Sandinistas' Pact partner: it was a Sandinista judge, named to the case by a Sandinista member of the Supreme Court of Justice (CSJ), who presided over Alemán's trial. How-ever, after a visit from the US secretary of state in 2003, the president began turning away from the one-time revolutionaries. Shortly thereafter, in 2004, the National Assembly approved a constitutional amendment that radically reduced presidential powers. Bolaños refused to publish the amendments, required for them to have the force of law, which led the assembly to investigate the president for alleged violation of campaign finance laws. In the end, an agreement was reached that saw the amendments approved but not enacted until after Bolaños completed his term.[12]

While the president was running the gauntlet set up by the Sandinistas and the PLC, which remained in Alemán's control, Nicaragua's party system began showing signs of change. In 2005, what had been for fifteen years a stable two-party system (Sandinista versus anti-Sandinista) suddenly saw the two main parties split, offering the chance for a four-way race. Combining this new pattern of competition with a Pact-based amendment to the electoral law that allowed a candidate to be elected president with 35 percent of the vote, providing there was at least a 5-point edge over the second-place candidate, was enough to bring Daniel Ortega the presidency again after a sixteen-year absence.

The Second Sandinista Administration

This is necessarily a brief and tentative treatment. It sketches how Ortega and the FSLN broke their electoral losing streak at three and retook the reins of government by winning 38 percent of the vote in the 2006 general elections. Then it offers what we believe is a sufficient overview of the Ortega administration's first years back in power to give a sense of the path it is laying out for the country. In particular, it notes the president's governing style, the direction of the administration's domestic policy, and the cut of its foreign affairs.

Regaining Office

Becauses Shelley McConnell examines the 2006 elections systematically in Chapter 6, we will just highlight two major themes. First, those elections produced an at least temporary realignment of the Nicaraguan party system. Two new contenders for national power emerged—the Sandinista Renewal Movement (Movimiento Renovador Sandinista, or MRS) on the left[13] and the Nicaraguan Liberal Alliance (Alianza Liberal Nicaragüense, or ALN) on the right. Each abandoned the old structure of Sandinistas versus anti-Sandinistas to protest the Alemán-Ortega Pact and thus gave Nicaraguan politics a different dimension. For one election, anyway, questions of probity, accountability, and governing style would compete with attitudes toward the Sandinista Revolution in defining people's votes.

Second, the Pact wrought an electoral modification (another structural factor). Although Nicaragua's politics have been resolutely two-party since independence, third parties have been part of the mix. Though none had ever drawn enough support to deny the winning presidential candidate a majority of votes cast, in 1996 the presence of other parties in the race had translated into a plurality legislative victory for the winning Liberals instead of a majority. Thus some provision for a presidential runoff was prudent. The provision adopted in 2000, however, was unusual: it set 40 percent, or 35 percent with a 5-point margin over the runner-up, as the thresholds for avoiding a second round of elections.[14] The latter of these was sought by the FSLN, whose share of the vote seemed set at around 40 percent. Although the amendment looked pointless when approved, it decided the 2006 election in Daniel Ortega's favor.

Part of what gave the Frente a chance was a change in Nicaragua's party system that put at least a temporary end to the polarized dynamic that had pitted the FSLN against the anti-Sandinistas. That system had produced landslide victories for the right in 1990, 1996, and 2001. The party realignment in 2006 saw four competitors seeking the public's support: the FSLN, two Liberal parties—the PLC of Arnoldo Alemán, whose standard-bearer was José Rizo, and the anti-Alemán ALN led by Eduardo Montealegre—and the anti-Ortega but progressive MRS that had formed from a sizable FSLN splinter group.[15] This produced three possible breakdowns: (1) the FSLN against all others, which would be a tweaking of the old bipolar system to let in the MRS on the anti-Sandinista side; (2) the left, meaning the two Sandinista parties FSLN and MRS, versus the right, meaning the two Liberal groups PLC and ALN; or (3) the pro-Pact parties, FSLN and PLC, against the anti-Pact ALN and MRS.

In Nicaragua's first serious four-way electoral campaign, the FSLN adopted a cautious stance. It appeared to have banked on doing nothing either to alienate its loyalists or to frighten undecideds into turning out and voting to ensure the Sandinistas' defeat. To this end, Ortega skipped the candidates' debate, spoke in generalities about the grave problems of poverty facing Nicaragua but said little about how he proposed to fix them, and, to neutralize the Catholic Church hierarchy that had opposed him in past elections, ordered the FSLN contingent in the National Assembly to support a bill criminalizing even therapeutic abortion (see Chapter 8). Moreover, as in the two previous campaigns, the Sandinista Hymn, which has the line, "We fight against the Yankee, the enemy of humanity," was dropped in favor of gentler tunes; this time they chose John Lennon's "Give Peace a Chance." This reflected the influence of Ortega's wife, Rosario Murillo, a well-known poet, who was his de facto campaign manager. Her strategy worked.

The final count of Nicaragua's 2006 election showed Daniel Ortega winning the presidency with 38 percent of the vote. The two Liberal parties divided 55 percent almost evenly between them, and the MRS trailed with 6 percent. Viewed from the first perspective above, the FSLN versus everyone else, the vote went 3 to 2 against Ortega. He won but could expect an uphill fight that would require careful compromises on his part to get his program approved. If the angle is left versus right, the outcome is 45 percent for the two Sandinista parties to 55 percent for the Liberals, giving Ortega a larger minority. However, if the Alemán-Ortega Pact is the focus, thus viewing the results in terms of how a party has governed and proposes to govern, Ortega is much more comfortable: 66 percent of the vote went to the candidates of parties committed to unaccountable hyper-presidentialism. In this view, that is, Nicaraguans voted 2 to 1 for top-down, personalistic politics. The first four years of the Ortega administration suggest that this latter perspective is the most accurate, though on some issues Ortega has faced a united opposition in the legislature.

Daniel Ortega Returns to the Presidency

After being inaugurated in January 2007, Daniel Ortega followed the path laid by George W. Bush six years earlier, abandoning conciliation and beginning to govern as if he were the landslide winner instead of a minority president. In each case, brazenness worked. Both presidents gathered around them a cadre of personal loyalists, Ortega outdoing Bush by making his wife Rosario Murillo, who had managed Daniel's campaign, his prime minister in all but name. Actually, the Nicaraguan president may have surpassed the former US leader in his efforts to construct a firewall around himself and his administration. Each president increasingly concentrated power in his office and became increasingly unresponsive to criticism from outside his administration. However, Ortega may have outdone Bush when he arguably resorted to fraud to let the FSLN win Nicaragua's 2008 municipal elections by a massive margin and then put young toughs onto the street in party colors—no longer red and black but a deliciously bright pink—to repress those who protested the results.

One should bear in mind that Ortega's second government is part of a broader movement that is led by President Hugo Chávez of Venezuela and that takes its name—Bolivarian—from the revolutionary regime he is endeavoring to build. Besides Chávez and Ortega, Bolivia's Evo Morales and Ecuador's Raphael Correa are also Bolivarians. Ortega, Morales, and Correa all received assistance, direct or indirect, for their election wins from Chávez. The four share, first, an outlook. They are radical democrats, seeking a peaceful transition to a socialism that offers a significant place for private enterprise, rather like the Sandinista model of the 1980s. In addition, they share a model for governing that includes an extremely strong president with a populist approach who deals directly with his supporters. It is personalist rule adapted to the requirements of electoral democracy. It is also a format well suited to a government seeking thorough and rapid political change, drawing comparisons (both nervous and supportive) to the transformative agenda and governance style practiced by the revolutionary Sandinista government of the 1980s.

Yet Ortega differs from the other Bolivarians in three important respects. First, the other three promised big changes and spelled out what those changes would be in their campaigns, whereas Ortega waffled through the 2006 race. Second, Ortega is very much a plurality president, and one might call him a minority president to stress that five out of every eight Nicaraguans voted against him; Chávez, Correa, and Morales won big majorities and then gained similar majorities in later votes as well.[16] Finally, Ortega must count on the Pact and Arnoldo Alemán; without those he would be in a 3 to 2 minority in the National Assembly and unable to pass legislation.

In the first four years of his second administration, President Daniel Ortega has changed Nicaragua's political trajectory. Never an ideal liberal constitutional democracy, between 1984 and 2007 Nicaragua was nevertheless a functioning electoral democracy. Although the nation's electoral machinery did not always work smoothly, published election results were broadly accepted as reflecting the actual distribution of voters' preferences. More importantly, after 1990 violence figured far less prominently as a political instrument than it had in the past (see Chapter 3). One could reasonably be optimistic about Nicaragua's chances to become a political system in which the rule of law (a government of laws, not of people) prevailed and political tolerance reigned. In 2011 such prospects seem more distant, due in no small measure to how President Ortega has ruled.

Since assuming the presidency in January 2007, Ortega has both broken new ground and continued old practices in his approaches to governing (organizing and applying state power) and governance (coordinating the state's actions with those of nonstate groups—parties, interest groups, civil society, and the citizenry). In itself this is unexceptional: every president and prime minister does the same. From the past, Ortega carries forward the president-centered, highly partisan politics seen in his first administration and in the Alemán government. In addition, the current president's foreign policy continues the practice of allying with a greater power that can offer material aid. In the past this great ally was either Washington or Moscow, but now it is Caracas (see Chapters 11 and 12). Finally, the second

Ortega government follows the economic policy path blazed by its conservative predecessors by adhering to the strictures required to qualify for loans from the International Monetary Fund (IMF).

Yet what is new, at least what deviates from the path laid down between 1984 and 2006, matters more. Here the most significant break with the past is the Ortega government's rediscovery of actively redistributive social policy (outlined in Chapters 9 and 10). Less positive but perhaps even more important for Nicaragua's future are the administration's return to using violence and intimidation as instruments of rule, seen after the 2008 municipal elections, and its taking constitutional manipulation to unprecedented heights. Since its adoption in 1987, Nicaragua's constitution has undergone three sets of significant amendments that substantially changed the relationships between the branches of government or between state and citizen. This by itself suggests that there is either serious and continuing conflict over the nature of the constitution, and hence over the Nicaraguan state itself, or that sitting governments amend the constitution to meet short-term needs; and the two are not mutually exclusive. However, when in 2009 the Nicaraguan Supreme Court's Constitutional Division issued an injunction declaring that the no-immediate-reelection clause of the country's constitution (Article 147a) did not apply to Daniel Ortega (see Chapter 5), it may have signaled the end of constitutional government in Nicaragua, at least for the time being.

Conclusion

In just over three decades since the 1979 Revolution, the Sandinistas, Nicaragua, and indeed the world have all changed greatly. The FSLN has matured as a political institution, having governed, known electoral defeat and life as a parliamentary opposition, and then regained the reins of power. Most importantly, the one-time movement, now a party, has come to be dominated by its leader Daniel Ortega to a degree unimaginable in 1979. Moreover, the second Ortega administration shows signs of concentrating power in the executive and governing heedless of its opponents, who outnumber it three to two, reflecting either a shrewd strategy or a reckless gamble.

It is worth noting that the Sandinistas' return to office corresponds with the waning of the Washington Consensus, the neoliberal economic policy prescription regnant through most of the party's time in opposition. Further, it occurred when Washington's foreign policy was oriented elsewhere and it was content to give even its old Sandinista foe a bit of space, which was definitely not the case in 1979. And it came at a time when Venezuela's

President Hugo Chávez had money to spend to support his allies abroad, among whose number one counts Daniel Ortega. The stars were aligned much more favorably for Ortega and the FSLN in the first decade of the twenty-first century than they were in the eighth decade of the twentieth. And now in 2011, it appears that Daniel Ortega is well positioned to win a third term in office, even though it is constitutionally prohibited. That is the reality the contributors to this book seek to explain.

Organization of the Book

Following this introductory chapter, Chapters 2, 3, and 4 provide historical context and introduce some of the key political actors. Chapter 2, by Salvador Martí i Puig, considers the trajectory of the FLSN from its founding to the present. Martí argues that the party never outgrew its clandestine, revolutionary roots, preserving a top-down command structure that both limited its policymaking capacity and facilitated the concentration of power in the hands of Daniel Ortega, its historic leader. In Chapter 3, David Close takes a similar look at the anti-Sandinistas—the various groupings, civil or violent, parties or other organizations, that have been the FSLN's adversaries over the years—to give a sense of how the politics of opposition work in Nicaragua. He concludes that between 1990 and 2008, the use of violence against political opponents nearly disappeared; electoral success became the only legitimate road to power.

Chapter 4 is a treatment of Nicaraguan political culture by Andrés Pérez Baltodano. Pérez takes the position that Nicaraguan political culture is best defined as "resigned pragmatism," the perspective on politics that says that the desirable must always be subordinated to the immediately possible. He then suggests that this helps explain the contradictions that often appear in Daniel Ortega's policies in his second administration, such as denouncing neoliberalism while following neoliberal policies.

The next three chapters focus on institutions. In Chapter 5, Elena Martínez Barahona addresses the judiciary and finds that Nicaraguan courts, above all the Supreme Court, are partisan instruments. The Sandinistas and Liberals not only divide the places on the Court among themselves, but Sandinista and Liberal magistrates often make their decisions on partisan grounds rather than legal ones. Elections and electoral law are the subjects of Chapter 6 by Shelley A. McConnell. She describes each national election since the Sandinista Revolution (1984, 1990, 1996, 2001, and 2006) in detail. McConnell also analyzes the politics surrounding electoral system reform in Nicaragua. She concludes that Nicaragua's democratic weaknesses indicate that competitive elections do not, by themselves, guarantee democratic accountability.

In Chapter 7, Miguel González and Dolores Figueroa consider the complex question of regional autonomy for Nicaragua's Atlantic Coast. In 1987 the Sandinista government enacted an Autonomy Statute for the Coast, which is ethnically and culturally distinct from the western regions of Nicaragua. Since then, years of neoliberal economic policy and the challenges of building an operating model of multiethnic government have made the achievement of meaningful political autonomy difficult. Their chapter combines institutional analysis with a description of the evolution of Managua's policy toward the Caribbean Coast, something only the FSLN has taken at all seriously, thus making it a natural bridge to the section on public policy.

Public policy is the focus of Chapters 8, 9, and 10, which look at policy questions in Nicaragua. Although all present an overview of the Sandinista period, each gives special attention to policies emerging under the Ortega administration that won election in 2006. In Chapter 8, Karen Kampwirth concentrates on gender politics, especially what she describes as the unintended consequences of the revolution. Although Sandinista efforts to mobilize women in the 1970s and 1980s produced Central America's most significant feminist movement, Kampwirth details the antifeminist countermovement that grew in the 1990s and the friction that developed then between the women's movement and the FSLN. Perhaps the most striking part of this chapter is her examination of the repeal of a century-old law permitting therapeutic abortion (performed only to save a woman's life) that was adopted in 2006 thanks to Sandinista votes.

In Chapter 9, Rose J. Spalding addresses the socioeconomic impact of economic policy. She traces the evolution of Nicaraguan economic policy as it passed from revolutionary socialist to orthodox neoliberal. Spalding argues that the effects of these neoliberal policies have been especially costly in health, education, and rural poverty. Rural issues are the theme of the final policy-related chapter, Chapter 10, in which Eduardo Baumeister considers agricultural reform and counterreform. Baumeister's focus is the correlation between Nicaragua's evolving sociopolitical environment and the country's agrarian structure. The last part of his chapter evaluates the changes to agricultural policy that are being implemented by the current Sandinsta government.

Hector Perla addresses an often overlooked element of Sandinista history in Chapter 11, namely the role of international solidarity movements, focusing on the Central American Peace and Solidarity Movement. With particular reference to the United States, he argues that the movement in the United States was especially successful in limiting the Reagan administration's scope of action in its attempts to overthrow the FSLN government. Perla then sketches how international solidarity works today, noting the extent to which relations with such like-minded states as Venezuela have assumed the roles formerly played by solidarity organizations.

In Chapter 12, Martí and Close ask if the transformation seen in the FSLN and Sandinismo since 1979 is exceptional. Their assessment stresses the continuity of the FSLN's structures and leadership, on the one hand, while pointing to the dramatic changes that have occurred in its environment on the other.

Notes

1. Throughout this chapter, indeed throughout the book, "FSLN," "Sandinistas," and "Frente" are used effectively interchangeably. When necessary for clarity, as when describing conflicts between former FSLN members, who still consider themselves Sandinistas, and the official party, headed, in practical terms, by Daniel Ortega since 1984, alternative formulations are used.

2. This section really is a primer, intended for those who are only now learning about Nicaragua. There are several newer books that would be of interest both to individuals discovering Nicaragua and those more conversant with its history. Among them are Luciano Baracco, *Nicaragua: The Imagining of a Nation from Nineteenth-Century Liberals to Twentieth-Century Sandinistas* (New York: Algora, 2005); Consuelo Cruz, *Political Culture and Institutional Development in Costa Rica and Nicaragua: World-Making in the Tropics* (Cambridge: Cambridge University Press, 2005); Michel Gobat, *Confronting the American Dream: Nicaragua Under US Imperial Rule* (Durham, NC: Duke University Press, 2005); and Mauricio Solaún, *US Intervention and Regime Change in Nicaragua* (Lincoln: University of Nebraska Press, 2005).

3. Generals in these civil wars were usually not career officers. Rather, they were caudillo-style leaders who amassed enough men and arms to be given a commander's responsibilities. Some, like Sandino, were naturally gifted military leaders and had substantial success.

4. Ernesto Guevara, *Guerrilla Warfare* (Melbourne: Ocean, 2006).

5. One attempt came from inside the system in 1947, when Leonardo Argüello, Anastasio Somoza's designated placeholder, tried to usurp power. Another came from outside the regime in 1956, when oppositionists, including newspaper publisher Pedro Joaquín Chamorro, attempted a coup. Both ended disastrously for the perpetrators.

6. Phil Ryan, in *The Fall and Rise of the Market in Sandinista Nicaragua* (Montreal: McGill-Queen's University Press, 1995), sets out the FSLN's economic thinking and policy in detail.

7. The 1984 Electoral Law not only set up the electoral system, defined the constituencies, and set the election date; it also defined the offices to be elected. In so doing, it structured the executive and legislative branches of the new, electoral Sandinista regime. It was a case of constitution making by stealth.

8. There was a seventh, unofficial, undeclared, but very real participant: the Nicaraguan Democratic Coordinator (CDN). Led by Arturo Cruz, who had once been a member of the JGRN and then Managua's ambassador to Washington, the CDN campaigned even though it declared it would not run. Less than a month before the vote, the CDN pulled out definitively.

9. Not everything about the FSLN's government was edifying, however. In a lame-duck period after losing power, when the Sandinistas moved to regularize the titles of properties that had been transferred under agrarian reform or had been allocated to house the urban poor, they also ensured that the party's leaders secured the mansions they had seized from fleeing, wealthy, Somoza sympathizers. This episode became known as the piñata, after the swagbag game played at children's parties.

10. David Close and Kalowatie Deonandan, eds., *Undoing Democracy: The Politics of Electoral Caudillismo* (Lanham, MD: Lexington Books, 2005). The Pact, habitually capitalized, figures prominently in most of the chapters of this book, too.

11. Article 133 of the Nicaraguan Constitution provides for this.

12. The amendments were not enacted. In 2008, Nicaragua's Supreme Court, with eight justices named by the FSLN and the other eight by the PLC, thanks to the Pact, declared the legislation unconstitutional.

13. The party was founded by Herty Lewites and is often called the Alliance for Herty–Sandinista Renewal Movement. In this book, we refer to the party simply as the Sandinista Renewal Movement or MRS.

14. See, Article 145, *Ley Electoral,* www.bcn.gob.ni/.

15. The MRS lost its first candidate when Herty Lewites died of a heart attack in July 2006. Lewites was a well-known politician, a popular former mayor of Managua, and a talented campaigner. His replacement, Edmundo Jarquín, was more of a technocrat who lacked Lewites's panache. With Lewites's death, the chances for the MRS to play a decisive role in the race also perished.

16. Although Correa's first majority came in a runoff, he was reelected in 2009 with 52 percent of the vote.

2

The FSLN and Sandinismo

Salvador Martí i Puig

NICARAGUA IS THE ONLY COUNTRY IN LATIN AMERICA TO have had a successful popular revolution since the Cuban Revolution of 1959. It thus joins Mexico, Bolivia, and Cuba as Latin America's fourth twentieth-century social revolution. Yet Nicaragua stands apart from the others in three respects. First is the character of the revolutionary coalition that overthrew the Somozas' dictatorial regime. The revolution's policies and how the revolution itself developed are the second singularity. Finally, how the Sandinistas lost power and their decision to accept a role as Nicaragua's leading opposition party is without parallel among Marxist revolutionary parties. To appreciate these distinctions, it is necessary to focus on the political organization that drove the process. This chapter pursues that objective by analyzing the following points: (1) the origins of the FSLN as a politico-military front and the unfolding of the insurrection, (2) the debates about democracy that took place within the revolutionary process, (3) how the FSLN was affected by its electoral defeat in 1990, and (4) the FSLN's subsequent internal crisis and its eventual adjustment to the new style of Nicaragua politics.

The Beginnings: Between the Rule and the Exception

The Sandinista National Liberation Front (Frente Sandinista de Liberación Nacional, or FSLN) was founded on June 23, 1961, in Tegucigalpa, Honduras,

---

This chapter was translated by David Close.

21

under the name Frente de Liberación Nacional (National Liberation Front). It was the creation of young dissident radicals from the Nicaraguan Socialist Party and the Conservative Party, the historic enemies of the Somozas. They had seen how Anastasio Somoza García had built a patrimonial regime and how skillfully he co-opted his opponents. But they had also seen the triumph of the 26th of July Movement in Cuba. In 1962, after the group's initial unsuccessful forays into guerrilla warfare, it changed its name at the suggestion of Carlos Fonseca, one of the Frente's charismatic founders, to become the Frente Sandinista de Liberación Nacional.[1]

Like almost all Latin American guerrilla organizations that arose in the 1960s, the FSLN built its identity around the myths of the Cuban Revolution, *foquismo* (the Fidelistas' strategy), and to some extent liberation theology. However, the FSLN was also heir to a nationalist, anti-imperialist tradition and a popular imagination that embraced Sandino's rebellion while resisting the Somozas' dictatorship. This gave the Frente fertile ground for the politics of revolution. For many, the FSLN was the continuation, with new strategies and methods, of a struggle against imperialism and dictatorial oppression that had continued for a century.[2]

Once established, the FSLN gave guerrilla action and establishment of a rural presence priority over internal organization, the political education of the masses, and urban agitation. From 1961 to 1965, Sandinista armed action was limited to a small guerrilla *foco* in the mountains of north-central Nicaragua, and its recruits were mainly students. For those four years, the FSLN's principal accomplishment was to have survived, having made little military progress. Yet those years gave rise to the mystique of the mountains, influencing Nicaraguan revolutionary poetry in the 1970s. This vision of the heroic guerrilla was the framework for guerrilla action and, later, after the Frente split into three factions, the hallmark of the Prolonged People's War tendency.[3]

Guerrilla activity began anew in December 1966 with the task "of patiently organizing the peasants, creating drops to send and receive messages, and building a solid information and communications network to achieve political dominance in the region that did not depend on firepower."[4] However, between May and August 1967, the National Guard, the Somocista military force, learned of the *foco* and, after a series of engagements, killed some of the guerrillas and dispersed the rest. The Somoza state then moved rapidly to destroy the guerrillas' urban network and rural enclaves, sending the Sandinista leadership into exile in Cuba, Panama, and Costa Rica. It was in exile that the reduced band of Sandinistas began to form a distinctive doctrine and a new organizational structure. In 1969 the results appeared in the form of a new National Directorate (DN) and a program that laid out the ideals and objectives of the organization, the Historic Program of the FSLN.[5]

Despite being founded in 1961, most analysts place the FSLN in the second, or 1970s, wave of Latin American guerrillas, because that was when it became politically relevant. Its transition to significance began with the Managua earthquake of December 23, 1972, and grew rapidly after 1975, when the dictatorship showed clearly that it would brook no reform. At that point, all political opposition effectively moved outside the official channels of the regime.[6]

It was in this period leading up to the insurrection that divisions emerged within the FSLN, reflecting differing strategic and tactical perspectives.[7] There was a greater emphasis on urban action and recruiting among the urban poor, the middle sectors, and even the rich.[8] It was then that the FSLN began to concentrate on urban areas. As a result of mobilizing an urban insurrection, the FSLN itself began to acquire an urban tint, and the Sandinista leadership began to take notice of the "new urban social subjects."[9]

The late 1970s saw the rapid and intense politicization of Nicaraguan society, and this radical energy was channeled through the FSLN. Sandinistas specialized in one form of politics (armed struggle, in a specific context—the repressive Somocista dictatorship) and had one goal (taking power). Unsurprisingly, the FSLN was a highly centralized politico-military organization, with a strict vertical chain of command, and a rigidly compartmentalized structure. Its leadership was, as it had always been, a military hierarchy. One level down were the regional commands, the Departmental and Zonal Command Committees. They reported directly to the National Directorate, the supreme authority in all matters. At the base were the *milicias* (militias), which included guerrilla columns and commandos, and *celulas* (cells), found only in urban areas.

Given the clandestine nature of the organization, its members (*militantes*) pledged themselves to carry out a wide range of responsibilities with a dedicated, disciplined, almost religious fervor. We can characterize the FSLN as what Maurice Duverger styled a *Bund* or *Order,*[10] since it was deliberately created, had a nearly sacred character, and demanded the complete allegiance of its members.[11] It must be recalled that this military structure was necessary for the FSLN to survive and succeed in an extremely hostile environment. The Nicaragua of the late 1970s was, after all, a place where "it was a crime to be young."

Mobilization and Insurrection

Until the end of 1977, when it began a series of attacks in different parts of the country, the Frente had not been deemed a relevant political actor. But then the various strands of opposition to the regime began mobilizing. In

October of that year, the FSLN launched two military operations, San Carlos (October 13) and Masaya (October 17), while the Group of Twelve (Los Doce) affirmed that it would be necessary to resort to arms to overthrow the dictatorship.[12]

However, it was the assassination of Pedro Joaquín Chamorro, publisher of *La Prensa* and a lifelong foe of the Somozas, on January 10, 1978, that set the Somocista state on the road to ruin. The act, for which the dictator's eldest son was believed responsible, had the effect of heightening tensions and putting the dictatorship's behavior in a new light. There was never any doubt that Somoza's National Guard (nicknamed the Genocidal Guard) could repress ordinary opponents with impunity. However, the economic elite and the nation's established families had always believed that they could dissent openly. No more. Chamorro's forebears included presidents, caudillos, and generals. With his murder, the elite's privileges and security came to an end, and panic spread through the ranks of the *haute bourgeoisie*.

It was in these conditions that the FSLN, following the savage repression of a series of popular uprisings (particularly in Monimbó), pulled off what was until then its greatest coup: seizing the Congress in August 1978. That audacious act catapulted the Sandinistas back into the public's consciousness and reestablished them as political actors. Thus, by the end of 1978 Nicaragua had acquired what Charles Tilly calls a condition of multiple sovereignty; that is, the Somoza government was not totally in control.[13] It was then, in December 1978, that the three tendencies of the FSLN agreed to coordinate their actions (see Chapter 1). The following March 13, the three wings were reunited after five years of separation. A nine-member Combined National Directorate (Dirección National Conjunta), with three representatives from each tendency, began to lead the Frente.[14]

Rather than describe the course of the revolution, I shall treat only the breadth and intensity of popular participation in the insurrection.[15] A central question here is what brought so many urban Nicaraguans into the streets. Obviously, there is a mix of structural and conjunctural reasons. Among the former are the country's rapid and unequal economic development since the 1950s and the unrelenting pressure the Somoza regime used against many different groups. Indeed, the system's characteristic behavior—corruption, political monopoly, and the brutality of the forces of order—sparked a consciousness among the people that led them to reject the misery, unemployment, and land hunger they experienced.

Turning to the immediate context, two things stand out: the high level of mobilization that would support the insurrection and the regime's indiscriminate repression. The two are closely linked, because indiscriminate repression turned rebellion into self-defense. In fact, being a victim of repression was no longer what happened to others—subversives, agitators, or those who were looking for trouble—but became something that could happen to anybody, even if they just minded their own business. So vicious repression stopped being exceptional and became ordinary, thus making "active defense" necessary for survival. One insurrectionist put it this way: "I started shooting them, because otherwise they were going to kill us all like sheep."[16]

Finally, there is this question: Who mobilized, pushed, and tried to organize the people? The FSLN. The murder of Pedro Joaquín Chamorro ended all hope of changes within the system. After January 10, 1978, even more people believed that the opposition mounted for nearly twenty years by the Sandinistas was the only answer. Thus any analysis of the fall of the Somocista regime cannot stop at the "primitive character of the dictator" or the "mistakes made by Washington," but must include the ability of the popular forces to carry on the struggle. The actions of the insurrectionists were the fruit of organizing done by the FSLN over the years. The Frente gave the people the room and the tools to make their claims, and the people took to the streets and gave the FSLN power. But the people also gave the Frente Sandinista a human base, a social foundation, a discourse, a set of demands, an image, and a face. That face was eminently urban and was the incarnation of the Revolución Popular Sandinista. And the Frente brought it into the state and the party and governed in its interest. But there was a flip side: the campesinos (subsistence farmers) of the rural borderlands who shared poverty and subordination with their urban counterparts, but had a different outlook, valued different symbols, and made different demands.[17]

Sandinismo in Power

The Debate over Democracy

The Nicaraguan revolutionary project, like any social revolution in an underdeveloped country, brought together varied objectives. Social revolutions in underdeveloped societies are simultaneously national liberation and antidictatorial revolutions. Consequently, they combine social and economic transformation with the rejection of prior forms of political domination. Such revolutionary processes face the challenges of building democracy and national sovereignty and increasing development.[18] In this section I consider the question of democracy and participation.[19]

First, during the revolutionary process, different political actors struggled to control the same political community and the same political instruments. The country needed both to unite to overthrow a dictatorship and to develop a project for building the material, institutional, and symbolic bases of a new Nicaraguan society. Consequently, the alliances formed to combat a common enemy grew weaker when it came time to build a new society. Some saw the fall of Somoza as ending the process, but for others it was just the beginning.

The twenty months following the triumph of 1979 saw the FSLN emerge as the force that would direct the revolutionary process. And by the mid-1980s, the Sandinistas were hegemonic actors, controlling the majority of the nation's material and symbolic resources and setting the public agenda without regard to the views of other political actors. As a result, the issue of elections, the role of traditional political forces in the new political framework, and legal guarantees for private property caused sharp disagreements between the FSLN and other parts of the political spectrum.

Arguably, the greatest conflict arose around the question of elections. Although the Sandinistas accepted that elections would have to be held, they did not put much emphasis on the vote. The FSLN's distrust of elections (seen in its initial decision to postpone them until 1985) grew from its rejection of "politics as usual" and its embrace of "real democracy." In this the Frente expressed the view of a generation of the Latin American left for whom elections, historically used by oligarchic regimes, could never be the cornerstone of democracy. For the FSLN, the repression, exclusion, and privation that marked the lives of the poor demanded a style of democracy that addressed the conditions of daily life far more than traditional questions of formal rights. Once in power, the Sandinistas declared that democracy went far beyond elections, arguing that popular participation had to develop first in the socioeconomic realm and only then in the political.

However, this stance overlooked serious problems.[20] Who controlled the government in the first stages of the revolution? Who decided what economic preconditions were needed to produce political democracy? Who determined when the initial period ended and a new epoch began? What would happen when policy decisions—social, economic, national security, and so on—were out of line with, or even clashed with, the needs and values of sectors of the poor majority?

All these questions were raised throughout the revolutionary process and assumed signal importance because the FSLN, due to its origins as a clandestine, politico-military organization, could not abide open debate. On too many occasions the Frente Sandinista created a political context in which the new forms of transformation and democracy came bundled with the command-style politics associated with the "infallibility of the vanguard." Thus the FSLN in the mid-1980s ran up against a paradox that would face every revolutionary movement: How could movements that were not pluralist and did not tolerate dissent within their own ranks build democracy and permit broad, free political participation?

The FSLN and Its Organization

From the triumph of the revolution, FSLN cadres progressively took over Nicaragua's state institutions, putting into effect Comandante Jaime Wheelock's words that "the state is just another instrument the people use to bring the Revolution into being."[21] Despite the Fundamental Statute of Rights and Guarantees (Estatuto Fundamental de Derechos y Garantias) of 1979, which defined the relations among the various state institutions, in practice the system was increasingly marked by the fusion of party and state.[22] Reinforcing this tendency was the vanguardist character of the FSLN, which had three bases: (1) the unquestioned leadership of the nine comandantes who formed the DN; (2) a party organization formed by a small number of highly involved, dedicated, and disciplined members (militants); and (3) a series of mass organizations organically linked to the party. These, plus the effects of operating in a wartime environment, pushed the FSLN inexorably toward a top-down, highly centralized mode of governing.

The first leg of the tripod was the DN, the nine comandantes who were the party's chiefs and the final arbiters in all political decisions.[23] During the revolutionary decade, the DN became the apex of both party and state, and the chant, "Direccion nacional ordene!" ("National Directorate, give us our orders!"), reflected the authority vested in this collegial body. Giving the party a collective leadership symbolized the organic integration of its three tendencies while signaling the FSLN's rejection of caudillismo and personalism. Nonetheless, the DN still came to be idolized, and the individualism of the nine frequently showed through in the so-called institutional feudalism, which left each comandante running specific ministries as near fiefdoms and fragmenting the machinery of government.[24] The FSLN's party machinery regulated its members with rules that were simple and brief and full of gaps. There were four levels of authority: national, regional, zonal, and base. But this was not a party with a mass membership. Rather, it was built on a small number of carefully selected and extremely loyal cadres, or *militantes,* which gave the Frente and its members a sectarian cast. The militants were shifted among posts in government, service in the armed forces, and work within mass organizations and the party itself. As the military conflict expanded and the accompanying economic crisis deepened, the FSLN depended ever more on its militants to mobilize and direct collective action, do public relations, and generally look after the public sphere. Little wonder, then, that ordinary citizens increasingly saw party and state as one.[25]

The party's mass organizations were the last component of its vanguardist character.[26] The FSLN believed that the masses had to be integrated into specialized organizations that were outside the party structure but still organically fused with the party. These organizations played a key role in the reconstruction of civil society in the postinsurrection period, although the role the FLSN assigned them was never clearly defined. At the outset (1979–1984), the combination of conventional political representation via parties and functional representation via sectoral groups in the Council of State gave the mass organizations substantial room to act.[27] After the 1984 elections and the creation of the National Assembly, whose seats were filled with the representatives of parties returned from geographic constituencies, the institutional weight of the mass organizations declined, and their legal and political subordination to the Frente Sandinista grew. In the end, the mass organizations became the occupational and sectoral "catch basins" where those sympathetic to the Sandinista Revolution gathered.[28]

If in the first years of the revolution the mass organizations channeled the outpouring of hope, enthusiasm, and activity of the many who had never before taken any part in public life, it was not long before their participation responded to directives coming from the state and the party. The intensification of the war of aggression sponsored by Washington and the worsening of economic conditions only intensified this top-down tendency. These circumstances saw ever more marked contradictions emerge between the immediate needs of the people and the strategic demands arising from the defense of the revolution. The result was that popular participation began to decline.

Under those conditions, the FSLN postponed looking after the immediate and more personal needs of the people and instead stressed defense in the war sponsored by the United States.[29] As happens in wartime, criticism was suppressed, civilian demands were deferred, and discipline was demanded. In addition, the government took the position that the counterrevolution was just a tool of Washington to defeat the Sandinista Revolution and thus its origins were foreign and not domestic. Although this rhetoric helped maintain international solidarity, thereby frustrating the Reagan-Bush efforts to isolate Nicaragua, it made it very hard for the Sandinistas to acknowledge that the policies and governing style of the revolution contributed to the rise of the Contra. Accordingly, the government was less able to modify its stands, which caused sectors of society that had been neither strongly with nor strongly against the Frente to align with the opposition.

After 1982, national defense became Nicaragua's top priority. The economy and every aspect of social life were subordinated to the war effort, leading to labor shortages and shortages of machinery in nondefense sectors, the resettlement of people living in war zones, the disruption of commerce, the depreciation and inconvertibility of the currency, and the growth of government deficits. By the end of the 1980s, almost half the budget and a fifth of the economically active population went to the war effort.

But the war's impact reached beyond the economy: it was also political. A sociologist who was part of this process described it in these terms:

> The situation of prolonged war took on its own logic, which implied a particular structuring of social relations and of the world of symbols, thus altering the political project it had once claimed to be building. . . . The armed forces grew rapidly. This meant bringing a large part of the population within a military structure, characterized universally by hierarchical organization. Under those circumstances, methods of work and organization became permeated by a military logic.[30]

Thus the war generated demands and laid the bases for strengthening verticalism and centralized control. This tendency was seen in the organization of the various state agencies and, above all, in the FSLN itself, as well as in the mass organizations. Against this background, it is easy to see why 1990 found the Sandinistas unable to accept an electoral defeat that called into question a project they had defended so energetically and unquestioningly.

All those problems were evident throughout the life of the revolution. They had great relevance because the FSLN had worked underground for many years, possessed a strict command structure, and had no history of open debates. For the Frente Sandinista, therefore, all too frequently the discourse of transformation and democratization joined a governing model rooted in the "infallibility of the vanguard," the watchword of two decades of clandestine struggle. During the 1980s, therefore, the FSLN, along with other Latin American revolutionary groups, experienced the paradox of being organizations uncomfortable with the pluralism that promoted democracy and an open political system.

The Legacy of the Revolutionary Experience

It must be recalled that the Sandinista Revolution was Nicaragua's first (and still only) attempt to build a state with a popular and national character. The project began when similar experiments were in crisis in Latin America and when the neoliberal international order worked against their success. Within the revolution, society's humble organized themselves, debated issues, and participated in a framework that consciously offered them space. The upsurge in the development of social organizations and the experience of people working together and discussing their common problems among themselves marked a break with the country's past. People felt themselves part of a social subject that was trying to build something better for the future. Most of the accomplishments of the 1980s—literacy, adult education, vaccination campaigns—were the product of collective action and involved the participation of ordinary people. But the quick arrival of the Contra war, orchestrated by the United States and backed by the country's reactionary sectors, rolled back many of the forces set in motion by the revolution, not least the people's enthusiasm. In this sense, lines written by Roque Dalton, referring to El Salvador, reflect the feelings of many Nicaraguans toward the revolution:

> thinking about how beautiful life
> and everything else would have been
> if the struggle had not been so fierce
> in this the tiniest country you can imagine[31]

Expulsion from Power

Defeat and Transition

Early on February 26, 1990, Daniel Ortega, presidential candidate of the FSLN, saw the projections based on 50 percent of the vote. At noon, the Supreme Electoral Council issued an update: 54 percent of the 1,101,397 votes counted had gone to the National Opposition Union (Union Nacional Opositora, or UNO) and 44 percent to the FSLN. Violeta Barrios de Chamorro was president-elect, her Liberal running mate Virgilio Godoy would become vice president, and her party, the UNO coalition, won 51 of 92 seats in the National Assembly. Thirty-nine seats went to the FSLN and two other parties, the Movement for Revolutionary Unity (Movimiento de Unidad Revolucionaria, or MUR) and the Social Christian Party (Partido Social Cristiano, or PSC), each of which got 1 seat.

The result surprised both the international observers and the politicians who ran in the election. I do not analyze the data but rather focus on four factors that eroded the Sandinista vote: (1) an economic crisis produced by the war and the administration's too numerous policy mistakes; (2) the apparently endless war; (3) the effects of austerity politics on large parts of the population; and (4) the questionable behavior of some Sandinista officials, seen, for example, in the reappearance of clientelism.

These elections would produce four unintended results that would significantly affect future Nicaraguan politics. First, they would strengthen political pluralism. Second, they would channel political action through the institutions created by the 1987 constitution. Third, they would shift the balance of social, economic, and political power within the country. Finally, the relations among political actors would have to change, based on the resources each now controlled. A number of challenges for the political system emerged from the Sandinistas' loss in the 1990 elections. Two of the most important were consolidating a new institutional framework for political life and winding up the armed conflict that dated from the early 1980s. However, those problems could only be addressed successfully if the main political actors changed how they saw politics. The central political instrument of the new era would be the pact, and it would significantly change Nicaragua's prevailing political attitudes.

The first pact, the Protocol for the Transition of Executive Power (PTEP), was struck between the Sandinista leadership and the president-elect's top advisers on March 27, 1990. The PTEP implied, first, that the new administration would continue to use existing state institutions, thus maintaining outward institutional stability and continuity with the revolutionary government. Interestingly, one sector of the FSLN leadership and the new administration shared an interest in perpetuating the current structure. To understand what this means, one must look at the PTEP as more than a technical instrument and see it as expressing the convergence of interests (here, economic and familial) shared by the negotiators. During the revolution, family links had played an important role, which continued during the transfer of power.[32] Thus the electoral outcome, along with the deal concluded between the outgoing and incoming governments, muddied Nicaragua's political waters, and the resulting turbulence would produce conflicts within the country's principal political forces.

For the FSLN, electoral defeat and the loss of power profoundly affected its self-image and its organizational outlook. Within the still fragile fourteen-party UNO coalition, the PTEP and the construction of an administration based more on personal loyalties than partisan identity increased internal tensions and conflict. For the next decade and more, this new political panorama would shape the perceptions of the political actors who defined issues and set agendas.

The Sandinista Labyrinth: The Internal Debate

The FSLN's initial response to its electoral defeat was complete confusion. A Sandinista leader had this to say a few months after the elections:

> When I heard about the electoral defeat I felt like shit. I asked myself what I had done to bring this about. I felt like what I had done wasn't enough

and I questioned myself about all the wild parties. . . . I turned to ice, thinking that there would be a bloodbath. . . . Then Juan Rivas, the painter,
showed up and we decided to form a commando [unit]. We got in his car
and drove all over the place. . . . We ended up drunk and bawling. We
laugh about it now.[33]

A little later, though, the various voices that were being raised within the
FSLN converged in the internal debate about the party's future. Party militants did not just talk about why the FSLN lost the election but also how it
had lost touch with Nicaraguan society and why its leadership had grown
distant from the rank and file, its base. They also wanted to talk about the
rapid, disorderly, and at times abusive way in which the Sandinista government passed out state-owned real estate and government goods to its top
officials in the so-called piñata.

The debate's first systematic installment appeared during the Asamblea
Nacional de Militantes (National Assembly of Members, a party conference), held in El Crucero. This conference marked the culmination of spontaneous meetings organized at various levels (base, local, and departmental)
by the membership, while the once almighty National Directorate did nothing. In its summary, the conference outlined the reasons why the FSLN
lost.[34] The report also rebuked the party officialdom for not accepting criticism and for its bureaucratic and top-down style of government, its tight
control over the mass organizations, and the sumptuous lifestyle of some
leaders during a time of bitter austerity for most Nicaraguans. A poem by a
former Sandinista deputy and one-time official of the Ministry of Culture,
Alejandro (el Negro) Bravo, sums up the feelings of the rank and file:[35]

> Ten years ago
> my kids were little
> and it was really hard
> to find milk for them
>
> Ten years ago
> the countryside was the same
> but from the overcrowded buses
> we felt that it was ours
>
> Ten years ago
> Reagan railed
> against Nicaragua
> and students brought in the coffee harvest
>
> Ten years ago
> things were totally fucked

you had to wait in line for everything
except hope

II

Hope,
the wife of a mid-level party official
who shopped at the *Diplo*[36]

What was worse, many of these criticisms had been aired before the elections, but they were ignored to preserve unity.[37]

Thus the FSLN faced two challenges: organizational renewal and rethinking its political project and social profile. Regarding the former, the loss of government for a party that had built a party-state during the 1980s was crucial, for the FSLN suddenly became a party with a small and weakened structure. Thousands of party members who had held government posts lost their jobs when the new administration was sworn in. Where once the Frente had 5,000 professional paid staff, within months of the 1990 election there were only about 500.[38] As Aldo Díaz Lacayo notes, Sandinismo "had lost the government and the Sandinistas had lost their jobs."[39] With regard to its social and political redefinition, the FSLN suddenly had to rethink a revolutionary program that had been applied unconditionally for over a decade.

Learning to Be an Opposition Party

The FSLN began confronting its organizational issues with new party statutes. Organizationally, losing office meant the loss of what had become combined party-state structures. This produced further problems, not least the ability of the DN to control the once strictly disciplined FSLN. In short, not having a party-state undermined the command-and-control system that had been carried over from the guerrilla war into the revolutionary state. However, the more basic question of redefining the organization's identity was harder to address because it brought into play a variety of interests, positions, and sensibilities at the FSLN's core.[40]

To put an end to its slide, the party held its first-ever congress in July 1991.[41] Its objective was to write statutes to redefine the FSLN's organization, platform, and principles. Therefore, the congress proposed a profound reorganization that touched both the Frente's official structure and its internal power relations. Despite these ambitious objectives, however, the party dashed the high hopes for renewal that had been growing since losing the

1990 elections. That was because the National Directorate of the FSLN was strong enough to control the congress and limit the scope of the reforms adopted.[42]

Even if the 1991 congress neither put an end to top-down internal control nor changed the old hierarchy of power, it could not prevent a split in the FSLN between the forces of continuity and those pressing for radical change. The congress only postponed the day of reckoning. Indeed, conflicts within the party continued to grow in the months following the initial congress, necessitating the calling of an extraordinary party congress in 1994 to settle the disputes raging not just among the members but even within the leadership.

Unlike the 1991 congress, the 1994 event focused on the FSLN as an opposition party. There were two distinct and incompatible positions. One, called "pragmatic," favored collaboration and negotiation with the government. It was made up principally of elected public officials, notably National Assembly deputies, and was led by former vice president Sergio Ramírez. The other, led by party insiders and including Daniel Ortega, was called "principled." It leaned toward more openly contentious opposition, including all the forms of struggle ever used by the Sandinistas, and drew its supporters from the FSLN-affiliated unions.

Both options had been clearly visible since 1990, giving the FSLN a contradictory image as an opposition party. The legislative caucus sought to support the president, leading some to see it as a "co-government," or disguised coalition.[43] However, another wing of the party promoted direct confrontation—strikes, building occupations, roadblocks, street violence—to show that it rejected consensus politics. The development of this "threat-negotiation" oppositional dualism produced fully fledged factions within the FSLN. And unlike 1991, the DN could not control these warring wings.[44]

Unsurprisingly, the extraordinary congress of May 1994 witnessed the direct confrontation of the two factions. Under the leadership of Daniel Ortega and Tomás Borge, the "principled" faction, now named the Democratic Left (DL), called for "a high level of combativeness from the FSLN in defense of the poor, its revolutionary vocation, and its vanguardist nature." The "pragmatists," labeled the Movement for the Renewal of Sandinismo and led by Sergio Ramírez, Dora María Téllez, and Comandante de la Revolución Henry Ruiz, wanted a party based on multiclass alliances that sought a broad social consensus. Thus, one faction wanted continuity with the past, meaning a party embracing the FSLN's revolutionary character and the principle of class struggle, whereas the other sought a clean break with the past and a party of the social democratic left that embraced the tenets of constitutional democracy.[45]

In the end the DL won when Daniel Ortega was elected secretary-general of the party over Henry Ruiz by a margin to 287 to 147. Nevertheless, some members of the "renovationists" still remained in the DN. Thus party unity was still absent, and conflict soon broke out anew. A crisis developed when the Sandinista parliamentary caucus, headed by Sergio Ramírez since 1990, opted to support a package of constitutional amendments that had been opposed by the Sandinista Assembly, the FSLN's highest decisionmaking body, and by Ortega. On September 9, 1994, the assembly removed Ramírez as the FSLN's house leader.

At that point, many party members began voicing their dissent. A significant section of the FSLN's militants, including a number of the Frente's historic leaders, publically broke with the leadership and rejected its political direction. One celebrated case was that of Ernesto Cardenal, a poet who had been minister of culture in the revolutionary government: "I am still a Sandinista and a revolutionary, with the ideas of Sandino and the revolution to the fore. And I remain a Marxist and a Christian. . . . My resignation from the FSLN has been caused by the kidnapping of the party carried out by Daniel Ortega and the group he heads."[46]

In this atmosphere of schism and mutual recriminations, the Sandinista Assembly met again in October 1994. With a quorum of 67 of its 130 members present, the assembly voted to fire the board of directors of the Sandinista paper *Barricada,* including its longtime editor Carlos Fernando Chamorro, for having supported the Ramírez faction. Chamorro was replaced, first by Lumberto Campbell, a newly named member of the DN, and then a few days later by Tomás Borge. This prompted eighteen of twenty-two journalists to leave the paper.[47]

Later, four members of the DN—Henry Ruiz, Dora María Téllez, Luis Carrión, and Myrna Cunningham—criticized the action. However, the schism was made complete on January 8, 1995, when, following attacks against him and his family made by a Sandinista radio station, Radio Ya, Sergio Ramírez quit the party. A significant number of FSLN notables followed Ramírez out of the FSLN and formed the Sandinista Renewal Movement (Movimiento Renovador Sandinista, or MRS) on May 21 of that same year. In 1996, the MRS ran in Nicaragua's general elections, taking just 0.44 percent of the presidential vote and only 1.33 percent of the legislative vote. This left the FSLN with near-monopoly control over the Sandinista trademark.

After the 1995 split, the FSLN entered a new era. However, it did not come with a reshaped organizational framework, revamped regulations that had been debated by all party members, or amended procedures designed to reduce friction between different factions, whether within the leadership councils or at congresses. Actually, quite the opposite occurred. Five years

of hard work aimed at reconciling internal differences and putting limitations on the leadership's power and ambitions were abandoned. The ab-
solute victory of Daniel Ortega's group and the withdrawal of Ramírez's
reformers meant that total control of the FSLN passed into the hands of the
leader and his loyalists.

From 1996 to 2006: Ortega Commands
the FSLN, and Pact Making Pays Off

It took little time for personalist principles to appear in Sandinista structures. Internal checks disappeared, procedural rules lost their force, and the
old collective decisionmaking institutions, the DN and the Sandinista Assembly, became dead letters. Particularly striking is the fate of the DN, once
the core institution of the FSLN. After 1995, the DN ceased meeting regularly, and when a meeting was called only Daniel Ortega, Tomás Borge, and
Bayardo Arce (until 1998) were invited. The others, the remaining original
members and those elected by the congresses of 1998 and 2001, no longer
even pretended to be Ortega's equals but merely rubberstamped his decisions. There was no place left for the DN, so it came as no surprise that the
FSLN's revised statues of 2002 eliminated the revolutionary holdover and
set in its place a politburo called the Sandinista National Council (SNC) to
run all aspects of the party's operations between meetings of the Sandinista
Assembly. However, the SNC has thirty-eight members, serving five-year
terms, so it is too big to actually manage the daily affairs of a political party.
    Since the split there have been six national congresses of the FSLN:
second extraordinary, 1996; second regular, 1998; third regular, 2001; fourth
regular, March 2002; third extraordinary, 2005; and fourth extraordinary,
2006. Unlike earlier congresses, they were models of tranquility, as everything was well under control. However, in 2005 attempts by two longtime
Sandinista leaders, Herty Lewites and Victor Hugo Tinoco, to run for the
party's presidential nomination did inject some excitement, but the end result was that both left the FSLN. National FSLN party congresses had become events to ratify the leader's decisions, perhaps approving pacts with
the Constitutionalist Liberal Party (Partido Liberal Constitutionalista, or
PLC) or conferring the party's nomination on those selected by the secretary-general. It is interesting to note, however, that since 1996, all Sandinista candidates, except for the presidential ticket and the candidate for mayor
of Managua, have been chosen by party primaries. The plum posts are Ortega's to hand out, but the rest are contested.

As to the FSLN's internal organization, a 2002 revision of the 1991 party statutes showed substantial continuity.[48] It still claimed to uphold the principles of promoting internal democracy, ensuring the unity of the FSLN, and being a national organization. In addition, the rules continued to distinguish between *militantes* (full members) and *afiliados* (probationary members) while setting out what one needed to do to become a member of the FSLN. However, although the changes were few, they were far-reaching.

First, there was more emphasis on discipline as well as the formal recognition of the centralization of power in the post of secretary-general. Then there is the electoral question. Article 7 states that the "FSLN is organized to win elections, which is how the power to govern is won today." This is reinforced in Article 97, which declares that "the FSLN will be permanently organized as an electoral party." Chapters VII and VIII of the document address the related question of party discipline, the former in the Nicaraguan National Assembly and the Central American Parliament and the latter extending the principles to municipal councils and the autonomous regional governments of Nicaragua's Atlantic Coast. Both cases make it plain that Sandinista legislators have no option but to toe the party line.

What becomes clear from the foregoing is that the ten years from 1996 to 2006 witnessed a radical concentration of effectively unaccountable power in the position of the party's secretary-general, hence in the person of Daniel Ortega. That man and party had become one is symbolized by the fact that during this period, the headquarters of the FSLN were moved to the Ortegas' house, a substantial compound that the FSLN expropriated from the man who became Ortega's vice president in 2006: Jaime Morales. Moving the party offices to the family home also bears witness to the growing influence in party and state affairs of Ortega's wife Rosario Murillo and likely some of his children.

During this period, the FSLN worked to establish a presence in Nicaragua's civic organizations and unions. This gave the party an extraparliamentary arm that could be activated even while the Sandinistas were in opposition. Ortega's opposition thus blended "outside" strategies, often literally taking to the streets but always using direct action, with "inside" ones based on negotiations with Nicaragua's president to gain "quotas of power," that is, the assured control of a number of appointments within state institutions, which gave the Sandinistas substantial influence over government.

Implementing this strategy took different forms during different presidencies. Accordingly, Ortega dealt with Alemán in a manner quite distinct from how he engaged Enrique Bolaños. With Alemán (1997–2002), Ortega established a reciprocity accord by which each would protect the other from the serious legal problems hanging over them.[49] From that came a power-sharing arrangement, the Pact. In the case of Bolaños (2002–2007), Ortega dealt both with the president and with Alemán and his PLC. This strategy netted the FSLN the presidencies of both the Supreme Electoral Council and the Supreme Court in 2002.

By the start of 2003, the Ortega-dominated FSLN had come close to controlling all the key political institutions in Nicaragua but the presidency itself. That year also saw the beginnings of a new political cleavage in the country. From 1979 to 2003, the country had split along Sandinista versus anti-Sandinista lines, but now there was a Pact (FSLN and PLC) versus anti-Pact (MRS plus supporters of President Bolaños) dimension. Although this new alignment would harm the Frente's public image, it was what would bring them back to power in 2006. Nevertheless, there were costs involved, most notably the effective de-institutionalization of the FSLN as a democratic political organization.

As has already been noted, the rules according to which the FSLN operated had been changed to concentrate exceptional power in the party's leader; these changes included dissolving the DN and granting the leader the ability to expel "bothersome" members from the party. As a result, the party became increasingly personalized, and as is common in such regimes, ties to the leader, whether among family or friends, became ever more evident. The rest of the party's elite and its permanent staff were converted into instruments that passively awaited the leader's call to implement his latest plan to increase the FSLN's quotas of power.

To conclude, I want to raise the issue of the autonomy of the FSLN's local branches and the various groups (unions, nongovernmental organizations, and professional organizations) affiliated with the party. Regarding the FSLN's local organizations, it should be recalled that the party has done reasonably well at the municipal level by being sound civic managers. That required a substantial measure of autonomy for mayors and councils, but that independence always came with explicit declarations of loyalty to the secretary-general. As to occupational organizations, two parallel processes can be detected. On the one hand, there are organizations that have an organic relationship with the Frente, such as the teachers' union, whose scope of independent action is limited. On the other hand, one finds more independent organizations with substantial power of their own (such as the taxi owners or the bus and trucking companies), which are actually able to negotiate with the FSLN and even with Ortega himself. In short, although Daniel Ortega has come to command the FSLN, exercise significant influence over the PLC because of the Pact, and use his party's quotas of power within the machinery of government to advance his agenda, there are still a few centers of power in Nicaraguan political life that lie beyond his reach.

The FSLN's Return to Power

Once sworn into office in January 2007, Ortega designed a low-profile cabinet, giving a preeminent role to his wife. There were no historic (or relevant) officials from the Sandinismo of the 1980s or, indeed, from the period when the party was in opposition. The majority of the ministers were Sandinistas with a limited public profile who could not hope to challenge the president. Key features of this governing model were the First Lady Rosario Murillo's considerable influence; the figure of the minister of the presidency; and the president's "direct advisers," who dealt with social groups and trade unions and enjoyed greater power than the cabinet ministers, whose job was simply to execute policies. This, together with the presence of the children and grandchildren of the Ortega-Murillo family in different official roles and at public functions (as well as their presence on diplomatic trips), brought the issues of privileges and nepotism into the national political debate. This was no small thing, taking into account the long history of family-dominated politics in Nicaragua.

Social Policy Instruments

With regard to public policy, Ortega's first messages as president were contradictory. On the one hand he announced a "total about-face" in the sphere of social policy, but on the other he maintained, despite the radical rhetoric used in international forums, complete continuity with the neoliberal economic policies of previous administrations. The new social policy had two pillars. The first was making primary and secondary schools as well as access to health care completely free. The second was the launching of focused social policies to alleviate poverty through programs such as Hambre Cero (Zero Hunger), Usura Cero (Zero Usury), Desempleo Cero (Zero Unemployment), and Calles para el Pueblo (The Streets Belong to the People).

These programs had a considerable impact on the FSLN's organization because they were implemented via new, highly partisan "political-administrative" mechanisms that were brought into being by a 2007 presidential decree.[50] They were created under the "Pueblo Presidente" plan promoted by the Communications and Citizenship Council (Consejo de Comunicación y Ciudadanía) of the Presidency of the Republic, presided over by the first lady. These new mechanisms, called Councils of Citizens' Power (Consejos de Poder Ciudadano, or CPCs), were designed to represent citizens from throughout the country and to deliver the majority of the new, targeted, antipoverty policies.

Although the format of the CPCs is reminiscent of the Sandinista Defense Committees (Comités de Defensa Sandinista, or CDSs) that existed during the 1980s, a closer look leads us to conclude that they are places where public goods are distributed to citizens. Furthermore, one of the characteristics of the CPC model is that decisions are made only at the very top, in the National Cabinet of the CPCs, while the other levels can only make proposals. This is an unusual notion of citizen empowerment, to say the least.

The FSLN's Party Structure

With regard to the FSLN's party apparatus, it is necessary to point out that the secretary of the party organization was Lenin Cerna until he lost the position in May 2011; he was director of the National Directorate of State Security (Dirección General de Seguridad Estatal, or DGSE) in the 1980s. However, some of his functions overlapped with those of the first lady since, as the president of the CPCs, she is able to deal directly with the Frente's officials and grassroots organizations. Furthermore, according to declarations made by Rosario Murillo in June 2008, we can see that the FSLN's party organization in the municipalities and departments has been integrated into the CPCs. However, despite this overlapping of functions, the party's secretary has never questioned the strategy employed by Ortega and his wife. Furthermore, shortly before the meeting of the Sandinista National Council in September 2009, Cerna declared that "up until now the FSLN's political strategies in order to reach power have been successful, although we need to design new plans so that the party can advance via new routes and in new ways, always under Ortega's leadership."[51] Two of these "new party strategies" are particularly striking: the selection of candidates by the party's top leadership (i.e., Ortega and Murillo) and the recruitment campaigns to sign up a mass membership. Obviously, these practices—the massive recruitment of members and appointment of candidates by the personal choice of the presidential couple—have grievously weakened the few mechanisms for accountability and control that were present in the party's structure.

Notes

1. A recent work on Fonseca is Matilde Zimmerman, *Carlos Fonseca and the Nicaraguan Revolution* (Durham, NC: Duke University Press, 2000).

2. The nationalist conscience of the Nicaraguan people was always nourished by anti-imperialist and anti-authoritarian tendencies drawn from its own history. These themes have been taken up by its leading intellectuals and can be seen in the poetry and prose of Rubén Darío, the exploits of Benjamin Zeledón, and the popular nationalism of Augusto César Sandino.

3. Omar Cabezas, *Fire from the Mountain: The Making of a Sandinista,* trans. Kathleen Weaver (New York: Crown, 1985).

4. Tomás Borge, *La Paciente Impaciencia* (Managua: Vanguardia, 1989), 47.

5. The Historic Program begins by defining the FSLN as a "Vanguard organization, capable of directly confronting its enemies and thereby seizing political power and establishing a revolutionary government based on a worker-peasant alliance, along with all the country's patriotic, anti-imperialist, and anti-oligarchic forces." Its objectives, spelled out in three chapters, were to create a revolutionary government based on the full participation of all the people, nationalize the property of the Somozas as well as foreign-held property, give control over foreign trade to the state, carry out an agrarian reform, extend public education, bring in new labor legislation, integrate the Atlantic Coast into the Nicaraguan nation, secure the emancipation of women, build a patriotic people's army, put an end to exploitation by the Yankee, and build bonds of solidarity with all people who struggle for their liberation. See FSLN, *Programa del Frente Sandinista de Liberación Nacional* (Managua: DPEP-FSLN, 1981 [1969]).

6. Timothy Wickham-Crowley, *Guerrillas and Revolution in Latin America: A Comparative Study of Insurgents and Regimes Since 1956* (Princeton, NJ: Princeton University Press, 1992).

7. The rise of two new tendencies with the FSLN was produced in no small measure by the physical separation of various members of the leadership due to the dictatorship's repression. Thus it was impossible to debate alternative views on organizational and strategic questions. The three tendencies that emerged were the Prolonged People's War (GPP), Proletarian Tendency (TP, also *proles*), and Insurrectionary Tendency (Terceristas or TI, or *terces*).

8. Carlos Vilas discusses the recruitment of the wealthy in "Family Affairs: Class, Lineage, and Politics in Contemporary Nicaragua," *Journal of Latin American Studies* 24 (1992): 309–341.

9. Much the same thing happened in Colombia within the M-19 (Movimiento 19 de abril, or 19th of April Movement) and in El Salvador within the groups forming the FMLN (Frente Faribundo Martí para la Liberación Nacional, or Faribundo Marti National Liberation Front).

10. Duverger sees the Order substituting dedication for membership: "Dedication is complete membership, the direction given to the whole of one's life; membership is only a restricted dedication, affecting only part of the member's activity and not committing his inner self." Maurice Duverger, *Political Parties,* trans. Barbara and Robert North, 3rd ed. (London: Methuen, 1964), 126.

11. This is discussed more fully in Salvador Martí i Puig, "El FSLN d'organització político-mililtar a l'oposició parlamentària," master's thesis in politcal science, Universidad Autònoma de Barcelona, 1992.

12. The Group of Twelve was composed of notable Nicaraguans with international reputations in their various fields of endeavor but without partisan ties. They were active opponents of the Somoza dictatorship who had permanent links with the Sandinistas. They played a crucial role in the development of the FSLN's international links.

13. Charles Tilly, *From Mobilization to Revolution* (New York: Random House, 1978), 198.

14. The National Directorate remained unchanged until the FSLN's 1991 National Congress, except for the death of one member, Carlos Nuñez, in 1990. Its members were Daniel Ortega, Humberto Ortega, and Victor Tirado from the Terceristas; Bayardo Arce, Tomás Borge, and Henry Ruiz from the Prolonged People's War tendency; and Luis Carrión, Carlos Nuñez, and Jaime Wheelock from the Proletarian Tendency.

15. See Carlos Vilas, *Perfiles de la Revolución sandinista* (La Habana: Ediciones Casa de la Américas, 1984).

16. Quoted in Elizabeth Maier, *Nicaragua. La mujer en la Revolución* (México, DF: Ediciones de la Cultura Popular, 1980).

17. Lynn Horton covers this complex issue in *Peasants in Arms: War and Peace in the Mountains of Nicaragua, 1979–1994* (Athens: Ohio University Press, 1998).

18. Salvador Martí i Puig, *Nicaragua 1977–1996: La revolución enredada* (Madrid: Libros de la Catarata, 1997).

19. The sectoral issues of agriculture and international relations are treated in Chapters 10 and 11.

20. Carlos Vilas, *Between Earthquakes and Volcanoes* (New York: Monthly Review Press, 1995), 10.

21. Quoted in Dennis Gilbert, *Sandinistas: The Party and the Revolution* (Oxford: Basil Blackwell, 1989), 61.

22. Orlando Núñez, ed., *La Guerra en Nicaragua* (Managua: CIPRES-NORAD, 1991).

23. See, Gilbert, *Sandinistas*.

24. Alejandro Martínez Cuenca examines this issue in detail in *Nicaragua: Una década de retos* (Managua: Nueva Nicaragua, 1990).

25. Núñez, *La Guerra*.

26. Included among the mass organizations were the several Sandinista-affiliated unions, various sectoral groups (e.g., women, youth, farmers), and neighborhood organizations called the Sandinista Defense Committees.

27. Translator's note: Although parties were present in the Council of State, they did not represent geographic constituencies. Their role was to represent ideological currents or simply to include parties as social groups similar to a business organization or church.

28. Luís Serra, "Organizaciones populares: Entre las bases y el poder," *Pensamiento Propio* 56 (March 1988): 41–45.

29. Carlos Vilas, "Especulaciones sobre una sorpresa: Las elecciones en Nicaragua," *Revista de Ciencias Sociales Desarrollo Económico* 118 (1990): 255–276.

30. Serra, "Organizaciones populares," 44.

31. Roque Dalton, *Las historias prohibidas del Pulgarcito* (La Habana: Casa de las Américas, 1974), 112.

> pensando en lo bonito que habría sido la vida
> y todo lo demás
> si la lucha no hubiera sido tan dura
> en el país más enano que le vino uno a tocar

32. The presence of members of the same "leading families" in the leadership of the Sandinistas, the Contra, and the UNO meant that there was always an

element of moderation and consensus on which later pacts and accords could be built.

33. *Barricada Internacional,* "Reflexiones después de la derrota," March 3, 1994, 40.

34. Envío, "FSLN Discussion Papers," *Envío* 109, August 1990, www.envio .org.ni/.

35. Alejandro Bravo, "Esperanza," in *Merecido Tributo* (Managua: ANE-CNE, 1995), 28–29.

> Hace diez años
> Mis hijos estaban pequeñitos
> Y me costaba mucho
> Conseguir leche para ellos.
>
> Hace diez anos
> El paisaje era el mismo
> Pero desde los autobuses atestados
> Sentíamos
> Que nos pertenecía
>
> Hace diez anos
> Reagan tronaba
> Contra Nicaragua
> Y los estudiantes
> Recogían las cosechas
>
> Hace diez años
> Las cosas estaban jodidas
> Se hacía fila para todo
> Menos para la esperanza
>
> II
>
> La Esperanza
> La mujer del cuadro intermedio,
> La que compraba en la *Diplo*

36. The *Diplo* refers to the Diplotienda, where those who could pay in US dollars and had the appropriate legal status—diplomats, journalists, and the Sandinista *nomenklatura*—could buy goods utterly unobtainable anywhere else in the country.

37. Carlos Vilas, *El debate interno sandinista* (México, DF: CIIH-UNAM, mimeo, 1991).

38. Salvador Martí i Puig and Salvador Santiuste, "El FSLN: De guerrilla victoriosa a oposición negociadora," in *La izquierda revolucionaria en Centroamerica: De la lucha armada a la participación electoral,* edited by Salvador Martí i Puig and Salvador Santiuste (Madrid: Libros de la Catarata, 2006), 173–202.

39. Aldo Díaz Lacayo, *El Frente Sandinista después de la derrota electoral* (Caracas: Centauro, 1994), 68.

40. Salvador Martí i Puig, "Nicaragua postrevolucionaria: El laberinto Sandinista y la difícil consolidación democrática," *Afers Internacionals* 34–35 (1996): 149–169.

41. Martí, in "El FSLN," 1992, 136–147, discusses the balance of power in that party congress and analyzes the organizational changes it prescribed.

42. For details see Salvador Santiuste, "La incompeta transformación del FSLN," *América Latina Hoy* 27 (2001): 75–98.

43. Salvador Martí i Puig, *Nicaragua, 1977–1996: La revolución enredada* (Madrid: Libros de la Catarata, 1997), 187–201.

44. Translator's note: There is no reason why threats and negotiations cannot be combined into a coherent oppositional strategy by a party. In fact, that is what the Sandinistas did from 1994 to 2006, under Daniel Ortega's undisputed leadership.

45. See Katherine Hoyt, *The Many Faces of Sandinista Democracy* (Athens: Ohio University Press, 1997), as well as her "Parties and Pacts in Contemporary Nicaragua," paper presented to the congress of the Latin American Studies Association, Washington, DC, 2001.

46. Ernesto Cardenal, "El FSLN está secuestrado," *Envío* 154 (November 1994), www.envio.org.ni/.

47. Translator's note: *Barricada* ceased publication in January 1998.

48. *Estatutos 2002 FSLN*, www.fsln-nicaragua.com. All references to the FSLN's 2002 statutes come from this document.

49. In Alemán's case the charges involved corruption; in Ortega's the issue was sexual abuse of his stepdaughter. Ortega never stood trial. Alemán was convicted of massive fraud in 2001, but the charges were dismissed by Nicaragua's Supreme Court in 2009; Elena Martínez Barahona provides details in Chapter 5.

50. The passing of this decree (3-2007) was particularly controversial because a majority of the National Assembly actually voted against it. Afterward, Ortega resorted to the Supreme Court of Justice and obtained a resolution in his favor.

51. Declarations taken from the weekly report *El 19,* published on the official webpage of the President of Nicaragua. See *Nicaragua Hoy,* "FSLN 'revisará estrategias' para seguir en el poder," August 27, 2009, www.nicaraguahoy.info.

3

The Politics of Opposition

David Close

IN 2006, FOR THE FIRST TIME IN SIXTEEN YEARS, THE SANDINISTA National Liberation Front (Frente Sandinista de Liberación Nacional, or FSLN) won a national election in Nicaragua (see Table 3.1). The FSLN did this while receiving just 38 percent of the vote and accomplished this feat because its opponents split three ways. The party's rightist opponents, the strongest electoral bloc in the country, suffered a schism that left each of two contenders—the Nicaraguan Liberal Alliance (Alianza Liberal Nicaragüense, or ALN) and the Constitutionalist Liberal Party (Partido Liberal Constitucionalista, or PLC), the governing party since 1996—dividing over 55 percent of the vote nearly equally between them. However, the FSLN also had a leftist opponent: the Sandinista Renewal Party (Movimiento Renovador Sandinista, or MRS), composed of those who were expelled from the FSLN or who tired of Daniel Ortega's centralized, personalist leadership and left on their own. Although the MRS ended up as an also-ran, it showed strongly through much of the campaign, hinting that Ortega and the FSLN were in danger of losing their monopoly on progressive politics in Nicaragua.

Although the Sandinista Revolution dramatically altered the fabric of Nicaraguan politics, making democratic electoral politics possible for the first time, it is clear from the 2006 election results that the FSLN is not the country's natural governing party. Since 2006, there have been two Liberal parties, but their politics and policies are actually conservative in the North American sense. They gained the support of 55 percent of Nicaragua's voters. Even putting the two Sandinista parties together, something neither would accept, leaves the country's left in the minority. Adding the MRS in with the ALN and PLC indicates the dimensions of anti-FSLN sentiment in 2006: nearly five-eighths of the Nicaraguan electorate preferred someone other than the Frente Sandinista.

Table 3.1 Nicaraguan Presidential Election Results, 1984–2006 (percentage)

Year	FSLN	Leading Opponent	Second Leading Opponent	Third Leading Opponent
1984	66.97	PCD, 14.04	PLI, 9.6	PPSC, 5.6
1990	40.8	UNO, 54.8	Others, 4.4	
1996	37.75	PLC, 51	Others, 11.2	
2001	42.3	PLC, 56.3	Others, 1.4	
2006	37.99	ALN, 28.3	PLC, 27.1	MRS, 6.3

Sources: For 1984 election, Envío, "Nicaragua's 1984 Elections—A History Worth the Retelling," Envío 102, January 1990, www.envío.org.ni/; for the others, Political Data Base of the Americas, *Nicaraguan Electoral Results,* pdba.georgetown.edu/.

Notes: PCD: Partido Conservador Democrático, or Conservative Democratic Party; PLI: Partido Liberal Independiente, or Independent Liberal Party; PPSC: Partido Popular Social Cristiano, or Popular Social Christian Party; UNO: Union Nacional Opositora, or National Union of the Opposition; PLC: Partido Liberal Constitucionalista, or Constitutionalist Liberal Party; ALN: Alianza Liberal Nicaragüense, or Nicaraguan Liberal Alliance; MRS: Movimiento Renovador Sandinista, or Sandinista Renewal Movement.

This chapter sets out who the FSLN's opponents are and examines how their behavior and policies have changed over time. In doing so, it necessarily lays out how the Sandinistas have acted, in both government and opposition. It proceeds in four steps. First, it introduces the two sides, Sandinistas and anti-Sandinistas. Next, it discusses political opposition as a concept. The third part examines the evolution of anti-Sandinista politics since 1961, with similar attention given to the Sandinistas. The conclusion discusses how the party's return to power in 2006 affects the balance of power between the FSLN and its opponents, as well as the way in which political competition is carried out in contemporary Nicaragua.

Sandinistas and Anti-Sandinistas

Even before the Sandinistas took power in 1979, there were anti-Sandinistas. They were concentrated in the Somoza regime, which the FSLN sought to overthrow, but also represented substantial swathes of the economic and social elites, the usual antirevolutionary interests. At the risk of overstating the case, those anti-Sandinistas were opposed to everything the then-guerrilla insurgents stood for. First, they were anti-Marxist and more broadly opposed to significant changes in the distribution of power and privilege in Nicaraguan society. There was also, therefore, a difference in the class composition of the Sandinistas and their opponents, for although the FSLN's leadership was drawn mainly from the middle and even upper classes, the anti-Sandinistas were the bulwarks of the country's establishment.

Later, important segments of the peasantry and the poor more generally came to oppose the Sandinista revolutionary government for its policies regarding land reform and the prosecution of the counterinsurgent war.[1]

Some of these foes of Sandinismo were domestic, like the Somoza dictatorship and its allies, but others were foreign, such as the government of the United States. That Washington's foreign policy interests would lead it to oppose Marxist revolutionaries everywhere during the Cold War was obvious.[2] In 2009, thirty years after the Somozas fell, opposition to the FSLN still had both domestic and international components. Domestic opposition came from political parties, the Catholic Church, much of civil society, the more conservative elements of society generally, and those who came to distrust the FSLN during the 1980s. Where their predecessors often used violence to first repress and later attempt to oust the FSLN, now anti-Sandinistas operated within the limits of electoral politics. International opposition still came from Washington, although there too resort to arms was no longer an option.

Paralleling this story is the Sandinistas' own journey from revolutionary guerrillas to radically transformational governing party to a decade and a half as a constitutional opposition party and now back to power as leader-dominated left-populists. As guerrillas, from 1961 to 1979, the FSLN's opponents were the state it was trying to overthrow, the interests—class, sectoral, and ideological—that state represented, and the foreign actors—the United States among others—who supported the regime in Managua. That state was a dictatorship run by two generations of the Somoza family, which like any state had full legal rights to defend itself. Thus both the first anti-Sandinistas and the then-insurgent Sandinistas relied heavily on force.

With the triumph of the Sandinista Revolution in 1979, the nature of the relationship between the Frente Sandinista and anti-Sandinista forces changed because the regime had changed and reordered the political system in the following ways:

1. Shifting the bases of the system's legitimacy, with the revolutionary seizure of power having become the key to the right to rule;
2. Altering the manner in which government was held accountable and to whom it was responsible with the coming to power of a vanguard party committed to radical change;
3. Installing new patterns of influence over and access to government that made Nicaragua's subordinate classes real stakeholders for the first time;
4. Creating new relationships among state, society, and citizens that privileged the formerly excluded and left the political system more pluralistic and competitive than it had been before the revolution.[3]

The revolutionaries now controlled the state, so anti-Sandinista politics assumed new forms. Some of the opposition targeted the FSLN more as a government than as the builders of a new regime. Another part was determined to end the Sandinista project but generally used pacific means, though often illegal ones. A third stream of opposition used violence and built a guerrilla insurgency, the contras.[4]

Electoral defeat in 1990 and only the second peaceful handover of power from one party to another in Nicaragua's history made the FSLN an opposition party until it won the presidency again in 2006.[5] The anti-Sandinistas controlled the state for sixteen years, winning the 1990, 1996, and 2001 elections by near-landslide margins. However, they acted generally within the limits of a constitution originally drafted by the revolutionary government in 1987. Although an array of conservative groups in Nicaraguan life (such as the Catholic hierarchy and business organizations) opposed the Frente, it is the political parties, most recently the Liberals (PLC), and, since 2006, the ALN and the MRS that really shape anti-Sandinista (better called anti-FSLN) politics. More critically, from 1990 until 2006, the anti-Sandinista side was unbeatable at the polls, whether led by the National Union of the Opposition (Union Nacional Opositora, or UNO) or the PLC. Indeed, Nicaragua's four national elections since 1990 have seen the Frente unable to garner more than 42.3 percent of the vote, their 2001 figure.[6] Although this no longer leaves the FSLN in opposition, it does show that it has three opponents for every two supporters.

Equally important are the effects of a succession of divisions within the Frente itself since 1990. Some of them resulted from doctrinal differences: those who wanted a party that retained its revolutionary identity and anti-imperialist style defeated, on several occasions, proponents of a more social democratic Sandinismo. However, these programmatic conflicts also had a personal component: if you supported Daniel Ortega, one of the original nine *comandantes de la revolución* and the only Sandinista ever to run for president in Nicaragua (1984–2006), you backed the party's status quo; but if wanted change, you challenged him. In fact, FSLN supporters are commonly called Danielistas. Thus the FSLN faces both anti-Sandinistas, who reject all the party stands for, and anti-Danielistas, whose opposition is focused on the party's current policies and its leader but not its revolutionary history or leftist politics per se.

In the forty-five years (1961–2006) from the founding of the FSLN to its return to power, Nicaragua went from personalist dictatorship to revolutionary democracy and, now, an electoral democracy.[7] Each of these three regimes has conditioned how anti-Sandinista interests have organized themselves, what objectives they have had, and how they have acted to minimize the Sandinistas' influence. Clearly, the FSLN has changed as well, learning to be an opposition party, shedding its less revolutionary wing, and becoming increasingly leader-centered. This makes examining these three periods the most effective way to present the non-FSLN side of Nicaraguan national politics. This analysis starts by reflecting on the theme of political opposition because it directs attention to both the relationship between a government and its opponents, and to what those opponents do.

The Politics of Opposition

Political opposition has two characteristics that interest us. First, it is about resistance and dissent, saying no to a government or even to a regime. Second, it is distinguished from other forms of political conflict because it offers an alternative policy, government, or entire political order. For example, during their eighteen years as a guerrilla front (1961–1979), the Sandinistas not only fought the Somocista dictatorship but also offered an alternative model for organizing the state and exercising power.

Opposition is a central concept in political analysis, but it is not especially well specified theoretically. Were we to ask political scientists to tell us about political opposition, most would say something like this: opposition is an integral part of all political processes; legally tolerated, openly exercised, peaceful opposition is a prerequisite for democracy; and in democracies, it applies principally to legislatures and political parties. We shall examine each of these briefly and then develop a number of implicit themes more fully.

Saying that opposition is always part of politics recognizes that politics is conflictual and that there are always those who seek change. What a state does will always be controversial because there are some interests (individuals, sectors, classes, etc.) whose demands will not be met to their satisfaction. Those who believe that government acts wrongly may try to change the government's position by lobbying, protest, or even insurrection. Throughout most of recorded history, opportunities for resistance to authority have been circumscribed, as authoritarian states were the norm. Resistance was risky, costly, and often unsuccessful. It is only with the arrival of constitutional regimes in Western Europe, the forerunners of democracy, that the role and prospects of political opposition change.

To the Encyclopedist Denis Diderot, "the right of opposition . . . is a natural, inalienable, and sacred right."[8] To later thinkers, opposition became an essential part of democracy, the natural consequence of a free, rational being's liberty to voice opinions and share in governing. In constitutional orders, where government functions according to law, opposition is accepted as normal and tolerated. In an ideal democracy, opposition is encouraged because it makes governments defend their decisions and fosters debate. But the true mark of democratic opposition is that success is possible. An opposition party can become the government, or a citizens' movement can see its views become law, and it happens within a legal framework that lets future oppositions know that they too can win.

Analysts agree that opposition is integral to democracy. Ghita Ionescu and Isobel Madariaga hold that "the presence or absence of institutionalized opposition can become the criterion for the classification of any political society into one of two categories: liberal or dictatorial, democratic or authoritarian, pluralistic-constitutional or monolithic."[9] In the same vein, Stephanie Lawson asserts that "constitutional political opposition is the *sine qua non* of contemporary democracy in mass polities and that its institutionalization in some form or another is required before a regime can be called 'democratic' with any real meaning."[10] Further, most commentators emphasize the role of political parties and legislative oppositions. Seymour Martin Lipset defines democracy "as a system of institutionalized opposition in which the people choose among alternative contenders for public office."[11] Robert Dahl is even clearer, stating that "one is inclined to regard the existence of an opposition party as very nearly the most distinctive characteristic of democracy itself, and we may take the absence of an opposition party as evidence, if not always conclusive proof, for the absence of democracy."[12]

Even if parties are the only oppositional actors that are able to win elections and govern, they are not the only instruments of democratic, constitutional opposition. The media often criticize an administration and frequently suggest alternative policies. Movements are another easily recognized source of resistance to a state. Finally, private actors, institutions, groups, or individuals can also work to hamper or even bring down governments. Opposition in democracy can obviously be mobilized outside elections, as the varied forms of political protest demonstrate. Indeed, in democratic states only violent opposition is unacceptable.

In authoritarian systems, though, violence is often the most effective, or even the only, way to express dissent. That was the reality that confronted the FSLN prior to 1979, although even the Somozas permitted "licensed opposition" (parties that could run for office but would never be allowed to win). After winning the revolution but prior to 1982, the Sandinistas too favored a system with licensed opposition. They abandoned it, proscribing only groups that advocated the return of the dictatorship, but still faced violent opposition from the contras and a civil opposition that was not restricted to parties but included the press (*La Prensa*), radio (Radio Corporación), the Catholic hierarchy, and business organizations.[13] Nevertheless, it meant that the focus of political activity would increasingly be on parties and elections, above all after the 1984 elections.

Although Nicaraguan politics are filled with personal invective, and violent conflicts occasionally erupt between police and protesters, armed struggle has all but vanished from the country's political life. The 1990 elections and subsequent peace agreements ended the war, and remaining banditry by remnants of the contras and demobilized soldiers from the armed forces was suppressed by 1993. The FSLN waged a multifaceted opposition during its sixteen years out of office, combining parliamentary, electoral, and protest-based direct action as it fought to retake power, yet it never attempted a violent overthrow. Parties are the main oppositional agents in Nicaragua, but they do not monopolize oppositional politics. Doctors, taxi and bus owners, and university students have staged long, violent strikes to protest state policies. In fact, parties are not always instruments of opposition: the two main parties, the Sandinistas and the Liberals, formed a power-sharing arrangement (conventionally called the Pact) in 2000 in an attempt to exclude other parties from the nation's political life. Thus between 1979 and 2006, Nicaragua's anti-Sandinistas went from waging counterrevolution to colluding with the FSLN.

The remainder of this chapter examines anti-Sandinista politics. For convenience and clarity, I treat each regime and the style of its oppositional politics separately. Within each period there is a description of the nature of the regime, an examination of the Sandinistas' role in the system, and a discussion of who the anti-Sandinistas are and how and why they oppose the FSLN.

The Somozas: The Original Anti-Sandinistas

It was natural that the Somoza dictatorship would oppose the FSLN with all its might.[14] In 1934, the patriarch of the clan, Anastasio Somoza García, commander of the National Guard, ordered the execution of Augusto César Sandino. Even without this personal involvement, the Somozas would have opposed the current Sandinistas for the simple reason that the FSLN sought to overthrow them. All states, regardless of how well or badly they behave, have the right to self-preservation. Faced with a guerrilla insurgency, the Somozas did the obvious and responded with military force.

The Regime

Adjectives abound to describe the political system that the Somozas built in the forty-three years (1936–1979) they ruled Nicaragua, but "sultanistic" figures prominently in the academic literature. Max Weber first used the term to describe extreme examples of patrimonial regimes: systems in which the ruler treated the state as a personal possession.[15] It was reintroduced into political science by Juan Linz[16] and adapted by Linz and Alfred Stepan[17] to the analysis of democratic transition and consolidation, and a more recent work by H. Chelabi and Linz[18] developed the concept further. Sultanism is characterized by the conflation of regime and ruler, a marked personalism, and sham constitutionalism.[19] It is a regime in which "all individuals, groups, and institutions are permanently subject to the unpredictable and despotic intervention of the [ruler], and thus all pluralism is precarious."[20]

John Booth's examination of the Somoza system as a sultantistic regime fleshes out those abstract criteria.[21] The most notable feature of Somocismo was that it spanned two generations. The father, Anastasio Somoza García (nicknamed Tacho), was able to bequeath the Nicaraguan state to his son, Luis Somoza Debayle, who on his death was succeeded by his brother Anastasio (Tachito).[22] A second distinctive feature was the existence of a licensed opposition, something earlier Nicaraguan strongmen, like José Santos Zelaya, had not permitted. These tolerated opponents could make deals ("pacts") with the regime, receiving "quotas of power"—guaranteed shares of government positions—in return for acquiescing in the Somozas' fraudulent electoral victories. The other attributes noted by Booth—a nonprofessional army controlled by the Somozas and high levels of corruption—are common characteristics of any caudillo-based political system.[23]

What brought the Somoza dynasty to an end was principally the cupidity of its last leader. The first Somoza fell to an assassin's bullet in 1956. The second sought to withdraw the family from direct political involvement, using instead its control of the Nationalist Liberal Party (Partido Liberal Nacionalista, or PLN), but he died of a heart attack in 1967 before he could make the necessary changes. Tacho and Luis had been able political operators, knowing how to mix coercion and cooptation to keep their rule secure. However, Tachito lacked their sense of balance. When confronted with the Managua earthquake of 1972, this last Somoza pilfered relief funds and supplies and then had the capital rebuilt in ways that benefited the Somozas at the expense of the rest of the economic elite. This set in motion a series of events that saw the bulk of Nicaragua's capitalists abandoning the Somozas.

Finally, a word about the Somozas' relationship with the government of the United States is necessary. Of the first Somoza, US president Franklin Delano Roosevelt supposedly said, "He's a son of a bitch, but he's our son of a bitch!" The Somozas worked hard at being America's "sons of bitches," for example by letting the B-26s that were to support the Bay of Pigs invasion take off from Puerto Cabezas on Nicaragua's Atlantic Coast. Although the Somozas were never anyone's lapdogs, the US government appreciated the family's reliable support in the Cold War and its ironfisted control of Nicaraguan politics that kept the country from being a "problem" for Washington for four decades.

The Sandinistas

The Sandinistas began as an insurgent guerrilla military force. In most guerrilla insurgencies, military action is integrated with political action: recruiting adherents, proselytizing, and gaining allies among the regime's nonviolent opponents. The FSLN was a subversive, antistate opposition. The state responded with force but did little political work. Thus the Somozas were ineffective counterinsurgents because they relied nearly entirely on repression and ignored reform. Perhaps the assassination in 1956 of the founding Somoza, Anastasio Somoza García, and the regime's fall to revolutionary Sandinista insurgents twenty-three years later were logical consequences of the Somozas' method of rule.

However, the FSLN brought with it its own antidemocratic baggage when it came to dealing with opponents. As a politico-military insurgent organization, it could not be open and pluralistic, and its relations with its opponents, especially the Somoza state, were most often carried out violently.[24]

The Anti-Sandinistas

From the Sandinistas' founding in 1961 until their revolutionary triumph in 1979, anti-Sandinista politics were military politics. In this effort the Somoza state was allied with the government of the United States, which supported and equipped the government in Managua. By 1961 the noninterventionism of the Good Neighbor Policy was long dead, a casualty of the Cold War. Fidel Castro's revolution in 1959 pushed anticommunist fervor to new heights, and the Alliance for Progress made money available for antiguerrilla military training. Although the Carter administration pressured Tachito to reform or retire, Washington never accepted the coming to power of a revolutionary regime.

More interesting than the response of either the Somozas or the US government was the reaction of Nicaragua's middle and upper classes. As already noted, many of those who should have formed the dictatorship's natural constituency began to abandon the Somozas after the 1972 earthquake. Through the rest of the decade, the children of the elite rallied to the Frente in significant numbers; and at least some of their parents, notably those who formed the Group of Twelve (see discussion of Los Doce in

Chapter 2), actively supported a Sandinista triumph. Even the once securely tame Catholic Church distanced itself from the Somoza regime, with the archbishop of Managua mediating between state and rebels on two occasions.

The Sandinistas Govern

Unlike the FMLN (Frente Faribundo Martí para la Liberación Nacional, or Faribundo Marti National Liberation Front) in El Salvador, the Sandinistas had never controlled extensive liberated zones, and thus they had little administrative experience. What they did have, though, was the support of much of the population and the tolerance of the upper classes and the Roman Catholic hierarchy. The revolutionaries also benefited from the extreme unpopularity of the Somozas, which let them nationalize the properties of the Somozas and their most important supporters, all of whom had fled the country, without provoking protests from Conservatives who had broken with the dictator.

The honeymoon did not last long. Anti-Sandinista guerrillas, the contras, directly supported by Washington, were soon operating in the same remote areas where the FSLN began its struggle. Moreover, the new revolutionary government, the Governing Junta of National Reconstruction (Junta de Gobierno de Reconstrucción Nacional, or JGRN), began moving quickly to revolutionize Nicaragua, implementing what the Sandinistas called "the logic of the majority." These plans did not include electoral politics because the FSLN declared that the people had voted for the revolution with their lives, yet they did allow some space for opposition, especially in the admittedly weak representative chamber, the Council of State.

Nevertheless, within two years of taking power, the Sandinistas saw many of their erstwhile anti-Somoza allies, notably a civic if disloyal opposition, the Nicaraguan Democratic Coordinator (CDN), boycotting state institutions and beginning to oppose the principles on which the revolutionary state was founded.[25] Over time, neutrals and even supporters began having doubts about the revolutionaries, with many of the skeptics, especially poor peasants, eventually taking up arms against the revolutionary regime. Foreign supporters, notably European social democratic governments, began pressing the FSLN to hold elections and bring more forces into the political system, making it more pluralistic.

Political pluralism means, at a minimum, that there exist sources of power that operate independently of the state. The Sandinista state always claimed to be pluralistic, but in 1983 Nicaraguan pluralism grew dramatically with the approval of a Parties Law, which allowed any party not advocating a return to Somocismo to govern if it won an election. Presumably the FSLN could not imagine that the people would not support their vanguard and thus supposed the new law posed few risks. Rather, by conforming to the institutional standards of orthodox liberal democracy, the Sandinistas saw themselves institutionalizing their revolution. The new institutions—competitive elections; an expanded role for political parties; and an executive, legislature, and judiciary that would have looked familiar in any democracy— would let the Frente steer the regime's development with fewer objections from abroad.

Things did not happen that way, yet pluralist politics worked well for the revolutionaries. The government wrote a constitution in 1987 that had many liberal elements and was not amended until 1995, five years after the FSLN lost power. It passed an autonomy statute for the ethnically distinct Atlantic Coast of Nicaragua. And the new legislature, the National Assembly, became increasingly important. However, the negatives outweighed the positives as the Contra war intensified and the economy neared collapse. A ruined economy and a seemingly endless counterinsurgency war were the record on which the FSLN had to run in the 1990 elections.

Those elections marked a turning point in Nicaraguan political history. First, the Sandinistas lost and, having lost, handed over power to the victorious UNO and its winning presidential candidate, Violeta Chamorro. Second, the election crystallized the Sandinista versus anti-Sandinista split that had characterized Nicaraguan politics since 1979. Third, it marked the beginning of sixteen uninterrupted years of right-of-center government in the country. However, it also saw oppositional politics lose its military flavor.

The Anti-Sandinista Opposition

One of the traits that most distinguished the FSLN from other revolutionary governing parties was its perspective on the role of opposition in its regime.

> They can be anti-Sandinistas, they can be against the Frente Sandinista as a political party, they can criticize us, but they cannot attack the bases of the new society that is in the historical interest of the people of Nicaragua . . . These people can even be nonrevolutionary, but they cannot be counterrevolutionary.[26]

Perhaps the best way to understand the opposition to the Sandinista government is to divide it into three categories. The first is naturally the counterrevolutionary armed opposition that waged an insurgent war. The other two forms of opposition the Sandinistas faced were a conventional or loyal

opposition and an opposition of principle, which rejected the very foundations of the revolutionary state but did so nonviolently.[27] We begin with the
contras and their sponsors.

The origins of the contras' story lie in 1919, when the World War I allies invaded the new Soviet Union, following Winston Churchill's advice
that "the only remedy for Bolshevism is bullets." This hot side of what became the Cold War arrived in Latin America in 1954 with the overthrow of
the reformist government of Jacobo Arbenz in Guatemala, and we should
not forget that the British government refused to recognize the electoral victory of the Marxist Cheddi Jagan in its Guyanese colony that same year.
There were replays in the hemisphere with the Bay of Pigs: counterinsurgency assistance via the Alliance for Progress; and the coups in Brazil, Ar-
gentina, Chile, and Uruguay that brought bureaucratic authoritarians to
power. Sandinista Nicaragua could not hope to escape the same fate.

Washington's chosen instrument in what was called a "low-intensity
war" against the Sandinistas was the contras.[28] Although the contras were an
insurgent force, using the military tactics of guerrilla warfare, they were not
guerrilla insurgents as the Sandinistas had been. Unlike the FSLN, or most
twentieth-century guerrillas, the contras did relatively little political work,
relying far more on violence. This was not accidental but rather the application of rational choice theory to insurgent and counterinsurgent warfare.
Its objective was to increase "the cost, through coercion and terror, of supporting . . . movements [that Washington opposed]."[29]

Obviously, the armed counterrevolution was an opposition of principle, a disloyal opposition rejecting all aspects of a regime, but oppositional
forces can deny the legitimacy of a state without resorting to violence. Indeed, they can operate within the confines of a constitution they absolutely
reject, even if they maintain contact with armed opposition groups. In Sandinista Nicaragua, the leading actors in this civic opposition of principle
were the CDN, whose members included businesspeople, unions, and political parties, and separately the hierarchy of the Roman Catholic Church,
and *La Prensa,* the newspaper that took on the Sandinistas much as it had
the Somozas.[30] Occasionally, these fierce and active critics of the FSLN
would find their members jailed or, in the case of *La Prensa,* be unable to
publish. It should be noted that these actions by the government occurred
under a state of emergency when the war with the contras was at its peak.

There was also a loyal opposition, defined as one that supports the constitutional framework of a regime, while objecting to specific policies or the
general conduct of government by a specific party or administration. The
Sandinistas' loyal opposition was built around the six parties that ran against
the FSLN in the 1984 elections: the Nicaraguan Socialist Party (Partido

Socialista Nicaragüense, or PSN), the Independent Liberal Party (Partido Liberal Independiente, or PLI), the Nicaraguan Communist Party (Partido Comunista de Nicaragua, or PCdeN), the Popular Social Christian Party (Partido Popular Social Cristiano, or PPSC), the Conservative Democratic Party (Partido Conservador Democrático, or PSD), and the Marxist-Leninist Popular Action Movement (Movimiento de Acción Popular-Marxista-Leninista, or MAP-ML). None of them was strong, well organized, or sophisticated in terms of its strategies. At times, Sandinista mass organizations, such as the Farmers' and Ranchers' Union (Unión Nacional de Agricultores y Ganaderos, or UNAG) or the women's organization Asociación de Mujeres Nicaragüenses (Luisa Amanda Espinosa, or AMNLAE), would also act as loyal opponents of the government by resisting or protesting specific policy initiatives.

Overall, the anti-Sandinistas had more legal avenues open to them than had the opponents of the Somozas. The civic side of the movement was not without effect, but had they not benefited from the counterrevolution and the implacable opposition of the US government, it is unlikely that either the loyal or disloyal segments of the Nicaraguan opposition would have dislodged the Sandinista administration in 1990.

The Reign of the Right: 1990–2006

On losing the 1990 elections, Daniel Ortega promised Nicaraguans that the Frente would henceforth govern from below. There were at least two ways to take this statement. The more benign interpretation had the defeated candidate saying that his party would combine extraparliamentary and parliamentary forms of opposition to push the new government of Violeta Chamorro as hard as it could, but that it would remain civic and loyal to the constitution. A more suspicious reading saw Ortega threatening to overthrow the legitimately elected government by force. Over time, the FSLN's behavior bore out the former interpretation. In fact, the Sandinistas went beyond what anyone could have read into the original statement by adopting the stance of the Conservatives during the Somoza era and entering into pacts with the governing party. Unlike those Conservatives, however, the Frente has managed to turn its pact into real power, not just a source of jobs for its followers.

Three Variations on the Politics of the Nicaraguan Right

Three different conservative, anti-Sandinista administrations, representing two different parties, governed Nicaragua from 1990 to 2006. These governments effectively rolled back most of the Sandinistas' social and economic agenda, setting Nicaragua squarely on the neoliberal straight and narrow. What they did not do, however, was completely abandon the shift to formal democratic procedures that the FSLN began in 1982. Although the second of these anti-Sandinista governments, in which Arnoldo Alemán Lacayo led the PLC, achieved levels of corruption that rivaled if not surpassed anything the Somozas had accomplished, there was never a return to the Somozas' use of coercion to manage opposition. That this was due to the independence of the military and the police does not change the fact that state violence practically disappeared as a regular instrument of rule in Nicaragua.[31]

These anti-Sandinistas generally sought to marginalize the FSLN as a political force, rather than repress it. In 1990, an "It's time for a change" campaign was enough to push the Frente from office. Perhaps if the UNO had not split into two camps over the issue of how forcefully to disarticulate the FSLN, the Sandinistas might have suffered a sharper and more permanent reverse. As it was, the Frente's leader, Daniel Ortega, was able to concoct strategies and seize conjunctural openings that let the party make a strong run at power in 1996, possibly losing only because of a last-minute intervention by Cardinal Miguel Obando y Bravo in favor of the PLC. The winning presidential candidate, Arnoldo Alemán, presumably thought he had a surer way of keeping the Sandinistas perennial runners-up by engaging them in a pact, which we examine below. In 2001, the PLC returned to power, led by former vice president Enrique Bolaños Geyer, as usual with assistance from Washington. Whether these maneuvers were needed remains an open question, because the Frente's electoral support still hovered around 40 percent, which is always second-best in a two-party race.

The Sandinistas in Opposition

So what did the FSLN do to try to stop being the perpetual runner-up of Nicaraguan politics? First, although the Frente has always called itself a revolutionary party, its everyday practice, the content of its campaigns, and its formal alliances in 2001 and 2006 with groups that included a number of former anti-Sandinistas revealed an appreciation of the need to at least appear moderate.[32] Second, the party and its veteran leader, Daniel Ortega, took advantage of any opening everyday politics offered to push the FSLN agenda and increase its power. During the Chamorro administration, this took three forms: supporting the president, a moderate, when hardliners in her party deserted her; establishing close relations with Chamorro's son-in-law and minister of the presidency, Antonio Lacayo, to give the FSLN a regular channel into the administration; and siding with protesters in the streets to push the president when that seemed the best alternative. With the Alemán government, some things remained the same, namely the judicious mixture of pressure through demonstrations and daily cooperation, but others changed dramatically. Chief among the latter was the PLC-FSLN Pact struck in 2000 between Alemán and Ortega.[33]

The Pact itself was at first an ad hoc alliance between the country's two biggest parties to pass a package of bills, containing both constitutional amendments and changes to ordinary laws. Together, these greatly strengthened the executive, reduced the accountability of all branches of government, and saw nonpartisan institutions converted to partisan strongholds. Both Ortega and Alemán sought to expand unaccountable presidential power and to secure a Liberal-Sandinista duopoly that legally kept other parties from contesting power. However, each also saw the Pact giving his party the inside track on becoming the dominant party in Nicaragua.

After 2001, the Sandinistas found themselves in a peculiar position. On the one hand, since President Bolaños, elected in 2001, started an anticorruption campaign that put his former boss, Arnoldo Alemán, under house arrest for fraud and corruption, the Frente found itself forced to turn on its old ally to maintain its credibility. On the other hand, however, the Sandinistas took advantage of the split in Liberal ranks produced by Bolaños's prosecution of Alemán to become the most powerful political force in the country. This was helped by local elections in 2004, in which the Frente captured 91 of the country's 152 municipalities, causing Ortega to predict that, like Brazilian president Luiz Inácio Lula da Silva, he would follow three straight losses by winning in 2006.

In 2005, the FSLN and PLC combined to pass another set of constitutional amendments, this time obliging Nicaragua's president to submit a wide range of appointments for legislative confirmation.[34] The unusual part of the measure was the 60 percent supermajority it set for confirmation of cabinet officers, a number that suggests that the objective was to ensure that both Pact partners had to approve an appointment. However, President Bolaños refused to publish the reforms, triggering a ten-month crisis in which the legislature and executive operated under different versions of the constitution. Eventually a "framework law" delaying the reforms' application until January 2007 settled the conflict.[35]

In fact, by 2006 the FSLN was the strongest it had been since 1990 and could think realistically about retaking power. Three factors explained this. One is that Daniel Ortega reconciled with the Catholic Church in 2005, thus losing a long-time foe. Second, the Frente was the only party talking about doing something for the 79 percent of the population who lived on less than $2 a day.[36] Finally, the breach within the Liberals, between the anti-Pact

ALN and the PLC, was well established. Though there was a corresponding division in the Sandinista ranks between the FSLN and the MRS, it would not be a decisive factor come election day. The prospects of an Ortega victory were strong enough that the United States again mounted a substantial effort against him,[37] yet even that could have been worse because Washington also targeted the PLC and Arnoldo Alemán.[38]

Sandinistas and Anti-Sandinistas Since 2006

For a decade and a half, it looked as if the anti-Sandinistas were unbeatable. The presidential election of 2006, however, gave power back to Daniel Ortega. Because Shelley McConnell deals with the election in detail in Chapter 6, I shall address several points that have arisen since then. Over its sixteen years in opposition, the FSLN witnessed a dramatic change in its relations with its foes. Political conflict between the two sides went from being mainly military to unfolding within the confines of an admittedly rancorous electoral politics. Thus, even though Nicaragua's political system in 2006 was no one's model of an ideal democracy, the country had managed to put partisan political contention on a civic basis that left little room for violence. Electoral parties, not armed forces, are the main combatants in the country's political struggles, and opposition parties do not plot the violent overthrow of the government.

Violence has not disappeared entirely from Nicaraguan politics, however. Not infrequently inspired by the FSLN, university students, doctors and other medical professionals, teachers, and the owners of taxis and buses have regularly used political violence to seek their objectives. Thus Nicaragua has not yet achieved what Bernard Crick labels "the political method of rule," which proceeds by negotiation and the reconciliation of competing interests rather than by intimidation and armed force.[39] By 2006, however, it had removed violence from the roster of standard political tactics employed by governments and opposition parties. This step is crucial if Nicaragua is to have a democratic future.

Key to reducing the political utility of violence has been an implicit agreement that electoral results had to represent voters' choices in some general way. Although not every election since 1990 has been a model of probity and flawless administration, the outcomes were accepted because the official numbers did not grotesquely distort the popular will. This condition may no longer be met after the disputed 2008 municipal elections. In fact, a number of developments in the management of government-opposition relations since Daniel Ortega became president in 2006 appear capable of undermining Nicaragua's political stability.

The most obvious of those is the Pact the FSLN maintains with the PLC. This alliance does not bind the two parties to always vote alike: they can be bitter foes on one bill and bosom friends on the next. Nonetheless, the Pact does let the FSLN govern much of the time as if it had a legislative majority instead of three-eighths of the seats.

A second factor is the concentration of executive power in the president's office, where Ortega's wife Rosario Murillo and old comrades from the 1980s like Bayardo Arce wield what seems to be great power but remain totally unaccountable to either the National Assembly or Nicaragua's citizens. Although this is a subjective assessment on my part, the operations of the second Ortega administration appear at least as opaque as those of the Alemán government and may be more impenetrable than those of Daniel Ortega's first presidency, when the Sandinista government was waging a counterinsurgent war. One effect of this style of governing is to make it impossible for opponents to get the information they need to criticize the government responsibly.

Third, opposition is not the monopoly of political parties, as anyone can criticize government, so the Ortega administration's relations with civil society are important. Like the Alemán administration before it, Ortega's government abhors civil society. It may be because they handle money the state cannot control or because they raise issues that are not on the administration's agenda, but for whatever reason, President Ortega has declared that civil society groups opposed to any of his policies are in the pay of foreign interests (read the United States) and seeking to destabilize his government.[40] Presumably the president's objective is to silence dissent from this sector of the political system.

Finally, the allegations of fraud arising from the 2008 municipal elections marked a dramatic shift in the relations between the Sandinistas and their foes. Not only did opposition parties cry fraud, led interestingly by the FSLN's Pact partners, the PLC, but the FSLN turned its members into the streets to defend the controverted results, and several incidents of violence occurred.[41] If the country's most important political actors cannot count on elections producing results that faithfully reflect the citizens' will and if day-to-day politics moves into the streets and become violent, the understandings that have let Sandinista and anti-Sandinista maintain a tense truce since 1990 could disappear. Should that happen, Nicaragua could find itself entering a period of open conflict, and heightened social conflict has often been used to justify restricting the political rights of not just organized oppositional forces but of ordinary citizens as well.

Notes

1. Lynn Horton, *Peasants in Arms: War and Peace in the Mountains of Nicaragua, 1979–1994* (Athens: Ohio University Press, 1998).
2. Some states—Costa Rica, Panama, Venezuela, and of course Cuba—gave active support to the FSLN.
3. For further elaboration, see David Close, *Nicaragua: The Chamorro Years* (Boulder, CO: Lynne Reinner, 1999), 37, 51–56.
4. The contras, short for *contrarevolucionarios* or counterrevolutionaries, were more formally known as the Nicaraguan Resistance in the late 1980s. They were financed and equipped by the United States, but even without Washington's aid there are two reasons why it is probable that an anti-Sandinista, counterrevolutionary insurgency would have evolved. First, Nicaraguan history would have taught the many powerful interests harmed by the revolution that armed insurrection was the only possible way to reclaim power. Less obviously, Sandinista policies, notably its land reform that originally favored cooperatives, its decision to keep food prices low, and its use of conscription to get troops to fight the contras, produced opposition among the rural poor. The latter provided a reliable base of recruits for the insurgents and a ready audience for their anti-Sandinista political message.
5. The first occurred in 1928, when the Conservatives recognized the Liberals' victory in elections organized and supervised by the United States. One might argue, however, that this case should not count because US troops occupied Nicaragua at the time.
6. The FSLN's post-1984 peak came in the 2004 municipal elections, when it won 43.82 percent of votes cast. However, as is common in local contests, turnout was low, 53.6 percent, compared to the usual 75 percent turnout for national elections. These 2004 elections were important, as they gave the first evidence of the Liberal split that brought the Sandinistas the presidency in 2006.
7. An electoral democracy is simply one where reasonably free, fair, and competitive elections determine who governs.
8. Quoted in Ghita Ionescu and Isabel Madariaga, *Opposition* (Harmondsworth, UK: Penguin Books, 1972), 29.
9. Ionescu and Madariaga, *Opposition,* 16
10. Stephanie Lawson, "Conceptual Issues in the Comparative Study of Regime Change and Democratization," *Comparative Politics* 25 (1993): 192; emphasis in original.
11. Seymour Martin Lipset, *The First New Nation* (New York: Anchor Books, 1967), 40.
12. Robert Dahl, "Preface," in *Political Oppositions in Western Democracies,* ed. Robert Dahl (New Haven, CT: Yale University Press. 1966), xviii.
13. Television was a state monopoly during the first Sandinista government.
14. General treatments of the Somozas and their political system can be found in Eduardo Crowley, *Dictators Never Die* (London: G. Hurst, 1979); Bernard Diedrich, *Somoza* (New York: E. P. Dutton, 1981); Knut Walter, *The Regime of Anastasio Somoza, 1936–1956* (Chapel Hill: University of North Carolina Press, 1993); Agustin Torres Lazo, *La saga de los Somoza: Historia de un magnicidio* (Managua: Hispamer, 2001); and Andrés Pérez Baltodano, *Entre el estado conquistador y el estado nación* (Managua: Fundación Friederich Ebert en Nicaragua, 2003), 450–574.

15. Max Weber, *Economy and Society: An Outline of Interpretive Sociology,* edited by G. Roth and C. Wittich (Berkeley: University of California Press, 1978).

16. Juan Linz, "Totalitarian and Authoritarian Regimes," in *Handbook of Political Science,* vol. 3, edited by Fred Greenstein and Nelson Polsby (Reading, MA: Addison-Wesley, 1975), 175–411.

17. Juan Linz and Alfred Stepan, eds., *Problems in Democratic Transition and Consolidation: Southern Europe, South America, and Post-Communist Europe* (Baltimore: Johns Hopkins University Press, 1996).

18. H. Chelabi and Juan Linz, eds., *Sultanistic Regimes* (Baltimore: Johns Hopkins University Press, 1998).

19. Chelabi and Linz, eds., *Sultanistic Regimes,* 10–24.

20. Linz and Stepan, eds., *Problems in Democratic Transition,* 52–53.

21. John Booth, "The Somoza Regime in Nicaragua," in *Sultanistic Regimes,* edited by H. Chelabi and Juan Linz (Baltimore: Johns Hopkins University Press, 1998), 132–152.

22. Instances of institutionalized personalistic rule are rare, precisely because of the individualized basis of the regime. The only other noteworthy examples of hereditary caudillismo in the Americas are those of Carlos Antonio López and his son Francisco Solano López, who ruled Paraguay from 1844 until 1870, and François and Jean-Claude Duvalier, who controlled Haiti from 1957 to 1986.

23. On the Somozas' military, the National Guard, see Richard Millett, *Guardians of the Dynasty* (Maryknoll, NY: Orbis Books, 1977).

24. For an introduction to problems revolutionary movements face in becoming conventional political parties, see David Close and Gary Prevost, "Introduction: Transitioning from Revolutionary Movements to Political Parties and Making the Revolution 'Stick,'" in *From Revolutionary Movements to Political Parties,* edited by Kalowatie Deonandan, David Close, and Gary Prevost (New York: Palgrave Macmillan, 2007), 1–16.

25. More information on the disaffection of the anti-Somocista conservatives from the Sandinista government is found in David Close, *Nicaragua: Politics, Economics, and Society* (London: Frances Pinter, 1988), 66–71, 120–126.

26. Jaime Wheelock, *El gran desafío* (Managua: Editorial Nueva Nicaragua, 1984), 84, quoted in Close, *Nicaragua,* 126.

27. The concepts "loyal opposition" and "opposition of principle" are developed more fully in Close, *Nicaragua,* 125–132.

28. See Michael Klare and Peter Kornbluth, eds., *Low-Intensity Warfare: Counterinsurgency, Proinsurgency, and Antiterrorism in the Eighties* (New York: Pantheon Books, 1988), for an introduction.

29. Greg Grandin, *Empire's Workshop* (New York: Metropolitan Books, 2006), 99.

30. The Coordinadora was composed of three small parties (Social Christians, Social Democrats, and the PLC), two rather weak unions, and COSEP (Consejo Superior de la Empresa Privada, or the Superior Council of Private Enterprise), the umbrella organization of the Nicaraguan private sector.

31. To say that violence is no longer an ordinary governing instrument does not mean that the police or military have not used force in dealing with the violent confrontations arising from the myriad strikes and demonstrations that now mark Nicaraguan politics. However, the controversial 2008 municipal elections saw violence and intimidation reappear as political instruments.

32. They were called the National Convergence (Convergencia Nacional) in 2001 and the United Nicaragua Will Triumph Alliance (Alianza Unida Nicaragua Triunfa), in 2006.

33. The Pact is analyzed thoroughly in David Close and Kalowatie Deonanadan, eds., *Undoing Democracy: The Politics of Electoral Caudillismo* (Lanham, MD: Lexington Books, 2004).

34. Government of Nicaragua, *Reforma parcial de la constitucion politica de la Republica de Nicaragua,* February 18, 2005, Political Database of the Americas, pdba.georgetown.edu/.

35. Government of Nicaragua, *Ley Marco para la estabilidad y gobernabildad del pais,* October 20, 2005, Political Database of the Americas, pdba.georgetown .edu/. In December 2006, the first indications appeared that the FSLN would not let the amendments take effect. See Ludwin Loásiga López, "FSLN: Ley Marco es negociable," *La Prensa,* December 14, 2006, www.laprensa.com.ni/. The law was declared unconstitutional in 2008; see Chapters 6 and 13 for details.

36. The figure is from the United Nations Development Programme, *Human Development Report, 2006* (New York: Oxford University Press, 2006), 228.

37. For an overview of US activities in the 2006 presidential campaign, see Nicaragua Network, *List of Interventions by the United States Government in Nicaragua's Democratic Process* (Washington, DC: Nicaragua Network, 2006).

38. With respect to Washington's views regarding the PLC, see M. J. Uriarte, "Fisk: Olvidense de Alemán," *La Prensa,* November 17, 2004, www.laprensa.com.ni; see also Ludwin Loásiga López, "Los liberales desilusionan a Estados Unidos," *La Prensa,* September 29, 2005, www.laprensa.com.ni. This continued throughout the 2006 campaign as Ambassador Paul Trivelli pushed the theme vigorously. For a good summary, see Nicaragua Network, "Ambassador Trivelli Tries Again for Right-Wing Unity While Momentum Shifts to the FSLN," *Nicaragua News Hotline,* September 5, 2006, www.nicanet.org/. Both Managua dailies, *El Nuevo Diario* (www.elnuevodiario.com.ni) and *La Prensa* (www.laprensa.com.ni), have extensive, free online archives where the 2006 campaign can be followed.

39. Bernard Crick, *In Defence of Politics* (London: Weidenfield and Nicholson, 1963).

40. See Rory Carroll, "Oxfam Targeted as Nicaragua Attacks 'Trojan Horse' NGOs," *Guardian,* October 14, 2008, www.guardian.co.uk/; and Blake Schmidt, "US-Nicaragua Relations Chill as Ortega Faces Domestic Tests," *World Politics Review,* September 19, 2008, www.worldpoliticsreview.com/. This point is considered again in Chapter 12.

41. See Lourdes Arroliga, "La ruta del fraude en Managua," *Confidencial* 610, November 16–22, 2008, www.confidencial.com.ni/; and Tim Rogers, "Why Nicaragua's Capital Is in Flames," *Time,* November 14, 2008, www.time.com/.

4

Political Culture

Andrés Pérez Baltodano

AFTER ITS ELECTORAL DEFEAT IN 1990, THE SANDINISTA NA-
tional Liberation Front (Frente Sandinista de Liberación Nacional, or FSLN)
adopted a position of resigned pragmatism toward both neoliberalism and
the power structures the Sandinista Revolution had sought to dismantle during the 1980s. Resigned pragmatism is a view of politics and power that
induces the members of an organization or a society to assume that the politically desirable must be subordinated to what is possible under existing
circumstances.[1] From the perspective of resigned pragmatism, the reality
of power defines what is socially possible and politically desirable. Politics, in other words, is about adjusting to reality.

Resigned pragmatism finds one of its principal roots in providentialism: divine providence. This theological concept views history as a process
controlled, organized, and administered by God.[2] Providentialism forms part
of the dominant religious cosmovision in Nicaragua and acts as a cultural
force that has inclined Nicaraguan society to accept, pragmatically and re-
signedly, history as a process determined by forces that transcend the country's political will. Like resigned pragmatism, providentialism is deeply
rooted in Nicaraguan political culture, the bedrock political values and be-
liefs of a people. Sandinismo sought to change that political culture, but
now it too has yielded to resigned pragmatism.

Political expressions of resigned pragmatism vary with the power of the
groups that form Nicaraguan society. Among the dominant sectors, it takes
the form of indifference toward poverty and social marginalization. Among
the marginalized, it is expressed as fatalism toward their own misery.

This chapter was translated by David Close.

Both the indifference of the elites and the fatalism of the masses reflect a sense of irresponsibility before history. Both attitudes assume that power and poverty are determined by forces beyond the control of Nicaraguans. In this view, the historical limitations imposed by the reality of the moment are accepted as the fundamental influence over human action. Thus, from the perspective of pragmatic resignation, politics becomes the ability to adapt to the reality of actually existing power, especially that of international forces that shape the nation's options. This perspective has severely limited the transformative power of dominant political ideologies throughout Nicaraguan history.

The pragmatic resignation that marks the political thought of Nicaraguan conservatism has simply expressed an instinctive tendency to defend an "order" rooted in particular and narrow traditional interests. In turn, the normative voluntarism of Nicaraguan liberalism has expressed an anti-oligarchic position, but not one capable of articulating a democratic philosophy that expresses and integrates the interests and hopes of the different sectors of Nicaraguan society. Finally, socialism tried to represent the interests of the masses without being able to articulate a body of thought that made explicit the values that unite the diverse social, ethnic, and cultural groups who make up the socially marginalized in Nicaragua.

Nicaraguan conservatism, liberalism, and socialism all adopted, superficially and uncritically, the principles and conceptual vocabulary of European political thought. The discursive expressions of this imported thought do not constitute an authentic representation of the thoughts and sentiments of Nicaraguans but are rather a falsification. For this reason, the revolutionary and reformist efforts that mark Nicaragua's history have been crushed by the weight of a reality that, by remaining pre-theorized, also remains independent of Nicaraguans' political will. Further, in the absence of political thinking, Nicaraguan elites—including those in the FSLN—end up internalizing the ideology and culture imposed by the structures of national and international power that have historically affected development in the country.

The Revolutionary Decade

In 1979, the FSLN succeeded, at least temporarily, in breaking with the attitude of resigned pragmatism that has characterized the political practice of Nicaraguan elites. If Somocismo was, as Edgardo Buitrago asserts, simply a *praxis* stripped of historical vision, Sandinismo was a vision of Nicaraguan society based on values that challenged and transcended the limits of the then-existing reality.[3] Confronting the external dependency of a country conditioned by constant foreign intervention, Sandinismo aspired to construct a sovereign nation. And faced with the reality of poverty and social inequality, the Sandinista Revolution sought to construct a society organized in accordance with the "logic of the majority."

However, Sandinismo never developed the capacity for political reflection necessary to give institutional expression to its fundamental values. The FSLN adopted a mechanical and imitative Marxism that gave rise to distorted interpretations of both Nicaragua's domestic reality and the international context within which the country operated. In turn, these erroneous interpretations produced an ambiguous and contradictory political practice that ended in confusion.

The theoretical poverty of the FSLN led the organization to value "revolutionary conviction" over understanding the problems the revolution faced. Public declarations of faith in Marxist socialism and the Leninist model—central planning, the revolutionary vanguard, and democratic centralism—became the scale the FSLN used to gauge the revolutionary commitment of its members. "Any voice of moderation within the party," observed Sergio Ramírez in his memoirs, "was seen as more than suspicious." He continues: "Immersing ourselves in the shimmering old waters of ideological orthodoxy, we obtained our certificate of virtue."[4]

To the theoretical weaknesses of the FSLN were added the practical difficulties of managing the politics of alliances promoted by the FSLN to let it take power. In an attempt to hide the incongruities between its thinking and the ideas and values of its allies, the FSLN chose to combine, in a confused and contradictory way, the Marxist-Leninist conceptual vocabulary that was part of its political discourse and thought and the markedly social democratic conceptual language contained in the program of the government of national reconstruction. Ramírez confirms that the political game of the FSLN consisted in "denying before both, allies and enemies, its identity as a Marxist-Leninist party."[5]

Divorcing Sandinista discourse from political practice eventually became a divorce between the FSLN's thinking and revolutionary action. Sandinista thought and its discursive expressions remained frozen in a theoretical scheme deprived of the enriching sustenance of experience. At the same time, the revolutionary experience degenerated into a political activism lacking the theoretical reference that the revolution required to make clear the framework of historical limitations and opportunities within which the country was operating. Eventually, the revolutionary activism of the FSLN deteriorated first into pragmatism and later into resignation when it confronted the weight of national problems that remained pre-theorized and immune to the constitutive and ordering force of ideas.

Thus Sandinista political thought, like that of José Santos Zelaya in 1893, fell before the force of reality that the FSLN was unable to make comprehensible, let alone domesticate. With the Frente's electoral defeat in 1990, Nicaragua's political development again set its course within a resigned, pragmatic vision of history, which perceived the future as determined by forces outside the nation's control.

From Revolutionary Sandinismo to Resigned Pragmatism, 1990–2006

The electoral victory of Violeta Barrios de Chamorro in 1990 initiated Nicaragua's transition to neoliberalism. On the political level, the change meant a legal and institutional reform that aimed to consolidate an electoral democracy. It would replace the verticalist model, a schizophrenic blend of democratic centralism and pluralism the FSLN used in the 1980s. The neoliberal transition's economic side sought to institutionalize a market economy to replace the mixed and planned economy of the Sandinista regime. Economic competitiveness would become the independent variable that would drive the rest of the social equation (employment, wages, social programs, etc.). Finally, the social objective of the new regime was a significant reduction in the state's social role. Concretely, this showed itself as the elimination of the principles of universality, free access, and public participation that guided the Sandinista's social policy.

The rationale and the objectives of the Nicaraguan neoliberal transition came from three international financial institutions (IFIs)—the World Bank (WB), the International Monetary Fund (IMF), and the Inter-American Development Bank (IDB)—and the US Agency for International Development (USAID). They shared an economic outlook and a social vision. This convergence of values and norms generated the Washington Consensus, which dominated official thinking about economic development throughout the 1990s.

Chamorro's victory and the reforms undertaken by her administration took place within a national context characterized by political fragmentation, economic backwardness, and a weakening of the bonds of social solidarity among Nicaraguans. By 1989, as the result of errors by the Sandinista leaders, the complexity of the revolutionary process, and aggression by the United States, the country's gross domestic product (GDP) had fallen to 42 percent of its 1977 level. Worse, in 1989 Nicaragua's per capita foreign debt was the highest in Latin America: $3,000, or 33 times the value of its exports.[6]

Besides political polarization and economic collapse, in 1990 Nicaragua also faced the torn social fabric left by its civil war. That war pitted Sandinismo against an armed counterrevolutionary movement financed by the United States. Paul Oquist described the human impact of the conflict:

> The 61,884 victims of the war represent 1.72 percent of the population of Nicaragua, roughly 3.6 million persons. The 30,865 deaths represent 0.86 percent of the population. If we apply this same percentage to the population of the United States, approximately 250 million, it would leave 2,125,000 dead, which almost equals the number of all American deaths in all the wars fought by the United States throughout its history.[7]

How was the FSLN to confront the neoliberal project imposed by the IFIs, welcomed by an important sector of the Nicaraguan economic elite, and enacted by the Chamorro government? That was what millions of Nicaraguans asked themselves after Daniel Ortega accepted electoral defeat in 1990. Two days after the election, on February 27, Ortega offered an enigmatic response. Before thousands of Sandinistas gathered in the Plaza de los No Alineados "Omar Torrijos" to receive directions from their leaders, Ortega said: "We were not born on top, we were born on the bottom, and we're going to govern from below. Now there is a people's power [*poder popular*], so we're in much better conditions to return, in a short time, and govern this country from above."[8]

Ortega's warning was not an empty threat. The FSLN was still the strongest political party in the country. It had been defeated by the National Union of the Opposition (Union Nacional Opositora, or UNO), a coalition of parties that, with assistance and pressure from the United States, united only around the common objective of defeating the Sandinistas. Yet despite the population's war-weariness and the economic pressures caused by the war, the FSLN remained a considerable political force. In 1990, the FSLN took 38 of 91 National Assembly seats and 30 of 131 municipalities.[9] On the Atlantic Coast, the Sandinistas won 22 out of 48 regional council seats in the North Atlantic Autonomous Region (Región Autónoma Atlántico Norte, or RAAN) and 19 of 47 in the South Atlantic Autonomous Region (Región Autónoma Atlántico Sur, or RAAS).[10]

Moreover, the FSLN now enjoyed the legitimacy that comes with having accepted the public's verdict in the elections. Thus *Envío,* a magazine of news and commentary published by the Jesuit Central American University (Universidad Centroamericana, or UCA) in Managua, declared the Sandinista electoral defeat an "ideological victory" against the Reagan administration, which had for years labeled Sandinismo "totalitarian." *Envío* stated:

The heroic solidity of the vote of 41 percent of Nicaraguans will have to be assessed with great responsibility and integrity alongside its other crucial component: President Daniel Ortega, who is widely recognized today as a symbol of the struggle against the dictatorship, the defense of [national] sovereignty, and the construction of pluralism and democracy. In these accomplishments lies the paradox of the FSLN's defeat. By [the Sandinistas'] political defeat, the revolutionary process of the small, heroic, worthy Nicaraguan people won the ideological battle with US imperialism, the brutality of Reagan, and the subtle, bipartisan pragmatism of Bush, because the project of Sandino lives on in Nicaragua.[11]

During the first two years of the new government, the "project of Sandino" indeed seemed to remain in force. Throughout that period, the FSLN maintained its revolutionary posture and discourse. In 1991, Daniel Ortega made this comment:

In Nicaragua those who think that the capitalist and imperialist option is the best have twenty-three parties that they can join. Our option is still the revolutionary one, to which we now add discussion and dialogue as a new expression of internal democracy. For the first time in its history, the Frente is discussing its statutes and principles. The elections themselves are a new element, an instrument to *reaffirm* our political and ideological positions, to modernize how we work, and to confront capitalism, which remains our enemy.[12] (emphasis in original)

Behind Ortega's public discourse, however, the FSLN had begun to suffer serious internal divisions. They arose from the electoral defeat and the different interpretations the Sandinista membership gave to that defeat, as well as to the different proposals for how best to face challenges that were coming from within the party. It was under these conditions that the group closest to Daniel Ortega, the party's secretary-general, closed ranks around Ortega's leadership to defend the organizational unity of the FSLN. As Erik Aguirre observed, "the existence of [competing] lines of thought was proscribed and Ortega's hegemony guaranteed."[13]

By 1993, the political and ideological tensions within Sandinismo were evident. In that year, a group of intellectuals affiliated with the FSLN stated publicly that the party suffered from "the lack of a clear identity, failing to have redefined the program and strategy of the FSLN, a crisis of leadership at all levels, and facing these crises with an organizational structure that had become dysfunctional or even the source of the problems."[14] Little by little, the revolutionary meaning attached to Sandinismo was fading in the midst of an accelerated process of institutionalizing the neoliberal values promoted by the IFIs and Nicaragua's government. Social conditions in Nicaragua were also being transformed to permit a resurgence of the old social structures that produced inequality, the same structures Sandinismo had sought to dismantle.

But not everything was marching back to the past. In these postrevolutionary conditions, the leadership of the FSLN became part of the economic elite pushing the neoliberal transition in the country. What made those Sandinistas rich was *La Piñata* (the Piñata).[15] That was the name Nicaraguans gave to the massive transfer of state property to the Sandinista elite during the FSLN's two-month lame-duck period. Ernesto Cardenal, who was minister of culture in the 1980s, lays out the dynamic of the Piñata:

> There was the theft of state properties undertaken by the leaders to give them to the Frente Sandinista, as well as the theft of state properties by the leaders to assign them to themselves; later they would take for themselves the properties they had first stolen for the Frente Sandinista. This was how the majority of the members of the National Directorate (though not all of them) and other party elites or top government officials and labor leaders got bank accounts, houses, cars, businesses, supermarkets, coffee haciendas and cattle ranches, sugar mills, banana plantations, restaurants, televisions, radios, firms that market meat or bananas, and financial institutions and banks. The people were left out of all this.[16]

The Piñata was one of the causes of the split in the FSLN. In 1995, Sergio Ramírez, Dora María Téllez, and many other leading thinkers left the FSLN to form the Sandinista Renewal Movement (Movimiento Renovador Sandinista, or MRS). The rise of the MRS was, as a former Sandinista activist observed, "just one part of a deeper fissure, a consequence of the loss of leadership and credibility by the party's National Directorate, as well as of the violent behavior and politics [characteristic of the FSLN] that an overwhelming majority of Nicaraguans now reject."[17] Since the formation of the MRS, other individuals and groups have taken up the fight to renew the ideology and policies of the party. However, the faction of the FSLN organized around Daniel Ortega—in which the new Sandinista tycoons play a prominent role—has been able to neutralize dissent and stifle open and democratic debate about the party's social outlook, political ideas, general strategy, and organization, especially concerning participation in decisionmaking.

The 1996 Elections:
A Political Defeat Degenerates into a Moral Defeat

According to the reports issued by the Supreme Electoral Council (Consejo Supremo Electoral, or CSE), Nicaragua's electoral authority, twenty-three parties and political alliances ran in the 1996 campaign. Yet it was the Liberal

Alliance (Alianza Liberal), led by the right-wing former mayor of Managua, Arnoldo Alemán Lacayo, and the FSLN, led by Daniel Ortega, that captured the public's attention. The Alemán campaign succeeded in capitalizing on "the declining political authority of President Chamorro's government, while maintaining intact the anti-Sandinista coalition that had carried the [UNO] to power."[18] For its part, the FSLN presented a new image to the electorate. Here is a description of the metamorphosis of the Sandinista leader at one campaign rally:

> For the first time in the history of the celebrations of the 19th of July, Daniel appeared with his wife Rosario Murillo and several of their children. The Sandinista Comandantes—including Humberto Ortega—abandoned their olive drab and the chants recalling the FSLN's guerrilla past. Daniel called the United States "our great neighbor," with whom the FSLN "is ready to continue working within a framework of respect, equality, and justice." There were white shirts and caps, and doves, and flowers tossed in the air. In his speech, Ortega called for "national unity" against what he styled the "Somocista Liberal project" of Arnoldo Alemán. And he proposed that Cardinal Obando [the archenemy of the Sandinistas] be the guarantor of a pact on campaign ethics that included the promise to accept October's electoral results.[19]

In that same rally Ortega explained to the crowd how the position assigned the FSLN in the middle of the ballot paper was a "providential" sign that confirmed the "centrist" position that, in his view, the FSLN occupied in the Nicaraguan political spectrum. The magazine *Envío* described the scene this way:

> "Here," said Daniel during the rally, "all the other parties have been searching for the center. But Providence gave the center to the Frente Sandinista." He meant that the FSLN had drawn slot 12 of 24 in the lottery to assign places on the ballot. "We are," said Daniel, "the point of convergence, which means we will get the votes of all Nicaraguans. As Sandino said: 'Neither the far right nor the far left. The Only Front is our slogan.' And the Only Front is the slogan of the Frente Sandinista de Liberación Nacional."[20]

Daniel Ortega's new image and message, however, convinced neither the Catholic Church nor the United States. Washington certainly made its distaste clear, but the church went further. On October 17, 1996, during the period when campaigning was to have stopped, Cardinal Miguel Obando y Bravo celebrated Mass in Managua's cathedral with Liberal presidential candidate Arnoldo Alemán present. The cardinal was wearing red vestments, the Liberals' color, even though the liturgical calendar called for green. During his sermon, moreover, Cardinal Obando invented a biblical passage to warn the public against the wickedness and snares of "vipers"; Alemán coincidently had called Ortega a "snake" during the campaign. Then, to make sure that the church's message got through, on election day the anti-Sandinista dailies, *La Prensa* and *La Tribuna,* published a color photo of Cardinal Obando literally giving his blessing to Arnoldo Alemán and his vice presidential candidate, Enrique Bolaños.

Washington and the church won. The results showed the Liberal Alliance with 51.03 percent of the votes and the FSLN with 37.75 percent. The remaining twenty-one parties split the rest, with nineteen of them unable to garner the support of even 1 percent of the voters. On the municipal level, the Liberal Alliance won 92 of 143 localities, including Managua; the FSLN captured 51.[21] In elections held two years earlier, in 1994, for regional councils in Nicaragua's two autonomous regions on the Atlantic Coast, the FSLN had captured 20 of 48 seats in the RAAN and 15 of 47 in the RAAS. In 1998, it had less success, taking 15 of 48 seats in the RAAN and 12 of 47 in the RAAS.[22] Nonetheless, the Frente clearly remained Nicaragua's second party.

While neoliberal democracy in Nicaragua was being refined in the 1990 and 1996 elections, the popular organizations that had arisen during the 1980s were weakening gradually due to the ideological bankruptcy of the FSLN and its entry into the new Nicaraguan social order. The crisis besetting these organizations was described by the Sandinista sociologist Oscar René Vargas in 1997.

> The figures and images that habitually served as points of reference for people's political orientations have faded rapidly from Nicaragua's fractured political and ideological scene. Gone are the coordinates, even the maps, established under the influence of "real socialism." So too is the thirst for social justice and equality that characterized several generations of activists and intellectuals of the broad left. All that remains on the horizon is a sense of emptiness, the feeling that something is missing from the national political scene that today cannot be found anywhere.[23]

What had disappeared was revolutionary Sandinismo. After the electoral defeat and the Piñata in 1990, the FSLN neglected its organizational work and began activating and deactivating popular organizations to serve its pursuit of quotas of power in the new order. Then in 1998, the FSLN began negotiating the Pact with the Liberals, making it clear that it brought all the organizations linked to the Frente into the deal as well.

The Pact between the FSLN and the Constitutionalist Liberal Party (PLC) led by Arnoldo Alemán aimed to give those parties total control of

Nicaragua's political system and state institutions. Through this deal, the two parties gave themselves key positions on the Supreme Court of Justice and the Supreme Electoral Council and in the controller's office, the attorney general's office, and the office of the superintendant of banks. But the Pact did not stop there. Hoping to perpetuate the dominance of the PLC and FSLN, it set serious obstacles to the formation of new parties. Moreover, it amended the property law in the FSLN's favor, thereby resolving legal questions lingering since the Piñata. And it left the way open for a constituent assembly to enshrine the Pact in a new constitution.

A key aspect of the Pact was its insistence on establishing a system of immunity from prosecution for the two party leaders. Daniel Ortega used this protection when, shielded by parliamentary immunity and counting on the support of the Sandinista and Liberal benches, he avoided charges of sexual abuse of a minor brought by his stepdaughter Zoilamérica Narvaez. For his part, Arnoldo Alemán got an automatic National Assembly seat via the Pact and thus diplomatic immunity from charges of corruption, though ultimately the legislature would strip him of that protection and permit his prosecution.

Dora María Téllez of the MRS offered this view of the significance of the Pact and its longer-term implications:

> One of Arnoldo Alemán's major objectives in the pact with the FSLN was to buy off the organized opposition. He correctly calculated that only the FSLN could put up any organized opposition to him in a crisis. The FSLN sold out to Alemán through the pact, and it sold out cheap. With the organized opposition in his pocket, Alemán has reduced his internal problems. The rest of the opposition is less organized and one of the pact's aims is to make it even harder for it to get organized. Now the Liberal government has only to face a dispersed opposition, one concealed within the conscience of the people.[24]

Because of the Pact, the popular organizations of Nicaraguan civil society were practically demobilized, creating conditions for the growth of corruption that became endemic in Alemán's administration, which some analysts estimate cost Nicaragua roughly $100 million between 1996 and 2000.[25] Further, during Alemán's presidency there were several fraudulent bankruptcies of private banks that some estimate cost the state the equivalent of five times the annual education budget or twenty-five times what government spends annually on medicine.[26] Losses from the failure of just one of those banks, Interbank, which had been "the deal-making center for Sandinista capital derived from the La Piñata of the '90s," amounted to $300 million.[27]

The attitude of the Catholic Church toward this corruption was scandalous. Statements by the bishops recognized the existence of corruption but treated it as a moral problem that called for spiritual solutions. The ambiguous and evasive language of the Conferencia Episcopal, the assembly of the country's Catholic bishops, contributed to the institutionalization of social values that saw abuses of power and impunity for bureaucrats involved in corruption become parts of the country's daily life.

This ambiguous, even complicit stance taken by the Catholic Church on the question of corruption is explained by the relationship of mutual convenience it maintained with the Alemán government. The church had backed Alemán's candidacy and contributed to legitimizing his power. His administration then supported the church's positions in education and reproductive health. Further, the Alemán government assisted the church economically.

In sum, Arnoldo Alemán's term in office was marked by five political characteristics: (1) corruption, (2) antidemocratic practices created by the FSLN-PLC Pact, (3) collaboration between the Catholic Church and the PLC, (4) loss of legitimacy by public institutions, and (5) serious poverty affecting the majority of the population.

A statistical view of his administration's economic management is similarly unimpressive. By 2001, GDP per capita was barely $30 higher than the $454 average of 1990. Unemployment rose from 7.6 percent in 1990 to 11.5 percent in 2001. Underemployment, which was 37.2 percent in 1990, remained high at 38.2 percent in 2001.[28] The social consequences of the economic situation were dramatic. According to a 2002 study by the United Nations Food and Agriculture Organization, 31 percent of the 5.2 million Nicaraguans suffered from malnutrition, making Nicaragua the most ill-nourished country in the Americas.[29]

This was the background for Nicaragua's 2001 general elections. The FSLN competed in these elections, employing a discourse based on a managerial view of government. Its platform contained a long list of promises: peace and security for all Nicaraguans; anticorruption measures; the promotion of participatory governance; programs to improve the status of women and children; respect for private property; promotion of investment and heightened production; antipoverty measures; programs for sustainable development; extensive public works projects, including the Dry Interoceanic Canal; full application of the Statute of Autonomy for the Regions of Nicaragua's Atlantic Coast covering Nicaragua's Caribbean Coast; and respect for freedom of religion, free speech, a free press, human rights, and the right to life.[30]

Thus by 2001, the FSLN viewed governing as implementing develop-ment projects within the limits set by the national power structure and con-gruent with neoliberal guidelines of the IFIs. The revolutionary spirit of the Sandinistas had disappeared.

The 2001 Elections

The resigned pragmatism of the FSLN showed itself clearly in the quest for alliances in the 2001 elections. To take power, the FSLN was ready to ally with anyone who, for whatever reason, could help them defeat the PLC can-didate, Enrique Bolaños. As a result, the FSLN came to head the National Convergence (Convergencia Nacional). In that coalition coexisted—without ever discussing their contrasting visions of how society should work—San-dinistas from the FSLN, dissident Sandinistas from the MRS, evangelical Christians, social Christians (from the Partido Social Cristiano), a sector of the Nicaraguan Resistance (the contras who fought the FSLN in the 1980s), as well as political personalities and sports stars recruited for their names. The pragmatism behind the National Convergence was confirmed by the Sandinista historian Aldo Díaz Lacayo.

> [The 2001 presidential elections were] an eminently political event in which the important thing is getting into power, literally capturing power, because that at least creates the possibility that some things can be done, and that's enough. Negotiate or accept the economic policies imposed by the international financial institutions without so much as questioning them.[31]

Instead of vision and critical thought, the FSLN offered a mystical dis-course that revealed the depth of providentialism in the country's political culture. *For the Highest Ideals* (*Por los ideales más altos*), a letter signed by Daniel Ortega and his running mate Agustín Jarquín, was practically a prayer.

> Nicaraguan brothers and sisters: We beseech God to guide us in the Way of Hope, where each of us is ready, as His Instrument, of His Will, His Peace, and His Love, to serve this country which, through our combined efforts, we shall move forward! We dedicate ourselves to organize and op-erate a government for all, without exception. We swear to serve all Nicaraguans with honesty, transparency, austerity, and efficiency. We shall promote peace, understanding and harmony among all Nicaraguans and between Nicaragua and the whole world, based on the principles of re-spect and cooperation. These times in which we live demand women and men full of strength and Love, and ready to work strenuously. And in this

way, working together, we can make ourselves better and enjoy the blessings that Life offers us. The shades of a difficult past will not take from Nicaraguans the possibilities and the certainties of a future built on experience and on the sense of justice and responsibility. We beseech God to illuminate our consciences, so that we may choose "the highest ideals." We ask that His Will permits us to show that we represent those highest ideals. We beseech Him to let us realize those ideals for you, calling on us all, together, to create in peace, decent conditions of work, education, culture, and progress for every Nicaraguan family. To vote for the party in Box 2 on your ballot [the Convergencia] is to vote with hearts willing to fill every corner of our country with joy and hope, confidence and tranquility, and general betterment! Nicaragua United is great. Nicaragua United promises Peace. Nicaragua United is . . . the Promised Land.[32]

The religious turn in Sandinista thinking was also evident during the celebration of the twenty-third anniversary of the revolution. On that occasion, Daniel Ortega gave thanks to "God and the Revolution" for the electoral democracy that had been consolidated in the country since 1990: "We had to throw out the Somocista dictatorship at gunpoint but now, thanks to God and the Revolution, governments change peacefully, through the vote, and this coming November 4th we will hold elections."[33] In the same speech, Ortega invited people to "conquer the fear" produced by the memories of war and of the economic hardship of the 1980s and thus reach "the Promised Land":

It's the same fear people felt when they went with Moses. We all remember the story when they came to the sea and all of a sudden it opened up. Well, naturally, Moses and everyone with him were afraid to cross, because, what might happen? If they were crossing and the sea suddenly shut around them they would all drown. This is the same fear that some Nicaraguans have now. They ask themselves, what if the Frente Sandinista wins. They're afraid to cross the sea, the sea that's open this coming 4th of November. But I'm sure, because I believe that this country will vanquish its fear, that the ordinary people will conquer their fear and will pass through the sea and reach the Promised Land.[34]

At the same event, Laureano Ortega, Daniel's son, sang "Ave Maria." Rosario Murillo, Daniel's wife, went before the crowd to affirm her support for the Sandinista candidate and to reject, implicitly, the accusations of sexual abuse that Zoilamérica Narvaez had leveled against her stepfather in 1998. Murillo used language that highlighted the new spiritualism of the FSLN: "I am here with my heart full, with nothing to hide, my breast bared, to tell you, Daniel, that we, your family, those closest to you, we offer Nicaragua the broadest horizon." She added that "nothing really changes unless the heart changes," that "there are no certainties, on searching and paths," and that the moment had come to "move from the shadows and let the Light of Nicaragua shine through."[35]

The mystical and religious tone was highlighted by *Envío* when it reported that the FSLN's platform had appeared "as blurry as the utopian horizon of the *Promised Land,* the central theme of the Sandinista campaign." It continued: "Asking for God's forgiveness and love, the FSLN diluted history, principles, style, and programs to embark on a pseudo-religious campaign that tries to paint over not just the difficult history of the eighties but also the real problems the country faces in the twenty-first century and the inability of the FSLN of the nineties to face those problems."[36]

Despite the efforts the FSLN made remaking its image and presenting itself as a nonrevolutionary organization—one adapted to the country's social and political realities—the Catholic Church again tilted the electoral process toward the PLC. In its *Exhortación en ocasión de las Elecciones Generales de 2001* (*Exhortation on the Occasion of the 2001 General Elections*), the church preached the need to distrust changes in candidates' style and the content of their speeches. Nicaraguans understood very well that this referred to Ortega and his attempt to project a more moderate and pious image.[37]

Come election day, the PLC captured 56.3 percent of the votes, whereas the Frente got 42.3 percent. The year before (2000), in municipal elections that were held separately from the national contest as specified by a 1995 constitutional amendment, the FSLN had won as many localities (52) as in 1996 and accounting for 60 percent of Nicaragua's population, with Managua among them.[38] Herty Lewites, who won Managua for the Frente, would in six years (in the presidential elections of 2006) be leading a strong Sandinista dissident movement, challenging Daniel Ortega for the presidency. In the Atlantic Coast elections of 2002, the party improved on its 1998 results, taking 18 of 48 seats in the RAAN and 14 of 47 in the RAAS.[39]

In the first months of Enrique Bolaños's Liberal government, the FSLN acted cautiously to see how relations between Bolaños and Alemán developed. The Sandinistas knew that ties between the two were fragile. Bolaños wanted to govern. Alemán, however, was not about to give up power and could control the government's agenda as president of the National Assembly as well as through his dominance of the PLC. The FSLN knew that a split between Bolaños and Alemán could turn the Sandinista deputies in the National Assembly into votes that Bolaños would have to count on to survive politically.

With FSLN support, Alemán became the National Assembly's president. Though protected by legislative immunity as a member of the assembly, he soon faced corruption charges. Alemán's role as speaker and the question of corruption soon came to dominate the Nicaraguan political agenda. Bolaños, keen to rid himself of Alemán, worked diligently to bring the former president and his principal collaborators to trial. In this, Bolaños had the support of the media and many civil society groups. The Catholic Church continued defending Alemán.

However, Bolaños's haughty bearing and inability to communicate with the people kept him from leading the popular protests that supported his anticorruption campaign. The Nicaraguan president preferred rather to use the support he received from the US embassy once Washington decided that Alemán's presence weakened the PLC and favored the FSLN.

For the FSLN, the fissure within the PLC offered an opportunity to expand its power to "govern from below." Taking advantage of its weight in the assembly and over the judiciary, the FSLN backed Bolaños and provided the votes necessary to strip Alemán of his legislative immunity. It then used its control of the judiciary to secure Alemán's conviction for corruption. An unavoidable result of the former president's conviction was the definitive break between the PLC and Enrique Bolaños, who became a traitor in Liberal eyes. Thus the president turned to the FSLN to keep governing.

Even while the FSLN was working toward Alemán's conviction, it maintained the Pact with the PLC. The Frente wanted to weaken Alemán to strengthen its hand when dealing with the Liberals, a blatant power grab. As a result, on his conviction Arnoldo Alemán became both an inmate and a prisoner of the Sandinistas, who could dictate the conditions of Alemán's imprisonment. The FSLN named the judges who controlled Alemán's fate, who approved or rejected requests that he receive house arrest instead of jail time. Whenever the FSLN needed the PLC's votes in the assembly, it threatened to send Alemán to prison. Once the Liberals accepted the Sandinistas' demands, Alemán was returned to his ranch and house arrest.

Eventually Alemán was permitted to travel throughout the department of Managua and finally to have the run of the country. Each of those changes in the conditions of Alemán's imprisonment was approved by a judiciary that received its directions from the FSLN. In this regard, it is important to recall that Alemán's freedom of movement became an important factor in the run-up to the 2006 campaign, as dissident Liberals, led by the banker Eduardo Montealegre, who were opposed to Alemán's leadership, grew stronger. The FSLN wanted Alemán able to travel freely to reinforce his leadership and avoid the unification of the Liberals.

This political opportunism of the FSLN reflected the ideological vacuum within which the organization functioned. The absence of conviction, the essential characteristic of any pragmatic position, was palpable in the party's *Program for the Twenty-First Century*. In that document, the FSLN defined itself vaguely as "a revolutionary party that stands for a modern socialism that is solidaristic, democratic, popular, pluralist, inspired by its love of the people and the country, created to serve the citizenry." According to this ambiguous but florid document, the party's principal objective was to "secure the happiness of all Nicaraguans, building a society with democratic politics, a democratic economy, social justice, and the rule of law."[40]

In fact, the FSLN had done very little to promote "the happiness of all Nicaraguans." Its pact with the PLC had benefited the organization's leaders and sold out the popular sectors. This was bitterly confirmed by the Sandinista journalist William Grigsby:

> What sector of the Frente Sandinista has come out ahead as a result of its strategy of wheeling and dealing, deal making, and log rolling? Which of the many sectors within the Frente Sandinista—the workers, peasants, the unemployed, women, youth, business—has done best from the Pact and its consequences? You know who, right? The [big guys:] the Coronel Kautzes, the Bayardo Arces, the *tutti quanti* of the businessmen, the Chico Lopezes. That's who is better off. Their businesses have prospered incredibly. They have more hotels, more import houses, better *fincas* [farms], improved access to bigger loans, and control more shares in banks. They're the ones who have gotten ahead. They're the ones who benefited from the politics of the Pact, from the deal making and sellouts. It certainly hasn't been the ordinary people who belong to the Frente.[41]

The 2006 Elections

The FSLN began getting ready for the 2006 elections right after their 2001 loss. As part of their strategy, they sought rapprochements with all who had opposed them. In that class were the Nicaraguan economic elites who were not already linked to the Sandinistas, the Catholic Church, the counterrevolutionary organizations that the Frente faced in the 1980s, and the government of the United States. Ortega's flirtation with Washington is best represented by a photo, dominated by the Nicaraguan and US flags, which shows the Sandinista leader entering the Plaza La Fe on horseback to celebrate the anniversary of the Sandinista Revolution.[42] The Frente also stopped using the Sandinista Hymn, which refers to the United States as "the enemy of humanity," at its rallies. Finally, it minimized the use of the colors of the Sandinista flag, red and black, substituting pink. Washington, however, remained intransigent.

Nicaraguan capitalists remained neutral toward Ortega. Their preferred candidate was the conservative Eduardo Montealegre, but they did not fear an Ortega administration. For many of them, it was clear that the FSLN had lost its ideology and become a party controlled by a business-oriented elite. A member of this elite, onetime member of the FSLN national directorate Bayardo Arce, declared during the campaign that the FSLN's economic policy would follow that of the neoliberal governments of Presidents Chamorro, Alemán, and Bolaños. When asked if he thought a Sandinista win would provoke capital flight, Arce responded: "If I look at what Carlos Pellas, Ramiro Ortiz, Roberto Zamora, and Ernesto Fernandez Hollman [all leading Nicaraguan capitalists] have said, none of them thinks that changing the government will change the rules."[43]

By 2006, the FSLN had converted itself into a confessional party that collaborated with the most conservative sectors of the Catholic Church and constantly invoked God's name in its speeches. To underline this religiosity, Daniel Ortega and his wife Rosario Murillo, who was also his campaign manager, renewed their vows before Cardinal Miguel Obando y Bravo. The media also captured the couple praying in Managua's cathedral and receiving communion. The growing closeness of the FSLN and the Catholic hierarchy reached its peak when the Sandinista Assembly caucus voted to criminalize therapeutic abortion, fully implementing the Church's position.[44] Rosario Murillo explained the action this way:

> Precisely because we have faith, we have religion. It is because we are believers, because we love God above all things that we have been able to endure so many torments without worry. We have learned from each difficulty the lesson that the Lord has wanted us to learn. This is also why we defend ourselves and fully agree with the Catholic Church and other churches that abortion principally affects women: because we can never get over the pain and trauma that an abortion produces. No woman who has ever had an abortion is ever again whole.[45]

Cuban author Celia Hart responded to Murillo with a letter decrying the behavior of the FSLN. Hart wrote indignantly: "No, Sra. Murillo! What we women can't get over is not being able to decide what to do with our own bodies or to determine our own priorities. What we can't get over is a girl of 12 or 13 who has been raped and has to have the baby, even though there's no way she can look after it by herself." Hart then turned to the shameless opportunism of the FSLN, concluding by quoting Marti: "Politics is a dishonorable occupation when it covers itself in shame, beneath a layer of wrongful activities, of patent misery and despair, the great misery and despair of the people that the arrogant and slow-witted habitually see instead of their own timidity and complacency."[46]

The complacency of the FSLN in the face of neoliberal and ultraconservative Nicaraguan politics found new expression in the theme of "love and reconciliation" on which the party campaigned. Keeping to this theme, neither Murillo nor Ortega spoke of class struggle or even social conflict. For Murillo, social cleavages and tensions were reducible to resentment and hatred that can be overcome with love and reconciliation. Love and reconciliation legitimated another coalition, which brought in individuals and political movements from even the extreme right. For example, Ortega's running mate was Jaime Morales Carazo, who in the 1980s was a civilian director of the counterrevolutionary forces. Alluding to this, Ernesto Cardenal declared that the "united Nicaragua" of which Ortega spoke was not a revolutionary Nicaragua. Cardenal also asked what kind of a union the FSLN proposed: "A union of exploiters and exploited? One with thieves? With Somocistas? With criminals? The rich embracing the poor, with the rich staying rich and the poor staying poor? Is this the revolution? Is this Sandinismo? The peace they propose is treason."[47]

Celia Hart also commented on the alliances the FSLN justified in terms of love and reconciliation:

> Daniel Ortega has openly allied himself with Arnoldo Alemán, perhaps the most corrupt politician Nicaragua has ever known, and, even more, has chosen as his vice president one of the Contras who, with the backing of Ronald Reagan and the CIA, killed hundreds of young Sandinistas who were trying to save the Sandinista revolution. . . . And as a finishing touch for this new, misnamed Sandinismo, those who once raised the Red and Black flag are now rubbing shoulders with the Church and the right who worked together to destroy the revolution.[48]

The FSLN campaign's message of reconciliation and love was congruent with the vision of consensual politics promoted by the IFIs and international aid agencies. From their perspective, class conflicts disappeared in this era of globalization. Thus any social conflicts that still exist are marginal and can be settled through dialogue among civil society actors interested in building democratic governability. By taking social conflict from the realm of the politically legitimate, this consensual view of politics treats conflict as a moral question. In doing so, it makes the status quo and its defenders the representatives of the good, because any challenge to this order must come from the forces of evil.

The nonconflictive view of politics adopted by the Sandinistas during the electoral campaign did not prevent their leaders from demonizing any who would challenge the presidential aspirations of Daniel Ortega. Note how Rosario Murillo reacted to the former Sandinista mayor of Managua, Herty Lewites, when he decided to run against her husband:

> Herty Lewites is a coward, an obscene manipulator, a walking swamp. He is a servile instrument of putrid interests, the aberrant and perfidious interests of the empire and its servants; of the snakes and bloodsuckers who live by slithering before this empire and from sucking the innocent and heroic blood of all Nicaraguans. I accuse that gelatinous star of imposture, that vile, twisted, mediocre figure who saturates our TV screens, with the biggest media circus we've had to suffer in recent years.[49]

There are several old and discredited anti-Semitic slurs that make their way into the FSLN's attack. Referring to Lewites's Jewish background, Rosario Murillo, Tomás Borge, and Daniel Ortega himself all warned against the "danger of the Levites" and spoke of Judas to discredit their adversary.[50] Daniel Ortega went so far as to warn that a "Judas could end up hanged." The "Lewites phenomenon" was celebrated by progressives hoping for the democratization of the FSLN. It was also well received by the Nicaraguan right, who understood that a split Sandinista vote could help its favorite, Eduardo Montealgre. Nevertheless, from the moment he became a presidential candidate, no one heard Herty Lewites present a leftist vision for Nicaragua. During the struggle against Somoza, Lewites was the Frente's treasurer. During the 1980s, he gained fame as the administrator of the diplomatic stores that were opened in Nicaragua to earn dollars. He was also minister of tourism. He was a good mayor of Managua, but many were surprised by his decision to lead the renewal of Sandinismo. In fact, neither Lewites nor Ortega thought about the world from a leftist perspective. Both accepted neoliberalism's rules, and each was pragmatic in his own way.

Herty Lewites did succeed in building a coalition of minor parties from the left and center-left, which took the name of Alianza-MRS. The MRS formed in 1995, when Sergio Ramírez and other Sandinista leaders left the FSLN. The alliance led by Lewites took the name of the MRS because that organization was already a legally recognized party and the alliance needed that legal status. In the end, Lewites died several months before the elections and was replaced by his running mate Edmundo Jarquín.

The Alianza-MRS was never able to specify what its "refounding of Sandinismo" actually implied. The movement was Sandinista because many Sandinista activists participated, not because it had an economic, political, and social philosophy that presented a framework for a renewed Sandinista left. This theoretical and doctrinal weakness led the Alianza-MRS to have many of the same weaknesses as the FSLN itself. Both platforms presented the same nonconflictive vision of politics, drawn from the same international financial institutions and aid agencies. Neither addressed the social tensions found in the country, even though Nicaragua had one of the worst levels of social inequality in the Americas.

The only conflicts the platform of the Alianza-MRS identified were those that fit within the neoliberal outlook that reigns in Nicaragua. That explains why the fight against the FSLN-PLC Pact and the corruption of those parties were its main planks. However, it was possible to put an end to political corruption in Nicaragua and undo the Pact and end up with nothing but clean, efficient neoliberalism.

Similarly, the Alianza-MRS promised transparent public management but never said what it understood by the word "public." Thus, the language used by the Alianza-MRS did nothing to show the people of Nicaragua that there were different conceptions of "public," "transparent," and "efficient." One can have a transparent and efficient administration, measured by an IFI's standards, and a very different one that is inspired by socialist or humanist values. And this difference can be measured in human lives.

The FSLN took the presidency in 2006 with 38 percent of the vote, due in part to their electoral strategy but perhaps more because Nicaraguans were tired of the indifference shown them by three consecutive rightist governments. But there was also the change in the electoral law, wrought by the Pact, that let a candidate avoid a runoff with 35 percent of the vote and a 5-point lead on the runner-up. Commentators joked that Ortega won the race riding a stationary bicycle, but in fact he went backward, taking 4.25 percent fewer votes than in 2001. What happened is that the FSLN-PLC Pact had moved the goalposts closer to where Ortega could get the ball.

In addition, the Sandinista win in 2006 was helped by a strong showing in the 2004 municipal elections, in which the FSLN took 43.82 percent of the vote, winning 87 of the country's 152 municipalities, including Managua.[51] The PLC received 37.7 percent of the vote and won 57 municipalities. In March 2006, elections in the two Atlantic Coast autonomous regions saw the Sandinistas take 17 of 45 seats in the RAAN and 11 of 45 in the RAAS, not greatly different from four years earlier.[52]

Sandinista municipal governments were good governments: an evaluation of municipal government performance, done for the Association of Municipalities of Nicaragua (Asociación de Municípios de Nicaragua, or AMUNIC) by the German Society for Technical Cooperation (Deutsche Gesellschaft für Technische Zusammenarbeit, or GTZ)) in 2006, found that twelve of the fifteen best-run municipalities had Sandinista administrations.[53] The success of Sandinista local governments reveals the existence of a party capable of winning elections and governing effectively. However, municipal governments in Nicaragua have limited powers: looking after roads and streets and collecting garbage are their principal tasks.[54] It is the central government and the political dynamic unfolding at the center that shape the country's destiny.

Quo Vadis FSLN? Quo Vadis Nicaragua?

The FSLN that reached power in 1979 was able to expand Nicaragua's historic horizons and present the option of a Nicaragua built around three basic values: national sovereignty, social justice, and popular democracy. In contrast, the FSLN that won the elections in 2006 was a party that had resigned itself to acting pragmatically within the traditional Nicaraguan political morality and the rules of the game set by neoliberal economics.

The profound transformation the FSLN has undergone was recognized by a leading Sandinista business executive, Ricardo Coronel Kautz, in an article published in 2005 and never disowned or criticized by any member of the party. He comments that "ethics are a bourgeois prejudice" and that Nicaraguan politics were nothing more than

> a witches brew of demagogy, manipulation, deception, the sale of illusions, traps, gamesmanship, buying and selling people's dreams, blackmail, cynicism, bribes, pacts to split spoils, nepotism, so-called corruption, influence peddling, breaking promises, half lies and half truths, and all the rest. And that is how it has to be. It is in the marrow of the system and cannot be removed. It is how the system works. It is the system.[55]

Coronel Kautz noted that the Nicaraguan right criticized the FSLN because the party had learned how to operate in Nicaragua's corrupt political system. The FSLN, he explained, "has had to learn that game." He added: "For the Frente learning that poses a grave risk because it has learned something contrary to its nature that lets it achieve indispensable tactical advantages at the cost of leaving [the party] permanently disfigured. But that is what is necessary to survive. In other words, do it or disappear. So in this game . . . the end justifies the means."[56]

Coronel Kautz's self-evident pragmatism explains the absence of substantive and stable political orientations and ideological principles in the political actions of the FSLN during its first months in office. This lack of direction was clear in statements made by Foreign Affairs Minister Samuel Santos during his first visit to Spain in March 2007. Meeting with sympathizers from the 1980s and representatives of the Spanish aid community, Santos could not answer questions regarding Nicaragua's relations with

Hugo Chávez or how Managua would square that relationship with its ties to Washington. Neither could he explain why the Sandinistas had changed their position on abortion.

One of those at the meeting observed that Santos would say only that Nicaragua wanted good relations with everyone. He spoke in favor of international integration but did not indicate how to achieve it. He talked a lot about the need to improve living conditions and to address the problems of illiteracy and poverty. The minister reiterated Nicaragua's friendship with the American people and acknowledged the importance of the oil received from the Venezuelan government. Finally, he affirmed that his government was committed to the IMF's program to maintain economic stability.[57]

The vagueness and contradictions of the FSLN administration were also noted by *Envío* in a review of Daniel Ortega's first 100 days in office.

> [Within the FSLN] criticisms of neoliberalism coexist with adherence to the neoliberal policies of the IMF. It confronts the United States but seeks its favor. It cultivates friendships with both Chinas and wants investments from both. It coexists with the ALBA [Bolivarian Alliance for the Americas] and with the FTA [Free Trade Agreement], which leads to FTAA [Free Trade Area of the Americas]. Power is "citizens' power," but it is organized by a family that arrogates power to itself. The ruling couple manages these contradictions not from the presidential residence but from their own home, which doubles as the seat of the FSLN's secretariat. The revolution those two propose is "spiritual" and promotes a cultural regression. The only thing that is clear is the Pact and permanent presence of the same individuals in the three sides of the triangle of power.[58]

Despite this confused political situation, there can be no doubt that the principal factor shaping the choices of the government of Daniel Ortega is his relation with Venezuelan president Hugo Chávez. Economic aid from Venezuela is crucial for Ortega's administration. And politically, Chávez has backed Ortega publicly and unreservedly. At Ortega's inauguration, in front of Arnoldo Alemán, who was the FSLN's guest, Chávez called Ortega an essential figure of the Latin American left. In this same visit to Managua, Chávez declared on television that he was one of Cardinal Obando y Bravo's admirers.

Still, from Ortega's perspective and perhaps from Chávez's too, the relationship between the two leaders is essentially pragmatic. Just as Ortega's behavior is little affected by principles or fixed values, neither is Chávez's twenty-first-century socialism clearly laid out. Henry Petrie Bejarano, a long-time Sandinista with a profound knowledge of the internal workings of the FSLN, commented that Daniel Ortega "can talk about socialism but can't conceptualize it." For Petrie Bejarano, "the sitting president [Ortega] is a man of action but lacks a compass; thus he often acts instinctively and focused on the day to day, the right-now." Petrie Bejarano concludes by saying that the Sandinista administration acts like "it's shooting craps: if it rolls a three and its opponent a four, it does everything it can to beat him, whatever the cost."[59]

In the game of short-term openings that the FSLN is playing, there is a debate about the future of a society that desperately needs a new vision. Political corruption and impunity have become institutionalized. The society that found the voice and spirit of Sandino in the 1970s and put an end to Somocismo today appears impotent when faced with the immorality created by the abuse of power by its leaders.

To date, none of the money stolen from the state during the Alemán administration has been recovered. No one is in jail serving time for those crimes. The primary architect of that corruption, Arnoldo Alemán, has been, since January 2009, a free man.[60]

The current political state of Nicaraguan society is inexplicable if one ignores the cultural context within which the struggle for power in Nicaragua unfolds. In particular, it is necessary to look to the reaffirmation of resigned pragmatism and providentialism that has taken root since the failure of the Sandinista Revolution. The consolidation of these cultural values reflects people's lowered expectations and is consistent with the country's depressed political, economic, and social conditions. The democratic experiment that began in 1990 has been turned into a quinquennial raffle for the right to act arbitrarily and with impunity. Current corruption is as bad as, if not worse than, under the Somozas. *La Piñata,* for instance, was worse than anything done by the Somozas, because it was done in the name of Sandino and of the people after a cruel war in which thousands of young Nicaraguans gave their lives to end corruption.

The Catholic Church has also lowered its ethical standards. The church collaborated with the Somozas, even though it pretended not to. It kept up appearances and tried to maintain its distance from the dictators. By way of contrast, the collaboration between the Catholic Church hierarchy and the government of Arnoldo Alemán was open and shameless. The audacity with which the hierarchy defended and participated in the corruption of that government is also an indicator of existing moral conditions in the country.

It is not madness to state that, since 1990, Nicaragua is living a nightmare more terrifying and painful than anything it experienced during the Somoza era. Somocismo was a corrupt regime, but Nicaraguan society maintained hope. Sandinismo offered hope. In those days the Catholic Church, under the influence of liberation theology, also offered hope. In today's Nicaragua, hope has faded and life is a punishment. Any movement that promises the material recovery of the country must first let Nicaraguans again dream of a better Nicaragua.

Notes

1. Andrés Pérez Baltodano, in *Entre el estado conquistador y el estado nación: Providencialismo, pensamiento político, y estructuras de poder en el desarrollo histórico de Nicaragua* (Managua: Fundacion Friederich Ebert en Nicaragua, 2003), canvasses the concept thoroughly.

2. Peter C. Hodgson, "Providence," in *A New Handbook of Christian Theology* (Cambridge, UK: Lutterworth Press, 1992), 394–397.

3. Edgardo Buitrago, "La intervención norteamericana y la política nicaraguense durante el período conservador (1910–1929)," in *Historia de Violencia en Nicaragua,* edited by Elisa Arévalo C. et al. (Managua: UPOLI, 1997), 309.

4. Sergio Ramírez, *Adiós, muchachos: Una memoria de la revolución sandinista* (Mexico City: Aguilar, 1999), 113.

5. Ramírez, *Adiós, muchachos,* 113.

6. Government of Nicaragua, "Nicaragua: Medium Term Development Strategy, 1992–1996," document presented to the Grupo Consultivo, Washington, DC, March 26, 1992.

7. Paul Oquist, "Sociopolitical Dynamics in the 1990 Nicaraguan Election," in *The 1990 Elections in Nicaragua and Their Aftermath,* edited by Vanessa Castro and Gary Prevost (Lanham, MD: Rowman and Littlefield, 1993), 7.

8. See Giorgio Trucchi, "Nicaragua: 17 Years of Governing from Below," *La Rel,* www.rel-uita.org/.

9. Envío, "¿Cómo votó Nicaragua?" *Envío* 102 (April 1990), www.envio.org .ni/.

10. Pierre Fruhling, Miguel González, and Hans Pettar Buvollen, *Etnicidad y Nación: El desarrollo de la autonomía de la Costa Atlántica de Nicaragua (1987–2007)* (Guatemala City: F y G Editores, 2007), 121.

11. Envío, "¿Cómo votó Nicaragua?"

12. Daniel Ortega, "Defender nuestro derecho a la rebelión," *Barricada Internacional* 339 (July 1991): 25.

13. Erik Aguirre, "De lucha ideológica a poder contranatura," *El Nuevo Diario,* April 4, 2007, www.elnuevodiario.com.ni.

14. Instituto de Estudios Nicaraguenses (IEN), *FSLN: De vanguardismo al acuerdo nacional* (Managua: Fundacion Friederich Ebert en Nicaragua, 1993), 13.

15. *La Piñata* is capitalized to distinguish the transfer of wealth effected by the FSLN's leaders from the children's party game.

16. Ernesto Cardenal, *La revolución perdida* (Managua: ANAMA, 2003), 660–661.

17. Augusto Zamora, *El futuro de Nicaragua* (Managua: Fondo Editorial Cira, 1995), 12.

18. Carlos Fernando Chamorro, "La elección del 20 de octubre y el nuevo escenario político," *Pensamiento Propio* (July–December 1996): 3.

19. Envío, "Nicaragua comienza la cuenta regresiva," *Envío* 173 (August 1996), www.envio.org.ni/.

20. Envío, "Nicaragua comienza la cuenta regresiva."

21. Envío, "Los 33 días que conmovieron a Nicaragua: El nuevo escenario nacional," *Envío* 176 (November 1996), www.envio.org.ni/.

22. Fruhling, González, and Buvollen, *Etnicidad y Nación,* 170, 205.

23. Oscar René Vargas, "¿Dónde está la izquierda?" *El Semanario,* January 17–23, 1997, 8.

24. Dora María Téllez, "A New Option for the Left," *Envío* (March 2000), www.envio.org.ni/articulo/1404 (accessed December 20, 2007). Editor's note: *Envío* publishes in Spanish and English, but the editions are not identical. Where there is an English version of a citation, it will be used.

25. *Vértice,* "La caída de Arnoldo Alemán," October 14–21, 2004, www.el salvador.com/.

26. Gobierno de Nicaragua, *Incontrolables desafíos, una sola voluntad,* www .presidencia.gob.ni.

27. Envío Team, "Dilemas en la lucha contra el cáncer," *Envío* (March 2002), www.envio.org.ni/.

28. Arturo Grigsby, "New Government, New Economy?" *Envío* 248 (January–February 2002), www.envio.org.ni/.

29. *El Nuevo Diario,* "Desnutrición campea en Nicaragua," June 17, 2002, www.elnuevodiario.com.ni.

30. FSLN, "El programa de gobierno del FSLN, *Visión Sandinista* 54, August 1–7, 2001.

31. Aldo Díaz Lacayo, "These Elections Are Devoid of Ideology," *Envío* 241 (August 2001), www.envio.org.ni/.

32. Daniel Ortega and Agustín Jarquín, "Carta a los nicaragüenses: ¡Por los ideales más altos!" *Visión Sandinista,* August 22–28, 2001, 10.

33. Daniel Ortega, "A vencer la pobreza," *Visión Sandinista,* December 22, 2001.

34. Ortega, "A vencer."

35. Rosario Murillo, "Es la hora de la luz," *Visión Sandinista,* July 25–31, 2001.

36. Envío, "The 'New Era' Begins Amid Check Scams and Blank Checks," *Envío* 246 (January–February 2002), www.envio.org.ni/.

37. Conferencia Episcopal de Nicaragua, *Exhortación en ocasión de las elecciones generales de 2001,* August 15, 2001.

38. Envío, "Nicaragua's Municipal Elections: The Good, the Bad, the Uncertain," *Envío* 232 (November 2000), www.envio.org.ni/.

39. Fruhling, González, and Buvollen, *Ethnicidad y Nacion,* 228.

40. FSLN, "Un programa para el siglo XX!" *Visión Sandinista* (February 2002): 6–8.

41. William Grigsby, "Todavía es tiempo para que el FSLN gire a la izquierda," *Sin Fronteras,* September 1, 2005, www.nicaraguita.org.

42. *La Prensa,* "Ortega ofrece condonación y subsidio," July 20, 2006, www.laprensa.com.ni.

43. Bayardo Arce, "Gobernadores en unidad nacional," *El Nuevo Diario,* June 25, 2006, www.elnuevodiario.com.ni.

44. Editors' note: A detailed description is found in Chapter 8 of this volume.

45. Sofía Montenegro, "El retorno de Daniel Ortega," *Pueblos,* March 16, 2007, www.revista.pueblos.org.

46. Celia Hart, "Las elecciones rosa de Nicaragua," *Argenpress,* November 16, 2006, www.argenpress.info.

47. Ernesto Cardenal, "Sandinistas, no voten por el falso Sandinismo," *El Nuevo Diario,* October 26, 2006, www.elnuevodiario.com.ni.

48. Hart, "Las elecciones."

49. Rosario Murillo, "Sin sorpresas en la vida de Pedro: Todo sobre sus navajas," *Con amor Nicaragua: Artículos,* no. 47, March 3–4, 2005, www.conamor nicaragua.org.ni.

50. Andrés Pérez Baltodano, "El veneno del antisemitismo," *Confidencial* 428, March 6–12, 2005, www.confidencial.com.ni.

51. William Grigsby, "2004 Elections: FSLN-Convergence Victories in Numbers," *Envío* 280 (November 2004), www.envio.org.ni/.

52. Fruhling, González, and Buvollen, *Ethnicidad y Nacion,* 257.

53. AMUNIC, "Municipios destacados en el primer evento de mediación del Sistema de Reconocimiento al Desempeño Municipal," *Acta* SIDREM, December 13, 2006.

54. Daysi Alvarado, Alejandro Bravo, and Carlos Fernando López, *Agenda municipal de los partidos políticos de Nicaragua.* Managua: AMUNIC, 2004.

55. Ricardo Coronel Kautz, "Política y ética en Nicaragua," *El Nuevo Diario,* September 23, 2005, www.elnuevodiario.com.ni.

56. Coronel Kautz, "Política."

57. Manuel Guedán, "¿Cómo ven nuestra política exterior?" *Confidencial* 527, March 18–24, 2007, www.confidencial.com.ni.

58. Envío, "Nicaragua: 100 Days in Babel," *Envío* 309 (April 2007), www.envio .org.ni/.

59. Henry Petrie Bejarano, "Ortega huérfano de estrategias," *El Nuevo Diario,* April 11, 2007, www.elnuevodiario.com.ni.

60. Editor's note: For details, see, Chapter 5 in this volume.

5

A Politicized Judiciary

Elena Martínez Barahona

YEARS OF CIVIL WAR AND A LEGACY OF PERSONALISM, COR-
ruption, and endemic poverty have influenced Nicaragua's political institutions, especially its judicial institutions.[1] Most political scientists say
Nicaragua is a country "that never had an easy time," that is "unpredictable,"
or whose democracy is "undone."[2] In fact, the history of Nicaragua has always been marked by civil conflict and periodic foreign intervention that reinforce a tendency to strongman rule (caudillismo). In this context, as
political analyst David Dye points out, "political-cultural proclivities interact with key institutional arrangements to perpetuate the clientelistic exercise of power by the dominant power-holders."[3]

Nicaragua's judicial system combines all these features. The weakness
of the judiciary has resulted in high levels of politicization within its structures. Nicaragua's courts are properly styled a captive of the executive.[4]
Consequently, the Nicaraguan judiciary in general and the Supreme Court
in particular have historically been tainted by partisan favoritism. Judicial
positions are used as patronage, and politicians interfere in court procedures.

In recent years, this tendency has been perpetuated through a political
accord reached in 2000 between the the Liberal politician Arnoldo Alemán
Lacayo and the Sandinista politician Daniel Ortega that most Nicaraguans
call "el Pacto," or the Pact.[5] Every March, the Pact partners must by law renew the Pact by replacing or reconfirming the occupants of top-level positions whose terms have expired.[6] The Pact aligned the distribution of power
within the National Assembly and other state institutions, including the
Supreme Court. Thus, after expanding the Supreme Court of Justice (Corte
Suprema de Justicia, or CSJ), the Supreme Electoral Council (Consejo
Supremo Electoral, or CSE), and the office of the Comptroller General
of the Republic (Contralor General de la República, or CGR), the pacting

caudillos proceeded to divide between them the top positions in each institution according to the political weight of each party. In fact, this two-party Pact produced the clientelistic colonization of certain state institutions, seriously affecting their performance. As a result, a shared interest in impunity between the top leaders of Nicaraguan politics has created a corrupt "bipartisan" administration that has dominated these institutions and distorted their behavior.[7]

This political struggle between the Sandinista National Liberation Front (Frente Sandinista de Liberación Nacional, or FSLN) and the Constitutionalist Liberal Party (Partido Liberal Constitutionalista, or PLC) conditions how all Nicaraguan democratic institutions, including the courts, work. The Pact determines not only the Court's membership, including its president (chief justice), but also how the four chambers (*salas*) of the Court are organized, judicial appointments at appellate and district levels, and how cases of interest to one of the pacting parties are decided. Although I show below that all the magistrates[8] have clear political loyalties, the imposition of party discipline over decisions is done subtly, appearing to be sporadic and decentralized, involving multiple networks of loyalties that ultimately converge in the two national caudillos, Daniel Ortega and Arnoldo Alemán.[9] On a day-to-day level, this implies that arbitrary judicial rulings more often stem from simple payoffs or from bargaining between higher-level magistrates than from direct instructions by the leaders of the dominant parties. These circumstances leave Nicaraguan democracy with two critical weaknesses: (1) there is no effective system of checks and balances and thus horizontal accountability is weak, and (2) the rule of law scarcely exists, making it nearly impossible to protect the rights of citizens.

This chapter asks how well the Supreme Court of Justice meets the definition of "politicization of justice." The Court is politically active but not independent because it is used by Nicaragua's caudillos to protect their interests, not least by assuring them freedom from prosecution. To demonstrate, I first briefly describe the political role played by Nicaragua's judiciary. Then I examine the CSJ's political role, using the concepts of judicial independence and political intervention, which determine the quality and the political impact of its actions. The former relates to the free exercise of the judicial function, and the latter refers to the effectiveness of a supreme court in the political arena. The term "political intervention" is used here to distinguish this approach from "judicial activism" because I emphasize the partisan political character of judicial activity.

My evidence shows that the Supreme Court of Justice exemplifies the politicization of justice. In addition, I examine the system-level variables associated with politicized justice in Nicaragua, using documents, press reports, structured interview-questionnaires (basically two surveys), and a small number of in-depth, semistructured interviews with Supreme Court magistrates that I conducted.[10] Admittedly, using interview data from judges when analyzing controversial decisions in which they participated can produce highly skewed results, as the justices will likely present themselves favorably. However, knowing what the actors themselves say about their role in controversial matters is critical to understanding the political function of Nicaragua's judicial branch.

The Path of Judicial Counterreform

"Nicaraguans have never known a judicial system free from political interference and manipulation," observes political analyst David Dye.[11] Indeed, studies of justice in Nicaragua have emphasized the personal character of its courts.[12] Some analysts have explained it by a past filled with caudillos who had no use for the rule of law.[13] This historical continuity of caudillismo, which should be viewed as a strongly entrenched informal political institution in Nicaragua, remains an obstacle to democratic consolidation.[14]

Historically, the nation's courts, including the Supreme Court, have been tainted by judicial appointments used as patronage and political meddling in judicial proceedings.[15] From 1936 to 1979, Nicaragua's Supreme Court was so dominated by the Somozas that Kenneth F. Johnson and Paul Paris called Nicaraguan justices "puppets of the Somoza family."[16] After the Sandinista Revolution, the judicial system did experience some changes, but they did not alter its trajectory. Judicial independence was formally guaranteed under the first elected Sandinista government (1984–1990) but in practice it was compromised by political factors. For example, one of the most severely criticized aspects of revolutionary justice was the creation of a number of special courts responsible to the executive, exacerbating the tendency to make the judiciary a partisan instrument.[17] During the first years of Sandinista rule, there was an effort to include members of the opposition on the Supreme Court (there were three non-Sandinistas out of seven justices). In 1987, however, when the agricultural ministry refused to comply with the Court's *La Verona* decision, the CSJ's independence from the executive branch was brought into question.[18]

Since the early 1990s, the FSLN has slowly extended its influence over the judicial system. According to Dye, it reflects a conscious effort to prepare party members to become lawyers and later place them as judges.[19] As a result, Sandinista-aligned judges began to dominate the criminal courts in Managua and increasingly the civil courts as well. Early in the Chamorro administration, growing Sandinista influence on the CSJ appeared to be a potential threat to the new liberal democratic government because the Supreme Court assumed an unprecedented role as the final arbiter in conflicts not resolved in the political arena. In an attempt to guarantee political equilibrium on the Court, the constitutional amendments passed in 1995 required that the National Assembly, which elects Supreme Court magistrates, receive at least two slates of candidates for each opening. The Court's membership was expanded, and justices were assigned to newly created *salas* (specialized divisions), but these changes came as a result of compromises and political deals.

Though President Alemán (1997–2002) initially had few friends on the Supreme Court, patronage soon gave him loyalists and favorable decisions.[20] Today, Supreme Court justices are still named through deal making and political manipulation, controlling the nomination process, or blocking a candidate's election. The most recent judicial reform process, initiated in 2005, is similarly subject to politics.[21] Although these arrangements are supposedly aimed at creating a more nonpartisan Supreme Court, they have seen the High Court effectively kidnapped by the PLC and FSLN.

The Performance of the Supreme Court

In this section, I first examine perceptions of judicial independence and then consider the political salience of matters coming before the Supreme Court.[22] I find a rather low level of judicial independence and a clear predisposition toward political intervention. Thus one can say that the decisions of the Nicaraguan Supreme Court politicize justice.

The Degree of Judicial Independence

Judicial independence means that courts (especially supreme courts) reach decisions without any restrictions, improper influence, pressures, threats, or interference, direct or indirect, from any quarter, for any reason.[23] Because there is disagreement on how to measure judicial independence, I employ a proxy: how actors involved in the judicial process perceive it.[24] This approach reflects the belief that a deeper analytical understanding of the judicial independence of a country can come from knowing how the judiciary itself perceives it. The data come from surveys that ask judges, citizens, and deputies about the independence of the judiciary.[25] Using these three sets of perceptions captures more fully the complexity of judicial independence.

Nicaraguan judges rated their own independence as 6 on a 10-point scale.[26] More interestingly, the in-depth interviews showed that views about the independence of the Supreme Court varied with the partisan loyalties of the justices. Justice Rafael Solís Cerda, a Sandinista, defended their independence: "I believe that despite what people say, we [justices] are quite independent."[27] However, his brother justice, Iván Escobar Fornos, from the PLC, voiced his doubts: "You can't ensure total independence . . . the problem is that some justices and some judges do take sides . . . even though they shouldn't."[28]

Regarding what undermines judicial independence, the justices point principally to appointment procedures (40 percent) and instability in office (30 percent).[29] Both obstacles signal the absence of mechanisms that guarantee judicial independence. When asked which institutions influence their decisions, CSJ justices listed the media (75 percent), the political parties (60 percent), pressure groups (40 percent), and the executive and legislature (30 percent). Indeed, when questioned about the principal problem of Nicaragua's judiciary, the justices point to its lack of independence relative to other political institutions, particularly the political parties (40 percent).[30]

However, Justice Guillermo Vargas Sandino had a different view:

> [There are] two individuals who are running things. Here, one of them calls and everybody in one party comes running. The other calls and the same thing happens in the other party. *[Those two] call up judges and pressure them.* This has never happened before, never in the history of Nicaragua. (emphasis added)

Thirty percent of Supreme Court magistrates also claim to have received threats or bribes while on the bench. Although they do not mention the source of the bribes, they do say that they have been threatened mainly by political parties, which again points to parties as the main obstacle to judicial independence.[31] The same proportion of justices also sees the mechanisms used to discipline judges as instruments of political control or pressure.[32]

Obviously, asking the judges themselves about the state of judicial independence runs the risk of getting self-serving answers. However, using survey material showing how legislators and the general public view Nicaragua's judges provides an independent standard against which to check the magistrates' self-evaluations.

Regarding whether citizens see judges as independent, when the Latinobarómetro poll asked Latin Americans if judges in their country are bribed to get a favorable verdict, more than a third of Nicaraguans, 35 percent, said yes (see Figure 5.1).[33] Similarly, regarding confidence in the courts' ability

**Figure 5.1 Perceived Probability of
Bribing Judges in Latin America (percentage)**

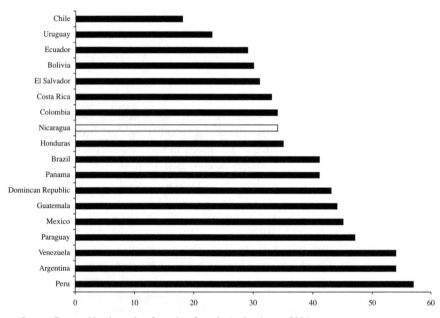

Source: Prepared by the author from data from *Latinobarómetro* 2004.

to provide a fair trial, Nicaragua again ranks in the bottom half of the scale.[34] These results are confirmed by a 2005 national survey in Nicaragua in which 44.4 percent of those interviewed considered judges unfair and 85.25 percent reported little or no confidence in the judiciary.[35] With respect to the CSJ, a 2007 Nicaraguan survey showed that 68.2 percent of those interviewed ranked the level of credibility of this institution as low or very low.[36]

Due to this perceived lack of judicial independence, many civil society organizations began mobilizing to protest Supreme Court decisions. Posters urging public participation in a 2005 protest featured slogans like that in Figure 5.2: "Reject the recent Supreme Court decisions that violate the rule of law. Come to the funeral procession for justice in Nicaragua, this Friday" and "The Supreme Court decisions are producing a two-party dictatorship."[37]

This absence of judicial independence on the Supreme Court is also widely reported by the media. Almost daily, headlines scream: "SCJ Promotes Impunity"[38] or "Political Circus in the Courts."[39] Furthermore, public opinion surveys showed citizens holding equally skeptical views about the Court. For example, on September 5, 2005, *La Prensa* reported a poll showing that 72.6 percent of those interviewed disapproved of a decision

**Figure 5.2 Poster Announcing a Protest Against
Recent Supreme Court Decisions**

RECHAZA LAS RECIENTES
SENTENCIAS DE LA CORTE
SUPREMA DE JUSTICIA POR
SER VIOLATORIAS AL ESTADO DE
DERECHO

Y

CONVOCA PARA
ESTE VIERNES 9 - SEPTIEMBRE

A la Caravana Fúnebre de la
Justicia en Nicaragua

Del Estadio Nacional - 5:00 PM
a la Corte Suprema de Justicia - 7:00 PM
NO FALTES !
HABRÁ TRANSPORTE!

JUSTICIA SÍ !   DICTADURA NO!
DEMOCRACIA SÍ !   PACTO NO!

ratifying the 2005 constitutional amendments, which threatened to strip the president, Enrique Bolaños, of key powers.[40] Supreme Court justices aligned with both big parties criticize such stories. Justice Iván Escobar Fornos, a PLC loyalist, argues:

> The media use this kind of poll . . . they use them a lot to see if the people agree with our decisions or not . . . but the people don't really know [because] there's no analysis in the press, nothing serious and from a legal standpoint to really cast doubt on our findings. [The media] may not even really know what this latest decision says, because they haven't even asked for certified copies, yet they keep right on doing those polls to see if the public approves of our decisions or not.

Justice Solis, a Sandinista, had this to say:

> The poll *La Prensa* published the other day was a telephone survey, done in Managua by one of the firms that *La Prensa* uses. It shows that 70 percent of the people are opposed to the judicial branch, with almost 80 percent

saying "they don't believe in us, that we're a disaster," based on three decisions we handed down last week. But this was a poll of the middle and upper middle classes, the ones who have telephones in Nicaragua, by *La Prensa*. So there you see the press acting, let's say "forcefully," because of its political leanings.

National Assembly deputies also highlighted this perceived lack of judicial independence. Unsurprisingly, opposition and government members hold starkly opposing views: the more independent a legislator thinks the judiciary is, the less likely it is that he or she sits on the government side.[41] Although 27.6 percent of opposition deputies rate judicial independence as high, 90.3 percent of the government deputies rate it low (see Table 5.1). This is counterintuitive, since one would expect that legislators in the majority caucus would rate the judiciary as more independent than the opposition would. The most likely explanation is that the survey was done in 2002, when the deputies on the government side (PLC) were worried about the impartiality of Arnoldo Alemán's trial for corruption, then being heard by a Sandinista judge.

From this analysis, it is apparent that there are serious doubts about the Supreme Court's independence. Judges, civil society organizations, and National Assembly deputies all express such doubts, not only in polls conducted by (potentially partisan) local media but also in sophisticated cross-time polls by international organizations and universities.

Court Intervention in Political Issues

Nicaragua belongs to the civil law tradition, which generally limits judicial activism. It has traditionally denied judges any power of judicial review: Supreme Court magistrates could only act when statutes are clearly against

Table 5.1 Nicaraguan Judicial Independence Evaluated by Government and Opposition, 2002 (percentage)

Judicial Independence	Opposition	Government	Total Deputies
Low	41.4	90.3	66.7
Medium	31.0	9.7	20
High	27.6	0	13.3
Percent total	100	100	100

Source: Author's calculations from the project Proyecto de Investigación Elites Parlamentarias Latinoamericanas (PELA), Instituto Interuniversitario de Estudios de Iberoamérica y Portugal, Universidad de Salamanca y Centro de Investigaciones Sociológicas (CIS), Agencia Española de Cooperación Internacional, 2002.

"the letter of the law," narrowly interpreted.[42] In practice, the norm of judicial deference to the elected branches, especially the executive, prevented judges from using the law to restrict government power. In Latin America, the combination of the civil law tradition, political norms regarding courts, and executive supremacy have historically left supreme courts politically ineffectual, with no real independence and thus little political importance in their own right.

However, these patterns are now beginning to break down.[43] Many supreme courts are now willing to engage "political" questions.[44] In this sense, the Nicaraguan case is paradigmatic. Not only has the CSJ become more interventionist, but it has been deliberately activated to oppose or support specific policies. This makes the Court's rulings controversial, leaves it with less credibility, and undermines the legitimacy of the judicial process.

Political intervention in judicial processes is evident in politically inspired Supreme Court decisions and the use of the courts as a battlefield in the corruption cases surrounding the Alemán administration, each of which will be considered here. Beginning with the Court's decisions, some see the Supreme Court of Justice as tending toward judicial dictatorship by treading on the legislature's prerogatives. However, partisan calculations lie behind many of the Court's actions. Delays in Supreme Court decisions are interpreted as products of negotiations with the executive (Alemán's administration) or with the National Assembly (the Bolaños administration) or with both (the current Ortega administration). Furthermore, in cases brought against the Pact, the Court has never acted quickly.[45]

In many landmark cases, the Supreme Court emerges as a partisan political actor. A November 2002 decision overturned portions of the highly restrictive Electoral Law of 2000. That law imposed draconian requirements for the registration of political parties and candidates, as well as the formation of electoral alliances. The Court ruled that the limitations were unconstitutional, "opening the way for at least some of the smaller parties to reappear."[46] Some magistrates, such as Justice Francisco Rosales, highlight this decision as the proof of the Court's freedom from partisan influences:

These small parties that you see today, like the Movimiento de Renovación Sandinista led by Herty Lewites or the Alternativa Cristiana, all of them [have] disappeared . . . because they didn't get 3 percent of the vote in the last elections . . . then, what happened? This Court found the regulation decreed by the Supreme Electoral Council to be unconstitutional, because it went beyond the law in establishing a series of prerequisites. Because of that, these parties again have political life. I'm giving you concrete examples where [responding to] the interests of Daniel Ortega or Alemán . . . would have put an end to those parties; they wouldn't exist. So because the Court said, "Look, gentlemen, this is unconstitutional": those little parties exist today.[47]

However, some see Daniel Ortega's hand behind this decision.[48] When Alba Luz Ramos, a Sandinista sympathizer, was elected president of the Supreme Court in October 2002, minor parties were immediately resuscitated. Thus some argued that the decision facilitated splintering the anti-Sandinista vote in future elections. Even the magistrates on the Supreme Electoral Council had suspicions about the political intentions of this decision. Justice Mauricio Montealegre had this to say: "I respect the Court, but it strikes me that they go out of their way to accommodate certain political interests. I feel quite certain that from a legal perspective the Court's decision to wait so long before declaring a law unconstitutional can hardly be deemed proof of seriousness of purpose."[49]

Throughout the Bolaños administration, the FSLN used the Supreme Court in the party's power struggle with the president. One example is found in the Court's decision of May 2004, in which the Supreme Court ruled that parties might seek injunctions (*amparos*) against draft laws—ones not yet passed. According to Dye, "as the court typically takes months or even years to process one *amparo,* this invitation to obstruction could potentially paralyze the legislative process."[50] The decision again reflected partisan interest. This view was expressed by Justice Iván Escobar Fornos, who dissented, arguing that "it is not right that the CSJ have the power to interfere in the process of debating a law."[51]

Furthermore, during the Bolaños administration, most petitions for injunctions from politicians targeted the executive. Taking advantage of the Supreme Court's activism, the National Assembly (particularly the Sandinistas, then the minority) used the judiciary to hobble virtually every form of executive authority. Thus, on August 30, 2005, after several months of political tension, the Supreme Court upheld the constitutionality of amendments reducing executive power passed by the National Assembly.[52] Many justices defended this decision increasing the power of the legislature. Justice Rafael Solís said, "I believe that legislatures in Latin America should have more power. It's a battle I've been waging since I was a deputy [in the 1980s]."[53]

> This amendment restores certain attributes to the legislature and takes them from the executive, and this is good for the country. They in no way create a parliamentary system, but were, in the Court's judgment, good for Nicaragua. Moreover, they were passed by the assembly following established procedure. The president [Bolaños] doesn't like them and lost the support of his party in seeking to have them declared unconstitutional.

This situation changed once Ortega became president in 2007, however. Another conflict arose between the legislature and the executive, here over the constitutionality of new executive decree powers that created the Councils of Citizens' Power (Consejos del Poder Ciudadano, or CPCs). In this case, the Supreme Court accepted the *recurso de amparo* (request for an injunction) filed by President Ortega against a bill that sought to revoke the decree.[54] The problem was that the Supreme Court granted the injunction one day *before* the law's passage, issuing a preemptive declaration of unconstitutionality. Thus the Supreme Court exceeded its powers by short-circuiting the legislative process to meet the wishes of the president, and the media quickly proclaimed the decision "politically inspired."[55]

Most of the magistrates justify these politically charged decisions by pointing to the incapacity of the other branches to solve their problems. Justice Fornos pointed out "that these cases come to the Court because the politicians can't solve their problems. So they send them to us, the judicial branch." None of this is new. Justice Solís said that he felt it has been normal throughout Nicaragua's history for the Court to decide cases with strong political connotations.

Further evidence that the judiciary is used as a partisan instrument may be found in its handling of the corruption trials of former president Alemán and his officials. The Alemán administration (1997–2002) was characterized by a pandemic of corruption, a "kleptocracy" in Close's terms, consented to by the judiciary.[56] During this period, Liberals and Sandinistas struggled fiercely for control of the judiciary, especially the Supreme Court, which rejected much of the evidence that the comptroller general of the republic, Agustín Jarquín, brought against Alemán's officials. When in 1999 Jarquín was accused of fraud, many took it as proof of a politicized justice system.[57]

In 2002, however, the circumstances seemed to change. Nicaragua faced up to the historical challenge of eliminating past abuses of authority. Newly elected Liberal president Enrique Bolaños mounted an anticorruption drive that saw three officials of the Alemán administration, including former president Alemán himself, indicted for corruption. These actions showed that for the first time in Nicaraguan history, politicians could be accused, tried, convicted, and jailed. The first set of cases came from an internal investigation into the accounts of the state-owned television network, Channel 6, in February 2002. Although several of those implicated were indicted, others were acquitted or became fugitives from justice.[58] Alemán protested his innocence and invoked parliamentary immunity to avoid answering the charges, but once details about the biggest fraud of all, the *huaca* (Quechua for "buried treasure"), became public, the case against Alemán in relation to Channel 6 grew stronger.[59]

The second set of cases, called the *checazo* ("check scam," or misappropriation of government checks) and the *camionetazo,* which involved pickup trucks, arose in April 2002 and were both closely associated with Byron Jerez, head of the national tax agency (Dirección General de Ingresos, or DGI) during much of Alemán's term and the second most powerful figure in that government. On December 12, 2003, Byron Jerez was acquitted by the Sandinista judge Juana Méndez Pérez, now a Supreme Court Justice, with the argument that he merely exercised "due obedience" (i.e. followed orders) and did not profit from any illegal activity. Judge Edgard Altamirano, another Sandinista, did the same in another case accusing Jerez of fraud involving the Banco Nicaragüense de Industria y de Comercio (BANIC). The Appeals Court ignored overwhelming evidence against Jerez and acquitted him on all counts. However, it is widely believed that Jerez was freed for turning state's evidence against Alemán.[60] Some jurists have argued that the acquittal was illegal for two reasons. First, the "due obedience" upheld by Judge Méndez cannot be applied when the acts are illegal. And second, under Nicaragua's penal code, a plea bargain cannot offset criminal responsibility.[61]

Finally, the most crucial case concerned the *huaca.* In August 2002 the *fiscalía,* Francisco Fiallos, presented evidence that former president Alemán, his family, and thirteen other people had directly engaged in an elaborately orchestrated plan to defraud the government and launder massive amounts of money (around $100 million) through front corporations registered in Panama.[62] However, victories over corruption in court have been few, fragile, and "in all probability will turn out to be temporary,"[63] because the fight against corruption is based on political circumstances instead of a commitment to honest government.[64]

Sandinista leader Daniel Ortega joined the anticorruption battle to eliminate Alemán as a political rival. He did this, first, by having all thirty-eight Sandinista deputies vote to unseat Alemán as president of the National Assembly. Then, to prolong Alemán's absence, Ortega ensured that a Sandinista presided over his opponent's trial. Both strategies were used to pressure Alemán to concede more power to Ortega.[65]

One of the first signs of partisan use of the judiciary appeared in 2002, when one of the six Sandinista Supreme Court justices was in charge of the office that assigns cases to courts of first instance (Oficina de Distribución de Causas). At that time, the *huaca* case was presided over by then-judge Juana Méndez of Managua's first district criminal court, whose Sandinista links were well known. Her actions in the case are representative of the judiciary's severe politicization.

As Close points out, "it was not by chance that the judicial processes against Alemán and officials of his administration moved along smartly."[66]

Ortega used Alemán's plight for leverage in negotiations to replace nine Supreme Court justices. As a result, in June 2003, the FSLN achieved parity on the High Court with the PLC. Then, in March 2004, another Sandinista was chosen as the Court's chief justice, giving the FSLN its first working majority on the Supreme Court. Ortega could now offer Alemán his eventual freedom in exchange for a new pact. The bargain included a judicial career law,[67] the election of a Supreme Court president and officers for the National Assembly, and the postponement of the 2004 municipal elections until 2006, to hold them concurrently with national elections.[68] In December 2003, however, Méndez convicted the former president of Nicaragua of corruption, handing him a twenty-year sentence in a "politically-inspired and directed" action that seemed meant to punish Alemán for his intransigence in the negotiations.[69]

The next move came from Alemán. In his quest for freedom, he sought a deal with President Bolaños, who resented Ortega's machinations against him. In the bargain, it was assumed that the PLC would resume its role as government party, supporting Bolaños's legislative agenda. Once the legislature's leadership was elected, however, the PLC reneged on the deal and returned to working to free their caudillo from prison.[70] Their failure to do so produced more negotiations between Alemán and Ortega in April 2004, aimed at undermining Bolaños's hold on power and replacing Alemán's preventive detention with house arrest. The result was that in September 2004, Judge Juana Méndez brought indictments against Alemán for fraud and money laundering and charged Bolaños with "electoral offences," related to the financing of his 2001 campaign. Indeed, Méndez repeatedly and capriciously altered the conditions of Alemán's confinement to fulfill Ortega's wishes.[71]

On July 25, 2005, Judge Roxana Zapata, a criminal court judge supervising sentencing and incarceration (Jueza Primera de Ejecución de Sentencia y Vigilancia Penitenciaria) who also was the wife of the current Supreme Court justice Sergio Cuarezma Terán, placed Alemán under a special form of house arrest called the Régimen de Convivencia Familiar. Her ruling allowed Alemán to move around the country (what Nicaraguans called "Nicaragua as prison," or *Nicaragua por carcel*). In August 2005, the Supreme Court also acted, replacing Alemán's preventive detention with house arrest. The decision was signed by the Liberal Supreme Court justices (Ramón Chavarría, Iván Escobar Fornos, Guillermo Selva Argüello, and José Damisis Sirias), because, by chance, the Sandinista justices (Camilo Argüello, Rafael Solís, and Francisco Rosales) were absent.

But the conditions of Alemán's detention kept changing. On December 13, 2007, a new decision by the Managua district Court of Appeals (Sala Penal Uno del Tribunal de Apelaciones, or TAM) revoked the Régimen de

Convivencia Familiar and again confined Alemán to his house. This decision was signed by two Sandinista judges, Ileana Pérez and Angela Dávila, with Liberal Rafael Avellán dissenting, and enjoyed broad public support.[72] Then on January 10, 2008, Judge Zapata reestablished *Nicaragua por carcel*. The president of the CSJ, Liberal justice Manuel Martínez Sevilla, accepted Zapata's decision, arguing that she, not the Court of Appeals, was authorized to grant house arrest.[73] Finally, on January 15, 2009, the majority of the Constitutional Division of the Supreme Court (Justices Cuarezma Terán, Escobar Fornos, Selva Argüello, and Gabriel Rivera Zeledón—all PLC sympathizers) dismissed all charges against Arnoldo Alemán.

The battle between the two major parties until then had centered on controlling Alemán's terms of confinement and the conditions for his freedom. Consequently, the legal arguments kept changing according to each party's immediate needs. The reactions of the Supreme Court magistrates to these political battles varied with their partisan loyalties. Then-justice Guillermo Vargas Sandino acknowledges that many magistrates from the PLC were on the Supreme Court to gain Alemán's release:

> The last four Liberals named to the Court came from Dr. Alemán's wing of the party. On their appointment, they declared: "We're here to set Alemán free. That's our mission." And that's what they've tried to do. Then everything here on the Court became paralyzed, because there was this emphasis on horse-trading of the "what do I have to give you for you to cut me some slack on Alemán" sort. The Liberals have spent three years trying to free their leader and the Sandinistas have not given an inch, effectively keeping Alemán as a hostage. This has produced judicial gridlock, because everything but everything relates back to this question. As a result, we, the Court, cannot function, which is truly lamentable.

All the magistrates justify their actions as normal in Nicaraguan political life. Justice Rafael Solís asserts that the complaints come from sectors that have no quota of power (representation) on the Supreme Court, such as big business.

The justices seem to accept that this creates impunity in democratic institutions. When they are questioned about levels of impunity, they consider it "very high" or "high" in the legislative branch (67.3 percent) and the executive (58.3 percent), underscoring their powerlessness to control those institutions.[74] Similarly, when questioned about the degree of collaboration among public authorities when an official is charged with some offense, the majority respond that it is "low" or "very low." This contributes to impunity by hampering investigations. Obviously, the Supreme Court does not provide horizontal accountability. It does not ensure that other branches of government obey the law because it follows the wishes of the two caudillos. The

Supreme Court has intervened in highly contentious political controversies with apparently partisan motives, and thus speculation about political intent always surrounds the Court's decisions.

Former justice Vargas Sandino confirms this, observing that "right now the courts have little credibility." In his view, it is due to partisan influences on Supreme Court decisions: "There has been a terrible politicization [of the Court], because since 1999, as magistrates leave on the expiration of their terms, their replacements are individuals who depend entirely on the big political parties for their jobs. There are deals, pacts, compacts . . . and then the whole judicial branch is politicized." He further declared that the Supreme Court can be manipulated by everyone. "That's been one of the problems: that political conflicts get passed on to the Court. Right now, everybody can manipulate the Court: the president, the deputies, anybody. To my mind, there has been a very serious blow to our institutional integrity that has grave consequences for the entire country." Having an active but politicized Supreme Court, with little judicial independence, makes Nicaragua a clear case of the politicization of justice.[75]

Why Justice Is Politicized
on the Nicaraguan Supreme Court

A combination of political control over judicial procedures and a highly partisan (*partidista*) composition of the Supreme Court, in a country with a polarized two-party system, has produced a politicized Supreme Court. External interference in judicial affairs, from the selection of judges to the absence of guarantees for judicial tenure, is central to understanding the lack of judicial independence on the Nicaraguan Supreme Court. This absence of independence has been a continual source of criticism of the Court. As Dye observes: "Since the end of the Sandinista revolution, political sympathy, if not outright party affiliation, has consistently been important in the selection of Supreme Court and appeals court magistrates."[76] All that is somewhat ironic because increasing judicial independence was a key objective of the 1995 constitutional amendments. It was to be secured by reducing the executive's power over Supreme Court appointments and by making judicial tenure more secure. Supreme Court nominees are now proposed by both the executive branch and the legislature through lists drawn up in consultation with interested outside groups. However, at the end, it is the National Assembly that elects the magistrates by a 60 percent vote, which implies bipartisan support. The assembly may also reject the pool of candidates proposed by the president. This limits executive powers, as Justice Francisco Rosales notes:

Today, the National Assembly is making a career out of amending the Constitution so as to limit executive power. The 1995 amendments gave the Assembly the right to make appointments to the Supreme Court, as well as to propose its own list of candidates [*terna*], something that was previously exclusively a presidential prerogative.[77]

The Pact expanded the Court from twelve to sixteen members. Initially, this favored the PLC and included three independents.[78] In subsequent years, the elections to replace the magistrates whose terms were expiring always returned candidates from the PLC or FSLN.[79] Although at the beginning, the FSLN controlled several divisions (*salas*)[80] as well as the Court's internal disciplinary commission,[81] by 2007 both Alemán and Ortega counted on eight loyal justices. Obviously, the two big parties determine judicial (re)appointments and shape judicial careers.

Justice Francisco Rosales defends the Supreme Court's appointment procedures and claims that President Bolaños "wants judges . . . who reflect [his] preferences."[82] He goes further, saying that "[Bolaños's] political incapacity makes him an enemy of the judiciary." In his view, criticisms from the executive stemmed from not having justices loyal to the president.

So, what's the president upset about? When he came to office in 2001, there were nine justices whose terms had expired so there were nine to elect. Simply put, the president, instead of negotiating and having someone in charge of relations with the assembly, acted irresponsibly, lost the initiative, and neither got his own choices elected nor agreed on a compromise candidate with the chamber.

Not surprisingly, the process of legislative appointment leaves the system open to charges of patronage politics and partisan bias, something the deputies recognize.[83] The partisanship involved in Supreme Court appointments is also reflected in the high percentage of justices who consider relations with government (63.6 percent) or having belonged to a political party (61.8 percent) to be determining factors in CSJ appointments.[84]

In different ways, all the magistrates criticize the appointment procedure. Justice Escobar Fornos recognizes the need for change to avoid the politicization of justice: "political parties . . . run the assembly and, logically, they are the ones who select the justices. . . . They should have sought another system to avoid the charge of politicizing justice." Justice Francisco Rosales criticizes the fact that sitting deputies can be appointed to the Supreme Court: "It should not be possible to name a sitting deputy to the Supreme Court. They come to the Court and keep acting as if they were deputies, saying 'I was elected by the people, thus I am sovereign.' That doesn't impress me. You came here; [if you don't like it] go back to the assembly."

Justice Solís, however, finds the criticisms ill-founded:

> Before, when the justices were former corporate lawyers, nobody said the Court had been captured by big business. That's how it was during the Chamorro administration and Dr. Alemán's first years. But then the FSLN got two magistrates elected . . . and now has [more]. This is when people talk about parties co-opting the Court.[85]

Regarding security of tenure, the 2000 Pact amended the constitution to reduce a justice's term from seven years to five, with the possibility of re-election (Art. 161). This short tenure means that, in general, the magistrates are more subject to political pressures.[86] All Supreme Court magistrates interviewed proposed a longer term to avoid politicizing justice and to depend less on the deputies' wishes. Justice Solís also addressed this topic:

> The current tenure of office is very short, which lends itself to political pressures or misunderstandings. When one is in one's last year, *there is more pressure from deputies, perhaps because they know you cannot be re-elected if you do not go along with them.* A longer period, ten years, if not a lifetime appointment, would be preferable. (emphasis added)

And the politicization of the Supreme Court permeates the whole justice system through the system of *feudos* (personal domains). As Justice Sergio Cuarezma points out,

> The judiciary is currently organized territorially, with each justice responsible for a specific region (called fiefdoms). There they control judicial appointments—even cancelling them—and promotions, transfers, etc. When I took my position, March 28, 2007, I was asked which "territory" I wanted to look after administratively. I said "none." From my perspective, which combines democratic and academic elements, the judiciary should not be run along lines better suited to running an eighteenth-century hacienda, but rather according to principles derived from the rule of law and constitutional governance.[87]

Then there is the Law of Judicial Careers, legislation that puts judges' careers in a nonpartisan, civil service–style system. It was passed in 2005 but not officially published into law until June 2008 due to disagreements between the PLC and FSLN over the law's specific regulations. Justice Cuarezma has some critical comments. "The Judicial Career Law is a good start but it does not reach the desired objective . . . [and] its regulations are defective." He signaled three problem areas:

> First, the constitution makes no reference to a National Council of Judicial Administration and for the Judicial Career. The council we now have,

as a recent study has shown, is just another patronage plum to be parceled out by the political operators. . . . Second, nontransferability for judges is no more than half done: the law says a judge cannot be transferred without her or his consent, *except* for reasons of administrative necessity [Article 37], which vitiates the original principle. The law leaves the legislator an "exceptional" means of control over judges they find undesirable. Third, disciplinary control is simply perverse. The law denies judges due process: the disciplinary procedures are secret, done by written submission [and] thus depersonalized, and frankly feudal. Worse, almost all disciplinary decisions are badly edited and too general.

According to Cuarezma, "the task before the Supreme Court . . . as well as the international donors who are underwriting this project, is to remove the sort of partisan control that now exists. That will take an act of political will that will see the Court abandon trying to control judges or look for a 'friendly' judge."

These findings confirm the perception that, in Nicaragua, excessive political control over the Supreme Court reduces judicial independence and creates partisan judicial behavior. Thus the country not only lacks an independent Supreme Court but also has Supreme Court justices appointing lower court judges for partisan reasons.

The Supreme Court: Mirroring Nicaragua's Political Elite

The sociopolitical background, ideology, and role orientations of Nicaraguan judges further condition the political role of the Supreme Court. The political role of appellate courts is similarly affected by the political background and ideology of their members and by the judges' perception of their own role (their role orientations, which reflect the broader legal culture).

In analyzing the profile of the CSJ, one must recall the judges' connection with the political sphere: 60 percent of them have been politicians or have had a relative in the political arena.[88] Although only 30 percent claim to have previously worked in the judicial branch, it is striking that 80 percent of Supreme Court magistrates claim to have worked in politics before joining the Court.[89] For example, in 2009, all sixteen members of the Supreme Court had been deputies in the National Assembly or owed some political loyalty to Daniel Ortega or Arnoldo Alemán (see Table 5.2).

Since 2000, this trend has become more evident and harmful. Whereas previously only a minority of judges were required to demonstrate their party loyalty, by 2004 at least 70 percent were plainly either Sandinistas or Liberals, with the former enjoying a significant numerical advantage.

Table 5.2 Composition of Nicaragua Supreme Court, 2009

Name	Elected	Former Profession	Proposed by . . .	Political Party
Alba Luz Ramos Vanegas	1988	Justice Department lawyer in the first Sandinista administration	FSLN	FSLN
Rafael Solís Cerda	1997	Lawyer and ambassador in the first Sandinista administration and an FSLN legislator	FSLN	FSLN
Armengol Cuadra López	1997	Judge and ex-judge in the anti-Somoza tribunals	FSLN	FSLN
Marvin Aguilar García	1997	Judge and ex-judge in the anti-Somoza tribunals	FSLN	FSLN
Francisco Rosales Argüello	1997	Labor minister in the Chamorro administration	FSLN, universities, and civil associations	FSLN
Yadira Centeno González	1997	FSLN legislator	MRS and FSLN	FSLN
Guillermo Selva Argüello	1997	PLC legislator	PLC	PLC
Iván Escobar Fornos	1997	PLC legislator; voted for his own appointment	PLC	PLC
Ligia Molina Argüello	2003	Appeals court judge	FSLN and universities	FSLN
Manuel Martínez Sevilla	2003	Labor minister in the Alemán administration	PLC	PLC
Edgar Navas Navas	2003	PLC legislator	PLC	PLC
José Damicis Sirias	2005	PLC legislator	PLC	PLC
Juana Méndez Pérez	2007	Career judge and magistrate	FSLN	FSLN
Sergio Cuarezma Terán	2007	Academic	PLC	PLC
Antonio Alemán Layaco	2008	Appeals court judge	PLC	PLC
Gabriel Rivera Zeledón	2008	PLC legislator	PLC	PLC

Source: Compiled by author from interviews with Dr. Moises Martínez in September 2005 in Managua, and anonymous contributors.

According to former justice Guillermo Vargas Sandino, the election of the Supreme Court magistrates depends directly on the political weight of the candidate: "a candidate isn't proposed due to honesty, seriousness of purpose, or qualifications but rather because of political influence or usefulness to a party . . . that's how it's been recently."[90]

The CSJ justices aligned with the two main political parties openly admit the existence of political caucuses (*bancadas*) inside the Court (see Table 5.3). Although in 2000 there were more identifiable ideological groups on the Supreme Court ("Sandinistas," "Liberals," "the Barefooted," and "Granadinos-tacón de hule"), there are now just Sandinistas and Liberals.[91] This situation was confirmed in the last Supreme Court election, in March 2007, when both the reelections and the election of new magistrates were pacted to maintain the Liberal-Saninista balance.[92]

In 2007, the Sandinistas reelected Justice Alba Luz Ramos and elected Judge Juana Méndez (from Alemán's trial), instead of the favored candidate of the Judges' Association, Martha Quezada. One can interpret the election of Méndez as a political payoff for her performance during the Alemán trial.[93] The PLC reelected Iván Escobar Fornos, Alemán's friend, and elected Professor Sergio Cuarezma, whose wife Roxana Zapata was the judge who sentenced Alemán to special house arrest in July 2005. Some of the media saw Cuarezma's election as a reward for favors done. When questioned about the independence problem and the partisan-patronage election of the justices, Cuarezma replied:

> It's the National Assembly's responsibility to improve how Supreme Court justices are chosen, in order to have a more independent judiciary and to ensure that justices named to this Court are chosen on their demonstrated

Table 5.3 Political Forces Represented on the Nicaraguan Supreme Court, 2009

FSLN	PLC
Alba Luz Ramos Vanegas	Iván Escobar Fornos
Rafael Solís Cerda	Guillermo Selva Argüello
Armengol Cuadra López	José Damicis Sirias
Yadira Centeno González	Manuel Martínez Sevilla
Marvin Aguilar García	Edgar Navas Navas
Francisco Rosales Argüello	Sergio Cuarezma Terán
Ligia Molina Argüello	Antonio Alemán Layaco
Juana Méndez Pérez	Gabriel Rivera Zeledón

Source: Based on Lourdes Arróliga, "Bancada en la Corte," *Confidencial,* June 15–21, 2003, and anonymous collaborators.

professional merits. Nevertheless, whatever mechanism is used to select candidates and elect Supreme Court justices, we must appeal to the conscience of every justice and ask that all set themselves above partisan concerns, not favor the party that backed their election, and dedicate themselves to fulfilling their constitutional duties and upholding the law.[94]

Justice Vargas Sandino was more pessimistic:

Just as the National Assembly is dominated by two parties, Liberal and Sandinista, *so too is the Supreme Court: it's a second National Assembly* and there is no way that should be . . . this has never been seen anywhere. . . . [The Court] should be pluralist, focused on jurisprudence to settle legal issues and not be concerned about mere political questions.[95] (emphasis added)

This politicization has serious consequences for the performance and legitimacy of the Supreme Court. The media report frequent confrontations among the justices.[96]

Regarding their role orientations, which mediate between policy preferences and behavior, Supreme Court justices are aware of the political importance of their decisions and freely acknowledge their partisan inclinations.[97] In this sense, the comments of Justice Solís are relevant. He openly admits that he is a Sandinista and that this influences his decisions: "I have been a Sandinistas and once one is named to the Court life as a political partisan is left behind, but that does not mean that there remains no sympathy for the old cause."[98] He then declares that "in strictly political cases you can certainly say that Dr. Rafael Solís did not go against the Sandinistas, because he obviously is a Sandinista!" Indeed:

I am not one of those justices who, on being named to this Court, says "well, now that I am a Supreme Court magistrate I must renounce my party loyalties and all that I have been." Well, I do not and I have said so publicly, even though it has cost me dearly . . . but it is my way of living and seeing the world, and if before coming to the bench I held political office in Nicaragua and still think that I could do so again in the future . . . But people want to box you in and have you erase all traces of political commitment . . . and that isn't right. Others don't do it: they remain the representatives of the bankers and big business interests and certain newspapers of Nicaragua, just as they were before becoming magistrates . . . obviously, your political views, your vision of democracy and of Nicaragua and where it should be going . . . is going to influence your decisions.

When I asked Justice Vargas Sandino about his political identity, he made the following comment: "They call me the only Bolañista [supporter of President Bolaños], but I'm the only justice who doesn't talk to the president. In the past I was a Liberal, but now I am the Court's only independent."[99]

When the justices were asked to place themselves on a 10-point political ideological scale, where 1 is furthest left and 10 furthest right, their mean score was 4.20, with a standard deviation of 3.24. This means that although the average Nicaraguan Supreme Court judge is ideologically close to the Sandinistas, the high standard deviation indicates the ideological divisions within the Court.

Differences in ideology, sociopolitical background, and role orientation influence the behavior of the Nicaraguan Supreme Court justices. This was expected, as the justices have strong role orientations and policy preferences that influence judicial decisions.

Conclusion: Confirming the Political Kidnapping of Judicial Institutions

As Close states, "for most of the more than 175 years that Nicaragua has been independent, it has been ruled by tyrants or oligarchs and democracy—government in the interest of, chosen by, and accountable to all the people—did not figure into the country's politics."[100] With this history, it is difficult to imagine a Supreme Court free from political pressures or corruption.

The current role of the Supreme Court is not just the product of institutional design but also reflects the political agendas of the dominant parties. Control of the Supreme Court has become a crucial power resource to be protected at all cost. As a result, the CSJ currently has enormous power that is compromised by the nonindependence of its members. That, in turn, stems from the 2000 Liberal-Sandinista Pact struck between Alemán and Ortega, which increased the power of the Court but harnessed that power to the parties' interests. The excessive partisan control over procedures that should guarantee judicial independence, together with a Supreme Court where election depends on partisan loyalties, undermines the Court's role as Nicaragua's final arbiter of justice by making it just another partisan instrument.

The close alignment of the Nicaraguan magistrates' party preferences with their judicial decisions casts doubt on those decisions. This ostensible partisanship has two principal consequences for the judicial system. First, it undermines collegiality among the justices. Second, it diminishes the perceived independence of the entire justice system. Therefore, political and social actors question the impartiality of judicial proceedings, which undermines the rule of law and weakens an essential component of state-society relations.

It must be stressed here that skillful "intrusions" into politics can let high courts in new democracies "build the institutional legitimacy required to survive, and eventually . . . assist in the consolidation of democracy."[101] This can happen because, by transforming political conflicts into constitutional dialogues, "these courts can reduce the threat to democracy and allow it to grow."[102] As long as the judiciary remains independent and demonstrates a high level of professionalism, judges can perform one of their most important functions: to check the power of the executive and the legislature and thereby protect citizens from political abuse. This is not the case with Nicaraguan courts, which have long been partisan instruments.

Though Nicaraguan politics is never very predictable, it seems obvious that the kidnapping of the country's highest judicial institution by the FSLN and PLC has weakened democracy and governability in the country while undermining the rule of law in the pursuit of partisan advantage. It seems appropriate to conclude with this observation by the former Supreme Court justice Guillermo Vargas Sandino: "The future of the Supreme Court is linked to the political future of the country . . . [and] it is quite difficult to make a prediction about how things will turn out."

Notes

This chapter is a revised version of a part of my PhD dissertation, which was published as Elena Martínez Barahona, *Seeking the Political Role of the Third Governmental Branch: A Comparative Approach to High Courts in Central America* (Saarbrüken, Germany: VDM Verlag, 2009). I would like to thank David Close for his insightful comments and his help editing and translating the interviews with the magistrates. Valuable comments on earlier drafts were provided by Selene Guevara, Alejandro Aguilar Altamirano, and Juan Carlos Gutierrez Soto.

1. Some political analysts believe that Nicaragua is undergoing a transition from a traditional oligarchic society to a democratic one, in which some features from the old regime (such as authoritarianism expressed through caudillos or caciques, political intolerance alternating with pacts between leaders, nepotism, patrimonialism, and corruption in the management of public goods) still predominate. For a more detailed analysis, see Emilio Alvarez Montalván, *Cultura política nicaragüense* (Managua: Hispamer, 2000).

2. David Close and Kalowatie Deonandan, *Undoing Democracy* (Lanham, MD: Lexington Books, 2004); and David Dye, *Democracy Adrift: Caudillo Politics in Nicaragua* (Brookline, MA: Hemisphere Initiatives, 2004).

3. Dye, *Democracy Adrift,* 17.

4. Luis Guillermo Solís and Richard Wilson, *Political Transition and the Administration of Justice in Nicaragua* (Miami: Florida International University, Center for the Administration of Justice, 1991), 1–12.

5. This has been the latest in a long list of Nicaraguan pacts—there have been a dozen. The common thread uniting all of them has been, in former foreign minister

Emilio Alvarez Montalván's words, "to limit partisan competition." Quoted in Isidro López, "Los más ricos de Centro América quieren gobernar Nicaragua: Recelo por participación abierta de al familia Pellas en la política." *Tiempos del Mundo,* February 24, 2000. www.tdm.ni.com.
    6. Dye, *Democracy Adrift,* 36.
    7. They shared an interest in having a guaranteed legislative seat with its associated parliamentary immunity. Ortega wanted immunity from prosecution for charges of sexual harassment brought against him by his stepdaughter, and Alemán wished to avoid the legal consequences of investigations into charges of corruption leveled against him throughout his presidency. For more details, see David Close, "Political Parties and Democracy in Nicaragua: Not Yet, Maybe Someday," paper presented at the Joint Sessions of Workshops of the European Consortium for Political Research, Edinburgh, Scotland, 2003. They also shared an interest in replacing the top personnel then in office, as a number of them were their enemies: the then-CSE president, Rosa Maria Zelaya (Ortega's enemy after his defeat in the 1996 elections) and the then-controller General Agustín Jarquín (Alemán's enemy for his investigations into corruption). David Dye examines this in greater detail in *Retazos de democracia: La política nicaragüense diez años después de la derrota* (Cambridge, MA: Hemisphere Initiatives, 2000).
    8. Editor's note: The judges on the Nicaraguan Supreme Court are called "magistrates," but this chapter also uses the term "justices," more familiar to North Americans.
    9. Dye, *Democracy Adrift,* 48.
    10. All quotes making reference to Supreme Court judges' opinion come from this source. Interviews were conducted in Managua with Supreme Court judges Iván Escobar Fornos (September 5, 2005), Francisco Rosales (September 6, 2005), Rafael Solís (September 6, 2005), Guillermo Vargas Sandino (September 7, 2005), and Sergio Cuarezma Terán (March 10, 2008).
    11. Dye, *Democracy Adrift,* 46.
    12. Joel G.Verner, "The Independence of Supreme Courts in Latin America: A Review of the Literature." *Journal of Latin American Studies* 16 (1984): 499.
    13. David Close, *Nicaragua: The Chamorro Years* (Boulder, CO: Lynne Rienner, 1999), 70.
    14. The bibliography on this topic is fairly limited. As Solís and Wilson point out, regular reports have only been issued by international human rights organizations. See also Vilma Nuñez de Escorcia, *Independencia del poder judicial* (Managua: Editorial Ciencias Socales, 1990); Alejandro Serrano Caldera, *La transformación judicial en Nicaragua (y otros ensayos)* (Managua: Ediciones Jurídicas, 1988); and Andrés Pérez Baltodano, *Entre el estado conquistador y el estado nación: Providencialismo, pensamiento político, y estructuras de poder en el desarrollo histórico de Nicaragua.* Managua: Fundación Friederich Ebert en Nicaragua, 2003.
    15. Solís and Wilson, *Political Transition,* 70.
    16. Kenneth F. Johnson and Paul Paris, "Nicaragua," in *Political Forces in Latin America,* edited by Ben G. Burnett and Kenneth F. Johnson (Belmont, CA: Wadsworth, 1970), 129.
    17. In 1983, the government established the Popular Anti-Somoza Tribunals (Tribunales Populares Anti-Somocistas, or TPAS) to try certain cases involving counterrevolutionary activities. These tribunals were abolished in 1988 due to international criticism; see Solís and Wilson, *Political Transition,* 28.

18. The *La Verona* case involved the expropriation of a farm by the agrarian reform ministry in 1987. An agricultural tribunal reversed the expropriation, but the ministry did not comply. The CSJ then issued a writ of *amparo,* similar to an injunction, again overturning the expropriation, which the minister of agriculture declared he would not obey. The Court's three non-Sandinista justices then resigned. For details, see Solís and Wilson, *Political Transition,* 29.

19. "In this way Sandinista caudillo Ortega compensated for the dwindling of other power resources and gained leverage over decisions of vital importance to his followers' patrimonies." Dye, *Democracy Adrift,* 48.

20. Dye, *Retazos de democracia,* 15.

21. The last judicial reform measure was adopted in January 2005 (Ley de Carrera Judicial, Ley 501; Law of Judicial Career). The law was passed in 2005 but the regulations needed to make it effective were not adopted until 2008.

22. The salience of an issue matters because the public tends to follow on the most salient cases coming before a court. S. B. Burbank and B. Friedman, eds., *Judicial Independence at the Crossroads: An Interdisciplinary Approach* (Thousand Oaks, CA: Sage, 2002), 6.

23. This is one of the principles adopted by the Seventh United Nations Congress on "Prevention of Crime and the Treatment of Offenders," held in Milan from August 26 to September 6 1985 and endorsed by General Assembly resolutions 40/32 of November 29, 1985 and 40/146 of December 13, 1985.

24. For a recent discussion of competing definitions of judicial independence and its measurement, see Julio Ríos-Figueroa, "Institutional Models of Judicial Independence in Latin America," paper presented at the Twenty-Sixth Meeting of the Latin American Studies Association (LASA), Puerto Rico, March 15–18, 2006; and Sebastian Linares, "La independencia judicial: conceptualización y medición," *Política y Gobierno* 11 (2004): 73–136.

25. The research for this chapter was drawn from three databases. My first source was the judges' database at the University of Salamanca, which is drawn from the Proyecto Política de Justicia y Calidad de la Democracia en Centro América (The Politics of Justice and the Quality of Democracy Project, or JDCA) and contains information about judges gathered through interviews carried out between 2000 and 2004. I looked at interviews of ten of the sixteen judges on the Supreme Court (62.5 percent of the Court) and at interviews of forty-five of the sixty-one lower court judges who received surveys (74 percent) conducted between October 2002 and June 2003. The second source I used was the polls done by Latinobarómetro. Third, I compiled information from Élites Parlamentarias Latinoamericanas (PELA), the parliamentarians' database at the University of Salamanca, which contains information about legislators from throughout Latin America. I focused on interviews with sixty members of the Nicaraguan National Assembly conducted from September to November 2002. This analysis also incorporates my previous work, which uses legislators' views on policy to analyze government-opposition divides in Costa Rica, Guatemala, and Nicaragua. See Elena Martínez Barahona, "Exploring Parliamentary Opposition in Contemporary Central America," thesis, Diploma Research Project in Social Science Data Analysis, University of Essex, UK, 2004.

26. There was a high standard deviation (2.4). The question (no. 14) read in Spanish: "En una escala del 1 al 10, entendiendo por 1 ninguna independencia y 10 plenamente independiente, ¿cómo valoraría la independencia del poder judicial en

su país?" From Proyecto Política de Justicia y Calidad de la Democracia en Centro América (JDCA), Universidad de Salamanca, Comisión Interuniversitaria de Ciencia y Tecnología (CICYT), SEC 20001-1779, 2004.

27. Supreme Court Justice Rafael Solís, Managua, Nicaragua, personal interview with author, September 6, 2005.

28. Supreme Court Justice Iván Escobar Fornos, Managua, Nicaragua, personal interview with author, September 5, 2005.

29. Question no. 12 read in Spanish: "¿Cuál considera Ud. que es el principal obstáculo para la independencia judicial de su país?¿Y en segundo lugar?" Source: Proyecto Política de Justicia y Calidad de la Democracia en Centro América (JDCA).

30. Question no. 10 read in Spanish: ¿Cuál de los siguientes problemas considera que es el principal que presenta el poder judicial en su país." Only two responses were counted: "a lot" or "almost a lot." From Proyecto Política de Justicia y Calidad de la Democracia en Centro América (JDCA). There were no follow-up questions.

31. Question no. 24 read in Spanish: "¿Alguna vez ha recibido amenazas en relación a algún caso concreto durante el ejercicio de su cargo? ¿Cuáles son los grupos o instituciones de los que sospecha?" From Proyecto Política de Justicia y Calidad de la Democracia en Centro América (JDCA).

32. Question no. 21 read in Spanish: "¿Podría decirme si Ud. está muy de acuerdo, de acuerdo, en desacuerdo o muy en desacuerdo con la siguiente afirmación? Los procesos disciplinarios son en realidad un mecanismo político para remover o presionar a jueces que no siguen las pautas dictadas por el gobierno o por la corte." From Proyecto Política de Justicia y Calidad de la Democracia en Centro América (JDCA).

33. The question (no. 23) read in Spanish: "Imagine que un amigo suyo extranjero, que no conoce nuestro país, le pregunta qué probabilidades hay aquí de poder sobornar a un juez para conseguir una sentencia favorable. ¿Qué diría Ud.?" Only two responses were counted: "Tiene muchas probabilidades" and "Tiene bastante." From Latinobarómetro 2008, www.latinobarometro.org.

34. The question read: "To what point do you believe that the courts in Nicaragua guarantee a fair trial?" For further discussion of this topic, see Mitchell Seligson, Luis Serra Vázquez, and Pedro López Ruíz, *The Political Culture of Democracy in Nicaragua* (Nashville, TN: Latin American Public Opinion Project [LAPOP], Vanderbilt University, 2004).

35. The national survey data included answers to these questions, asked in the order of their appearance here: (1) "¿Cree usted que los jueces son imparciales al aplicar las leyes?" (2) "¿En qué medida cree usted que los jueces y magistrados cumplen con el principio de independencia en el derecho de las partes?" From Instituto de Promoción Humana–Centro de Investigación y Asistencia Económica y Social (INPRHU-CINASE) survey, March 2005.

36. The question read in Spanish: "¿Cuál es el nivel de credibilidad de la Corte Suprema de Justicia?" See Instituto para el Desarrollo y la Democracia (IPADE), *Encuesta Cultura Política y Valores Democráticos,* January 2007.

37. On September 9, 2005, 1,500 citizens participated in the protest organized by the civil society network Coordinadora Civil: "Movimiento por Nicaragua." Posters advertised a "Caravana Fúnebre de la Justicia en Nicaragua. Del Estadio

Nacional a la Corte Suprema de Justicia. NO FALTES! JUSTICIA SÍ! DICTA-DURA NO! DEMOCRACIA SÍ! PACTO NO!" ("Funeral Cortege for Justice in Nicaragua. From the National Stadium to the Supreme Court. Be there! Justice, yes! Dictatorship, no! Democracy, yes! The Pact, no!").

38. Mirna Velázquez Sevilla and Carolos Martínez Moran, "Magistrados 'pactan' por narcodolares," *La Prensa,* December 14, 2005, www.laprensa.com.ni/.

39. Oliver Bodan and Lourdes Arróliga, "Circo político en las cortes," *Confidencial* 448, July 31–August 6, 2005, www.confidencial.com.ni/.

40. Mirna Velazquez Sevilla, "Mayoría rechaza sentencia de CSJ," *La Prensa,* September 5, 2005, www.laprensa.com.ni/.

41. From Martínez Barahona, "Exploring Parliamentary Opposition."

42. C. Neal Tate and Torbjorn Vallinder, *The Global Expansion of Judicial Power* (NewYork: New York University Press, 1995), 519.

43. Alec Stone Sweet, *Governing with Judges* (New York: Oxford University Press, 2000).

44. Rachel Sieder, Line Schjolden, and Alan Angell, eds., *The Judicialization of Politics in Latin America* (New York: Palgrave, 2005).

45. Eloisa Ibarra, "Suprema da largas a recursos contra las reformas del pacto," *El Nuevo Diario,* April 26, 2000, archivo.elnuevodiario.com.ni/.

46. Close, "Political Parties," 15.

47. Supreme Court Justice Francisco Rosales, Managua, Nicaragua, personal interview with author, September 6, 2005.

48. Lourdes Arróliga, "CSJ: Luz verde al pluripartidismo," *Confidencial* 317, November 24–30, 2002, www.confidencial.com.ni/.

49. Arróliga, "CSJ: Luz verde al pluripartidismo."

50. Dye, *Democracy Adrift,* 18; Eloisa Ibarra, "¿Visión clasista para rechazar la politización?" *El Nuevo Diario,* August 23, 2004, archivo.elnuevodiario.com.ni/.

51. Dye, *Democracy Adrift,* 58.

52. On October 2005, to avoid a deeper political crisis, the leaders of the executive and legislative branches, Bolaños and Ortega, respectively, signed an accord witnessed by the Organization of American States (OAS) and Cardinal Miguel Obando y Bravo. This accord froze the constitutional amendments until January 20, 2007.

53. Supreme Court Justice Rafael Solís, Managua, Nicaragua, personal interview with the author, September 6, 2005.

54. This was the CSJ's Decree 333, December 5, 2007.

55. Carlos Tunnerman, "Una sentencia eminentemente política," *El Nuevo Diario,* December 12, 2007, impreso.elnuevodiario.com.ni/. The *amparo* law has since been amended to prevent the issuance of anticipatory injunctions.

56. David Close, "President Bolaños Runs a Reverse," in *Undoing Democracy: The Politics of Electoral Caudillismo,* edited by David Close and Kalowatie Deonandan (Lanham, MD: Lexington Books, 2004), 174.

57. Oliver Bodan, "Sala Constitucional pone manos arriba al Contralor," *Confidencial* 121, November 22–28, 1998; and Oliver Bodan, "Hay indicios de dictadura," *Confidencial* 168, November 14–20, 1999, www.confidencial.com.ni.

58. Dye, in *Democracy Adrift,* 46, reports that by mid-2004, "most of the indictments in the Channel 6 case had moreover been dropped by the presiding judges (some with the government's acquiescence), leaving Arnoldo Alemán and his finance minister as the only defendants."

59. Close, "President Bolaños," 175–182.

60. Both the *procurador general de la república* (attorney general or minister of justice) and the *fiscalía* (solicitor general) dissented, and most newspapers reported this; see Iván Olivares y Lourdes Arróliga, "Un precedente en la justicia," *Confidencial* 342, June 8–14, 2003, www.confidencial.com.ni/; *El Nuevo Diario*, "Jerez sabía y se lucraba," December 9, 2003, archivo.elnuevodiario.com.ni/; *El Nuevo Diario*, "Fallo infame," archivo.elnuevodiario.com.ni/2004/octubre/07-octubre-2004/; Mirna Velasquez Sevilla, "Jerez declarado inocente," *La Prensa*, October 7, 2004, www.laprensa.com.ni/; Jorge Loaisiga Mayorga and Mirna Velasquez Sevilla, "'Limpian' a Byron Jerez," *La Prensa*, March 19, 2005, www.laprensa.com.ni/.

61. Centro Nicaragüense de Derechos Humanos (CENIDH), *Derechos Humanos en Nicaragua, 2003* (Managua: CENIDH, 2003).

62. Editor's note: a *fiscal* is the equivalent of a district attorney or a crown prosecutor.

63. Dye, *Democracy Adrift*, 38.

64. The media and citizens began to question irregularities in the Court's behavior. See, for instance, *El Nuevo Diario*, "Lavan a corruptos," July 21, 2004, archivo.elnuevodiario.com.ni/; Ludwin Loasiga López, "Otro intento para liberar a Alemán," *La Prensa*, September 14, 2004, www.laprensa.com.ni/; Lourdes Arróliga, "Sigue Pacto PLC-FSLN en la justicia," *Confidencial* 430, March 20–April 2, 2005, www.confidencial.com.ni/; and Ludwin Loasiga López, "PLC celebra round judicial a favor de Arnoldo Alemán y reiteran que en Nicaragua justicia es de Ortega," *La Prensa*, May 27, 2006, www.laprensa.com.ni/. One can also see the report of the nongovernmental, Sandinista-affiliated human rights group Centro Nicaragüense de Derechos Humanos (CENIDH), *Derechos Humanos en Nicaragua*, for a detailed document treating the irregularities in the judicial decisions.

65. Dye, *Democracy Adrift*, 31.

66. Close, "President Bolaños," 178.

67. In civil law systems, judges do not serve first as lawyers but join the bench directly. A judicial career law protects judges just as a civil service law protects bureaucrats.

68. For a synopsis of the bargaining, see Dye, *Democracy Adrift*, 32, and Xiomara Chamorro, "Así nació la crisis," *La Prensa*, November 28, 2003, www.laprensa.com.ni/. See also Envío, "The Twelve Days That Shook Nicaragua," *Envío* 269 (December 2003), www.envio.org.ni/.

69. Dye, *Democracy Adrift*, 46.

70. Dye, *Democracy Adrift*, 35.

71. Dye, *Democracy Adrift*, 14, 46.

72. *El Nuevo Diario*, "Sentencia TAM cortó rabo y oreja," December 13, 2007, www.elnuevodiario.com.ni/.

73. *La Prensa*, "Restituyen convivencia familiar a Alemán: Otra vez tiene Nicaragua por cárcel," January 11, 2008, www.laprensa.ni.com.

74. This situation could have worsened had the National Assembly passed an amnesty bill under discussion in 2010.

75. The combination of judicial independence and political independence generates other types of political roles for supreme courts, depending on how they actually move within this two-dimensional space. Thus, these different types of

political roles correspond to different degrees of judicial independence and political intervention. For a fuller discussion of these categories, see Elena Martínez Barahona, "Seeking the Political Role of the Third Goverment Branch: A Comparative Approach to High Courts in Central America." PhD diss., European University Institute, Florence, Italy, 2007.

76. Dye, *Democracy Adrift,* 46.

77. Supreme Court Judge Francisco Rosales, Managua, personal interview with the author, September 6, 2005.

78. Oliver Bodán, "Complejo reacomodo en la CSJ," *Confidencial* 185, March 26–April 1, 2000, www.confidencial.com.ni/.

79. Supreme Court Justice Vargas Sandino, Managua, Nicaragua, personal interview with author. The press also expressed concern about this. See Oliver Bodán, "Temor por retroceso en CSJ," *Confidencial* 151, June 18–24, 1999, www .confidencial.com.ni/, and Carlos Fernando Chamorro, "Elección política en la Suprema," *Confidencial* 156, August 22–28, 1999, www.confidencial.com.ni/.

80. These are divisions of the Court specialized in administrative, civil, constitutional, and criminal cases.

81. This situation is also reflected in the media: *La Nación,* San Jose, Costa Rica, "Eligen a cuatro magistrados más para la CSJ," March 21, 2000; Edgardo Barbarena, "Dos para vos . . . dos para mí," *El Nuevo Diario,* March 21, 2000, archivo.elnuevodiario.com.ni/.

82. The full quote is: "The executive wants judges and magistrates who reflect its preferences; that's what it tries to do. The president seems to think he's some sort of monarch because he was elected by popular vote!"

83. Nicaraguan deputies principally mention the appointment procedure (42.2 percent) as the main obstacle to judicial independence. Question no. 25a read in Spanish: "¿Cuál es en su país el principal obstáculo para que el poder judicial actúe de forma independiente?" Proyecto de Investigación Élites Parlamentarias Iberoamericanas (PELA), Instituto Interuniversitario de Estudios de Iberoamérica y Portugal, Universidad de Salamanca y Centro de Investigaciones Sociológicas (CIS), Agencia Española de Cooperación Internacional, 2002.

84. Question no. 16 read in Spanish: "¿Podría decirme qué grado de importancia estima que tienen los siguientes factores que le mencionó para el nombramiento de los jueces?" Only "very important" and "important" responses regarding the more relevant issues are included. Proyecto Política de Justicia y Calidad de la Democracia en Centro América (JDCA).

85. Supreme Court Judge Rafael Solís, Managua, Nicaragua, personal interview with the author, September 6, 2005.

86. In 2007, there was a FSLN-PLC proposal for lifetime appointments that was not acted upon.

87. Supreme Court Judge Sergio Cuarezma Terán, personal interview with the author, Managua, Nicaragua, March 10, 2008.

88. Question no. 59 read in Spanish: "¿Algún familiar suyo se ha dedicado a la política, aunque actualmente no lo haga?" From Proyecto Política de Justicia y Calidad de la Democracia en Centro América (JDCA).

89. Question no. 53 read in Spanish: "¿Podría decirme cuáles fueron los últimos cargos que ha ejercido dentro de la judicatura desde que fue nombrado juez o magistrado?" Question no. 55 read: "¿A qué actividades se dedicaba antes de haber

sido nombrado juez?" Proyecto Política de Justicia y Calidad de la Democracia en Centro América (JDCA).

90. Former Supreme Court judge Guillermo Vargas Sandino, personal interview with the author, Managua, Nicaragua, September 7, 2005.

91. The "Sandinistas," the most coherent group on the Supreme Court, comprised Solís, Aguilar, Cuadra, Centeno, Ramos, and Rosales. The "Group of Five," also called the "Barefooted" ("Descalzos"), were magistrates Cuadra Ortegaray, García Vílchez, Plata, Enríquez, and J. Ramos. The PLC "loyal" magistrates were Selva and Guerra (called the "granadinos," because they came from Granada, or "rubber heels" in opposition to the "Barefooted" group). See Oliver Bodán, "Arrancan cabildeos en CSJ," *Confidencial* 205, August 20–26, 2000, www.confidencial.com.ni/.

92. The following citations show how the media present the issue: Marvin Palacios Paiz, "Elección de nuevos magistrados: Un sainete más del pacto," *El Nuevo Diario,* March 31, 2007, impreso.elnuevodiario.com.ni/; Lourdes Arróliga, "Partidización en elección CSJ," *Confidencial* 529, April 1–7, 2007,www.confidencial .com.ni/2007-529/politica2_529.html; and *La Prensa,* "De la votación en plancha y otros demonios," April 3, 2007, www.laprensa.com.ni/.

93. Palacios Paiz, "Elección de nuevos magistrados.

94. Supreme Court Justice Sergio Cuarezma Terán, personal interview with the author, Managua, Nicaragua, March 10, 2008.

95. Former Supreme Court judge Guillermo Vargas Sandino, personal interview with the author, Managua, Nicaragua, September 7, 2005.

96. For example, on March 6, 2008, both *El Nuevo Diario* and *La Prensa* ran the following articles: "Trapos Sucios en la CSJ," impreso.elnuevodiario.com.ni/; and "Se sacan trapos sucios en la CSJ," www.laprensa.com.ni/.

97. P. C. Magalhães, *The Limits to Judicialization: Legislative Politics and Constitutional Review in the Iberian Democracies.* Unpublished PhD diss. (Columbus: Ohio State University, 2003).

98. This quote and those immediately following come from Supreme Court Justice Rafael Solís, Managua, Nicaragua, personal interview with the author, September 6, 2005.

99. Former Supreme Court judge Guillermo Vargas Sandino, personal interview with the author, Managua, Nicaragua, September 7, 2005.

100. Close, *Nicaragua,* 1.

101. Theunis Roux, "Legitimating Transformation: Political Resource Allocation in the South African Constitutional Court," in *Democratization and the Judiciary: The Accountability Function of Courts in New Democracies,* edited by Siri Gloppen, Roberto Gargarella, and Elin Skaar (London: Frank Cass, 2004), 108.

102. Tom Ginsburg, *Judicial Review in New Democracies: Constitutional Courts in Asian Cases* (Cambridge, UK: Cambridge University Press, 2003), 247.

6

The Uncertain Evolution
of the Electoral System

Shelley A. McConnell

SHORTLY AFTER COMING TO POWER VIA ARMED REVOLUTION in 1979, the Sandinista National Liberation Front (Frente Sandinista de Liberación Nacional, or FSLN) pledged that it would hold elections within five years. The announcement satisfied almost no one. Socialists within the revolutionary coalition considered elections a sop to bourgeois values. Liberals saw the five-year timetable as a delay and feared it signaled the emergence of authoritarianism. The US government doubted meaningful elections would be held, given the FSLN's intention to carry out a transition to socialism, which US policymakers assumed would follow the Cuban model.

The FSLN established a five-member Governing Junta of National Reconstruction (JGRN) to govern in the interim and organized political participation through mass organizations. Sandinista revolutionary leaders transformed their politico-military movement into a party and cast it in the role of a vanguard for the transition to socialism. Although other political parties were allowed, their leaders were sometimes harassed and jailed. Moreover, the new legislature, the Council of State, represented not districts but functional groups: peasants, labor, women, indigenous groups, religious denominations, and others, including parties. It would, however, be something of a rubber stamp body.[1]

By 1982, prospects for liberal representative democracy looked decidedly grim. Historically, no revolutionary government that had come to power via force of arms and espoused Marxist ideology had ever held free and fair elections that put control over state power in play. It thus came as a surprise to many that Nicaragua not only held the promised elections in 1984 but went on to hold competitive and honest elections in 1990, which were won by an antirevolutionary opposition group that then took over government in a peaceful transfer of power. The country would later hold three more general elections, in 1996, 2001, and 2006, all of which would be deemed acceptable by domestic and international observers despite some variation in quality. A series of elections for municipal offices and regional representatives on the Atlantic Coast would also meet acceptable standards prior to 2008.

This chapter reviews those elections and their political significance, including the evolution of electoral law and administration, with supporting material on the party system.[2] What is most striking about this story is the extent to which the revolutionary government's crafting of the rules for party formation and elections shaped new state institutions in the 1980s, thus having an impact well beyond the electoral realm. The rules for party formation changed the basis of representation from functional to territorial and altered the mode of interest intermediation from monism via mass organizations affiliated with a vanguard party to pluralism via competing political parties. The 1984 Electoral Law provided for competitive elections and changed the basis for government legitimacy from winning the revolution to winning public support at the polls.

The chapter makes the argument that Nicaraguan elections are not only a well-institutionalized characteristic of the political system but are championed as the centerpiece of a democracy that is weak in other respects. Indeed, there has been a tendency toward *electoralism,* meaning the faith that "merely holding elections will channel political action into peaceful contests among elites and accord public legitimacy to the winners in these contests."[3] One reason that elections hold such a peculiarly important position in Nicaraguan political life is that the 1990 transition elections substituted for a peace process as a means of ending the counterrevolutionary war that had wracked Nicaragua for a decade. Subsequent elections also were highly polarized events that pitched Sandinistas and Liberals against one another in a struggle for power that echoed the revolution and counterrevolution of the 1980s. Nicaraguans fearing a return to war and foreigners fearing the reelection of the revolutionary party perceived the stakes of these elections as inordinately high.

In 2000, the Pact between the Constitutionalist Liberal Party (Partido Liberal Constitutionalista, or PLC) and FSLN gradually reduced polarization by guaranteeing both parties access to government power regardless of who won the elections. The pact gave Sandinistas and Liberals control over leadership appointments in the judiciary, comptroller general (which has five members), and electoral authority. It politicized the electoral branch at all levels—national, departmental, and local—in both its leadership and staff. The Pact virtually eliminated the independence of branches of government, making them accountable solely to caudillo party bosses. In this system, horizontal accountability scarcely existed.[4] Accountability came through a free press and free and fair elections—a burden the electoral system was increasingly unable to bear.[5]

The First Sandinista Elections

Because of a Cold War mindset, US policymakers dismissed Nicaragua's 1984 elections as a sham staged by the revolutionaries to refute those who criticized its authoritarian tendencies, bolster aid from Europe, and delegitimize the counterrevolution launched with help from the Central Intelligence Agency (CIA) in 1981. Although there was some truth to this view, it underestimated the crucial role that the 1984 election preparations played in establishing the electoral system that would end Nicaragua's transition to socialism in 1990. Indeed, the bargaining process by which the Sandinistas and their internal opposition created the 1983 Political Parties Law and 1984 Electoral Law would substantially alter the main contours of Nicaragua's state institutions, the form of representation, and the basis for government legitimacy.

The 1983 Political Parties Law

As early as 1980, the Sandinista government took steps suggesting it would make good on its promise of elections, reaffirming via the JGRN's Decree 513 that elections would be held by 1985. On November 18, 1981, the government presented a draft law to regulate the formation and function of political parties. A legislative committee was formed to debate the proposal. The bill stipulated that parties winning elections would co-govern with the FSLN, since the revolutionary vanguard would necessarily control the state. The Sandinistas favored broad participation to express Nicaragua's political pluralism, but only with FSLN hegemony to assure that the "logic of the majority" prevailed in policy decisions. The other parties and proto-parties objected to this formula and put forward alternative drafts. Nonetheless, the original bill was only slightly amended, and it defined political parties as "groups of Nicaraguans with shared political ideas who form a party in order to participate in public administration."[6] In February 1982, the special committee published a working document with that language in the Nicaraguan newspapers and invited public discussion.

These early steps were halted by the beginning of the counterrevolution, which had gained covert backing from the United States in 1981 after President Ronald Reagan took office. In March 1982, the counterrevolutionaries, or contras, blew up two bridges in northern Nicaragua. In response, the JGRN declared a state of emergency, and discussion of the Political Parties Law was suspended. Debate was not reinitiated until the end of the year, this time with a new and more politically balanced committee that included members from six political parties as well as the FSLN. The center and right wing were represented, including those in the Nicaraguan Democratic Coordinator (CDN) alliance of political parties and business groups that was the largest right-wing opposition bloc.

After six meetings, on January 22, 1983, two of the CDN parties withdrew, arguing that the FSLN dominated the proceedings and intended to impose a one-party state.[7] The FSLN reacted by convening a three-day bargaining session parallel to the legislative process to offer a more neutral setting for negotiations. The CDN parties still refused to attend, but others did and struck a deal with the FSLN that would profoundly affect Nicaragua's prospects for democracy. A revised draft of the Political Parties Law defined political parties as organizations that would compete for power and control of the state through elections, not merely to co-govern. In exchange, participating opposition groups accepted the FSLN's insistence that counterrevolutionary "Somocista" parties would be illegal.[8]

The CDN parties refused to endorse the final draft of the bill. It went to the floor of the assembly, the Council of State, in May 1983, where it dominated proceedings for nearly three months before being approved in August. Despite the CDN's dismissal of the bill as "unilateral," the proceedings revealed a degree of inclusion of opposition forces well beyond anything that political scientists would have expected of a revolutionary socialist government.

In a stunning reversal, the law set aside the revolutionary model of participatory democracy based on mass organizations in favor of liberal representative democracy centered on political parties. It was much criticized within the FSLN's social base and was rightly viewed as a concession to international pressures. Nonetheless, it would not likely have occurred at all had the revolutionary coalition been narrowly based on Marxist elements under the influence of Cuba, as the United States contended. In fact, the revolutionary ideology was nationalist and Christian as well as socialist, and the coalition of forces that rose up in insurrection included peasants and capitalists who sought liberation from Somoza's tyranny and whose vision for the future was not a socialist utopia but rather democratic government based on honest elections.

Free and fair elections had been held in 1928 and 1932 under the supervision of the US Marines. However, under the Somozas from 1934 to the revolution in 1979, political pacting between their Liberal Party and the opposition

Conservatives had awarded each a set percentage of legislative seats via repeated fraudulent elections. Communist and socialist parties were banned, and voters had little choice at the polls. Even so, just holding elections inculcated the notion that government ought to be selected via the vote. For many Nicaraguans the problem had not been the elections per se but the fraud Somoza perpetrated, and they viewed the overthrow of the dictatorship as an opportunity to correct that flaw.

The revolution increased the opportunities for political parties to organize and participate in politics, despite some repression and curtailment of civil liberties during the early years of the counterrevolutionary war. This opening of political space would be cemented via the Political Parties Law, which made party formation easy, would let the winner govern, and altered the basis of representation from functional to territorial. Nicaraguan politics would not be organized on a Soviet or Cuban model of one-party rule in which mass organizations affiliated with the vanguard party acted as conveyor belts for state policy. Instead, they would feature a pluralist mode of interest intermediation and multiparty competition.

The 1984 Electoral Law

The following year, the legislature approved an Electoral Law that stipulated the rules for elections. In the process it roughed out the contours of new state institutions. The revolution had swept aside the old regime, leaving a tabula rasa with respect to the form of government. By determining what positions would be elected, the Electoral Law effectively defined the future form of the state as well as the regime. Although the Sandinistas had the power to invent a system that would have guaranteed their stay in government while meeting the letter—though not the spirit—of their promise to hold elections, they did not. Instead, they opted for liberal democratic electoral rules and procedures that held the potential to frame competitive elections that could curtail Sandinista power. That choice would not have been anticipated by scholars of revolution or socialism, much less by political practitioners; thus it demands explanation.[9]

What the Sandinistas wanted was pluralism within the hegemony of the FSLN. That is, they imagined a political system characterized by limited competition and continued FSLN domination that would meet minimal international standards for democracy. It was modeled less on Cuba than on Mexico, with the important difference that the Sandinistas were convinced of their own popularity and believed they could win elections without fraud.

Arguing that the people had already "voted" in 1979 by taking up arms in insurrection against the Somoza dictatorship, some Sandinistas viewed elections as primarily for an international audience. The government hoped that elections would delegitimize the Contra war in the eyes of the US Congress and European states, but to do so the electoral rules would need to conform to liberal democratic principles. Victor Hugo Tinoco, deputy foreign minister in 1979, explained, "The government and the Sandinista revolution said, okay, let's demonstrate that Nicaragua is a democratic country. Let's remove the United States government's pretext for the war and hold elections in the Western and Christian style."[10] Asked whether the Electoral Law might have taken a different form, Jesuit social scientist Álvaro Argüello, who helped draft the law, argued that Nicaraguans as well as foreigners understood elections in liberal democratic terms. "No one would have believed in a system that was not liberal democratic. It would have been a mockery," he said.[11]

On September 21, 1983, the legislature formed a special committee to draft the Electoral Law and named Sandinistas and members of their mass organizations to six of the nine seats. All three opposition seats were granted to representatives of parties allied to the FSLN. A more neutral advisory council, composed of members of the Supreme Court and university faculty, was also formed. The CDN was not offered seats. It had boycotted the legislature to protest the passage of a military conscription law, leading the FSLN to conclude it was unpatriotic and possibly allied to the counterrevolutionary cause.

To offset Nicaragua's inexperience with democracy, the legislative committee members drafting the bill visited a wide variety of other countries to assess their laws. The resulting report compared "socialist" to "bourgeois" political systems, allocating much more attention to the latter. It discussed and defined the division of powers, universal suffrage, and parliamentary versus presidential and semipresidential systems. A separate paper discussed various electoral systems, including majoritarian, proportional representation, and mixed systems, as well as methods for calculating remainders.[12]

The committee drafted an Electoral Law that was liberal democratic in most regards and sufficient to meet both international standards and domestic expectations for free and fair elections. Indeed, the 1990 elections that many scholars see as the founding elections in Nicaragua's transition to liberal democracy were held under a minimally amended version of that law. The FSLN stipulated that Nicaragua should directly elect a president and National Assembly, which would later also draft a constitution. The party shaped the debate as much through its superior resources as its votes, sending technical advisers to committee meetings to explain electoral options. Throughout the process, the FSLN showed an overarching concern for stability. Consensus was reached on all but thirteen articles, with the Independent Liberal Party (Partido Liberal Independiente, or PLI) raising most objections with periodic support from three other opposition parties.[13]

Elections were convoked the day the draft law was reported out of committee. Within the Council of State, the CDN immediately withdrew from the debate, objecting to the fact that the elections would be held prior to adopting a constitution. The remaining legislators went on to approve a presidential system with a legislature elected by proportional representation on closed lists for each of nine districts. There was no threshold for winning a seat, perhaps to discourage opposition alliances. The voting age was set at sixteen at the insistence of the FSLN, which was favored by youth. Citizens were required to register, but voting was optional. Members of the military were forbidden to run for office but were eligible to vote. A Supreme Electoral Council (CSE) would administer the elections through lower level bodies. Each political party would have access to state and private communications media.[14]

Two parties agreed with the FSLN, while four others opposed almost every issue, giving some credence to the charge that the Electoral Law was "unilateral." However, the small parties had leverage because the FSLN needed at least some of them to participate in the election in order for the exercise to be seen as legitimate. In July 1984, the law was reformed to accommodate some opposition concerns, including providing them two of the five seats on the CSE, increasing government funding for the parties, increasing media time available, and offering the presidential candidates of any party meeting the electoral quotient a seat in the legislature (thus expanding its size by an indeterminate number).[15] In August, a second reform increased the number of persons administering the balloting at each election location and allowed those individuals to be named by the Assembly of Political Parties, where opposition parties had influence; it was agreed that when possible those positions should be held by an opposition party member. Candidates were guaranteed the right to campaign full-time without losing their jobs or suffering income losses.[16]

Between October 9 and 20, 1984, eighteen representatives from the parties that had registered to participate in elections met in seven rounds of informal dialogue, signing an accord on October 22 that reformed the Electoral Law and campaign rules even further.[17] The reform guaranteed the opposition the right to name one of the electoral officials that administered elections at the voting sites, extended the campaign by twenty-four hours, gave the opposition greater access to state-owned media, and required voters to relinquish their voting identity card when they voted to prevent double voting. Moreover, the parties would keep their legal status regardless of the outcome of the vote and would retain their negotiated access to the state-owned media during subsequent constitution making. Municipal elections would be held after the constitution was approved, and national elections would be held at regular intervals. In addition, the parties agreed to a set of civil liberties that were functionally a bill of rights to be incorporated into the constitution. Finally, the legislature would decide whether to pardon some of those convicted by the special tribunals formed after the Sandinista victory to try members of the old regime for criminal acts. These were significant reforms that might have gone further, had the CDN participated in the dialogue.

The 1984 Elections

Elections were held on November 4, 1984. In addition to the FSLN, six opposition parties ran candidates, including the PLI, the Conservative Democratic Party (Partido Conservador Democratico, or PCD), the Popular Social Christian Party (Partido Popular Social Cristiano, or PPSC), the Nicaraguan Socialist Party (Partido Socialista Nicaragüense, or PSN), the Nicaraguan Communist Party (Partido Comunista de Nicaragua, or PCdeN), and the Marxist-Leninist Popular Action Movement (MAP-ML). The CDN named its candidates for the presidency and vice presidency but did not formally register them, saying it would not do so until further reforms were made.

On July 19, the fifth anniversary of the revolution, the government lifted key elements of the state of emergency, allowing unrestricted travel and freedom of assembly. Press freedom improved, and then the government restored the right of *amparo* (here akin to habeus corpus) and the right to strike. Over 1.5 million citizens registered to vote over a four-day period at the end of July.[18] The government extended the deadline for registering candidates and undertook the reforms noted above to provide fairer rules, but the CDN nonetheless decided not to run. The parties in that coalition lost their legal status because they did not register candidates as required by law.

On election day, 75.4 percent of registered voters cast ballots, and only 6 percent were blank or damaged despite the CDN's call for abstention. The count was honest. The allocation system was close to perfect proportionality, with the main deviation coming from the allocation of seats to presidential candidates winning more than one-ninetieth of the national vote, a provision that favored the opposition.[19] Sandinista leader Daniel Ortega won the presidency with 66.97 percent of the vote (see Figure 6.1). His closest rival, Clemente Guido of the PCD, won 14.04 percent. The Sandinistas won

Figure 6.1 1984 Legislative Elections, Seats by Party

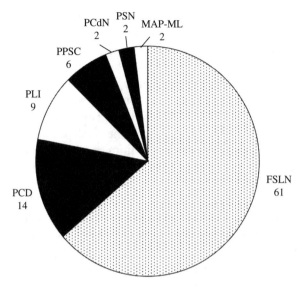

Source: Adapted from *Envio*, http://www.envio.org.ni/articulo/2578, 1990.

61 seats in the legislature, followed by the PCD with 14 seats and the PLI with 9 seats. The remaining parties all won at least 2 seats.[20]

Only sixty-two complaints were filed with the CSE, and election observers from the Irish parliament and churches from Holland and elsewhere hailed the process as clean and legitimate.[21] The European Parliament conceded that the elections indicated Nicaragua was not a totalitarian regime, as the Reagan administration contended, but credited the opposition (participating and nonparticipating) with the progress and proclaimed their courage in not allowing the country to become a one-party regime. Among US observer groups, the Washington Office on Latin America/International Human Rights Law Group delegation concluded that the election was a step in the direction of a pluralist polity because Nicaraguans would not likely tolerate closure of the political space, having had a taste of an open political system.[22] The US government rejected the elections as a sham designed to bolster the Sandinista regime in power and insisted Nicaragua was a Soviet client.

The elections served several important functions. First, they placed six opposition parties in the legislature, which would also serve as a constituent assembly. The Sandinistas won sufficient seats for approval of constitutional provisions, putting the FSLN in a position to ramrod through constitutional elements it viewed as matters of principle not open to amendment. But on other matters, opposition parties would have an opportunity for input, and indeed the government modified the constitutional draft in accordance with their criticism so that it respected liberal as well as socialist principles. A second important outcome of the 1984 elections was that they structured the state along classical liberal representative lines, with a presidential system and a legislature composed of party representatives from geographical constituencies chosen via periodic, openly competitive elections. Third, the elections created an electoral administrative body that was genuinely independent of the executive and legislative branches, a status later confirmed when the 1987 constitution made it a fourth branch of government. These elements would provide the basis for more broadly competitive elections six years later.

There were two things the 1984 elections could not deliver. The first was a social contract. The CDN refused to participate and rejected the outcome, meaning that an important domestic sector denied the legitimacy of not just the election process and resulting government but also the constitution that would be made by the elected legislature. Internal dissent would continue unabated, and opposition would eventually crystallize into the National Union of the Opposition (Union Nacional Opositora, or UNO), which would win the 1990 elections. Nor could the 1984 elections deliver peace. The US rejection of the process meant that it would continue to fund counterrevolutionary forces, and indeed the worst years of the war lay ahead. The US economic embargo and constraints on capital flows further debilitated the economy, which was already wrecked by poor policy decisions and the demands of wartime production. The economic crisis that resulted and Nicaraguans' desperate desire for peace would affect the way many people voted in 1990 in elections that the Sandinistas would lose, bringing an end to the revolutionary experiment.[23]

The Electoral System in the 1990s

The 1990 Elections

The 1990 elections can be called the "founding elections" in Nicaragua's transition to democracy because they were the first since the dictatorship to draw the participation of all political parties. They occurred within the framework of the Esquipulas II Peace Agreement (1987) and drew international attention as a possible means of ending Nicaragua's civil war. The Esquipulas accords stipulated that if Nicaragua held free and fair elections

by February 1990 in which all parties participated, Honduras would deny ir-
regular forces the use of its territory, meaning that the contras would be confined to Nicaragua, where the militarily superior Sandinista army could win
the war.[24]

The winding down of the Cold War framed the election process as well.
Nicaragua had never received much support from the Soviet Union, but now
that question was moot. Former Soviet satellite countries were beginning
their own transitions to democracy. Although Ronald Reagan had once
declared Nicaragua his number one foreign policy priority, his successor,
President George H. W. Bush, sought an exit from the Central American
quagmire. The political arm of the contras saw their financial support cut
and rightly understood this as a signal that the political game was now to be
won or lost in Nicaragua, not Washington. Many returned home to lead political parties that opposed the Sandinistas.

The Nicaraguan government declared a cease-fire, and although the
contra armed forces did not reciprocate, their options for action were limited because the United States was now only supplying humanitarian aid.
Had the elections been fraudulent, the country would surely have returned
to war and might possibly have faced a US invasion, as Panama did that
very year after holding fraudulent elections. Some speculated that a legitimate victory by the FSLN would have triggered a similar result, but the
presence of hundreds of international observers from the United Nations, the
Organization of American States (OAS), and the Carter Center would have
made US rejection of a free, fair and honest election result politically costly.

The elections would be held under the revolutionary constitution of
1987. The opposition parties initially insisted that constitutional reform pre-
cede elections, which would have made it difficult to meet the Esquipulas
timetable. However, a UN analysis concluded that free and fair elections
were possible under the existing constitution, and opposition forces ultimately settled for making constitutional reform one of their campaign planks.

The opposition also demanded reform of the Electoral Law, which
began in the spring of 1989. The FSLN once again dominated the reform
process, and since it was carried out by the National Assembly where the
most right-wing opposition parties had no representation, they condemned
the process. In fact, there were few changes from the 1984 text. Even though
a Library of Congress report concluded that the law was not biased against
the opposition, it was by no means clear that the opposition would participate in the elections under those rules.[25]

In June 1989, fourteen opposition parties formed the UNO coalition.
The core of the UNO was the set of political forces that had been in the
CDN, and their participation in the election was vital to its acceptance by

the United States and Central American governments. One difference between the UNO and the CDN was that the UNO was composed solely of political parties, whereas the CDN was led by the High Council on Private
Enterprise, a business association. Political parties had more incentives to
participate in elections. Despite this, the UNO's participation was sufficiently in doubt that Costa Rican president Oscar Arias (whose role in the
Esquipulas process was so instrumental it was often called the "Arias Plan")
visited Nicaragua to try to bridge the differences between the government
and the UNO over the Electoral Law.

The matter was ultimately resolved via a marathon meeting convened
by President Ortega in August 1989, just prior to the next summit of the
Central American presidents in Tela, Honduras. All the political parties were
represented, including the far-left-wing opponents of the FSLN and the
UNO. Witnessed by international observers, the meeting resulted in an
agreement wherein the parties would participate in elections if the government ended military conscription and made minor adjustments in the Electoral Law.[26] The government complied promptly with the terms of this
political agreement, and for the first time it appeared a broadly competitive
election would be held.

For the UNO, the tricky question was who should be the presidential
candidate. Businessman Enrique Bolaños sought the post, as did longtime
PLI leader Virgilio Godoy, and multiple rounds of voting at the UNO's nomination meeting resulted in repeated tie votes. Waiting in the wings was the
widow of the slain newspaper publisher Pedro Joaquín Chamorro. Politically inexperienced, Violeta Barrios de Chamorro nonetheless came from
one of Nicaragua's most prominent families and had married into another.
She enjoyed wide popular sympathy and the support of both Cardinal
Miguel Obando y Bravo and the US embassy. Chamorro's four children
were politically divided, with one a leader of the contras and another serving the Sandinista government, but first and foremost they were family, and
it became a metaphor for Nicaragua's civil war. Nicaraguans hoped that Violeta Chamorro could reconcile their countrymen. A final round of voting
put her name in the mix, and the UNO selected Violeta Chamorro as their
candidate and made Virgilio Godoy her running mate.

Further concessions by the government helped to keep the UNO in the
race and the elections on track. The registration of parties and alliances went
smoothly. At the urging of former US president Jimmy Carter, the government permitted exiled Miskitu Indian leaders to return to register as candidates. The registration of voters on four consecutive Sundays in October
1989 succeeded in registering most voters, despite a contra ambush killing
seventeen soldiers that led the government to end its unilateral cease-fire.

As the campaign got under way, there were few signs of harassment of opposition candidates such as those seen against the CDN in 1984. The relatively positive tone of the campaign was jeopardized when a pro-government newspaper published a headline equating the UNO to Somoza's old National Guard (and by extension the contras), but the electoral authorities intervened to sanction the publication. International observers weighed in, and no further incidents transpired. Then in December, a squabble at a UNO rally resulted in the death of one person, and although his political affiliation was uncertain, the event riveted the country. Investigations by international observers from the OAS and UN were inconclusive, but it was clear that the police monitoring the rally had not taken appropriate action. Former president Carter visited the country again and negotiated a nonviolence accord between the parties, and the electoral authorities published guidelines to improve policing at rallies.

The watchword at the Supreme Electoral Council was "inclusion." A special registration was held well past the normal deadline to accommodate contra forces that had given up their arms. After a number of candidates withdrew, the United Nations Observer Mission for the Verification of Elections in Nicaragua (ONUVEN) conducted an investigation and concluded that most did so for personal reasons rather than because of intimidation or bribery, but the electoral authorities nonetheless ruled that the parties should be able to replace those candidates. Given that the FSLN and its allies had nominated four of the five CSE magistrates, ONUVEN also examined CSE proceedings for bias. It found that in all cases the CSE decisions had been unanimous and the viewpoints of the opposition representative were regularly aired in CSE meetings, noting "attention was drawn once again to the electoral authority's concern to ensure effective implementation of the basic principle that political participation should be broad and pluralistic."[27]

Despite these consistently inclusive CSE decisions, the opposition remained at a disadvantage in two important respects. The first was campaign funding. The FSLN had at its disposal the resources of the state, whereas the UNO initially had quite limited resources. The war and US embargo had left few operative vehicles on the road. The UNO's shipment of vehicles was held up in customs, while the FSLN was able to use state-owned vehicles, technically by renting them, although documentation of payment was never provided. President Carter successfully resolved the customs issue and also the payment of funds from the United States to support civic activities by opposition-affiliated support groups, but not until January 1990—roughly six weeks before the election.[28]

The second problem for the UNO was media time. The Chamorro family owned *La Prensa,* the most widely circulated newspaper in the country and one that had been censored in the 1980s. They could count on good print press, some of which would be repeated over the radio. However, all television was state-owned, and although the electoral rules allocated media time to all parties, opposition spots were generally not aired during popular hours or on the one channel that broadcast outside Managua. The quality of production of the UNO television spots was poor by comparison as well. Meanwhile, the FSLN enjoyed its own newspaper, *Barricada,* and the advantages of incumbency, including the opportunity to build the government's image through public spending and by generating news coverage.

These factors combined to make the FSLN confident of its victory. Polls conducted at the time mostly reinforced this confidence by incorrectly predicting Ortega would win the presidency. Postelection analysis of the polling identified some of the problems that engendered this false confidence. One was the "Güegüense" phenomenon, in which Nicaraguans were reluctant to tell pollsters their intentions.[29] A more concrete analysis showed that pollsters had misallocated the "not sure/don't know" responses, assuming they would split roughly in the same proportion as those who did respond. In fact, a large percentage of those votes went to the UNO. Some analysts speculated that respondents were afraid to say they planned to vote for the opposition, but that was not confirmed.[30]

Several other reasons were given for the FSLN's false sense of confidence. The party had a vertical structure, and although cadres at the base appear to have known the party was not doing well, the bad news was downplayed and did not reach top officials. Another reason was the FSLN's final rally in Managua, which drew an estimated 300,000 participants. Looking out at the sea of faces, Ortega could easily have assumed they all intended to vote for him, but in fact they did not. For many Nicaraguans, election rallies were simply a public fiesta, the biggest thing in town and a no-cost opportunity to listen to music, dance, and receive free T-shirts. It was rumored that Ortega intended to announce a permanent end to military conscription, which had been temporarily suspended for the election but was presumably about to resume. His failure to do so no doubt disappointed some voters.[31]

The outcome of the election was a surprise landslide victory for Chamorro. She received 54.73 percent of the vote to Ortega's 40.82 percent. The hush that fell over Managua spoke of the tension as the rumor of the FSLN's debacle spread and citizens wondered whether the party would accept its loss or attempt to alter the numbers and send the army to the streets. International observers met with Ortega and urged him to concede, showing him the results of their quick count that accurately estimated the final results. After initial hesitation while awaiting his party's own analysis of the results from Managua, Ortega agreed to concede and asked Jimmy Carter to intercede with Violeta Chamorro to delay her victory announcement until he could make a concession speech.[32]

It soon became apparent that the legislative results mirrored the presidential race, giving the UNO 51 seats, the FSLN 39 seats, six other parties 3 seats each, and two trailing parties 1 seat each (see Figure 6.2). Although there were as yet no direct elections for mayors, elections for city council were held and gave the UNO control of 98 municipalities, the FSLN control of 31 municipalities, and the Central American Unionist Party (Partido Unionista Centroamericano, or PUCA) control of 2 municipalities.[33]

Following the election, the FSLN took advantage of its lame-duck period to rush legislation through the National Assembly to protect its adherents and give them title to lands transferred under the agrarian reform. Departing officials also stripped government offices of material goods in what Nicaraguans termed *La Piñata,* leaving the FSLN tainted with a new reputation for corruption. Daniel's brother and commander of the army Humberto Ortega met with president-elect Chamorro's son-in-law Antonio Lacayo to hash out the terms of the transition. Important agreements were reached. The military declared itself autonomous, and officers resigned their posts in the FSLN. Chamorro insisted on choosing her own cabinet but kept

Figure 6.2 1990 Legislative Elections, Seats Won by Party

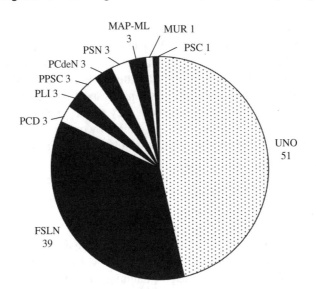

Source: Adapted from *Envio,* http://www.envio.org.ni/articulo/2587, 1990.

Daniel Ortega's brother Humberto as chief of the army, a move that was seen as a significant concession to the FSLN, though it may also have been the only practical way to achieve a peaceful reduction in the size of the armed forces from roughly 100,000 to 15,000 troops. That appointment carried a heavy cost as it caused most members of the UNO coalition to denounce Chamorro's decision and go into opposition.

Following Chamorro's inauguration in April 1990, cease-fire agreements and disarmament accords were signed with various contra groups, and the UN and OAS assisted with the disarmament and resettlement of former combatants.[34] Although full pacification of the countryside would take another three years, the election had for practical purposes ended the war. Future struggle between the Sandinistas and their opponents would be confined to the political battlefield.

The 1996 Elections

In 1995, the erstwhile UNO deputies in the legislature joined with a Sandinista splinter group that formed the Sandinista Renewal Movement (Movimiento Renovador Sandinista, or MRS) to amend the constitution. Most of the amendments were designed to reduce the powers of the presidency, but others changed the electoral system. Given the burgeoning number of parties, the law was reformed to require a presidential candidate to obtain 45 percent of the vote or go to a run-off. Relatives of the president were also forbidden to run for executive office, and the presidential term was shortened from six to five years.[35]

Mariano Fiallos, a Sandinista who had presided over the CSE since its inception in the mid-1980s, resigned his post to protest reforms that altered the way regional and local election authorities would be selected. They had been selected from a pool of capable citizens irrespective of party, with preference for nonpartisan members, but now they would be chosen from party lists, a change that Fiallos accurately predicted would politicize the electoral apparatus. Fiallos also argued that the electoral administration should function year-round at all levels to ensure access of citizens and parties to the electoral system, but due to budgetary constraints, the municipal-level electoral councils only operated for a period of about six months surrounding elections.

The presidency of the CSE was taken up by Rosa Marina Zelaya. She had extensive experience but took over less than a year before the election. Zelaya was understood to be sympathetic to the MRS: her husband headed the MRS list of deputies. She faced the daunting task of running an election when staff at the lower levels of the electoral administration were often new and inexperienced. The technical staff at the national level were largely holdovers from the 1980s and quite capable, but staff at the departmental/regional and the municipal levels were frequently administering an election for the first time.

The dissolution of the UNO coalition had left open the question of how Liberals and Conservatives would organize themselves against the FSLN in future elections. This dilemma was resolved in an unexpected way. A Managua city councilman of no particular consequence was selected by his fellows to serve as mayor. That man was Arnoldo Alemán Lacayo, who turned out to have far more political acumen than previously thought. He recognized that the shame heaped on the Liberals for their association with the Somoza dictatorship could be converted to an anti-Sandinista asset and went about forging a new Liberal identity under the slogan "proudly Liberal." Stressing that Augusto César Sandino was a Liberal, Alemán even competed for the historical legacy that the Sandinistas had claimed. He then skillfully crafted a Liberal Alliance (Alianza Liberal, or AL) to contest the 1996 elections, flying the historic red flag of Somoza's Liberal Party, and rode it to the presidency.

The 1996 election campaign was highly polarized. Concerned about the tone of the campaign, international observers again accepted invitations to monitor the elections. The OAS, European Union, and Carter Center sent sizable delegations and systematically collected data; their work was matched by a new civil society organization, Ethics and Transparency, that conducted an accurate quick count.

The FSLN and AL were not the only contenders. Indeed, the presidential ballot ultimately featured twenty-three candidates ranging from the far left to the far right. This was in part due to ease of registration and the availability of public funding prior to the election rather than as a reimbursement. These microparties had equal status with the FSLN and AL in the eyes of the Supreme Electoral Council, which was at pains to include them. For example, each party had to approve the quality of the colors used to represent their symbols on the printed ballots. The host of small parties made the CSE's administrative burden inordinately high.

In the end, Arnoldo Alemán won the presidential election in the first round with 51.03 percent of the vote, Daniel Ortega placed second with 37.75 percent, and no other candidate received more than 5 percent of the vote. A total of 92 seats were awarded in the National Assembly (see Figure 6.3). Of these, 42 went to the AL and 36 to the FSLN, and no other party received more than 4 seats.[36] The municipal elections were the first to allow direct election of mayors. The AL won control of 92 municipalities, the FSLN won 51 municipalities, and the MRS gained 1 municipality. In addition, the

Figure 6.3 1996 Legislative Elections, Seats Won by Party

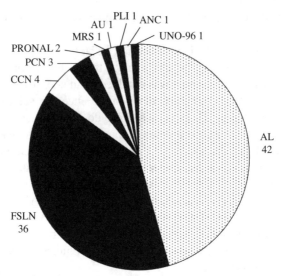

Source: Adapted from *Envio*, http://www.envio.org.ni/articulo/1990, 1996.

elections permitted "popular subscription candidates," who did not belong to a registered political party but had registered via a petition from citizens constituting at least 5 percent of the electoral rolls, and this resulted in one municipality being controlled by the Civic Association of Potosí (Asociación Cívica de Potosí ACP).[37]

The late change in leadership on the CSE and plethora of microparties demanding attention provides a partial explanation for the poor planning that produced a messy vote collection process in some departments in 1996. Although the election itself ran smoothly, with material arriving on time and voting locations opening as planned, and attained a high turnout level even in the former war zones, the process began to unravel after the polls closed. Poor planning for the collection and storage of ballots and tally sheets resulted in long lines at the collection facility in Managua. Some poll workers who had been working diligently for little pay for three days straight simply left their ballots and election materials in the street. Inside the warehouse there was insufficient space and poor organization, so that ballot boxes were heaped in piles with their contents sometimes spilling to the floor. Other problems occurred in the second most populous department, Matagalpa. At the end of the day, the CSE was forced to annul the results of 14 percent of the polls in the department of Managua and 11 percent in

Matagalpa and conduct a recount of some ballots at the national level. The disorganization at the end did not blind election observers to the broad picture of careful electoral preparations, proper conduct of the balloting, and an honest count, and they concluded that the elections were acceptable overall.

The Sandinistas saw things differently. They suspected a political motive behind these administrative snafus, calling it "organized disorder" and refused to accept the results of the presidential race. Ortega was convinced that he merited a runoff against Alemán. The party compiled a massive record of complaints reported by their cadres and sent it to the Supreme Electoral Council, demanding a response. However, it was really an ad hoc collection of uncorroborated testimony, because Sandinista party workers had not been trained to document these incidents properly and failed to build a case that the poor procedures constituted fraud. The Carter Center was prepared to back a Sandinista request to rerun the municipal races in municipalities where the number of ballots annulled exceeded the difference between the top two candidates, but the FSLN did not pursue that matter, focusing instead on the presidency. There was no indication of a systematic pattern to the annulments, and many were from locations where surrounding ballot boxes showed AL victories, so it was by no means certain that the annulled votes favored Ortega. In any case, the gap between Alemán and Ortega was sufficiently large that even if all the annulled ballots had been for Ortega, he would have fallen just short of the number needed for a second round.[38] Eventually, the FSLN legislators took their seats in the National Assembly, but under protest. Because he was the second-place finisher in the presidential race, Ortega also won a seat. As the leader of the largest single party and one that practiced party discipline, Ortega would wield substantial leverage, and the FSLN held enough seats to block constitutional changes.

The Electoral System in the Twenty-First Century

In 2000, the PLC and FSLN forged a political pact to divide up control over leadership positions in the judiciary, electoral branch, and other agencies.[39] Calling the pact a "governability accord," the parties reformed the Electoral Law drastically to reduce the number of options citizens had at the polls.[40] The new law required that groups seeking to form political parties establish representative boards in the then-151 municipalities, and the installation of those boards had to be certified before election authorities. They also were required to collect signatures showing support of 3 percent of eligible voters. Once a signature had been used by one party, it was not valid for another, although citizens could cast their votes for a different party on the legislative and presidential ballots. The FSLN proceeded to collect many more than the required number of signatures, in effect shrinking the pool of available signers for parties that tried to register later (the Liberals were grandfathered in).

Parties also were required to run candidates in all races for every election in order to retain their legal standing. To help induce local candidates to run for office on party tickets, the popular subscription association candidacies permitted in the 1996 municipal elections were abolished. To retain their legal standing after the election, parties needed to win 4 percent of the presidential vote or, in the case of alliances, 4 percent for each party in the alliance. Those that did not win a legislative seat would not be reimbursed for campaign expenditures, and no funds were available prior to the election to assist new parties. Alliances were required to run under the banner of just one legally recognized party, meaning the others lost visibility and had to swallow their pride and reorient their voters to cast ballots for erstwhile opponents. In the view of some experts, the FSLN and PLC legislators had constructed the most exclusionary electoral law in Latin America.[41]

The situation was worsened by the lack of accountability in Nicaraguan political institutions, a consequence of Nicaragua's thin democratic history and the new pact. This pact, often capitalized as "the Pact" to stress its significance beyond typical deal cutting, divided leadership in government institutions between Liberals and Sandinistas, excluding all others. Among these institutions was the CSE, whose composition was changed from five to seven magistrates to be chosen by the two largest "political forces" in the country (the FSLN and PLC). In stark contrast to the 1996 elections, in which the CSE presidency was held by a party that won a single seat, the institution was now to be controlled by magistrates from the two largest parties and would not provide others any representation at all. The membership of the CSE was changed less than a year before the next scheduled elections. Unlike other parties, the FSLN and PLC were guaranteed representatives on the regional, departmental, and municipal electoral councils and had reserved positions for themselves in polling site administration as well. In May 2001 they extended this principle to the technical and administrative posts in the electoral bureaucracy, dividing up the positions between their parties.

The first test of this new system came in the 2000 municipal elections, which were held separately from national elections for the first time. Some of the CSE's decisions were controversial. Although each decision was within the CSE's scope of authority and the CSE was constitutionally empowered to interpret electoral law, the readings were shaded in ways that many Nicaraguans saw as partisan. For example, prior to the 2000 municipal elections, the city of Managua had been divided into three municipalities, and the city limits of the capital neatly fell just short of the home of the most popular mayoral aspirant, an independent. The law required candidates to live in the municipality, so he was denied the opportunity to run for mayor of Managua. In another example, the Organization of the Peoples of Mother Earth (Yapti Tasba Masraka Nanih Aslatakanka, or YATAMA) party, which represented Miskitu Indians on the Caribbean Coast, was denied the opportunity to register candidates due to a technical flaw in its application, a decision that the Inter-American Court of Human Rights would later reject as unwarranted and discriminatory.[42]

The result was another victory for the Liberals. The Constitutional Liberal Party, which had consolidated the members of the Liberal Alliance into a single, more coherent party, won 94 municipalities. The FSLN took 52 municipalities, and the Conservative Party (PC), five. The FSLN candidate Herty Lewites won the mayoralty of Managua, the country's capital, where about one-third of the population lived.[43]

The 2001 Elections

In the lead-up to the 2001 general elections, two proto-parties were stymied in their efforts to register when they were unable to form boards in enough municipalities by the deadline. One complained that its efforts had been hindered by the CSE, whose magistrates declined to attend the board inaugurations needed to make them official. The other of these proto-parties was a vehicle for presidential aspirant José Antonio Alvarado, a former cabinet minister and Alemán protégé who had publicly broken with Alemán and now sought to replace him. Alvarado was prohibited from running when it was ruled that he had not published his renunciation of his US citizenship in the *Gazeta Oficial* by the required date. He then produced documents showing that he had submitted the declaration to the *Gazette,* but its publication was inexplicably delayed, implying the journal publishers had discriminated against him because they worked for the government.

The truth of these matters could not be verified prior to elections, and appeals were complicated by the fact that the Pact politicized the judicial system, too. Nonetheless, it was evident from the low number of parties that were able to register and run candidates that the Electoral Law reform had drastically narrowed choices at the polls. In the end, the legislative seats would be split between the FSLN and PLC. The PCN would be the only other party represented in the legislature, and they won just one seat. In a report measuring democracy, the United Nations Development Programme rated the 2001 contest slightly lower than the 1990 and 1996 elections with respect to presentation of candidates and party formation.[44]

Equally disturbing was how the politicization of the CSE produced internal problems, making that body periodically dysfunctional. The magistrates nominated by either of the two political parties represented on the CSE could boycott CSE meetings and prevent a quorum, bringing decisionmaking to a halt. They did this on several occasions, sometimes for extended periods, putting the election process in jeopardy because of the tight schedule. This pattern would emerge again in 2006, during both the Atlantic Coast and national elections, and was a blatant example of the damage that politicization of the electoral system had done.[45]

Despite the quorum problem, the preparations in 2001 were sufficiently good for elections to be held on time. Two parties and one alliance registered candidates—the PCN, the FSLN, and an alliance consisting of the PLC and the Nicaraguan Resistance Party (Partido de la Resistencia Nicaragüense, or PRN), the former contras. Daniel Ortega stood for the FSLN for the third time. Former president Alemán was ineligible to run in consecutive terms and chose his vice president Enrique Bolaños to carry the PLC colors. The Conservatives nominated Noel Vidaurre, but an internal party crisis led to his resignation and replacement by Alberto Saborio, which produced a sharp decline in support for the party.

Civil society groups and international observers had expressed concerns about technical elements such as the vote transmission process and distribution of voter documents, but eleventh-hour efforts by the CSE and additional funds from foreign donors mitigated these problems.

The tone of the campaign was initially less polarized than in 1996. However, competition sharpened over time as polls showed the FSLN and PLC running neck and neck. The US ambassador made it clear he opposed Ortega's reelection and on one occasion appeared with candidate Enrique Bolaños while distributing US food aid in a drought-stricken area. After the 9/11 attacks, a heightened concern for US security further colored foreign relations and was reflected in the election campaign. The PLC played to Nicaraguan fears of a return to a US-sponsored war should Ortega win the election, hanging banners that touted Ortega's cordial relations with Saddam Hussein and implying he consorted with terrorists. Two days before the election, army troops dressed in camouflage were deployed in Managua and several other towns, which may have had the effect of reminding citizens of the war years. President Alemán said he would declare a state of emergency if there was disorder following the vote, though election observers insisted that the conditions justifying such a heavy-handed maneuver did not exist.[46]

The election itself ran smoothly, and the difficulties that some departments had in collecting ballots in 1996 were not repeated. The political climate was less polarized than in the past, perhaps because each party knew the Pact guaranteed it a quota of power in state institutions regardless of the outcome. Tabulation of the votes was slowed by a last-minute change in personnel, but quick counts showed PLC candidate Enrique Bolaños with a decisive lead, later borne out by the release of official statistics showing Bolaños with 56.3 percent and Ortega with 42.3 percent of the vote. Alberto Saborio garnered just 1.4 percent. Daniel Ortega accepted defeat in a timely manner and needed no encouragement from international groups to do so. Results in the legislature were similar, with the PLC obtaining 53 seats, the FSLN 38 seats, and the Conservative Party 1 seat (see Figure 6.4).[47]

Analysis of the 2001 election raised the question of whether the pacted change in the Electoral Law and structure of the electoral administration had converted Nicaraguan democracy into a *partidocracia*—rule by the parties rather than the people. The two largest parties controlled leadership selection for the important state institutions without offering any opportunity for public input and left no room for nonpartisan or third-party influence. Because the leaders of state agencies owed their appointments to either the FSLN or PLC and could be replaced by them at any time, they were sensitive to the parties' interests. In the electoral realm, CSE magistrates voted in partisan blocs. The FSLN and PLC asserted that parties should control the electoral system because they were the ones most affected by it, rejecting the idea that the CSE should be composed of nonpartisan "notables." The magistrates

Figure 6.4 2001 Legislative Elections, Seats Won by Party

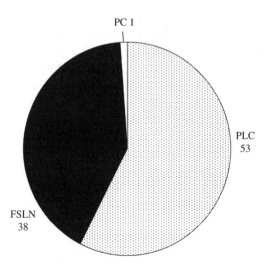

Source: Adapted from *Envio,* http://www.envio.org.ni/articulo/1547, 2001.

were comfortable with the practice of large parties having more input than smaller ones since they had demonstrated their relevance at the polls. The position was plausible given the proliferation of microparties in the early 1990s. Nonetheless, the pendulum had swung to the other extreme, creating an artificial two-party-dominant system in which others competed at a disadvantage, if they could compete at all.

The dearth of interparty competition *between* elections rendered horizontal accountability moot and left elections the only instrument to deliver accountability. However, the ability for citizens to "throw the rascals out" was limited by the closed party list system and the Electoral Law that excluded some parties and candidates. Nonetheless, the presence of high-profile election observers and Nicaragua's dramatic electoral history kept citizens and foreigners focused on elections as the keystone to democracy. They relied on the electoral system to deliver accountability when other aspects of the regime could not, despite evidence that its ability to do so was constrained. In this sense, Nicaraguan politics continued to suffer from electoralism.

Municipal and Coastal Elections, 2004 and 2006

What neither party could have predicted was that President Bolaños would promptly turn on his predecessor, allying with the Sandinistas to strip Arnoldo Alemán of his legislative immunity and prosecute him for corruption.[48] The subsequent trial and conviction of Alemán on fraud and money-laundering charges meant that he could not stand for the presidency in 2006. The PLC would make a series of concessions to the Sandinistas in an effort to win relief from the courts and a pardon that would restore Alemán's eligibility, all to no avail. The FSLN had entered into the Pact as the junior partner but now found itself in the driver's seat. Although Alemán's control over the party lists and ability to finance the party meant that the bulk of the Liberal deputies remained loyal to him, President Bolaños and his handful of "blue and white" bloc deputies were able to forge a working relationship with the Sandinistas to pass legislation between 2001 and 2003.

Then, as so often happens in Nicaragua, the United States intervened, sending Secretary of State Colin Powell to meet with President Bolaños and press him to end his dealings with the FSLN. Bolaños did so, and the Sandinistas struck back, blocking his bills and threatening impeachment. When the international community signaled that impeachment was not warranted and the armed forces continued to back the president, the FSLN and PLC abandoned impeachment and focused on the 2004 municipal elections.

The municipal elections were important both in their own right and as an indicator of party strength in advance of the 2006 general elections.

Working in alliance with the National Convergence (Convergencia Nacional), a group of well-known individuals representing splinter groups from diverse ideological currents, the Sandinistas swept the election. They won 14 of the 17 departmental capitals and 25 of Nicaragua's 42 largest cities. In all, the Sandinistas emerged with control of 87 municipalities, and the PLC with just 57. The Alliance for the Republic (Alianza para la República, or APRE), which tried to present an anti-Pact alternative, won just 4 municipalities. The Miskitu Indian party YATAMA won 3 municipalities, and the PRN won control of a single municipality. The PLC's drop is best explained by its preoccupation with Alemán's legal problems and a shift in Nicaraguan demographics toward an urban populace, eroding its traditional peasant base. The FSLN's alliance with the National Convergence, though, let it run mayoral candidates who were popular even if they were not FSLN members.

Those who opposed the Pact had focused their hopes on the APRE alliance of Conservatives and disaffected Liberals. Overall it performed poorly, but its most significant loss came in Granada, Nicaragua's third-largest city and historically a Conservative stronghold. There the FSLN candidate was pronounced the victor after a highly controversial decision by the departmental electoral office to accept as genuine a tally sheet that did not match those given to agents from other parties at the polling site. A decision in the other direction would have handed the victory to APRE, whose lack of representation on the departmental electoral council barred the party from participating in the discussions leading to the decision, which it then rejected. Election observers from the OAS could do little to illuminate the grounds for decision and maintained a low profile around the affair. Nonetheless, the municipal elections were of acceptable quality overall, and the success of the Sandinistas reflected genuine frustration that eight years of Liberal government had not brought relief from poverty.[49]

Immediately following the elections, the PLC and FSLN resumed their efforts to clip President Bolaños's wings. In December 2004, they amended the constitution to trim the powers of the presidency yet again, this time giving the legislature the right to fire cabinet ministers at will and transferring control over leadership selection in key government agencies to the legislature. Bolaños's refusal to publish the amendments and their subsequent publication by the legislature produced a constitutional crisis that endured for ten months in 2005.[50]

The FSLN and PLC again threatened the president with impeachment, demonstrating the lengths to which the pacting parties would go to consolidate their hegemony. Civil society, which had normally been quiescent, took to the streets in the summer of 2005 to protest the political maneuvering by the FSLN and PLC. This in turn gave a boost to anti-Pact candidates, including Liberal leader Eduardo Montealegre, who had sought the PLC nomination only to be booted out by Alemán, and the former Sandinista mayor of Managua, Herty Lewites, whom Daniel Ortega ousted from the FSLN. In 2006 these men would lead anti-Pact parties in their bids for the presidency with substantial success.

In October 2005 the FSLN ended its feud with Bolaños and agreed to delay implementation of the constitutional reforms until after his term. Ortega's motives in reaching that accord were mixed, but one element was the need to stem the public's growing anti-Pact sentiments. Another was Ortega's desire to focus the FSLN on the coming elections. The party wanted to repeat its municipal electoral success on the Atlantic Coast in the March 2006 regional elections to create momentum for the national elections seven months later. Moreover, impeachment of Bolaños or a shortening of his term might have worsened the crisis and brought international involvement in it. This could have delegitimized the 2006 presidential election, which Ortega wished to avoid since the deepening Liberal split gave him a good chance of regaining the presidency.

The 2006 Elections

The 2006 elections brought Nicaraguan politics full circle as former president Daniel Ortega was finally reelected. Three factors facilitated his victory.[51] The first was simply Ortega's own political skills. He had so continually dominated his party since the 1980s that he was guaranteed the FSLN's nomination despite three straight failures to gain the presidency. In most parties, repeated failures would have caused a leadership crisis and brought new contenders to the fore, but Ortega managed to expel his most serious rivals and sideline others, keeping a firm grip on the party machinery. He weathered personal scandals, including an allegation that he had sexually molested his stepdaughter Zoilamérica Narváez. His marriage to Rosario Murillo emerged stronger than ever, and the two renewed their vows before Cardinal Obando y Bravo, an act of contrition that helped realign the church with the Sandinistas. Murillo would go on to design a low-key campaign strategy for her husband that differed markedly from his grandiose stump speeches of the past. This time Ortega held a series of small reconciliation meetings in which he welcomed everyone from former contras to lapsed Sandinistas back into the fold. That did not earn him any more votes than he had received in the previous elections, but it put forward the notion that Ortega had changed and reduced the fear that a Sandinista victory would mean a return to the violence of the 1980s. His strategy helped ensure that voters did not unite behind a single alternative candidate to oppose Ortega.

The second key factor facilitating Ortega's victory was a split in the Liberal camp. Arnoldo Alemán hand selected former vice president José Rizo as the PLC candidate in a traditional "smoke-filled room" session. Eduardo Montealegre, a scion of the upper class and former finance minister, had sought the nomination and pressed unsuccessfully for a party primary. When it became clear he could not get the PLC nomination, Montealegre formed a second Liberal coalition, the Nicaraguan Liberal Alliance–Conservative Party (Alianza Liberal Nicaragüense–Partido Conservador, or ALN-PC), which had the tacit blessing of the US government. He went on to finish second in the presidential race, with 28.3 percent of the vote to Ortega's 38 percent. Although Rizo would place third with 27.11 percent, the PLC party finished in second place in the legislature because Liberal voters rallied to the traditional red flag. These numbers suggested that had the Liberals united around a single candidate, they could well have won the presidency outright and controlled the National Assembly.[52]

Ortega won the election with a plurality, 38 percent. A third crucial factor in his victory was the Electoral Law reform permitting a presidential candidate to win with just 35 percent of the vote if that candidate had at least a 5 percent lead over the runner-up. The provision had been in place since 2000 but was moot while there were two-party straight fights.

With the Liberals divided, polls predicted that Ortega would lead in the vote, but because the MRS was running a fourth candidate competing for votes on the left, there was some doubt whether Ortega could win in the first round. If not, his chances in a run-off against either of the Liberals were poor, as most Liberal voters likely would prefer the remaining candidate to Ortega. The untimely death of the popular MRS candidate, former Managua mayor Herty Lewites, in July 2006 may therefore have affected the outcome. At the time he was polling ahead of Ortega, but his replacement Edmundo Jarquín fell behind in the race, winding up with just 6.44 percent of the vote. Had the left wing been as deeply split as the Liberals, a run-off would likely have occurred.

The FSLN did not win a majority in the legislature, emerging with 38 of the 90 seats in competition (see Figure 6.5). In the event that the two Liberal parties and MRS joined forces against the FSLN, they had enough votes to block constitutional changes. The FSLN would be able to pass legislation in cooperation with either the PLC's 25 votes or the ALN-PC's 22. President Bolaños would receive a seat as the outgoing president, as would Eduardo Montalegre as runner-up in the presidential race, raising the total seats to 92.

Figure 6.5 2006 Legislative Elections, Seats Won by Party

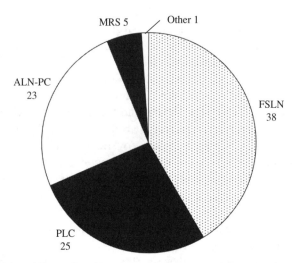

Source: Adapted from *Political Database of the Americas,* http://pdba.georgetown.edu.

This gave the ALN-PC 23 seats and a likelihood of receiving Bolaños' vote when needed.

After the ballot storage debacle and forced recounts and annulments in 1996, and the exclusion of parties and candidates in 2001, the 2006 elections were in many respects the best elections Nicaragua had held since 1990. Nonetheless, they did not bring the end of the FSLN-PLC Pact or a definitive shift to a multiparty system. The ALN-PC was largely a Liberal offshoot, and the MRS came from a split in the FSLN. The decision of the ALN and PLC to run in coalition in the 2008 municipal elections suggested that the old fault lines still defined the political landscape. The conflict between Liberals and Sandinistas that had begun with the 1979 revolution continued to play itself out on the electoral stage.

The 2006 election demonstrated just how much the electoral system relied on political parties. In comparison to the 1990 election, when the CSE was credited with building confidence in the process, despite the ongoing civil war, by adopting extra measures to register voters, in 2006 the CSE took on less responsibility for assuring that all citizens obtained voting credentials and were informed about their rights and opportunities to vote. The system placed a tremendous burden on parties not only to cultivate adherents but also to help them register and pick up voting credentials that the CSE manufactured. The CSE did little to advertise the election date and urge voter participation, leaving that role to parties as well. Such practices are sometimes used in developed countries, where most citizens have the resources to register and obtain information, but were questioned in Nicaragua, where poverty and illiteracy increased the barriers to participation in the electoral system. This party-based approach to electoral administration gave advantages to larger, better-resourced, and better-organized parties.

Nicaragua's electoral system was robust, with multiple safeguards against fraud, but ultimately it relied on the principle of party monitoring of the process. In 2006, the MRS and Alternative for Change (Alternativa para el Cambio, or AC) parties were unable to recruit sufficient party agents to staff all the 11,274 polling sites, despite their fears that the PLC and FSLN might collude rather than monitor one another against fraud. Fortunately, the ALN-PC was also able to place its party agents at nearly all the polling sites, and the national observers from Ethics and Transparency also had near-universal coverage. The parties were able to place their observers in the counting centers, where they helped identify summation errors and stopped an outright fraud attempt in a legislative race. This showed the verification system could work but also suggested the procedural safeguards in the law were insufficient unto themselves and in the end the prevention of fraud fell to the watchdog efforts of partisan actors. In sum, under this system the political parties assumed many of the responsibilities shouldered by the state in 1984, 1990, and even 1996. The system lent support to the suggestion that Nicaragua was increasingly becoming a *partidocracia* because the Pact left the election administration more vulnerable to partisan interests and the electoral system relied heavily on parties to help carry out basic administrative tasks.

Electoral Erosion Under the Ortega Administration

Concerns about the weak institutional basis of the electoral system and its growing partisanship deepened substantially under the Ortega administration. In 2008, Nicaragua held municipal elections that opposition parties and domestic observer groups said were fraudulent.[53] Aside from ongoing concerns about the accuracy of the voter list and delivery of voter identification cards, widespread inaccuracies in the vote tabulation were revealed. Copies of the tally sheets given to opposition parties did not always coincide with the final numbers reported by election authorities, nor were opposition complaints adequately addressed. Dozens of mayoral posts may have been affected, most seriously Managua, where Eduardo Montealegre was denied victory.

Members of the FSLN rejected the claim of fraud, some viewing it as part of an effort to discredit the Ortega government for ideological reasons. The international community was unable to provide data on the crisis because, for the first time since the revolution, the CSE had not invited the most credible international election observer groups to monitor the elections. Nonetheless, the European donor community was sufficiently persuaded by the evidence of fraud to cut budgetary support, and the United States also curtailed funds from the Millennium Challenge account.

Had the 2008 elections been an anomaly, or if the electoral system has been an isolated weakness within an otherwise robust democracy, there would have been less cause for concern. Instead, the 2008 fraud was soon followed by other indications of creeping authoritarianism. Most tellingly, in October 2009, the Constitutional Chamber of the Supreme Court of Justice suspended the application of the constitutional clauses limiting a president to two terms and prohibiting immediate reelection. The ruling came in response to an *amparo* appeal, here essentially an injunction, by President Daniel Ortega and over 100 Sandinista mayors, who claimed their constitutional rights to political participation were constrained by reelection limits imposed during the 1995 constitutional reform. The chamber convened without its Liberal members, calling up Sandinista substitutes to reach a quorum and deliver a partisan decision in record time.[54] No longer barred from running, President Ortega would still have to mount a winning campaign to claim victory at the polls in 2011. Nonetheless, his presumed candidacy cast the 2008 erosion of electoral credibility in a deeply troubling light.

The 2010 regional elections on the Atlantic Coast were a missed opportunity to restore some level of trust in election authorities. Donor countries had explicitly offered to restore budgetary support if the government held good elections. Instead, domestic observers found serious faults in the quality of four races in the South Atlantic Autonomous Region. The most experienced observer group on the Atlantic Coast, the Institute for Development and Democracy (Instituto para el Desarrollo y la Democracia, or IPADE), reported in no uncertain terms that there were critical problems in the handling of data in the regional-level counting centers such that "even if the elections were not fraudulent in terms of their general results, we cannot affirm they were transparent, just and equitable."[55] Whether this outcome reflected an inability or simple unwillingness to reform the gravely impaired electoral system, it meant that many Nicaraguans would enter the 2011 general elections with deep doubts about the validity of the exercise.

Among the main demands of domestic observers and opposition parties was that the Supreme Electoral Council be reappointed with new, nonpartisan members, reversing the Pact. International observers had expressed support for such a proposal in past reports. The fact that Eduardo Montealegre had placed second in the presidential race in 2006 seemed to imply that he represented the second-largest political force in the country and could therefore name three members from his party to the CSE once the terms of sitting magistrates ended. Some hoped this would rupture the Pact between Alemán and Ortega. It was the PLC, however, not the ALN, that had won the second-largest number of seats in the National Assembly in 2006, and that body was required to approve appointments. Meanwhile, Montealegre and the ALN had drifted apart, and he was courting Liberal support by treating with Alemán over the appointments process. The bargaining centered on who should serve on the CSE, not whether the main parties should control the appointments.

Indeed, politicking about the appointment of new magistrates bogged down other key appointments. This provided President Ortega with a ex post facto rationale for his decree in January 2010 that high-level appointees could retain their posts until the National Assembly acted to reappoint them. This use of a decree to sanction continuation in power smacked of authoritarianism, especially when Sandinista magistrates on the Supreme Court took advantage of their extended stay in office to threaten opposition deputies in the National Assembly with arrest when they tried to overturn the decree. This approach stood in stark contrast to the 1995 principled decision of CSE members to leave their posts vacant rather than usurp office while the legislature reached a decision on new appointments. It was hard to avoid the conclusion that the partisan penetration of the electoral system had compromised its integrity to a degree that threatened democracy.

Conclusion

The development of Nicaragua's electoral system in the three decades since the revolution has not been a linear progressive path toward democratic deepening. Overall, substantial progress toward democratic consolidation was made in the electoral realm—indeed, perhaps more so than in other areas—but the review of Nicaragua's electoral system in this chapter identified deficits and noted the steady increase since 1996 in partisan influence in administrative structures and processes. In the end, elections are a blunt instrument that can periodically provide a crude form of accountability, but they cannot substitute for more frequent forms of participation, the independence of branches of state, or the give-and-take that characterizes policy formation in a democracy.

In contrast to much other literature, this chapter has argued that the development of a democratic electoral system began not in 1990 but rather with the revolution that eliminated an entrenched authoritarian regime that used fraudulent elections to legitimate its rule. The Sandinistas promised to hold elections within five years and did so, making substantial concessions to opposition groups in constructing the rules for party formation and electoral competition. The 1984 elections were not broadly competitive due to the boycott by right-wing parties, and therefore their role in electoral development is often overlooked, but the laws and institutions developed in 1983–1984 were sufficiently democratic that with little revision, they framed the much-hailed "transition" elections of 1990. The 1990 elections not only ended the revolutionary experiment with socialism but also ended Nicaragua's civil war, serving as a substitute for the type of lengthy peace negotiations seen elsewhere in the region. Those elections also demonstrated that Nicaragua had a fully competitive electoral system that met international standards for a democracy.

The establishment of a democratic electoral regime by a revolutionary government seeking a transition to socialism was astonishing, forcing scholars and policy practitioners to rethink the potential for one-party-dominant and revolutionary political systems to evolve in a democratic direction. Furthermore, this chapter has explained how decisions in relation to the Political Parties Law and Electoral Law had far-reaching consequences for the political system, establishing parties rather than mass organizations as the basis for representation, adopting territorial rather than functional representation in the legislature, and shifting Nicaragua from a participatory to a liberal representative model of democracy. These laws helped sculpt the state, for in the process of their making the revolutionary government had to determine such elemental matters as whether there would be a parliamentary or presidential system. The 1987 constitution would largely codify the state structure, not invent it. The 1984 election process also shifted the basis of legitimacy from participation in the revolution to popular election, a form of procedural legitimacy that could stabilize democracy by allowing citizens to change governments without also inducing a change in regime.

Beginning in 1996, the electoral system became increasingly politicized. From an administrative standpoint many important tasks continued to be carried out well, and indeed some improvements were made via technological upgrades. Nicaragua continued to hold good elections on schedule, but they were not able to build public confidence in democratic institutions to the degree that the 1990 election had done. The decision to give parties control over selection of staff at lower levels of the electoral apparatus provoked the resignation of the CSE's long-standing president, whose politically neutral and inclusive leadership had generated confidence. The 1996 elections were marked by substantial disarray in some departments that eroded the Sandinistas' trust in the system. This caused them to join with

Liberal opponents in an electoral reform that was designed to increase governability by reducing the number of parties through draconian registration and finance requirements. The 2000 Pact accelerated the politicization process as the two largest parties excluded others from the CSE. Third parties and independent candidates in municipal and national elections found themselves sidelined, and their lack of access to the system contributed to a growing impression that the electoral system lacked transparency. The CSE's interpretation of the law was publicly questioned in various cases, and among parties not represented on the CSE, trust in the electoral apparatus eroded.

The 2006 elections alleviated some concern about the exclusionary nature of the electoral system, in part because Nicaragua's Supreme Court had overturned several of the most extreme elements of the law concerning party registration and also because no parties or candidates were excluded from running. Yet this shift reflected not a principled position but political expediency as the FSLN and PLC tried to encourage splinter groups that might reduce the other's chances at the polls. The CSE's makeup continued to exclude third parties, and at lower levels of administration the two largest parties enjoyed a privileged status. The CSE was once again paralyzed by partisan disputes that resulted in boycotts and an inability to form a quorum for decisionmaking. Some of the tasks it had carried out in earlier elections were now left to the parties, and the CSE also relied on parties to monitor one another in order to prevent fraud. The reasoning behind CSE decisions on electoral challenges was not made public, reducing confidence in their fairness and generating complaints about the CSE's lack of transparency.

Nicaragua remained a democratic polity. Nonetheless, amid scholarly debate about the limits of formal democracy, there was some suggestion that it would be helpful to qualify that label in order to express the shortcomings of the pacted regime. The list of potential qualifiers was long, but broadly speaking, the concern was that Nicaragua might be developing an illiberal democracy where the forms and procedures of democratic governance were followed, but politics were to an important degree determined by other means over which citizens exercised no control. The electoral system provided the best evidence to the contrary because it did give citizens a voice in political affairs and provided some measure of accountability. However, to the extent that FSLN-PLC collusion penetrated electoral affairs, it generated suspicions of potential bias in the system that hampered the fostering of public trust needed for its consolidation.

The foregoing analysis has further suggested that the intense focus on elections as the central mechanism for democratic politics constitutes unwarranted electoralism. As a consequence of the dramatic role elections played in forging the state in 1984 and bringing peace in 1990, Nicaraguans and the international community have tended toward overreliance on elections to generate democratic outcomes. As Terry Lynn Karl notes in an essay on electoralism, "If the mere holding of elections is taken as *the* central indicator of democratization, the political legitimacy conferred by such contests may be used to ratify existing concentrations of power rather than change them. In the process, not only might countries and people suffer, the very notion of democracy might be devalued."[56] Scholarly analysis should reflect the fact that elections occur in a political context, and the successful, regular completion of electoral exercises is not enough to consolidate a liberal, representative democracy.

It is worth bearing in mind that Nicaragua's transition to democracy was an inauguration, not a restoration of the sort undertaken in South America. Seen in that light, its electoral development was impressive. Democratization theorist Philippe Schmitter argued in 2007 that there has been "an ever-expanding set of criteria" for evaluating the quality of democracy and that diminutives like "low-intensity," "delegative," "illiberal," or "defective" tend to mask the substantial progress Latin America's new democracies have made.[57] Nicaragua's initial progress in establishing a democratic electoral system under a revolutionary government was unprecedented, and the faults that developed later in that system were remediable since they stemmed from a presumably transitory pact between the FSLN and PLC. However, underdevelopment was another, more enduring constraint.

Progress toward development of the state and democratic regimes is rarely smooth. The 1984 elections were not fully competitive but otherwise provided a strong start, and the 1990 elections were exemplary. The 1996 elections were marred by annulments and the 2001 elections by an exclusionary electoral law. The 2006 elections restored competition and proved that the FSLN could win back the presidency without provoking a political crisis. However, the municipal elections of 2008 brought multiple charges of fraud and deepened uncertainty about the autonomy of the electoral authorities and the electoral system itself. The 2009 partisan manipulation of the Supreme Court to permit Daniel Ortega to renew his candidacy for the presidency raised the perceived stakes of holding honest and transparent general elections in 2011, which some Nicaraguans came to view as a test of whether Nicaragua was becoming a competitive authoritarian regime.

This ebb and flow of electoral system performance was not unusual in a new democracy. Setbacks did not automatically preclude Nicaragua from eventually consolidating its democracy on liberal democratic terms. For the time being, however, and given the weaknesses in Nicaragua's democracy as a whole, the electoral system was heavily burdened with providing accountability, but its pacted structure sowed mistrust and impaired its ability to do so.

Notes

1. Nicaragua's early revolutionary political system is discussed in John Booth, *The End and the Beginning: The Nicaraguan Revolution* (Boulder, CO: Westview, 1985).

2. The various regional elections held on the Atlantic Coast are covered in Chapter 7 of this volume.

3. Terry Lynn Karl, "Electoralism," in the *International Encyclopedia of Elections,* edited by Richard Rose (Washington DC: CQ Press, 2000), 95–96.

4. The distinction between horizontal and vertical accountability was first made in Guillermo O'Donnell, "Illusions About Consolidation," *Journal of Democracy* 7, no. 2 (April 1996): 34–51. An expanded discussion may be found in Andreas Schedler, Larry Diamond, and Marc F. Plattner, eds., *The Self-Restraining State: Power and Accountability in New Democracies* (Boulder, CO: Lynne Rienner, 1999).

5. In the interests of full disclosure, it should be noted that a great deal of the information herein was gathered firsthand as a participant in and leader of election observation missions for the United Nations (in 1989–1990) and the Carter Center (1996, 2000, 2001, 2006). Other information on the 1984 elections and 1990 elections was obtained while conducting research for the author's doctoral dissertation. See Shelley A. McConnell, "From Bullets to Ballots: Nicaragua's Revolutionary Transition to Democracy," PhD diss., Stanford University, 1998.

6. February 1982 draft of the Political Parties Law as cited in David Close, *Nicaragua: Politics, Economics, and Society* (London: Pinter, 1988), 123–124.

7. Envío, "Update," *Envío* 21 (March 1983), www.envio.org.ni/.

8. Law of Political Parties, English translation, as published in Marlene Dixon, ed., *Nicaragua Under Siege* (San Francisco: Synthesis Publications, 1985), 174–182.

9. An influential article in policy circles was Jeane J. Kirkpatrick, "Dictatorship and Double Standards," *Commentary* (November 1979), in which she argued that right-wing authoritarian regimes sometimes became democratic, but left-wing ones did not.

10. Victor Hugo Tinoco, interview with the author, October 16, 1990.

11. Padre Álvaro Argüello, interview with the author, November 5, 1990.

12. Government of Nicaragua, Council of State, "Los sistemas electorales," paper presented at the Seminar on Electoral Material and Political Systems, Managua, January 1983.

13. The observations concerning the construction of consensus between the FSLN and opposition parties on the committee established to draft the Electoral Law are based on an examination of the committee minutes, loaned to the author by a member who requested anonymity.

14. Government of Nicaragua, Council of State, *Ley Electoral* (Electoral Law), 1984.

15. Government of Nicaragua, JGRN, *Decree 1472,* July 1984.

16. Government of Nicaragua, JGRN, *Decree 1496,* August 1984.

17. "Accords of the Meeting of the Registered Parties," English translation in the appendix to Jose Luís Coraggio, *Nicaragua: Revolution and Democracy* (Boston: Allen and Unwin, 1985), 100–104.

18. Registration, turnout, and null vote from Envío, "Nicaragua's 1984 Elections—A History Worth the Retelling," *Envío* 102 (January 1990), www.envio .org.ni/.

19. See the analysis in Daniel Wolf, "Falling Off the Bandwagon: Speculations on Electoral Politics and the Scope Available to Loyal Oppositions in Nicaragua," paper presented to the Latin American Studies Association, New Orleans, LA, March 18, 1988.

20. Election results from "Resultado de las elecciones para Presidente y Vicepresidente de la Republica y representantes ante la Asamblea Nacional, 4 de noviembre de 1984," *Monexico: Revista del Consejo de Estado* 8 (January 1985): 1–20. These data are also available online at www.envio.org.ni/. Note that the Supreme Electoral Council has only sporadically published the full election results in a hardcopy *memoria*. The CSE website (www.cse.gob.ni/) only gives results for elections since 2000, and they are given by department rather than for the country as a whole, with no indication of the resulting seat assignments for the legislature. For this reason, election results throughout this chapter are cited from reliable secondary sources.

21. The findings of election observers were relayed in unpublished reports. See Irish Inter-Party Parliamentary Delegation, "Report of the Irish Inter-Party Parliamentary Delegation on the Elections in Nicaragua," Dublin, November 21, 1984; "Declaration of the Delegation That at the Petition of a Group of Churches of Holland Attended the Elections Celebrated in Nicaragua November 4, 1984," Managua, 1984; Observation Mission of the Official Delegation of the European Parliament, "The Presidential and Legislative Elections That Took Place in Nicaragua November 4, 1984," Managua, 1984.

22. International Human Rights Law Group/Washington Office on Latin America, *A Political Opening in Nicaragua: Report on the Nicaraguan Elections of November 4, 1984* (Washington, DC:Washington Office on Latin America, December 11, 1984).

23. For a thorough discussion of how US policy affected the election, see William I. Robinson, *A Faustian Bargain: US Intervention in the Nicaraguan Elections and American Foreign Policy in the Post–Cold War Era* (Boulder, CO: Westview, 1992).

24. The nature of the Esquipulas Peace Process in comparison to others is discussed by Terry Lynn Karl, "Central America at the End of the Cold War," in *Beyond the Cold War: Conflict and Cooperation in the Third World,* edited by George W. Breslauer, Harry Kriesler, and Benjamin Wards (Berkeley: International and Area Studies, University of California, 1991), 222–251.

25. Gisela von Muhlenbrock, *Nicaragua: Amendments to the Electoral Law* (Washington, DC: Hispanic Law Division, Law Library, Library of Congress, April 1989).

26. Envío, "Political Agreement (Unofficial Translation)," *Envío* 98 (September 1989), www.envio.org.ni/articulo/2740.

27. The United Nations Observer Mission for the Verification of Elections in Nicaragua (ONUVEN) issued a series of five reports. The studies mentioned are in

the third report, UN General Assembly, *The Situation in Central America: Threats to International Peace and Security and Peace Initiatives,* A/44/917, January 31, 1990.

28. There was, of course, widespread speculation that the CIA had funded Chamorro, although the US Congress had promised President Carter no covert funding would flow. See Carter Center, *Observing Nicaragua's Elections, 1989–90* (Atlanta: Carter Center, 1990); available online at www.cartercenter.org/. For a critical perspective, see Holly Sklar, "Washington's Trying to Buy Nicaragua's Elections Again," *Z Magazine* 12 (December 1989): 49–64.

29. The name refers to a folkloric play in which Nicaraguan peasants fool the Spanish conquistadores as they were thought to have fooled the pollsters. The drama is one of the best-known cultural references in Nicaraguan society.

30. William A. Barnes, "Rereading the Nicaraguan Pre-Election Polls in the Light of the Election Results," in *The 1990 Elections in Nicaragua and Their Aftermath,* edited by Vanessa Castro and Gary Prevost (Lanham, MD: Rowman and Littlefield, 1992), 41–99. Poll results from 1988 to 1990 are given in appendix 4 of the volume. More in-depth polling analysis for the period 1990–2001 may be found in Leslie E. Anderson and Lawrence C. Dodd, *Learning Democracy: Citizen Engagement and Electoral Choice in Nicaragua, 1990–2001* (Chicago: University of Chicago Press, 2005).

31. An excellent analysis of the military conscription law and other factors leading to the UNO victory is Paul Oquist, "The Sociopolitical Dynamics of the 1990 Elections," in *The 1990 Elections in Nicaragua and Their Aftermath,* edited by Vanessa Castro and Gary Prevost (Lanham, MD: Rowman and Littlefield, 1992), 1–40.

32. For an insider's account of former president Carter's role, see Robert A. Pastor, "Nicaragua's Choice: The Making of a Free Election," *Journal of Democracy* 1, no. 3 (Summer 1990), 13–25.

33. Results for the 1990 elections were reported in Envío, "Election Data," *Envío* 104 (March 1990), www.envio.org.ni/.

34. For a full discussion of the postelection pacification, see Rose J. Spalding, "From Low-Intensity War to Low-Intensity Peace: The Nicaraguan Peace Process," in *Comparative Peace Processes in Latin America,* edited by Cynthia J. Arnson (Stanford: Stanford University Press and Woodrow Wilson Center Press, 1999), 31–64.

35. The 1995 constitutional reform is covered in more detail in David Close, *The Chamorro Years* (Boulder, CO: Lynne Rienner, 1999).

36. The complete results for the 1996 presidential elections are available on Georgetown University's Political Database of the Americas, pdba.georgetown.edu/Elecdata/Nica/nica96.html. Votes cast for the legislative races can be found at pdba.georgetown.edu/Elecdata/Nica/nicax96.html. Among smaller parties competing for legislative posts in the 1996 elections, 4 seats went to the Nicaraguan Party of the Christian Path (Camino Christiano Nicaragüense, or CCN), 3 to the Nicaraguan Conservative Party (Partido Conservador Nicaragüense, or PCN), 2 to the National Project (Proyecto Nacional, or PRONAL), and 1 seat each to the MRS, Unity Alliance (Alianza Unidad, or AU), Independent Liberal Party (PLI), National Conservative Action (Accion Nacional Conservadora, or ANC), and UNO-96 Alliance (Alianza UNO-96), as reported by Envío, "How Nicaraguans Voted," *Envío* 185 (December 1996), www.envio.org.ni/.

37. Results for the 1996 municipal elections from Envío, "How Nicaraguans Voted," *Envío* 185 (December 1996), www.envio.org.ni/articulo/1990 (accessed May 15, 2007).

38. Carter Center, *Observing the 1996 Nicaragua Elections* (Atlanta: Carter Center, 1997).

39. For a detailed description of the 2000 Pact and Electoral Law reform, see David Dye, Jack Spence, and George Vickers, *Patchwork Democracy: Nicaraguan Politics Ten Years After the Fall* (Cambridge, MA: Hemisphere Initiatives, 2000).

40. The 2000 reform of the Electoral Law was published in Government of Nicaragua, Supreme Electoral Council, *Ley Electoral.* Managua: *La Gaceta Diario Official,* January 24, 2000, 361–388. www.cse.gob.ni/.

41. Daniel Zovatto and Tatiana Benavides, "Analisis de la reforma electoral nicaraguense promulgada el 24 de enero 2000," mimeo, n.d., cited in David Dye, Jack Spence, and George Vickers, *Patchwork Democracy: Nicaraguan Politics Ten Years After the Fall* (Cambridge, MA: Hemisphere Initiatives, 2000), 8.

42. The complaint in case 12.388, *YATAMA v. Nicaragua,* was presented to the Inter-American Court of Human Rights on June 16, 2003. The merits of the case and final decision are reported in Inter-American Court of Human Rights, *Case of Yatama v. Nicaragua, Judgment of June 23, 2005 (Preliminary Objections, Merits, Reparations and Costs),* www.corteidh.or.cr/.

43. 2004 municipal election results from William Grigsby, "2004 Municipal Elections: FSLN-Convergence Victory in Numbers," *Envío,* 230 (November 2004), www.envio.org.ni/articulo/2672 (accessed October 17, 2007).

44. United Nations Development Programme, *Democracy in Latin America: Towards a Citizens' Democracy* (Buenos Aires: Aguilar, Altea, Taurus, Alfaguara, 2005), 82.

45. The details of these periods in which the CSE could not operate for lack of a quorum are given in the Carter Center's reports, *Observing the 2001 Nicaragua Elections* (Atlanta: Carter Center, March 2002) and *Observing the 2006 Nicaragua Elections* (Atlanta: Carter Center, May 2007).

46. The evolution of the campaign is covered in Carter Center, *Observing the 2001 Nicaragua Elections.*

47. Results for the 2001 elections are reported in José Luis Rocha, "PLC: The Resounding Winner," *Envío* 244 (November 2001), www.envio.org.ni/.

48. For an assessment of Nicaragua's transition to democracy during this period and how it was constrained by the pact, see David Dye, *Democracy Adrift: Caudillo Politics in Nicaragua* (Managua: Prodeni, November 2004).

49. In 2004 Nicaragua was the second-poorest country in Latin America after Haiti. Its per capita GDP in 2005 was US$3,674. See the United Nations Development Programme, *Human Development Report* 2007, hdrstats.undp.org/.

50. The details of the constitutional crisis are reviewed in Shelley A. McConnell, "Can the Inter-American Democratic Charter Work? Nicaragua's 2004–05 Constitutional Crisis," paper presented at the International Studies Association forty-eighth annual convention, March 2007, Chicago, Illinois.

51. For a lengthier discussion of the dynamics of the 2006 election, including the influence of foreign actors, see Shelley A. McConnell, "Nicaragua's Turning Point," *Current History* 106, no. 697 (February 2007): 83–88.

52. The 2006 election results are reported in Georgetown University's Political Database of the Americas, pdba.georgetown.edu/Elecdata/Nica/nicax06.html (parliamentary) and pdba.georgetown.edu/Elecdata/Nica/nica06.html (presidential).

53. One of these groups, the Institute for Development and Democracy (Instituto para el Desarrollo y la Democracia, or IPADE), issued a report. See, IPADE, *Elecciones Municipales 2008/2009 Informe Final,* www.ipade.org.ni/.

54. For a comparative perspective on the 2009 constitutional ruling that struck down limits on presidential reelection, see Shelley A. McConnell, "The Return of *Continuismo?" Current History* 109, no. 724 (February 2010): 74–79. Although the two-term limit and no immediate reelection prohibition cannot be applied to Ortega or the mayors involved in the *amparo,* it may still be applied to others in the future because the ruling is not equivalent to a constitutional reform.

55. IPADE, "IPADE brinda informe final de Observación de las Elecciones Regionales 2010," March, 18, 2010, www.ipade.org.ni/.

56. Terry Lynn Karl, "Electoralism," in *International Encyclopedia of Elections,* edited by Richard Rose (Washington, DC: CQ Press, 2000), 96.

57. See Philippe C. Schmitter, remarks to the forum "Democratic Deficits: Addressing Challenges to Sustainability and Consolidation Around the World," September 18, 2007, as reported in *Noticias* (Washington, DC: Woodrow Wilson International Center for Scholars, Spring 2008), 26.

7

Regional Autonomy on the Caribbean Coast

Miguel González and Dorlores Figueroa

IN THIS CHAPTER WE ARGUE THAT THE FOUNDING OF THE AU-
tonomous regime on the Atlantic Coast and the passing of legislation by the
Nicaraguan state to recognize specific group rights (notably land claims and
collective control over natural resources), as well as territorial self-governance
(in the form of regionally based, multiethnic governments), have contributed
to the attainment of peace and reconciliation both among the indigenous
and ethnic communities and in the broader national society. Nonetheless, the
effective implementation of autonomy rights under the post-1990 national
neoliberal regime remains an outstanding and challenging issue.

Since 1990, internal conflicts within political organizations and the subordination of regional authorities to successive national governments have
limited the exercise of regionally based self-government, leaving the local
indigenous and Afro-Caribbean communities with a restricted say in the autonomy process. At the same time, legally recognized group rights to land
and access to and control over natural resources have been hindered by national authorities, which used their power over the regional governments to
impede the effective use of those rights. That said, autonomy (which is not
federalism but a status analogous to that of an autonomous community in
Spain) still remains the basis for the historic aspirations of indigenous and
Afro-Caribbean communities and their existing practices of governance.
Those aspirations and practices inform the content of democracy in the autonomous regions.

The alliance of the Sandinista National Liberation Front (Frente Sandinista de Liberación Nacional, or FSLN) with the Organization of the Peoples of Mother Earth (Yapti Tasba Masraka Nanih Aslatakanka, or YATAMA)
in 2002 was animated by short-term political goals to exclude electoral competitors on the coast as well as the two groups' shared understanding of factors

that had hampered the implementation of autonomy rights. However, how the alliance will work in practice and what it will accomplish remain unclear. Indeed, some of the terms on which YATAMA and the FSLN have come to agree—the reform of the Electoral Law and the Autonomy Statute—will necessarily require National Assembly approval. On other, more immediately practical matters (notably on land demarcation, i.e., surveying and titling), substantive support from the communities in the Caribbean Coast will be needed. For YATAMA and the FSLN, as well as for other social and political actors, there is a pressing need to move ahead with implementation, which will require intercultural dialogue and consensus building beyond the realm of electoral politics.

Nicaragua and Its Caribbean Coast: Divergent Historical Trajectories

After winning independence from Spain in 1821, the Nicaraguan state was faced with two divergent and culturally distinctive societies on each of its coasts. Through the process of Spanish colonization, the Pacific region emerged bearing the imprint of Catholicism and was populated overwhelmingly by Spanish-speaking people, yielding a predominantly mestizo society. Although indigenous communities continued to exist in various parts of Pacific, central, and northern Nicaragua and were able to maintain important cultural and political traits, their very continuation after independence as a distinct society was eclipsed by Nicaraguan nationalism.[1]

On the Caribbean Coast, the colonial experience of its native population could not be more different. Inhabited by indigenous peoples who would later be joined by immigrants of African descent, the Caribbean Coast developed into a multiethnic society. The early British presence (in the form of settlers in the mid-seventeenth century and as a protectorate in the nineteenth century) not only evolved various forms of collaboration with the indigenous population, including trade, but was also seen as benevolent by the local communities.

While the Nicaraguan state was able to suppress cultural identities that challenged mestizo nationalism and the idea of a culturally homogeneous country expanded during the nineteenth century in the Pacific region, the Caribbean society flourished with assertive indigenous and Afro-descendant cultures. This assertiveness was based on their ability to maintain a certain level of control over local political institutions, community land, and natural resources while coexisting with the presence of the British and later on with the US enclave economy.[2] In 1849 Moravian missionaries (of German origin first, who were then followed by Moravian missionaries from the United States) initiated a long-lasting evangelization program that would also affect the cultural identities of the local population.

In 1860 the British recognized Nicaragua's sovereignty claims and terminated its protectorate. However, a mechanism was established to protect the coastal population from potential encroachment by the Nicaraguan state: the Miskitu Reserve, which provided a limited form of self-rule. The reserve's regulations, which created deliberative and executive bodies, envisioned a mechanism through which the local population could consider its full integration to the Nicaraguan state. The reserve lasted until February 1894, when the Nicaraguan Liberal government of José Santos Zelaya deposed the reserve's chief and disbanded its political institutions. A few months later, Nicaraguan political representatives brought together indigenous chiefs, who opted for their "incorporation" as "citizens" of the Nicaraguan state. In local indigenous narratives and social memory, the Miskito Reserve is viewed as the "first Autonomy experience" in the history of the Caribbean Coast and as an indication of its peoples' drive for self-determination.

As astutely noted by Baron Pineda, the society that emerged from this interaction with the English-speaking world was perceived as a "suspect internal other" from the perspective of Nicaraguan nationalism. In sharp contrast to this negative perception, *Costeño* (the multiethnic society of the coast) society saw itself as "cosmopolitans whose continuing ties to the English-speaking world place them above Pacific Nicaraguans."[3]

The result of this national composite was considerable cultural, historical, and political divergence between Caribbean and Pacific societies. The intense conflict that surfaced between the Nicaraguan state and the indigenous and Afro-Caribbean communities on the coast early in the 1980s cannot be explained without taking into account the cultural and political tensions underlying the historical relationship between the Pacific and coast societies.

The Caribbean Coast's particular history within the context of Nicaragua gave birth to a diverse, multicultural society. Data from 1981 showed 280,000 people on the Caribbean Coast (10 percent of the national population at that time), of which 24 percent were Miskitus, 1.7 percent Sumu (later called Sumu-Mayangnas), 0.2 percent Ramas, 8.9 percent Creoles, 0.5 percent Garifunas, and 65 percent mestizos.[4] Miskitu and Sumu (with three subsets, Tuahka, Panamaka, and Ulwa) were able to maintain their distinctive indigenous languages over time, but the Rama language has been affected by cultural assimilation and a dwindling population of native speakers.[5] Creoles and Garifunas are English-speaking, Afro-descendant communities. Mestizos speak Spanish.

Now three decades after the 1981 census cited above, migration (internal as well as external), population displacements, and above all, the increase of mestizo numbers, boosted by migrants from the western parts of Nicaragua, have significantly altered the composition of the Caribbean Coast's population. According to recent estimates, the population of the Caribbean Coast has 631,795 individuals—about 12 percent of the total of the country. The regional demographic make-up was as follows: 72.5 percent mestizo; 18.04 percent Miskitu; 6.22 percent Creole; 2.45 percent Sumu-Mayangna; 0.43 percent Garifuna; and 0.32 percent Rama. Although the literature on the region's population has often portrayed ethnic groups and their identities as neatly distinctive configurations, recent studies have noted more interethnic complexity and social interaction, particularly among indigenous and Afro-descendant peoples.[6]

The History of Autonomy and the Coast Society

During the mid-1970s, an intense process of political and social organizing along ethnic lines became apparent in the coast. Catholic missionaries and the Moravian Church were instrumental in this process of grassroots organizing and ethno-political activism that made land, agricultural development, and education the central demands among indigenous communities. In this context, two organizations were formed: the Agricultural Association of the Coco River (Asociaciones de Club Agrícolas del Rio Coco, or ACARIC) in 1967, and the Alliance Promoting Miskitu and Sumu Development (Alianza para el Progreso de Miskitus y Sumus, or ALPROMISU) in 1973. ACARIC was more focused on socioeconomic demands and geographically based in Rio Coco (on the Honduras border), whereas ALPROMISU assumed a broader agenda that included political and cultural rights. In the Creole communities, an important process of grassroots organizing took place during the same period. The Southern Indigenous and Creole Committee (SICC, founded in 1977) demanded educational opportunities, socioeconomic development, and political participation.[7]

In Pacific Nicaragua, the Somoza regime was facing increasing opposition from popular sectors (students, teachers, workers, and segments of the middle class) that had become alienated by the dictatorship's repression and violence. By the mid-1970s, it was plain that a civil war was likely to engulf the entire country. Although the tensions were known and developments closely followed by the coastal society, the war was perceived as a conflict among "Pacific mestizos" and therefore mostly irrelevant to the Caribbean Coast.

The FSLN triumph on July 19, 1979, almost went unnoticed on the Caribbean Coast. World media images of Nicaraguans celebrating the overthrow of Somoza did not convey the initial indifference of the coastal people toward the emergence of revolutionary Nicaragua. The FSLN and its leadership, for their part, did not have a sophisticated understanding of the history and culture of the coastal society.[8] References to the coast in the FSLN programmatic documents ranged from nonexistent at worst to folkloric at best. It was not surprising, therefore, that considerable challenges lay ahead for the new revolutionary government in its relationships with the Caribbean Coast. National unity and mutual understanding were being promoted between two societies, which, for the most part, had diverging historical trajectories. As things developed, the FSLN's early policies generated optimism and collaboration among indigenous and Afro-descendent communities in the early 1980s. Miskitu, Sumu, Rama, and Sandinistas United (Miskitus, Sumus, Ramas y Sandinistas Unidos, or MISURASATA), the new organization created in November 1979 to build the relationship between indigenous peoples and the Sandinista government, was rapidly able to mobilize support from local communities. However, unwise government decisions combined with a radical response from indigenous organizations and their leadership to the FSLN's missteps to evolve into mounting tensions and later into military confrontation. This confrontation deepened in the context of the US opposition to the Sandinista government. Indigenous opposition, formulated in terms of ethnic discourse, was hastily interpreted by the Sandinista administration as a "counterrevolutionary" and "separatist" movement.

From Initial Optimism to Open Conflict, 1981–1984

The literature on the origins and consequences of the conflict that unfolded during the early 1980s in eastern Nicaragua is abundant. We review here some of the events that transformed the coastal population's initial optimism and acquiescence to the Sandinista Revolution's plans, raised political tensions, and later precipitated far-reaching military confrontation.

In the period between 1979 and 1981, the relationship between the FSLN and MISURASATA grew increasingly conflictive. Initially, the Sandinistas sought to gain political support for the revolutionary government among the indigenous communities. However, the Sandinistas tried to downplay the identity-based organizations of those communities and instead proposed that MISURASATA be replaced by the national, class-based, mass organizations. The FSLN, however, finally recognized MISURASATA as the legitimate representatives of coastal indigenous communities. In

1980, a national literacy campaign (in Spanish) was launched by the Sandinistas. A few months later the literacy campaign *en lenguas* (in indigenous and Creole languages, after the Spanish-only campaign was challenged by Miskitu and Creole representatives) was completed successfully, though it was overshadowed by increasing tensions. Various authors suggest that the literacy campaign was particularly instrumental in organizing indigenous and Afro-descendant identity.[9]

In 1981 MISURASATA presented its vision of landed property rights for the Caribbean Coast to the FSLN government. This proposal—even though it is not clear that it was officially submitted to the Sandinistas—indicated that one-third of the lands of the coast legitimately belonged to the indigenous communities and should therefore be legally recognized as such by the Nicaraguan state. In the context of increasing US opposition to the Sandinista Revolution, MISURASATAS's proposal was considered separatist and counterrevolutionary by the Sandinistas, who responded with repression of the organization's leadership. From here on, the context became politically charged, and tensions rose in coastal communities. A series of particularly tragic incidents between Sandinista soldiers and young indigenous activists seems to have sparked military confrontation.[10]

In 1981 various communities fled to Honduras and Costa Rica, seeking protection from the escalating conflict. Indigenous leaders, after being released from prison by the Sandinistas, decided to join their communities and took up arms to fight the FSLN government. From 1981 through 1984, military confrontation prevailed, which would have a long-lasting socioeconomic impact on the society of the Caribbean Coast.

By 1984 the Sandinistas, under great political and military pressure, acknowledged that a different approach should be pursued in the conflict on the coast. After introducing a distinction between contras, who were fighting to overthrow the revolutionary government, and indigenous insurgents who sought their historic rights, the Sandinistas began peace negotiations with indigenous leaders while simultaneously launching an on-the-ground dialogue with field commanders of the indigenous guerrillas. A national commission "for autonomy," created in December 1984, and two analogous regional commissions received the mandate to oversee local consultations for peace and autonomy. At the same time, community leaders, women, churches, and civic authorities became involved in the peace efforts at the local level, seeking to put an end to military confrontation.

From 1984 through 1987, major changes took place on the coast. Broader consultations for autonomy began and produced a draft for an autonomy arrangement between the Nicaraguan state and the Caribbean Coast, while peace negotiations on the ground produced impressive results. However, negotiations between the FSLN government and YATAMA leadership in exile were not successful. There were important differences between the FSLN and YATAMA on the subjects of autonomy and indigenous self-determination. YATAMA held the position that indigenous peoples constituted "nations," whereas the FSLN maintained they were "groups." According to YATAMA, indigenous autonomy should be granted over the traditional territory of *Yapti Tasba* (mother earth), where internal self-determination would be exercised for the benefit of the indigenous nations. The FSLN avoided recognizing the specific collective rights (autonomy and territorial self-determination) of one ethnic group, the Miskitu. Instead, it proposed a multiethnic scheme in which both collective and individual rights would be exercised.

By 1986 armed conflict was almost over, and displaced communities in Honduras and Costa Rica began to return to their homelands on the coast. Indigenous leaders, though not totally persuaded by the Sandinista autonomy proposal, conceded that it might in the future serve as a legal platform from which to advance their collective rights and vision of indigenous autonomy.

Autonomy, 1987

The autonomous regime of the Caribbean Coast of Nicaragua was inaugurated in 1987 with the approval of the Autonomy Statute (Ley 28) by the National Assembly. The passage of the law followed broad public consultations on the coast and put an end to a five-year-long war between the indigenous armed resistance (mostly Miskitu) and the Sandinista government. In 1990, when the Autonomy Statute was first implemented, two regional councils (one for the north and one for the south) and their administrations were founded. The law also granted equal political representation in regional councils to the different ethnic groups that make up the region's population. These councils presided over nearly half of Nicaragua's national territory. The Sandinistas anticipated that the creation of the autonomous regime would bring about peace and reconciliation among the multiethnic population. Observers sympathetic to the FSLN expected that autonomy would eventually create the foundations for new relationships between the historically distant and dominant Nicaraguan state and the indigenous and other ethnic communities of the Atlantic Coast.[11]

From the perspective of the Sandinista government at that time, three elements formed the basis of the autonomous regime: (1) the recognition of universal citizenship rights (civil, political, and social), as well as group-specific rights for the ethnic communities; (2) the simultaneous recognition of the multiethnic and multicultural character of Nicaraguan society and of national unity as the condition to enable the effective implementation of universal citizenship and group rights; and finally, (3) the promotion of new social values, such as fraternity, solidarity, equality, and respect among the ethnic communities and between them and the rest of the nation in order to create an inclusive democratic society.[12] From the perspective of the indigenous resistance—which was disarmed in 1989 through negotiations with the Sandinistas—the autonomy framework created the essential, minimal conditions necessary to permit abandoning armed conflict and moving to political struggle in a new democratic setting.[13] However, in the eyes of the indigenous resistance, political accommodation within the Nicaraguan state would eventually demand substantial changes to secure indigenous self-determination in new legislation and daily political practice.[14]

Autonomy in the Making:
From Recognition to Implementation

The Autonomy Statute recognized important rights and granted administrative powers to regional governing bodies. Besides creating two regional councils and granting multiethnic representation, the Autonomy Statute assured recognition of communal rights to lands that "traditionally [had] belonged" to indigenous communities and the "use, enjoy[ment], and benefit from the communal waters, forests, and lands, within the plans for national development." According to the statute, community lands "are indissoluble; they cannot be donated, sold, leased, nor taxed, and they are eternal." This recognition was crucial, considering that communal land was a key demand of the indigenous uprising of 1981. However, Ley 28 did not mention any specific regulation through which the recognition of communal titles would be implemented. Ley 28 also recognized communities' rights to "freely develop their social and productive organizations—as well as their own authorities—in accordance with their own values." Although the bill did not clarify the association between land rights and indigenous territorial self-determination, it did open the possibility of further developing this provision.

Administratively, the autonomy law formally granted regional institutions important authority over local social and economic development. The regional councils are empowered

1. "to participate in the formulation, planning, implementation, and supervision of the economic, social, and cultural policies and programs which affect or concern the Region;"

2. "to resolve boundary disputes between the different communities of the respective Region;"
3. "to draft the regional budget" as well as the regional tax plan;
4. "to ensure the correct use of the special fund for the development and social progress of the Region;"
5. "to resolve boundary disputes between the different communities of the respective Region;" and
6. "to elect the Regional Coordinator from among its members and to find a replacement if and when necessary."

Even though the Autonomy Statute brought a novel legal regime and meant a key shift in the historical relationships between the coast and the Nicaraguan state, its language on fundamental matters (such as property rights and natural resource management) remained ambiguous. On this issue of how the coast would benefit from the exploitation of natural resources, the provisions were too general and made no reference to concrete mechanisms by which revenues derived from concessions granted by the state over natural resources in the Caribbean Coast would be allocated to the regional governing bodies. Moreover, the final decision on disputes over administrative matters between regional governments and national authorities remained largely in Managua's hands.

When the Autonomy Statute was approved, it required enabling legislation to be implemented. However, in the period between 1987 and 1990, the efforts made on both sides (the coast and the national government) to draft the regulations reached no accord. Among the political actors of the Caribbean Coast—convened through the regional commissions on autonomy—the viewpoint that enabling legislation should be prepared by the proposed regional councils to be elected in 1990 seemed to have gained currency.

For the FSLN government, autonomy implementation became less pressing (the war was over), and other national issues (such as the peace talks with the contras) eclipsed the coast's autonomy agenda. In addition, an unanticipated factor that further delayed the implementation of autonomy rights was Hurricane Joan, which devastated the southern region in October 1988 and necessitated significant emergency assistance and economic reconstruction.[15]

In sum, in 1990 autonomy was still a piece of innovative (though not yet implemented) legislation whose practical effects in a new national political and economic context remained to be seen. Although the Autonomy Statute let peace be achieved, meaningful advancement of the rights of the indigenous and Afro-descendant inhabitants of the coast had yet to be produced. The emerging context—both regional and national—in 1990 was one of uncertainty for the Caribbean Coastal society. There was a combination of hope and the traditional distrust that *Costeños* had always held toward Nicaraguan governments.

Therefore, it was clear that the successful implementation of autonomy rights depended on three factors. First, it would be necessary to achieve cooperation with and political commitment from the national authorities to develop the specific mechanism through which the provisions granted by the statute would be given effect. Further, a democratic consensus among the coast's social and political actors would have to emerge in order to build a common platform to make autonomy a reality. Lastly, the new regional governing bodies would need to develop the institutional capacity required to put autonomy rights into practice.

Achievements of the Autonomous Regime

In retrospect, several important achievements of the autonomous regime with regard to peace and reconciliation can be identified. First and foremost, the recognition of autonomy constitutes an official acknowledgment that Nicaragua is not composed of just one culture and one national identity; on the contrary, it is a multiethnic society. This principle has laid the basis for building mutual trust and understanding among ethnic communities, as well as between them and the rest of Nicaraguan society. Concretely, it has meant that there is an increasing consensus among indigenous peoples and the Caribbean Coast's ethnic communities that autonomy rights can be pursued through the 1987 Autonomy Statute. This has been confirmed by the Institute for Development and Democracy (IPADE), a Nicaraguan nongovernmental organization (NGO) dedicated to promoting political rights, which has conducted a series of surveys in the region since 1997. The results are summarized in Table 7.1.

Second, regional governments have confronted a wide-ranging neoliberal economic program at the national level, as well as internal political conflicts within the regional councils, which together have undermined the implementation of autonomy rights and limited the creation of institutional capacity within the regional councils and their administrations.

Since 1990, national governments and the political elite have tried in different ways to undermine autonomy rights. The following is just a partial list of how this attempt has unfolded. To begin, national governments have granted natural resource concessions to transnational corporations without consulting regional or community authorities. Further, national public policies have been applied in the autonomous regions with little or no coordination between Managua and the regional authorities. In addition,

Table 7.1 Perceptions of the Regional Governments' Performance and of the Autonomous Regime (percentage)

	1997 Agree	2001 Agree	2004 Agree
The problem with the autonomous regime is that regional authorities have not performed well.	72.6	78.1	70
Autonomy is the best solution to solve the problems of the Atlantic Coast.	75	75	59
The main problem of the autonomous regime is that the national government does not have the will to support it.	69	76.9	66
Autonomy contributes to democracy in Nicaragua.	n.a.	n.a.	72.7

Source: Adapted from IPADE, *Encuesta cultura política y actitudes hacias las elecciones y el régimen de autonomía en las regiones autónomas* (Managua: IPADE, 1997), 42.

Managua has created intermediate structures that have destabilized governance procedures and structures at the regional and local levels. Though it is perhaps unsurprising given Nicaragua's perilous fiscal state since 1990, the national authorities have limited public spending—especially in the fields of education, health, and infrastructure—that is needed to compensate for the region's historic marginalization. Finally, successive governments have delayed the process of demarcation and titling of community lands.

As pointed out by Andrés Pérez Baltodano, the Nicaraguan ruling elite tried to undermine autonomy rights during the 1990s whenever possible. However, these elites have not developed a consensus about what national strategy should be pursued in the matter of the Caribbean Coast. In practice, then, the resulting state response to autonomy has been enduring opposition to the emergence of a unifying force in the autonomous regions that could potentially challenge Managua's role as the "guarantor of political order."[16]

Nevertheless, in the midst of these constraints, the National Assembly passed constitutional amendments (approved in 1995) and relevant enabling legislation (in 2002 and 2003) in response to pressures from below. That pressure, in turn, was exerted through consensus building among social and political organizations at the national and regional levels, partly shielding the autonomous regime from the neoliberal economic program.

In this process, four important pieces of legislation were approved and are being implemented:

1. the indigenous land demarcation law of 2003 (Ley 445);
2. the Autonomy Statute's enabling legislation (*reglamentación*): the operational administrative procedures of the Autonomy Statute;

3. the law granting a veto to regional autonomous councils over concessions of natural resources granted by the national government on the Caribbean Coast. Thus regional authorities formally have the final say over the granting of rights to exploit natural resources in the autonomous regions; and

4. the law decentralizing control over education and designing the new system to accommodate the sociocultural characteristics and administrative arrangements of the autonomous regions.

It is important to note that this legislation and other related public policy initiatives obtained important levels of support from social organizations across the entire political spectrum of the autonomous regions. Eventually, however, this consensus produced recurrent conflict within the regional councils. In these governing bodies, local as well as national political organizations have engaged in periodic clashes over state funding and legal controversies about appointments within the regional governing structures. These conflicts, in turn, have often impeded the proper functioning of the autonomous regional councils.

Finally, it should also be mentioned that, in the context of the autonomous regime, two community-based, regional universities were created: the University of the Autonomous Regions of the Caribbean Coast of Nicaragua (URACCAN) and the Bluefields Indian and Caribbean University (BICU). These institutions are developing important educational outreach programs that respond to the needs of local communities. The main goal of these universities is to strengthen the autonomous regime, and they have established training programs to assist indigenous, mestizo, and Afro-Caribbean communities with the management of their natural resources and have designed and implemented local economic development projects.[17] These universities, which employ decentralized forms of administration, have had to cope with the state's shrinking budget for higher education during the 1990s. They also had to face strong opposition from conservative national institutions that still uphold a centralized conception of public universities.

The FSLN and YATAMA: Old Enemies, New Allies

The FSLN and YATAMA organizations in the North Atlantic Autonomous Region (Región Autónoma Atlántico Norte, or RAAN) acquiesced to a temporary alliance in 1994. This alliance was short-lived, and pragmatic concerns overshadowed the long-term objectives of both organizations.[18] Again in 2002, when the regional councils were beginning a fourth term, the two parties agreed to a new alliance, this time seeking to address both their short-term objectives and longer-term, strategic goals. After achieving agreement on five basic components in 2002, the FSLN and YATAMA were able to maintain and even expand a set of political accords around the autonomy regime up to 2006.

One of their short-term objectives in 2002 was to exclude the PLC from power. As a result, the FSLN and YATAMA have shared leading public posts in the regional governing bodies. When first agreed upon, the platform envisioned by the FSLN and YATAMA included the following elements:

1. establishing a regional planning commission and the special fund foreseen in the autonomy statute;
2. using legal advocacy to advance autonomy rights, in particular over communal land demarcation and the enabling legislation of Law 28; and
3. promoting effective decentralization in favor of the autonomous regions.

When the regional councils' terms were over in early 2006, only legal advocacy of autonomy rights had been promoted by both parties. The approval of both Law 445 and the enabling legislation of the Autonomy Statute was the concrete result. Even though other aspects of the accords were not met, YATAMA and the FSLN were able to maintain this alliance through the whole term without a significant crisis.

In 2006, in the context of the fifth regional elections, the FSLN and YATAMA decided to cement their political agreement in what was publicly announced as an "Alliance for Peace and Autonomy."

The 2006 accords stressed four points. One was that the bipartisan control of the regional governing institutions in the north should continue. The second objective was to reinvigorate the land demarcation (and titling) process that had stagnated since June 2005 because of political differences between the presidents of the regional councils. Further, the parties agreed to implement the Inter-American Court of Human Rights's judgment on YATAMA and the Awas Tingni community.[19] Finally, the FSLN and YATAMA committed themselves to amending the Autonomy Statute and the Electoral Law. A few months later, the Alliance for Peace and Autonomy was made public, and in the context of the national elections the FSLN opened its electoral lists to YATAMA's candidates for the National Assembly and the Central American Parliament. As a result, YATAMA's representatives were elected for the first time to these two important bodies. Combined, the 2006 regional electoral results favored YATAMA and the FSLN in the RAAN, while the PLC maintained its stronghold in the South Atlantic Autonomous Region (Región Autónoma Atlántico Sur, or RAAS) (see Table 7.2).

Table 7.2 2006 Regional Elections Results in Both Autonomous Regions of the Caribbean Coast

Region	PLC	FSLN	CCN	PAMUC	YATAMA	ALN-PC	APRE	MRS
RAAN	23,783	19,212	830	1,316	12,330	3,414	1,268	1,441
RAAS	17,577	7,690	685	0	3,561	5,643	229	1,373
Total	41,360	26,902	1,515	1,316	15,891	9,057	1,497	2,814

Source: Government of Nicaragua, Supreme Electoral Council, *Electoral Results, 2006,* www.cse.gob .ni/intro.php.

Notes: Parties: PLC, Partido Liberal Constitucionalista, or Constitutionalist Liberal Party; FSLN, Frente Sandinista de Liberación Nacional, or Sandinista National Liberation Front; CCN, Camino Christiano Nicaragüense, or Nicaraguan Party of the Christian Path; PAMUC, Partido Movimiento de Unidad Costeña, or Party Movement for Coastal Unity; YATAMA, Yapti Tasba Masraka Nanih Aslatakanka, or Organization of the Peoples of Mother Earth, Organización de los Pueblos de la Madre Tierra; ALN-PC, Alianza Liberal Nicaragüense–Partido Conservador, or National Liberal Alliance–Conservative Party; APRE, Alianza por la República, or Alliance for the Republic; MRS, Movimiento Renovador Sandinista, or Sandinista Renewal Movement.

The alliance between the FSLN and YATAMA should be interpreted, first, as their mutual recognition of each other as legitimate and contending political organizations, which acknowledges their capacity to exclude other local and national political organizations, such as the PLC, as electoral competitors. It is also apparent that the organizations have similar opinions of the autonomy regime. Their regional electoral gains (more obvious in the north) and the Alliance for Peace and Autonomy have opened a range of possibilities that would have been difficult to imagine in 2002, let alone in 1990, when YATAMA and the FSLN could barely tolerate each other.

With the return of the FSLN to power in 2006, its alliance with YATAMA takes on new importance. YATAMA's leverage over the FSLN should not be underestimated. The accords themselves constitute a key political platform through which YATAMA's agenda is now being placed on the public agenda. However, the FSLN may be tempted to treat YATAMA as the only audible voice in the complex choir of the Caribbean Coastal society. In order to meet the terms of the agreements, both parties will need to include other social and political actors to address the advancement of autonomy rights.

Challenges: A Confined Autonomy

At least formally, the Nicaraguan Caribbean Coast autonomous regime has been presented as one of the most advanced examples of internal self-determination in Latin America. For example, collective, communal property rights have been officially granted in the constitution, and territorial self-determination at a regional level for ethnic minorities has been formally instituted. Moreover, intercultural educational programs in various indigenous languages have been implemented, and decentralized health and education programs are being negotiated and implemented. These autonomy rights shine in comparison with other cases in Central and South America, where at best, only a limited degree of internal self-determination and group rights have been granted to indigenous peoples and where the process still faces strong political opposition.[20]

Notwithstanding the fact that important legislation regarding natural resources, land claims, and decentralizing initiatives has been approved in Nicaragua since 2000, critical obstacles hinder implementation of autonomy rights, despite the national government's constitutional responsibility to promote the autonomous regime. There are three challenges here, the first being the diminishing degree of political representation and participation of indigenous peoples and their organizations in the governance structures of the autonomous regime. Beyond that is the still limited extent to which group rights of indigenous and Afro-Caribbean communities to land and natural resources have been honored, which is particularly true in the matters of surveying and titling communal land. Finally, there is the as-yet-unmet need to strengthen the capacities of autonomous councils and regional governments to cope with the challenges of poverty, the overexploitation of natural resources, and economic development. We now consider each in turn.

Decreasing Political Representation

Since armed conflict ended, there have been important changes in the makeup of the region's population. One is the increasing migration of mestizo peasant families moving eastward, from the central, northern, and Pacific zones of Nicaragua to the Caribbean Coast regions. Although this is a long-term trend, it has accelerated significantly due to widespread poverty in rural areas, the generalized decline of the Nicaraguan agricultural sector, and recent environmental disasters that have affected peasant livelihoods. Mestizos now account for almost 70 percent of the population in the two autonomous regions. This shift has created two interrelated dilemmas for the autonomy regime. One is the underrepresentation of indigenous peoples and Afro-Caribbean communities and their organizations in municipal and regional governments, a fact that is most apparent in the RAAS. The second is the rising mestizo influence in regional politics. This implies that mestizos may gain control over autonomy rights, including those that protect the access to land and natural resources of indigenous peoples and Afro-Caribbean communities.

The *mestización,* as an indigenous leader characterized the increasing power of mestizos in the decisionmaking process, of both regional councils and other state institutions on the coast has been identified by YATAMA and Afro-descendent organizations as one of the most significant obstacles to the exercise of autonomy rights granted to the indigenous peoples and Afro-Caribbean communities in the constitution and the Autonomy Statute (see Tables 7.3 and 7.4).

Indigenous and Afro-Caribbean Community Rights over Land and Natural Resources

Even though specific legislation on indigenous land claims was passed in 2003, the Nicaraguan government has shown insufficient political will to

Table 7.3 Ethnic and Party Representation on RAAN and RAAS Regional Councils, 1990–2014

| | RAAN | | | | | | | |
	FSLN	PLC	UNO	YATAMA	PAMUC	Total	% Seats Regional Government	% Regional Population
Mestizos	63	64	3	0	0	130	45.1	56.7
Miskitu	33	24	0	71	1	129	45	36.2
Creole	10	2	0	4	0	16	5.6	1.2
Mayangna	8	4	0	1	0	13	4.5	5.9
Total	114	94	3	76	1	288	100.2	100

| | RAAS | | | | | | | |
	FSLN	PLC	UNO	YATAMA	PIM	ALN/PC	Others	Total	%
Mestizos	47	82	10	0	2	7	0	148	52.5
Miskitu	6	4	2	13	1	0	0	26	9.2
Creole	21	15	12	9	3	1	5	66	23.4
Mayangna	4	3	1	3	1	0	0	12	4.2
Garifuna	6	7	2	0	0	0	1	16	5.8
Rama	5	6	1	0	1	1	0	14	4.9
Totals	89	117	28	25	8	9	6	282	100

Source: Based on Miguel González, Dolores Figueroa, and Arelly Barbeyto, "Genero, etnia, y partidos en las elecciones regionales de la Costa Caribe: Retos de la diversidad," *Wani: Revista del Caribe Nicaragüense,* no. 44 (2006): 16.

Notes: FSLN: Frente Sandinista de Liberacion Nacional, or Sandinista National Liberation Front; PLC: Partido Liberal Constitucionalista, or Constitutionalist Liberal Party; UNO: Union Nacional Opositora, or National Opposition Union; YATAMA: Yapti Tasba Masraka Nanih Aslatakanka, or Organization of the Peoples of Mother Earth; PAMUC: Party Movement for Coastal Unity; PIM: Partido Indigena Multietnico, or Indigenous Multiethnic Party; ALN/PC: Alianza Liberal Nacional–Partido Conservador, or Nicaraguan Liberal Alliance–Conservative Party.

Table 7.4 Ethnicity of Local Councilors

Regions	Council Members by Ethnic Group					
	Mestizo	Miskitu	Creole	Mayangna (Sumu)	Garifuna	Rama
North (RAAN)	3	3	0	1	0	0
South (RAAS)	8	0	2	1	0	0
Total	11	3	2	2	0	0

Source: Compiled from Mario Rizo, "Citizenship and Identity in the Autonomous Regions of the Caribbean Coast of Nicaragua." In *Contributions to the First Human Development Report of the Autonomous Regions.* Managua: CIDCA-UCA, 2004, 77.

support the process of surveying, demarcation, and legalization of indigenous and Afro-descendant claims to land and territories.[21] From 2003, when the legislation passed, until December 2008, only five territories were demarcated and titles granted. And, even though titles were granted, the government refused until 2006 to authorize the registration of those titles—which was needed to complete the legal process to assert property rights—arguing that Law 445 conflicts with the agrarian code. Indigenous organizations contended that the Nicaraguan state did not act in good faith when granting those titles and therefore is contributing to indigenous historical distrust of national governments.[22] For its part, by the beginning of 2009, the current Sandinista administration had abandoned the legal objections put forth by the Bolaños government and issued titles to land in two territories: Awaltara Luhpia Nani Tasbaya, in Desembocadura del Rio Grande and in the community of Awas Tingni.[23]

This combination of lack of interest and manipulation by the national government is very significant for indigenous peoples, considering their struggle for land and self-governance over the last three decades. YATAMA has been a critical voice in this matter. In their view, "the indigenous land-demarcation bill will eventually create the material and organizational basis for indigenous communities to counterbalance the growing powers of regional autonomous bodies, and that of the national government."[24] This type of community-based autonomy "from below" within the autonomous regime has been identified by indigenous organizations as essential to halting the regional and national encroachment on the autonomy rights of indigenous peoples. Even though the specific form that community-based autonomy will take is not explained in the FSLN-YATAMA accord, there is no doubt that indigenous self-determination will eventually be addressed within this platform.

Increasing Human Development Policy Capacity

According to the United Nations Development Programme (UNDP), the Caribbean Coast of Nicaragua has one of the most acute human development gaps in the country. While Nicaragua's human development index (HDI) of 0.710 ranked one-hundred-and-tenth in 2008, both autonomous regions' HDIs (0.466 for the RAAN and 0.454 for the RAAS), would rank one-hundred-fifty-ninth and one-hundred-sixtieth, respectively.[25]

The incidence of poverty has increased, particularly in rural areas, and education, health, and other basic social services remain inaccessible to most people in the region. In 2001, according to the UNDP, 61 percent of the region's population was considered poor, and of the ten poorest municipalities in the country—where more than 70 percent of the local population live in extreme poverty—six were located in the Caribbean Coast. Ironically, as Table 7.5 indicates, the Caribbean Coast contributes significantly to Nicaragua's national wealth through exports of sea products (lobster, fish, and shrimp), timber (mahogany and pine), and various minerals (particularly silver and gold). Its participation in the national agricultural sector (including livestock) is also crucial, and the community-based, subsistence economy provides livelihoods for hundreds of rural communities.[26] The UNDP has estimated that the two regions contribute 6.1 percent of Nicaragua's GDP. However, extractive activities on the coast account for almost 20 percent of the national figure.[27]

It is not easy for regional governments to cope unaided with the challenges of growing inequality, human development gaps, and overexploitation of natural resources. These challenges are very significant, given the institutional weaknesses of regional authorities caused by internal political conflicts, a limited capacity to shape national public programs implemented in the autonomous regions, and most importantly, the scant support Managua gives the autonomous regimes.

Undoubtedly, many of the problems facing the autonomous regions cannot be explained without considering the impact of Nicaragua's neoliberal economic policies. The Sandinista revolutionary state that granted autonomy to the Caribbean Coast's indigenous peoples and ethnic communities during the 1980s ceased to exist in 1990. The approval of the Autonomy Statute by the revolutionary government manifested its commitment to advancing autonomy rights. However, since 1990 the contradictions between exerting autonomy rights on the coast and promoting a neoliberal economic agenda nationally by every government—including the second Ortega administration—have been evident and have shaped the development of the autonomy regime in Nicaragua.

Table 7.5 Caribbean Coast and Nicaragua, Selected Social and Economic Indicators, 2001

Component	Caribbean Coast	Rest of Nicaragua
Economy		
Fishery (volume)	67.00%	33.00%
Fishery, contribution to GDP (2001)	1.01%	0.50%
Gold production	24.00%	76.00%
Forest cover	70.00%	30.00%
Cattle	32.00%	68.00%
Pigs	37.00%	63.00%
Basic grain crops (area)	23.00%	77.00%
Small and medium-size enterprises (2001)	1.90%	98.10%
Transfers to municipalities (2001)	10.00%	90.00%
Poverty		
Poverty	45.80%	61.30%
Number of municipalities in extreme poverty	12	7
Social services		
Houses with potable water	21.00%	60.00%
Schools	7.60%	92.30%
Houses with electricity	33.90%	52.30%
Education		
Literacy rate	31.4%	20.9%
Life expectancy	65.8 years	68 years

Sources: The following sources may be consulted: Instituto INEC (Nacional de Estatidisticos y Censos), *Censos nacionales* (Managua: INEC, 1995); INEC, *Encuesta nacional de hogares sobre medicion del nivel de vida* (Managua: INEC, 2001); Banco Central de Nicaragua, *Informe Anual, 2001* (Managua: Banco Central de Nicaragua, 2001); Government of Nicaragua, Ministry of Natural Resources and the Environment (MARENA), *Informe del Estado Ambiental de Nicaragua* (Managua: MARENA, 2001); AMUNIC (Asociación de Municipios de Nicaragua), *Transferencias Municipales* (Managua: AMUNIC, 2001); INEC, *Censo Agropecuario* (Managua: CENA-GRO-INEC, 2000); Programa de las Naciones Unidos para el Desarrollo, *El desarrollo humano en Nicaragua: Equidad para superar la vulnerabilidad* (Managua: PNUD, 2000).

The FSLN's return to power after the 2006 elections opened new possibilities for both the coast and the autonomy process. The Sandinistas agreed with YATAMA on an agenda for legal reforms and political actions that may indicate what the future holds. First, progress has been made in titling indigenous land.[28] Second, numerous *Costeños* were named to important posts in the national government.[29] Third, a Development Council for the Atlantic Coast was formed.[30] In other areas, however, little has happened. For example, no progress has been made with respect to reforming the Autonomy Statute or addressing pressing issues regarding electoral administration.[31]

Further, news reports and complaints from a number of communities suggest that the FSLN government still wants to build a so-called dry canal, essentially a rail line linking the Atlantic and Pacific coasts, south of Bluefields. Although the projected line will cross the Rama and Creole indigenous communities of Monkey Point, which already hold indigenous title, the government has not held the legally stipulated consultations with either the regional authorities or the communities affected.[32]

Conclusion

The Nicaraguan autonomy process meant a radical shift in the context of the traditional historical relationships between the state and the ethnic communities of the Caribbean Coast. Further, it has allowed political actors who were formerly engaged in violent struggle to compete peacefully in a democratic setting.[33]

It is apparent that twenty years after the legal recognition of the autonomous regime in Nicaragua, peace and reconciliation have gained an important foothold, and real advances in autonomy rights have been secured in national legislation. These achievements have helped to counterbalance the neoliberal policies enacted at the national level by right-wing governments from 1990 to 2006. However, effective implementation of autonomy rights entails more than just "protecting" the coast's territories from the encroachment of neoliberal, no-holds-barred, economic development or advancing democratic stabilization. It also means the state's genuine collaboration with regional governments and the *Costeño* leadership to implement autonomy rights. It must also strengthen local institutional capacities to effectively govern both regions (most critically to decentralize programs in health and education). Finally, work must be done to build consensus among the people of the coast regarding how to advance autonomy. These actions are needed to repair the harm caused by the restrictive political and institutional environment under which autonomy has operated since 1990. As we have already explained, national governments between 1990 and 2006 displayed the traditional attitude of imposition (for example, making unilateral decisions to delay land titling in indigenous territories) that has characterized the Nicaraguan state in the past and has further fed the historical distrust of *Costeños* toward national institutions.

And even though legal action has led to legislation to secure the autonomy regime, other, extralegal factors are in play. One is the changing population structure, in which the coast now has a mestizo majority. Increasingly, both indigenous and Afro-descendant organizations are becoming aware that this trend may disrupt autonomy rights. This places greater pressure on the indigenous inhabitants and their political organizations to act effectively.

In this context the YATAMA-FSLN accords have included a wide range of topics backed by both organizations in order to "guarantee the defense of the historic rights and legitimate aspirations of the indigenous and Afro-descendant peoples."[34] The Alliance for Peace and Autonomy has created a new momentum for autonomy debates on the coast that could advance the consolidation of autonomy rights. However, for YATAMA deepening rights implies not only securing indigenous communities' voices in regional and national politics but also expanding its constituency to include nonindigenous *Costeños* to create a democratic, multicultural setting where an exchange of ideas on autonomy can take place.

If the autonomy project is to advance in the coming years, a key task for the coast's social organizations and governance structures is to continue designing implementation mechanisms and encouraging intercultural dialogue and consensus building among all the peoples of the coast. To be truly intercultural, this dialogue must transcend ethnic-based claims without suppressing them and thus move forward the effective exercise of autonomy rights for the peoples of the Nicaraguan Caribbean Coast autonomous regions.

Notes

1. Jeffrey Gould, *To Die in This Way: Nicaraguan Indians and the Myth of Mestizaje, 1880–1995* (Durham, NC: Duke University Press, 1998).

2. Charles Hale, "Wan Tasbaya Dukiara: Nociones contenciosas de los derechos sobre la tierra en la historia Miskita," *Wani* 12 (1992): 1–19.

3. Baron Pineda, *Shipwrecked Identities: Navigating Race on Nicaragua's Moskito Coast* (New Brunswick, NJ: Rutgers University Press, 2006), 3–4.

4. CIDCA (Centro de Investigación y Documentación sobre la Costa Atlántica), *Demografía Costeña: Notas sobre la historia demográfica y población actual de los grupos étnicos de la Costa Atlántica Nicaragüense* (Managua: CIDCA, 1982).

5. Colette Grinevald and Maricela Kauffmann, "Toponimia del Territorio en la Lengua y Cultura Rama," in *The Rama: Struggling for Land and Culture,* edited by Miguel González et al. (Managua: URACCAN and University of Tromso, Norway, 2006).

6. Pineda, *Shipwrecked,* 224.

7. Edmund T. Gordon, *Disparate Diasporas: Identity and Politics in an African Nicaraguan Community* (Austin: University of Texas Press, 1998).

8. Juliet Hooker, "Beloved Enemies": Race and Official Mestizo Nationalism in Nicaragua," *Latin American Research Review* 40, no. 3 (October 2005): 14–39.

9. Martin Diskin, "Ethnic Discourse and the Challenge to Anthropology: The Nicaraguan Case," in *Nation States and Indians in Latin America,* edited by Urban Grez and Joel Sherzer, 156–180 (Austin: University of Texas Press, 1991).

10. Evaristo Mercado, Lestel Wilson, and Miguel González, *YATAMA: La lucha por una verdadera autonomía en la Moskitia nicaragüense* (Managua: URACCAN, 2005), 18.

11. CIDCA/Development Study Unit, *Ethnic Group and the Nation State: The Case of the Atlantic Coast of Nicaragua* (Stockholm: University of Stockholm, Department of Social Anthropology, 1987); and Héctor Díaz Polanco, *Indigenous Peoples in Latin America: The Quest for Self-Determination* (Boulder, CO: Westview, 1997).

12. Manuel Ortega Hegg, "Conceptualización de la Autonomía de la Costa Atlántica," paper delivered at the *Fourth Simposio Internacional de Autonomía de la Costa Caribe de Nicaragua,* Managua, September 9, 2004.

13. Miguel González and Yuri Zapata, "Miskitu Politics: Fragmentation or Accommodation?" paper delivered at the annual meeting of the American Anthropological Association, New Orleans, November 20–24, 2002.

14. Charles Hale, *Resistance and Contradiction: Mískitu Indians and the Nicaraguan State, 1894–1987* (Stanford: Stanford University Press, 1994); and *Wani: Revista del Caribe Nicaragüense,* "En la Costa, ¿La frustración mediatizará la democracia? Entrevista con Brooklyn Rivera," no. 9 (1991): 52–56.

15. Peter Sollis, "The Atlantic Cost of Nicaragua: Development and Autonomy," *Journal of Latin American Studies* 21 (October 1989): 481–520.

16. Andrés Pérez Baltodano, *Entre el estado conquistador y el estado nación: Providencialismo, pensamiento político, y estructuras de poder en el desarrollo histórico de Nicaragua* (Managua: Fundacion Friederich Ebert en Nicaragua, 2003).

17. Phillip Dennis, "Higher Education in the Miskitu Coast," *Texas Techsan Magazine* (March–April 2000): 20–21.

18. González and Zapata, "Miskitu Politics," 2002.

19. See Maia S. Campbell, "The Rights of Indigenous Peoples to Political Participation and the Case of *YATAMA v. Nicaragua,*" *Arizona Journal of International and Comparative Law* 24, no. 2 (2007): 499–540; and James Anaya and Claudio Grossman, "The Case of *Awas Tingni v. Nicaragua:* A New Step in the International Law of Indigenous Peoples,"*Arizona Journal of International and Comparative Law* 19 (2002): 1–15.

20. Donna Lee Van Cott, "Constitutional Reform in the Andes: Redefining Indigenous-State Relations," in *Multiculturalism in Latin America: Indigenous Rights, Diversity, and Democracy,* edited by Rachel Sieder (Basingstoke, UK: Palgrave Macmillan, 2002), 45–73; see also Willem Assies, Gemma van der Har, and Andre Hoek, eds., *The Challenge of Diversity: Indigenous Peoples and Reform of the State in Latin America* (Amsterdam: Thela Thesis, 2000).

21. Edmundo T. Gordon, Galio Gurdian, and Charles Hale, "Rights, Resources, and the Social Memory of Struggle: Reflections on a Study of Indigenous and Black Community Land Rights on Nicaragua's Atlantic Coast," *Human Organization* 62 (4) (Winter 2003): 369–381.

22. This is based on information drawn from the letter, made available to the authors, that was sent by representatives of the Mayangnas territory (Indian Tashbaik Kumy Mayangna Sauni Bu) to the president of Commision Nacional de Demarcacion y Titulacion (CONDETI), the body responsible for applying Law 445, on October 3, 2006; for a general overview of the problem of surveying and titling indigenous lands in the Atlantic Coast autonomous regions, see Margarita Antonio,

"Who Do the Coast Lands Belong to and Who Will Get Them?" *Envío* 329 (December 2008), www.envio.org.ni/.

23. See Sergio León, "Gobierno quitara los cayos de los nuevos dueños," *La Prensa,* May 5, 2009, www.laprensa.com.ni/; and CONADETI (Comisión Nacional de Demarcación y Titulación), *Informe técnico y financiero para el traspaso ordenado y transparente del proceso de demarcación de los pueblos indígenas y las comunidades étnicas de la Costa Atlántica de Nicaragua y de los Rios bocay, Coco, Indio y Mais, Junio 2006–Junio 2008* (Bluefields, Nicaragua: CONADETI, 2008).

24. Brooklyn Rivera, interview with Miguel González, Managua, Februrary 17, 2004.

25. United Nations Development Programme, *Human Development Report, 2008* (New York; Oxford University Press, 2008), 231–232; Programa de las Naciones Unidas, *Informe de Desarrollo Humano 2005: Las regiones autónomas de la Costa Caribe ¿Nicaragua asume su diversidad?* (Managua: PNUD, 2005), 220–223, hdr.undp.org/.

26. Miguel González, Edward Jackson, and Yuri Zapata, "Analisis de la Economia y los Sistemas Politicos de la Costa Caribe," *Wani: Revista del Caribe Nicaragüense,* no. 31 (2001): 6–29.

27. PNUD, *El desarrollo humano en Nicaragua 2002: Las condiciones de la esperanza* (Managua: PNUD, 2002), 176, 181.

28. Besides issuing titles in the territories of Awatltura and Awas Tingni, the FSLN government also issued a decree creating a special region in the Mayangnas lands in the Jinotega region. Several *Costeño* organizations objected, arguing that the decision violated both the Autonomy Statute and Law 445.

29. Three cabinet ministers (for Fisheries, Forestry, and Health) and at least two vice ministers—similar to a US undersecretary or Canadian deputy minister—(Natural Resources and International Cooperation) were *Costeños*, drawn from the ranks of both YATAMA and organizations affiliated with the FSLN. Similarly, a relatively large number of *Costeños* were made directors general of departments, and some received appointments to diplomatic posts.

30. The Development Council succeeded the Secretariat for the Atlantic Coast, created by the Bolaños administration. A former minister from the Chamorro administration who was from Nicaragua's Pacific region directed the secretariat, whereas a *Costeño* directs the council. The latter is responsible for facilitating communication between the regional authorities and the central government and overseeing the application of Law 445. Further, it has begun to develop a conceptual framework for the "regionalization" of autonomy, instead of "decentralization," thus meeting a long-standing demand of YATAMA. Less positively, the council intervenes in what should be part of the jurisdiction of the regional governments, such as development planning and appointing government employees in the autonomous regions.

31. For its part, YATAMA became involved in postponing municipal elections held in November 2008 in the rest of the country until January 2009 in the RAAN, asserting that the effects of Hurricane Felix (which hit in September 2007) in indigenous communities precluded holding elections. Others on the coast, though, suspected that YATAMA feared the elections would be a referendum on the performance in office of its mayors in Waspám, Puerto Cabezas, and Prinzapolka, all of whom were suspected of misusing public funds. The vote, held January 18, 2009, showed

YATAMA losing Waspám and Puerto Cabezas to the FSLN but keeping Prinzapolka; see IPADE (Instituto para el Desarrollo y la Democracia), *Informe final preliminar: Elecciones municipales RAAN 2009,* www.ipade.org.ni/.

32. Gobierno Territorial Rama y Kriol, *Indígenas Rama y comunidades Kriol de la RAAS demandan a Presidente Ortega.* Press release, Bluefields, Nicaragua, December 3, 2008; Moisés Martínez and Carlos Salinas, "Canal interoceánico seguirá esperando," *La Prensa,* December 6, 2008, www.laprensa.com.ni/.

33. Marc Weller and Stefan Wolff, *Autonomy, Self-Governance, and Conflict Resolution: Innovative Approaches to Institutional Design in Divided Societies* (New York: Routledge, 2005), 65.

34. FSLN-YATAMA, *Acuerdos YATAMA-FSLN, Plan de Gobierno de la Unidad Nicaragua Triunfa para la Costa Caribe* (Bilwi-Bluefields: FSLN and YATAMA, 2006), p. 20.

8

The Feminist Movement

Karen Kampwirth

FROM THE VANTAGE POINT OF THE TWENTY-FIRST CENTURY, it seems that the unintended consequences of the Sandinista Revolution of the 1980s were at least as important as the intended consequences. Certainly that is true regarding gender politics. For among the unintended consequences of the Sandinista Revolution was the emergence of the most significant feminist movement in Central America. That autonomous movement, which was born in the early 1990s, came into existence in no small part because of the Sandinistas' attempts to mobilize Nicaraguan women during the 1970s and 1980s. But in the 1990s, there was also a clear gendered backlash against the revolution. Supporters of the antifeminist movement tend to remember feminism and the revolution as being part of the same process, despite long-standing tensions between the Sandinista National Liberation Front (Frente Sandinista de Liberación Nacional, or FSLN) and the Sandinista-inspired feminist movement.[1]

In October 2006, days before the presidential election, there was a convergence of long-simmering conflicts between Daniel Ortega's FSLN, the organized feminist movement, and opponents of the feminists. The result was the abolition of what Nicaraguans call therapeutic abortion, that is, abortion to save the life of the pregnant woman. The unanimous votes of FSLN congressmen and women were critical. Without them, the exception to save the life of the woman, a reform that dated to the nineteenth-century Liberal revolution of José Santos Zelaya, would not have been overturned. The story of the abolition of therapeutic abortion, with which I will conclude this chapter, shows how memories of gender and revolution continue to be contested, with real consequences for women's lives.

185

Feminists and Antifeminists
Remember the Sandinista Revolution

Many have suggested that about 30 percent of the Sandinista combatants who fought the Somoza dictatorship in the 1960s and 1970s, including many of the top guerrilla leaders, were women, though there is some controversy regarding these figures.[2] The guerrilla war that ushered in the Sandinista Revolution marked the revolution in profound—and contradictory—ways. In the guerrilla struggle of the 1960s and 1970s, thousands of women gained the opportunity to break the constraints of their traditional roles. During that time, many women who were to go on to be feminist activists first gained the skills and consciousness that made their later activism a real possibility. And Sandinismo would forever mark Nicaraguan feminism, even in the case of women who were to reject their formal ties to the party. "Without the revolutionary movement, feminism would undoubtedly still be the province of a privileged few."[3]

María Lourdes Bolaños, the first director of the Women's Legal Office (Oficina Legal de la Mujer, an institute created by the FSLN government) and then founder of the autonomous feminist organization IXCHEN Women's Center (Centro de Mujeres IXCHEN) in 1989, spoke of how the Sandinista Revolution created the conditions for the feminist movement that emerged in the late 1980s and especially in the 1990s. "The Sandinista Front made an opening that allowed for a new kind of social relations. . . . I think that in the first place we women had the right to make demands and to say that we should have control over changes. They treated us like we mattered. At the beginning of the revolution that was extremely important."[4]

But the actions of many Sandinista leaders were also responsible for impeding the emergence of feminism. Hazel Fonseca, who was also an active participant in the Sandinista Revolution of the 1980s as a volunteer in the Sandinista army and became an autonomous feminist activist (as a cofounder of the Xochiquetzal Foundation [Fundación Xochiquetzal] in 1991), remembered the Sandinista mobilization of women in the 1980s, but she also remembered the downside to that mobilization.

> What the Sandinista Front did was a sort of two-sided morality game. There was a lot of talk about women, but in practice there was a world of difference. I think there is a great fear of the word "feminist." I think more than anything it is a fear of losing power, of having to share power with a woman. . . . I think their intentions were good, but they were not capable of overcoming their machismo. They never proposed that changes would have to be carried out on their part as well.[5]

Fonseca's memory of the Sandinista leaders' desire to mobilize women and simultaneous fear of feminism is widely shared by contemporary feminist activists.

During the 1979–1990 revolution, three different currents of women's organizing emerged in Nicaragua. First, the Luisa Amanda Espinoza Association of Nicaraguan Women (Asociación de Mujeres Nicaragüenses Luisa Amanda Espinoza, or AMNLAE), a mass organization that was always very tightly linked to the Sandinista party, emerged in the final years of the war against the Somoza dictatorship. Second, a number of women's secretariats within the trade unions emerged in the early to mid-1980s. They tended to be more feminist and more independent than AMNLAE, though they were not fully autonomous given the close relationship between the Sandinista party and the unions to which they belonged. Finally, in the late 1980s, a few autonomous feminist organizations (especially women's clinics) were started by women who had become disillusioned with the party but who retained their identities as revolutionaries. At that time, there were also some attempts to organize for lesbian rights, which for the most part were stifled by the FSLN.[6] The story of the revolution told by participants in all three currents within the women's movement tends to be a story of women's mobilization by the Sandinista party, while attempts at feminist organizing, especially autonomous feminist organizing, were discouraged or even forbidden by the FSLN, which saw itself as a vanguard party.

But not all Nicaraguans remember the Sandinistas' gender policies in those ways. Opponents of today's feminist activists, the people I call antifeminists, often frame their opposition to feminism in terms of the Sandinista Revolution. While they share some memories of the guerrilla struggle and revolution with feminists—both remembering a generation of social upheaval—their memories differ in many ways.

Antifeminists remember upheaval that corrupted a formerly moral social order. For them, the revolution and its side effects—especially the mobilization of women prior to 1990 and the growth of the autonomous feminist movement following 1990—are legacies to be rejected. In many ways, Nicaraguan antifeminism is a form of anti-Sandinismo. So to fully understand the continuing importance of Sandinismo in Nicaragua requires attention to movements that, like the feminist movement, emerged in ambivalent relationship with the FSLN, and attention to the movements that emerged unambiguously against the FSLN, like the contemporary antifeminist movement.

After the Fall: Autonomous Feminists in the 1990s

The war was the central topic of the 1990 presidential campaign, and the language with which both sides spoke of war and peace was highly gendered. Daniel Ortega, "the fighting cock," was portrayed simultaneously as a loving father, hugging his baby daughter Camila, and as a horse-riding cowboy leading a charge of other men on horses.[7] At one such rally in Chontales, Ortega promised to respond to the Contra that "continues to assassinate and threaten the people, so we will respond to its threats with the arms of peace; with this cavalcade of peace."[8] These masculine images were tied together with the slogan "Everything will be better," a remarkably poor choice for a party that had already governed for ten years.

Ortega's major challenger, Violeta Barrios de Chamorro, or Doña Violeta as she was consistently called, always dressed in white, invoking the image of the Virgin Mary. Through her words and image, she made the claim that she, a woman with almost no formal political experience, would be able to end the war and reconcile the Nicaraguan family, just as she had reunited her own politically divided children. Instead of formal political experiences, Doña Violeta promised to draw on her experiences as wife, widow, and mother.

Doña Violeta is the widow of one of the most important political figures in recent Nicaraguan history—Pedro Joaquín Chamorro—an outspoken opponent of the Somoza dictatorship whose murder in January 1978 set off a wave of protests that contributed to the FSLN's overthrow of Somoza in July 1979. Throughout her 1990 election campaign, Doña Violeta reminded the public that she was the widow of that heroic figure. For instance, in a rally in Granada, she told the crowd, "I love this city because it was the city of Pedro Joaquín's childhood and of his parents. From Pedro Joaquín I learned his values, and I never thought that I would come to Granada as a candidate, carrying the bloodied flag of Pedro Joaquín."[9]

Doña Violeta emphasized that she had been a good traditional wife to Pedro Joaquín. As she told a reporter, "I am not a feminist, nor would I want to be one. I am a woman dedicated to my home, just as Pedro taught me." Later in the interview, she claimed "to be marked with the Chamorros' branding iron."[10] Appealing to an imagined past in which men protected women in exchange for their loyalty and subservience, a past in which families were not divided by politics, she promised to end the war, reconcile the Nicaraguan family, and end the suffering of mothers.[11] Based on that platform, she won with almost 55 percent of the vote.

When Doña Violeta took office in April 1990, she fulfilled many of those promises. The central promise of the campaign—to end the war—largely did occur that same year as the contras demobilized, mainly because their main source of funds (the US government) withdrew its support. Sporadic political violence continued for several years after Doña Violeta took office, but the draft was abolished, and for the most part, the war ended. To a significant extent Doña Violeta also came through on her promise of reconciliation, even making an alliance with some FSLN legislators against more radical right-wing members of her own political coalition. And Doña Violeta also carried through the implicit antifeminist promise of her political campaign by seeking to overturn many Sandinista-era gender reforms, especially in the areas of health, education, and social welfare.[12]

The early 1990s brought major changes for Nicaraguan feminists. The electoral loss of the party of the revolution, the Frente Sandinista, meant that they lost an ideological ally in government, and many of the laws and social programs that had promoted gender equality were overturned or underfunded. But they were also freed from the constraints that the vanguardist FSLN had tried to place on feminist activists. The most unanticipated result of the 1990 election was not the peaceful end of the Sandinista Revolution or the demobilization of the contras; it was the explosive emergence of autonomous feminism, including lesbian feminism.

The official coming-out party of the new branch of women's organizing was held, appropriately enough, on International Women's Day. The Festival of the 52 Percent, held at the Piñata fairgrounds in Managua during the weekend of March 8, 1991, was a critical turning point. It represented a definitive and public break between AMNLAE and other currents within the women's movement. Although the break did not mean the end of AMNLAE, it did signal a mass exodus of AMNLAE dissidents to the new independent feminist movement. Among those dissidents were members of a new lesbian-feminist rights movement that made its first public appearance at the Festival of the 52 Percent. A few gay and lesbian rights organizations existed as early as the mid-1980s, but they occupied a precarious space during the revolution, ordered by FSLN leaders to lie low and refrain from making waves.

Also, many lesbians were loyal revolutionaries who accepted those limits. For example, Mary Bolt, who helped found the sexual rights organization Fundación Xochiquetzal in 1991, had a long history as a Sandinista, having become an urban guerrilla in 1974. I asked if she was an open lesbian when she joined the FSLN.

> Nobody ever asked me, what sort of thing are you? Never [laughing]. You just joined and that was it, it isn't as though they asked me what I thought, what I believed. I just joined. . . . At that time, before the triumph [the overthrow of Somoza] I never had problems. And I wasn't interested much in lesbian organizations after the triumph either. For me the main goal was defending the revolution.[13]

But after the Sandinistas lost the 1990 election, she reconsidered her political goals. "Later after the election, an emptiness opened up, and I think that happened to large numbers of Nicaraguan men and women. It was a political emptiness . . . for us it was a strong thing, a cause for mourning. . . . So for me this emptiness was filled by the feminist movement."[14]

A single thread tied together Mary Bolt's life as guerrilla, party activist, and autonomous feminist. She never rejected the earlier activism; instead, she moved on from one form to another when circumstances changed: from guerrilla to party activist after Somoza was overthrown and from party activist to autonomous feminist after the Sandinistas lost the 1990 election. Many gays and lesbians did the same thing in the early 1990s. Freed from the constraints of the FSLN, a political party that tried to limit their activism, and faced with a hostile new government, many gays and lesbians tried to organize themselves.[15] The year 1990 saw the founding of the gay rights organization SHomos, the AIDS prevention organization Fundación Nimehuatzín, and the lesbian feminist collective Nosotras. In 1991, the sexual minority rights organization Fundación Xochiquetzal opened its doors. It was soon followed by the lesbian organizations Entre Amigas, and Grupo por la Visibilidad Lésbica. And in 1992, more than twenty-five groups united in the Campaña por una Sexualidad Libre de Prejuicios.[16]

If the March 1991 Festival of the 52 Percent was a declaration of independence for the autonomous feminist movement and the lesbian rights movement, that independence was ratified less than a year later. In January 1992, more than 800 women attended the first National Feminist Conference, entitled "Diverse But United." By early 1992, the autonomous feminist movement was large, diverse, capable, and increasingly daring.[17]

The major disagreement that divided the newly autonomous activists was autonomy itself. Some activists—the majority—were so afraid of being controlled once again by an organization like the FSLN or AMNLAE that they rejected proposals to form any sort of coordinating organization. Yet efficiency required them to be able to unite their individual groups in some way, and so they agreed to form a series of networks. Eight were formed at the conference to work on issues such as sexuality, economics, and environmentalism. By the early twenty-first century, two of the networks formed in early 1992—the Network of Women Against Violence (Red de Mujeres Contra la Violencia) and the María Cavallieri Network of Women for Health (Red de Mujeres por la Salud María Cavallieri)—still were active and large. There were between 120 and150 member organizations in the first network, and 96 alternative clinics, collectives, and women's houses in the network for women's health.[18]

Those who preferred the network model were in the majority at the 1992 conference. But there was a large minority that feared that failing to create something more centralized than the networks was risky. Without a coordinating body and without an explicit commitment to feminist goals, the new autonomous movement might stagnate. So they formed the National Feminist Committee (Comité Nacional Feminista) in May 1992. To join the committee, groups had to agree to support a set of feminist demands. The organizations belonging to the committee all publicly declared that they were against violence, domestic and otherwise, that they were in favor of gay rights, and that they were pro-choice. Though the committee disbanded in 1994, it recreated itself with twenty-five organizations and five individual members in November 1998.

By the mid-1990s, the autonomous feminist movement in Nicaragua was influential, not just in Nicaragua, but in the whole region.[19] So when the autonomous feminist five-country Central American Feminist Current (Corriente Feminista Centroamericana) was created in 1995, it was no surprise that its office and staff were based in Managua. But the internationalization of Nicaraguan feminism was not the only innovation of the 1990s; in mid-decade, some members of the emerging autonomous feminist movement made alliances that would have been unimaginable in earlier decades. There were a number of reasons for that organizational change. It was not that the women who traced their roots to the struggle against the Somoza dictatorship had dropped the commitment to greater class equality that had driven that struggle. But with time, they began to reevaluate the relationship among the multiple axes along which inequalities often revolve.

Though the classic Marxist understanding of inequality would have a vanguard party lead the class struggle, with the understanding that gender inequality would disappear of its own accord once women had access to well-paying jobs, the experience of the revolutionary period had made a lot of autonomous feminists think that the relationship between class and gender was not so simple. In the 1980s, gender inequality did not just disappear as class inequality was attacked through measures such as land reform, nationalization of health care, and the literacy crusade. Instead the very vanguard party that was supposed to lead the struggle for class justice was often hesitant to disturb gender inequality, especially when the interests of the male members of the party were at stake.

Two of the most visible examples of the new cross-partisan, cross-class alliances for gender justice were the Women's and Children's Police Stations (Comisaría de la Mujer y la Niñez) and the National Women's Coalition (Coalición Nacional de Mujeres). In 1993, a number of groups whose relations were often hostile came together behind a project that helped to make legal protections against domestic violence a reality. The plan was to create a series of Comisarías de la Mujer y la Niñez that would be staffed by women and would offer a holistic range of services, including legal, psychological, and medical support, very much like the women's houses that had been originated by AMNLAE in the 1980s and like similar women's police stations in Brazil. Seventeen organizations sponsored the pilot project: AMNLAE, the Association for the Well-being of Nicaraguan Families (Asociación Pro-Bienestar de la Familia Nicaragüense, PRO-FAMILIA), the Center for Constitutional Rights (Centro de Derechos Constitucionales), the Women and the Family Center (Centro Mujer y Familia), the 8 of March Women's Collective (Colectivo de Mujeres 8 de Marzo), the XOCHITL Collective (Colectivo XOCHITL), Defenders of Women Who Have Been Raped (Defensoría de Mujeres Violadas), Wholistic Services for Women (Servicios Integrales para la Mujer, or SI MUJER), the Nicaraguan Women's Institute (Instituto Nicaragüense de la Mujer, or INIM), the National Police (Policía Nacional), Berta Calderón Hospital (Hospital Berta Calderón), Manolo Morales Hospital (Hospital Manolo Morales), the Nicaraguan Institute for Social Security and Well-being (Instituto Nicaragüense de Seguridad Social y Bienestar, or INSSBI), the Ministry of Health (Ministerio de Salud, or MINSA), the Attorney General's Office (Procuraduría de Justicia), the Pedro Altamirano Health Center (Centro de Salud Pedro Altamirano,), and the Foundation of Nicaraguan Women (Fundación de la Mujer Nicaragüense, or FUNIC-MUJER). That these seventeen organizations and institutions united behind the *comisarías* was surprising, given their often opposing roles in the revolution, Contra war, and gender battles of the 1980s and early 1990s.[20]

Yet despite the apparent instability of the coalition, the Comisarías de la Mujer y la Niñez continued to grow: four years after the beginning of the pilot project, there were twelve centers in operation nationwide, three of them in the capital. By 2000, thousands of women had been served at one of fourteen centers nationwide.[21] Nicaragua stood out among Central American nations with regard to women and law enforcement. According to Tracy Fitzsimmons, "Nicaragua currently boasts a higher percentage of women police officers, more women officers in the highest ranks, the most institutionalized system of women's police stations, and the most extensive police training on gendered crimes in Central America."[22]

Another cross-class and cross-partisan women's coalition was formed in 1995. The Coalición Nacional de Mujeres sought to extract promises from all the parties in the months leading up to the 1996 national election, which was the first election for any national office since 1990. The coalition included women who belonged to the two biggest parties—Arnoldo Alemán Lacayo's Liberal Alliance (Alianza Liberal, or AL) and Daniel Ortega's FSLN—along with women from many of the smaller parties, including the Sandinista Renewal Movement (Movimiento Renovador Sandinista, or MRS), the Nicaraguan Conservative Party (Partido Conservador Nicaragüense, or PCN), the

Nicaraguan Resistance Party (PRN) (the contras), and the National Project (Proyecto Nacional, or PRONAL), an alliance of centrist parties. All three currents within the women's movement—AMNLAE, the women's secretariats, and the autonomous feminist organizations—were also well represented.[23]

At a rally of more than 2,000 women on March 8, 1996, the National Women's Coalition presented its "Minimum Agenda" to the parties. Three parties and coalitions—the FSLN, the MRS, and PRONAL—eventually signed the agenda, committing themselves to a series of gender reforms. Of course, the most controversial demands—abortion, contraception, gay rights— did not appear on the agenda. But even so, had the demands included in the agenda been met, politics would have been transformed in some important ways at the level of the nation and the family. As it happened, the big winner of the 1996 election, Arnoldo Alemán of the Alianza Liberal, refused to sign the agenda or to even meet with members of the coalition, even though it included many women from his own party.[24]

The Antifeminist Response from the State

Why did Alemán refuse to even consider signing the Minimum Agenda? Though he never really explained, his response to the National Women's Coalition was consistent with the general patterns of his political career. Both as a young man in the Somoza Youth and as the mayor of Managua from 1990 to 1995, his political style was one of right-wing populism: appealing to excluded groups, especially the very poor, and seeking to mobilize those groups from above. Arguably, Alemán refused to sign the Minimum Agenda of the National Women's Coalition because the coalition could not be squeezed into his political framework. It was nonpartisan, whereas he was fiercely partisan; it was an autonomous organization, whereas his organizations were all controlled from above; it demanded rights with no strings attached, whereas he preferred to dole out privileges in exchange for loyalty. Finally, the coalition's demands for gender equality might have been problematic: Alemán was very closely allied with the most conservative sectors of the Catholic Church.

During the first year of the new administration, that church-state alliance was strengthened. In one of his first acts as president, Alemán named a new cabinet, replacing all the ministers from the Chamorro administration with the exception of the minister of education, Humberto Belli. A member of the right-wing Catholic organization Opus Dei—and one of the most nationally and internationally prominent opponents of the feminist movement— Belli had been at the forefront of efforts to combat various revolutionary legacies. Although the 1987 Constitution, ratified on the Sandinistas' watch, had guaranteed free public education, Belli led the drive to privatize public education. While the women's movement promoted sex education, AIDS awareness, and egalitarian gender roles, Belli promoted legal matrimony, abstinence, and traditional gender roles.

Of course, the retention of Belli did not signal a break with Violeta Chamorro's administration—quite the opposite. Yet despite her efforts to turn back the clock on gender politics, Doña Violeta was also committed to reconciliation. Thus the state women's institute, or INIM, an agency that was formed under the Sandinistas, continued to exist. In fact by the end of the Chamorro administration, the INIM was one of the central actors in the coalition that created the Comisarías de la Mujer y la Niñez. Under Alemán, there would be far less ambivalence toward the feminist movement and feminist nongovernmental organizations (NGOs).

In 1999, in the wake of the devastation of Hurricane Mitch, and the subsequent formation of the alliance of NGOs known as Civil Coordinator (Coordinadora Civil), Alemán began a campaign against the NGO sector, attempting to shut down organizations and expel particular NGO leaders from the country. As I have shown elsewhere, this campaign was characterized almost entirely by attacks on women, especially foreign-born women, and women who identified with the feminist movement.[25]

In the campaign against the NGOs, Arnoldo Alemán united the church and state on one side, while he and his allies conflated foreigners and feminists on the other side. Marching in a September 2000 demonstration[26] with Cardinal Miguel Obando y Bravo of Managua, Alemán asserted his support for a proposal to abolish Article 165 of the constitution, the provision of the civil code that gave women the right to an abortion in cases when three medical specialists from the Ministry of Health had determined that the pregnancy endangered their lives.[27] Supporters of banning abortion under all circumstances asserted that the church and Alemán administration, not those NGO activists who defended women's right to life, were the real Nicaraguans. According to "Dr. Rafael Cabrera of the Catholic University [Universidad Americana], the NGOs 'are foreigners who do not represent Nicaraguans, feminist movements that promote lesbianism and organizations that promote sexual licentiousness and homosexuality.'"[28]

Journalist Sofía Montenegro has suggested that, of all the sectors of civil society, the feminist movement is the most threatening to the interests of the Catholic Church. According to Montenegro, "the Church has demanded the head of the feminist movement" as part of its pursuit of the "reevangelization of the continent [which is necessitated] by secularization and, on the other hand, [by] competition with the Protestants." She suggested that the very close ties between the Alemán administration and the hierarchy of the Catholic Church can be seen as an unofficial pact with the ultimate goal of forming a hegemonic alliance between the AL, the FSLN, and the church. Given that the Pact negotiated in 2000 between the AL and the FSLN undercut all other parties' ability to compete, and given the weakness of private enterprise and the unions in neoliberal Nicaragua, the main impediments to the AL/FSLN/church alliance were the feminist movement and the press. For a time, Arnoldo Alemán largely succeeded in co-opting and controlling the FSLN through the provisions of the Pact. In contrast, the feminists were not so easily co-opted or controlled.[29]

Antifeminists Remember the Revolution

The backlash against the feminist movement directed by Arnoldo Alemán was not unique to Alemán. In fact, anti-Sandinismo in Nicaragua is often gendered. Consider the words of two sisters who lived together in the Altagracia neighborhood of Managua, comparing life before and after the revolution. They directly linked Sandinista programs to what they saw as a negative change in gender relations: "Before the Sandinistas, life was different. Due to the night watch many men lost their women. There was disunion at that time."[30] Her sister similarly condemned the coffee-picking brigades in gendered terms: "They prostituted young girls by sending them off to harvest coffee, where they had to practice free love. That was what made those people fall."[31]

Elida de Solórzano, one of the most prominent opponents of the feminist movement, also remembered the Somoza years as a time when what she called family values were strong.[32] "Education [under the Sandinistas] was devoid of a lot of traditional family values that Nicaragua had known under the Somozas. . . . Christian values were lost."[33] But that does not necessarily mean that Solórzano was a Somocista or even that she sympathized with the Somoza dictatorship. Instead, identifying the time of Somoza as the time of family morality was a way of identifying the Sandinista Revolution, and the feminist groups that emerged indirectly out of the revolution, as the forces that destroyed previous moral stability.

Asael Pérez, executive director of the Nicaraguan Pro-Life Association (Asociación Nicaragüense por la Vida, or ANPROVIDA), hoped to recuperate the values of paternal responsibility, monogamy, and celibacy before marriage that he said were the norm in the past, a past that he did not date or identify with any particular government. His references to the past came up in replying to my question regarding what, in his opinion, Nicaraguan feminists want. He began answering my question by noting, "I think there is a justification for the feminist movement that no one can deny, which is the inequalities that at certain moments have existed between men and women." Like many feminists, Pérez identified his work as fundamentally about values. "You can't see the results of our work in very physical ways, because what we try to do is to arrive at the *conciencia* of problems."[34]

Conciencia is a term Nicaraguan feminists use often, which could be translated as "consciousness" or, in the case of work to create *conciencia,* as "consciousness raising." But when I noted that I had previously interviewed feminists and that they and Pérez seemed to have some things in common, both concerning themselves with *conciencia* and with changing values, he objected. "We don't talk about changing values; we think there is a loss or an absence of values. We try to recuperate values; in contrast I think the feminists really are trying to change values, even to denaturalize values. I don't think being an irresponsible father is a Nicaraguan value. It is an antivalue."[35]

The disagreement over the terms "values" and "antivalues" runs through the politics of feminism and antifeminism in Nicaragua. In part, this disagreement is based on different definitions of the word "value." By "values," Pérez seemed to mean things that are good, so for him, fathers abandoning their children could not be called a "value." But feminists use the word in an anthropological sense, referring to an aspect of culture or a particular tradition. Using the word as feminists do, paternal abandonment of children clearly is a Nicaraguan value. Studies of family structures, going back as early as 1950 (long before the Sandinista Revolution), consistently show a significant percentage of households were headed by single women.[36] Also, with some frequency men and women have told me that it is "natural" for a Nicaraguan man to have more than one woman.

Fundamentally, the dispute over values and antivalues is a dispute over two views of the past. One position is that families have always had their conflicts and inequalities but they can be reduced by working to transform values into greater equality. According to this position, which is the feminist position, the Sandinista Revolution created opportunities for the evolution of values, opportunities that feminists have built upon. According to the other position, the values of the past were good, and Nicaraguan families used to be characterized by complementarity and respect, not conflict and inequality. According to this antifeminist position, the problem is that something transformed age-old values into antivalues, and the way to end social problems like sex out of wedlock or paternal abandonment is to reject that something, to reject antivalues in favor of the values of the past.

For Max Padilla, head of the Ministry of the Family under Arnoldo Alemán, the something that turned values into antivalues was the Sandinista

Revolution. Padilla explicitly linked the political upheaval of the Sandinista Revolution to the threat of foreign imperialism in the postrevolutionary period, explaining in an address to the World Congress of Families II: "Family autonomy was under attack in my country under the Marxist government that ruled during the 1980s. . . . In that decade, the Constitution recognized common-law relationships as equal to marriage, and also unilateral divorce. What great wrongs against the family!"[37]

Padilla suggested that this internal Nicaraguan conflict also plays out on a global stage and that the fundamental battle in the post–Cold War world is no longer between socialism and capitalism but between feminism and antifeminism: "Perhaps the Berlin Wall has come down, but the ideology, the atheist and antifamily vision of Marxism, continues to be very much alive at the end of this century. Today the class struggle has been transformed into a struggle to eliminate sexual classes or for the triumph of the 'neuter sex.'"[38] In June 2000, Padilla was fired or chose to resign (depending on the source) under pressure from leaders of international development agencies who said that "they could not work with Max Padilla"[39] and ordered "Padilla to change his government's definition of gender to say that it was only a social construct."[40]

Rosa and the Competing Legacies of the Revolution

How one remembers and how one acts on those memories matters a great deal. In fact, it may be a matter of life and death, as it was when feminists and antifeminists clashed over a little girl. In November 2002, a Nicaraguan girl who became known as Rosa was raped in Costa Rica. She was not quite nine years old. As though that were not enough, Rosa had the bad luck to become pregnant and contract two venereal diseases as a result of the rape. When the Costa Rican health ministry refused her migrant worker parents' request that she be given an abortion, the three of them returned to Nicaragua. Fearing for her life (because of her physical immaturity and because of the infections that resulted from the venereal diseases), her parents sought an abortion in Nicaragua. Though they had a legal right to the abortion, given the unusual circumstances, Rosa was not quietly treated. Instead, her case became a public scandal that pitted feminists against antifeminists.[41]

In addition to her parents, major players in Rosa's case included the president of Nicaragua, Enrique Bolaños; staff at the Ministry of Health (Ministerio de Salud, or MINSA); staff at the Ministry of the Family (Ministerio de la Familia, or MIFAMILIA); the hierarchy of the Catholic Church; the mass media; the Network of Women Against Violence; and the international feminist community, organized by a Spanish group known as Feminist

Network (Red Feminista). Within Nicaragua, activists on both sides held demonstrations and collected signatures on petitions. In the end, Rosa received her abortion, not at the public hospital where she had been treated but in an unnamed clinic in the middle of the night.

Afterward, according to one of the psychologists treating her, it was "as if she recovered her childhood."[42] But Rosa had come close to losing her childhood and perhaps her life. During the month that the case dragged on, the minister of the family sought to have her held indefinitely in the hospital (a "kidnapping," according to some); at another point the minister of health tried to deny her parents the right to take her out of the country to Cuba, the only country in Latin America where abortion is legal without restrictions.[43] On the Sunday after she had the abortion, Cardinal Obando y Bravo announced during mass that everyone who was responsible for the abortion (with the exception of the rapist) was automatically excommunicated.[44]

That purely symbolic attack (for the archbishop of Managua lacks the authority to unilaterally excommunicate) was met by an equally symbolic counterattack by the international feminist community. A feminist group in Spain initiated an email petition campaign entitled "I also want to be excommunicated for collaborating in the interruption of the pregnancy and the saving of Rosa's life." The petition, which was to be presented "to the most recalcitrant sectors of the Catholic Church in Nicaragua," collected 7,500 signatures in its first day. On March 4, 2003, barely a week into the campaign, 27,126 people had signed the petition in solidarity with Rosa.[45]

Election 2006: Antifeminists Win Over the FSLN

Feminists won the battle over Rosa, in two ways. Most obviously because Rosa had a therapeutic abortion and because most Nicaraguans thought that a nine-year-old should not be forced to carry a pregnancy to term.[46] But the next time the issue of therapeutic abortion became a matter of public debate, feminists would lose. And in 2006, the battle was not about the life of one little girl but about the lives of the hundreds of girls and women who faced life-threatening pregnancies every year.[47]

During the 2006 campaign, the FSLN seemed to reimagine the legacy of the revolution. And that new vision of what it meant to be a revolutionary aligned with traditional Catholicism rather than with liberation theology Catholicism, and with antifeminist rather than feminist views. One could question in what sense this legacy of the revolution was revolutionary.

On the billboards that sprang up everywhere in Nicaraguan cities, there was little of the FSLN's traditional red and black, replaced instead with an array of brilliant colors, especially hot pink. Daniel Ortega, the Marxist-Leninist in military fatigues, was replaced with Daniel the practicing Catholic in white shirt and jeans. The rhetoric of anti-imperialism and class struggle was replaced with the rhetoric of peace and reconciliation. In fact, many historic enemies of the FSLN were incorporated into the Sandinistas' electoral coalition, most prominently, vice presidential candidate and former Contra commander Jaime Morales Carazo.[48]

Weeks after the election that returned Daniel Ortega to the presidency, Sandinista supporters that I interviewed in Managua's Altagracia neighborhood consistently praised the new Daniel who, in the spirit of forgiveness, silently turned the other cheek. "Today we see a Daniel that is different from the one at the time of the triumph of the revolution. . . . He showed that through the campaign, he was attacked very hard but he did not respond to those offenses. Rather he spoke of peace, of reconciliation."[49] "The propaganda against him was dirty, very dirty . . . [but] he did not allow them to provoke him."[50] Ortega himself spoke of the dirtiness of the campaign against him in religious terms, indirectly comparing himself to Christ.[51]

> They defamed Christ, they slandered him, they whipped him . . . and finally, when he was being crucified, that was when He said: "Forgive them, Father, for they know not what they do." And it is those people who carry the weight of those grudges and those dirty campaigns, for that reason we should forgive them, for they do not know the harm that they themselves are doing in their hearts.

One of many signs that Daniel had changed was his marriage to Rosario Murillo, his partner of twenty-seven years, in a Catholic ceremony presided over by former cardinal Obando y Bravo, a little over a year before the 2006 election.[52] Not only did he marry Murillo, mother of six of his eight children, but he often allowed her to speak for him. Daniel was silent when his wife—who also headed his electoral campaign—advocated the abolition of therapeutic abortion, firmly allying herself with the Catholic Church.

In an interview on Radio Ya, Murillo was asked about the position of the Gran Unidad Nicaragua Triunfa coalition (the electoral coalition to which the FSLN belonged) with respect to therapeutic abortion.[53]

> Precisely because we have faith, because we have religion; because we are believers, because we love God above all things. . . . For those reasons we also defend, and we agree completely with the Church and the Churches, that abortion is something that affects women fundamentally, because we never get over the pain and the trauma that an abortion leaves us! When people have had, or have had to resort to that, they never get over it. And this pain is something that we don't want for anyone. . . . The

[Sandinista] Front, the Great Nicaragua Unified Triumphs says, "No to abortion, yes to life!"

With these words, Murillo cemented the pact with the Catholic Church and with Cardinal Obando y Bravo in particular (whom she praised elsewhere in the interview). These words represented a real shift in the position of the Sandinista party regarding therapeutic abortion. It also represented a shift for Rosario Murillo herself as she wrapped herself in the folds of the Catholic Church. It was a fold to which she had only recently returned, as Giaconda Belli noted. "Her words, which would not be at all startling coming from someone who had lived within the Church for many years, cannot fail to surprise coming from someone who, until a few months ago, signed her opinion pieces according to the phases of the moon and who was openly influenced by lights, stars and all the magical paraphernalia of the Age of Aquarius."[54]

Murillo's interest in New Age religion had been well known, and on a number of occasions I have heard or read suggestions that she was a witch (*bruja*). No doubt most of those who called her a witch disliked her politics, but some of them were loyal Sandinistas. Moreover, the witch accusation continued to be made long after she married in the church and endorsed the church's teachings on women's roles. When the topic of Rosario Murillo came up in the context of discussing the November election, one Sandinista commented, "They say she is a witch. She wears rings on all her fingers. I don't know if they are made of gold. Or are they costume jewelry? No I think they are costume."[55]

I do not intend to imply that she actually is a witch (and, in fact, I do not think witches exist). But I think the ongoing accusation is telling, and not just about her interest in New Age religion. At least in the above quote, the witch accusation is clearly linked to her typically ostentatious and sometimes mismatched jewelry, something that may not befit the first lady of what many see as the party of the poor. It may also speak to popular discomfort with her position as an unelected power behind the throne and perhaps to her alienation from many other women in her society. Although her conversion to traditional Catholicism might be new, the mutual hostility between Rosario Murillo and organized feminists was not new in 2006.[56]

But despite long-standing tensions between the leadership of the FSLN and autonomous feminists, I think it is highly unlikely that the FSLN would have voted to ban abortions performed to save the life of the mother, if not for the fact that the election was days away. In other words, the FSLN's newfound opposition to therapeutic abortion does not indicate an ideological shift to the right. What it does show is that, after a decade and a half out of power and close to a decade of political pacts with the right—first with the Constitutionalist Liberal Party (Partido Liberal Constitucionalista, or PLC) and later with Obando y Bravo's faction within the Catholic Church— the FSLN was quite willing to oppose its former base in the women's movement, to say nothing of the vast majority of Nicaragua's women.[57] It was part and parcel of the FSLN's long-term evolution from a revolutionary party to one that was often a personal vehicle for Daniel Ortega and his family.

The vote to abolish therapeutic abortion in October 2006 tells us much about the evolution of the FSLN. But perhaps it tells us even more about the evolution of civil society, both feminist and antifeminist organizing, in the aftermath of the Sandinista Revolution. In 2006, the feminist movement was torn by significant divisions. There was no disagreement over the need to defend therapeutic abortion, but the movement was damaged by personality clashes and disagreements regarding language and symbolism. One position, promoted by activists in the feminist organization Common Ground (Puntos de Encuentro), among others, was that therapeutic abortion should be defended using "positive messages." They participated in various vigils dressed in white and carrying candles.[58]

> From the perspective of Puntos it was very worrisome that other women [from the Movimiento Autonomo de Mujeres, or MAM] were calling for a *carnaval*-style march [i.e., dressing up in costumes] a week after the church's march. . . . Later, the MAM began to have a public presence with a message that was quite full of negativity: "murderers," "killers of women," "you don't know your own laws," "don't vote for a rapist."

Ana María Pizarro, director of Sí Mujer and member of the MAM, was on the other side of this disagreement over tactics, but she also saw the divide as being whether radical or moderate strategies were the most effective. In her opinion, the cause had been hurt by the moderation of many members of the women's movement, who over the years took the position that "therapeutic abortion is the most we can hope for and don't even talk about legalizing abortion."[59] From her perspective, the problem was not that the tactics were too forceful, but that they were not forceful enough and that organized women would never successfully lobby if they continued to forgive and vote for the Sandinista party no matter what it did. I suggested that the dilemma was that a vote for the dissident Sandinista party, the MRS, was a wasted vote, as it was too small to win. In effect, not voting for the FSLN was giving a vote to the right. But she objected, "Your starting point is the idea that the Sandinista Front is a leftist party. . . . We keep on forgiving the [Sandinista] Front because we think they are the same revolutionaries that they have always been, and they are not." But whether women's movement activists were too radical or not radical enough in 2006, there is no question that the movement was more divided and less effective in lobbying than it had been in previous years.

In contrast, the antifeminist movement had never been so united and sophisticated as it was in 2006. This movement, which I argue is an indirect legacy of the revolution—a reaction to the autonomous feminist movement that traces its roots to the revolution—first became identifiable as a group of organizations after the Sandinistas were voted out of office in the 1990s. These organizations had strong ties to the state, especially to the state ministries that dealt most directly with personal politics: the ministries of health, education, and the family. Over the course of the seventeen years when the Sandinistas were out of power, one major goal of the antifeminists was to abolish Article 165 of the penal code, the article that gave doctors the right to perform therapeutic abortions.

Rafael Cabrera, president of the pro-life organization ANPROVIDA, told me that the abolition of Article 165 was a good thing because it was a nineteenth-century anachronism. In that time before the invention of antibiotics, before tuberculosis had been brought under control, before cardiac problems could be treated, Nicaragua was characterized by what he called "a hostile environment."[60] In the nineteenth century, pregnancy could threaten a woman's life, and so therapeutic abortion was permitted to allow doctors to try to save patients faced with life-threatening pregnancies. But over the course of the twentieth century, that medical environment became less hostile, until the point at which, according to Cabrera, all pregnancies could be safely carried to term. I brought up a case of a Nicaraguan woman I knew personally who died at the age of twenty-seven after her first pregnancy caused irreparable heart damage. He told me that since she died months after the baby was delivered by cesarean section, her death could not be attributed to the pregnancy. Cabrera's position—that therapeutic abortion was never medically necessary and so Article 165 was just a loophole to permit abortion for social reasons—was the most common position among the anti–therapeutic abortion activists that I interviewed.[61]

Cabrera and likeminded Nicaraguans had opposed therapeutic abortion for many years prior to 2006. That they succeeded in abolishing that nineteenth-century medical reform in 2006 cannot be understood outside the electoral context, which abortion opponents had not taken advantage of previously. Perhaps more critically, Catholic and evangelical abortion opponents had rarely worked together. But that started changing in the late 1990s.

Elizabeth de Rojas, a minister with the Evangelical Alliance (Alianza Evangélica), explained that her work first came to the attention of traditional Catholic leaders in December of 1998 when she helped organize what she called a "crusade" and "campaign" called "Festinavidad." That festival involved distributing more than 300,000 gifts to Nicaraguan children that had been provided by supporters of US-based evangelical minister Franklin Graham. Festinavidad culminated in a two-day cultural event in the Dennis Martínez National Stadium.[62] Rojas told me that through the event in the stadium, they hoped to "present the word of God to the children [and] to strengthen family values."[63] Rojas estimated that 160,000 children were mobilized by local church networks to participate in the two-day event.

That massive event attracted press coverage, and Max Padilla, the minister for the family at the time, saw the great gathering of children on TV. Believing that the evangelical organizers of this event shared values with the traditional Catholic leaders of the movement I have called antifeminist, he invited Elizabeth de Rojas to a meeting at his office in the Ministry of the Family. It was there that she met Elida de Solórzano, adviser to Padilla and founder of the Nicaraguan Association of Women (Asociación Nicaragüense de la Mujer, or ANIMU), Evangelina de Guirola of ANIMU and founder of Yes to Life (Sí a la Vida), and Rafael Cabrera of ANPROVIDA.[64]

That was the beginning of the alliance between Catholic and evangelical abortion opponents that culminated in a mass march against therapeutic abortion on October 6, 2006, and the vote in the National Assembly a few days later to abolish the exception in the civil code for abortions to save the life of the woman. During the march, a team from the feminist organization Puntos de Encuentro interviewed some of the approximately 200,000 participants. Many agreed with a young woman who explained that, in case of threat to a pregnant women's life, "That should be left up to God. The mother or the child. If it is put in God's hands, he is the one who will decide if the two of them are going to live or not."[65]

But given that the purpose of the march was to abolish therapeutic abortion, it was surprising that many of the marchers were not comfortable with the effects of a ban on therapeutic abortion, that is, the chance that some pregnant women facing high-risk pregnancies would die. One young man, when asked if a doctor should let a woman die rather than perform a therapeutic abortion, simply said, "That is hard; I cannot make a statement." A young woman who recommended that the pregnant woman die rather than having a therapeutic abortion was less sure what to recommend if she already had children. "I don't know." One teenage girl proposed the pro-choice position (though she did not call it that): "If it is a situation like that, it would depend on the person. In my case, I would prefer to have my child with the risk. Like a personal decision." And a fifty-four-year old woman explained that she was at the march "as the Catholic that I am, to support the ideas of our priests." But if the pregnant woman would die along with her unborn baby, the women said that in that case, "Yes [the abortion] would be the right thing." The interviewer clarified, "They should save one of the two?" and she answered, "Yes, that would be the right thing."

I also found some confusion over the meaning of "therapeutic abortion" in interviews I did with people who had voted for Daniel Ortega. A few weeks after the election, I interviewed sixteen voters in Managua's Altagracia neighborhood, five men and eleven women ranging in age from nineteen to eighty-three. The questions addressed the election, their hopes for the Sandinista government that was to be inaugurated in January, and the debate over therapeutic abortion.

When I introduced the topic of therapeutic abortion, I asked them to tell me what it was. Eleven out of sixteen (including all the men) offered examples of cases when a therapeutic abortion might be performed. The eleven who offered at least one example distinguishing therapeutic abortion from abortion in general (usually rape or risk to the woman's life) all thought it was a mistake for the National Assembly to have abolished therapeutic abortion, generally attributing that vote to pressures from the Catholic Church during the electoral campaign.

Five of the sixteen people I interviewed described therapeutic abortion in ways that were identical with abortion in general. Those five all thought it was a good thing that the National Assembly had abolished it. Patricia said, "That is when doctors take babies out and for me it is wrong. God made man and woman to multiply, to reproduce. We are like the tree, the tree of the Bible"[66] She and the others who described abortion in general in response to my question about therapeutic abortion thought it was a good thing that it had been overturned in the National Assembly.

I conducted all of these interviews in people's houses, three of them with members of the same family on a small covered porch decorated with a flyer from two months earlier. The flyer read: "The Catholic Church invites you to participate in the Great March against abortion on October 6th. At 9:00 it will leave from the Metropolitan Cathedral toward the National Assembly."[67] The flyer was illustrated with a drawing of a crying Jesus, holding a fetus in the palm of his hand.

As happens occasionally when interviewing working-class Nicaraguans in their always crowded houses, I asked fifty-five-year-old Diana to tell me what therapeutic abortion was and was answered by her thirty-three-year-old daughter Janet. "When the life of a woman is in danger, because they have to remove it; if not, she will die." Her mother looked displeased at that answer, saying, "To be perfectly honest, I don't understand therapeutic because abortion is killing a life."

Janet, who spoke of the importance of her Catholic faith, also told me that therapeutic abortion "should be accepted. I think so when there is really a risk." Janet's cousin, Magda, told me she would have liked to have been at the October march. Responding to my question on what therapeutic abortion is, she said: "With me it is not okay; I do not agree with abortion; it is killing an innocent, of one's own blood." But when I asked her what to do if a pregnant woman's life were in danger, she said, "Better to take it [the fetus] out."[68]

My findings (from interviewing Sandinista supporters) and those of the Puntos de Encuentro team (interviewing participants in the march against therapeutic abortion) were similar. Many who said they opposed therapeutic abortion were actually against abortion for social reasons, and sometimes they favored therapeutic abortion. A poll conducted by CID-Gallup similarly found a large majority of Nicaraguans opposed to abortion (79 percent were against it, 12 percent were in favor, and 9 percent didn't know or didn't respond).[69] However, 55 percent of the 79 percent of those reported as opposing abortion rights indicated that they favored allowing an abortion to save the life of the woman. Thus to the 12 percent who favor abortion rights, one can add another 43.45 percent of those polled who favor therapeutic abortion (55 percent of the 79 percent recorded as opposed) to show that 55.45 percent of those sampled in this poll would support therapeutic abortion.

Conclusion

The day after the FSLN voted to eliminate therapeutic abortion, a cartoon was published in the newspaper *El Nuevo Diario*. Two women chat over coffee. One of them, apparently exhausted and wearing a "Women's Vote" T-shirt, tells her friend:

> He used me, he humiliated me, he abused me, he hit me, he ignored me . . . he pushed me to the side . . . and still he very cynically asks me to be faithful to him . . .
> Her friend responds: Idiot! . . . What did you say his name is?
> The answer: FSLN

As I argued above, the abolition of therapeutic abortion is the logical outcome of four separate trends in Nicaraguan politics in the years since the end of the revolution in 1990: (1) the FSLN becoming a less ideological party, seen most clearly in the 2006 electoral theme of reconciliation rather than revolution, (2) the FSLN's pact making with the right over nearly a decade, (3) the alienation of the feminist movement from the FSLN and divisions within the feminist movement, and (4) the increasing sophistication of the antifeminist movement.

As of October 2006, Nicaragua is one of a handful of countries (Chile, El Salvador, and Malta being the others) in which abortion is illegal without exception.[70] Six months after therapeutic abortion was abolished, an estimated forty-two women had died as a result of that legal change.[71] Most of these cases were women like twenty-two-year-old Francis Zamora, who died as a result of a miscarriage, leaving behind three orphaned children. Zamora's mother explained:

> They let my daughter die. The doctors at the *Alemán* [Hospital] told me that they could not do the curettage [*legrado*] until she expelled the fetus. She suffered from when we arrived on the January 25th in the morning, until 4:00 in the afternoon the next day when she expelled the fetus. . . . They told me they could not do anything, that the laws in the country had changed, and that they had to wait until the fetus came out on its own. Maybe if they had done the curettage earlier, she would not have died.[72]

Sandinista representatives in the National Assembly voted against therapeutic abortion in 2006 because they feared that the party would otherwise lose the election. Tragically, there is little reason to believe that their votes affected the electoral outcome at all. Most of the Sandinistas I interviewed disagreed with the abolition of therapeutic abortion, but they voted for the FSLN anyway, as did the Sandinistas who agreed with the abolition of therapeutic abortion. Similarly, none of the anti-abortion activists I interviewed gave me any reason to believe they had voted for the FSLN. Quite the opposite, many suggested that they thought the FSLN's anti–therapeutic abortion vote was only a response to the election, and so of course they voted for one of the two right-wing parties (the PLC and the AL), which better represented their values. Nationwide, none of the FSLN's electoral strategies—expensive advertising, the rhetoric of "love and reconciliation," the electoral alliances with contras and Somocistas, the alliance with the Catholic Church and various evangelical leaders, the vote against therapeutic abortion—seem to have made any difference. As analysts from the magazine *Envío* noted, the FSLN "won without growing," that is, it won with the votes of its traditionally loyal voters and few others, and the FSLN would have lost had the right not been divided in two. "Ortega won this time with 38 percent of the votes. In the three previous elections he obtained similar or greater percentages: in 1990 against Doña Violeta de Chamorro, 41 percent; in 1996 against Arnoldo Alemán, 38 percent; and in 2001, against Enrique Bolaños, 42 percent."[73]

But whether or not they win votes, electoral strategies have consequences. They set the stage for the government that is to follow, and they
may serve to reset the balance of power among different groups in society.
The gendered components of Daniel Ortega's 2006 electoral strategy certainly had the effect of weakening feminists, who had formed part of the
base of support of the FSLN, and strengthening the hand of antifeminists.
That strategy also had the consequence of making life more precarious for
pregnant women who depended on public health services.

It is worth noting that for many antifeminist activists or their supporters, abolishing therapeutic abortion is not the final goal. Instead, it could be
seen as part of a broader project of restoring Nicaraguan women to their
rightful place. Asked about the poor care pregnant women generally receive
in the public health care system in Nicaragua (which makes the abolition of
therapeutic abortion more dangerous than it would be in a country with good
prenatal care), Noel Pereira Majano, a PLC deputy and chair of the National
Assembly's Justice Commission, responded, "One has to keep one's cool in
making statements about the effects of abortion. We have to study the
causes; there has to be a coordination of governments and state agencies to
avoid prostitution and free love. We must work against the liberated woman,
who thinks she can control all the parts of her body."[74]

Notes

This chapter is a significantly revised version of "Revolución, feminismo, y an-
tifeminismo en Nicaragua," which was published in *De lo privado a lo público: 30
a os de lucha ciudadana de las mujeres en América Latina,* edited by Elizabeth
Maier and Nathalie Lebon (México, DF: Editorial Siglo XXI, 2006). It is published
here with the permission of the editors.

1. The activists I identify as "antifeminist" rarely use that term to describe their
own work, instead calling it pro-family or pro-life. But I contend that the term "antifeminist" is appropriate for at least three reasons. First, feminist activists are also in
favor of families (albeit egalitarian families), and their work against maternal mortality and domestic violence is also pro-life work. Second, activists in this movement are
not simply social conservatives any more than feminist activists are simply social liberals. In both cases, the movements are centrally concerned with the politics of intimacy
and daily life. Finally, the term "antifeminist" identifies it as a backlash movement.

2. Helen Collinson, ed., *Women and Revolution in Nicaragua* (London: Zed
Books, 1990), 154; Patricia Flynn, "Women Challenge the Myth," in *Revolution in
Central America,* edited by Stanford Central American Network (Boulder, CO: West-
view, 1983), 416; Linda Reif, "Women in Latin American Guerrilla Movements: A
Comparative Perspective," *Comparative Politics* 18, no. 2 (January 1986): 158.

3. Norma Chinchilla, "Nationalism, Feminism, and Revolution in Central America," in *Feminist Nationalism,* edited by Lois West (New York: Routledge, 1997),
201–219.

4. María Lourdes Bolaños, interview, May 7, 1991, Managua, Nicaragua.

5. Hazel Fonseca, interview, June 10, 1991.

6. On these three currents, see Karen Kampwirth, *Feminism and the Legacy of Revolution: Nicaragua, El Salvador, Chiapas* (Athens: Ohio University Press, 2004), 21–46; also Lorraine Bayard de Volo, *Mothers of Heroes and Martyrs: Gender Identity Politics in Nicaragua, 1979–1999* (Baltimore: Johns Hopkins University Press, 2001); Ada Julia Brenes et al., *La mujer nicaragüense en los años 80* (Managua: Ediciones Nicarao, 1991); Ana Criquillón, "The Nicaraguan Women's Movement: Feminist Reflections from Within," in *The New Politics of Survival: Grassroots Movements in Central America,* edited by Minor Sinclair (New York: Monthly Review Press, 1995); Clara Murguialday, *Nicaragua, Revolución y Feminismo (1977–1989)* (Madrid: Editorial Revolución, 1990).

7. Editors' note: Having the candidate lead a parade of mounted horsemen into a town before a rally is standard procedure in Central American electoral campaigns.

8. Photo from *Barricada,* January 5, 1990, 1.

9. *La Prensa,* January 22, 1990, 1.

10. Scarlet Cuadra, "Electorado femenino por la revolución," *Barricada,* January 13, 1990, 3.

11. Karen Kampwirth, "The Mother of the Nicaraguans: Doña Violeta and the UNO's Gender Agenda," *Latin American Perspectives* 23, no. 1 (January 1996): 67–72.

12. See Karen Kampwirth, "Legislating Personal Politics in Sandinista Nicaragua, 1979–1992," *Women's Studies International Forum* 21, no. 1 (January 1998): 48–54.

13. Mary Bolt, interview, July 1994.

14. Mary Bolt, interview, July 1994.

15. In 1992, Article 204 was presented to the National Assembly. It read: "The crime of sodomy is committed by anyone who induces, promotes, propagandizes, or practices relations with a person of the same sex in a scandalous way. The penalty will be between one and three years in prison." On the politics of Article 204, see Kampwirth, "The Mother," 77–80, and "Legislating Personal Politics," 60–63. Although the FSLN bloc in the National Assembly voted unanimously against Article 204, it passed anyway. For more than a decade, it remained on the books, and although it was rarely enforced, it was a threat to gays and lesbians. Then in 2006, in the process of revising the civil code, Article 204 was quietly deleted (interview, Elizabeth de Rojas, December 4, 2006). Rojas, an evangelical and anti-abortion activist, told me she hoped that Article 204, "which refers to sodomy," would be reinstated. But unless there is a campaign to publicize its quiet elimination, Article 204 will still have the same chilling effect on the lives of gays and lesbians and their supporters as it did when it was in the civil code.

16. On the gay and lesbian rights movement, see Rita Arauz, "Coming Out as a Lesbian Is What Brought Me to Social Consciousness," in *Sandino's Daughters Revisited: Feminism in Nicaragua,* edited by Margaret Randall (New Brunswick, NJ: Rutgers University Press, 1994), 265–285; Florence Babb, "Out in Nicaragua: Local and Transnational Desires After the Revolution," *Cultural Anthropology* 18, no. 3 (2003): 304–328; Mary Bolt González, *Sencillamente diferentes: La autoestima de las mujeres lesbianas en los sectores urbanos de Nicaragua* (Managua:

Centro Editorial de la Mujer, or CEM, 1996); Kampwirth, *Feminism and the Legacy,* 7–63; Margaret Randall, "To Change Our Own Reality and Our World: A Conversation with Lesbians in Nicaragua," *Signs* 18 (1993): 907–924; Millie Thayer, "Identity, Revolution, and Democracy: Lesbian Movements in Central America," *Social Problems* 44 (1997): 386–407.

17. On that conference and some of its results, see Kampwirth, *Feminism and the Legacy,* 63–65.

18. Kampwirth, *Feminism and the Legacy,* 64.

19. See Kampwirth, *Feminism and the Legacy,* 96–108; María Teresa Blandón, "The Coalición Nacional de Mujeres: An Alliance of Left-Wing Women, Right-Wing Women and Radical Feminists in Nicaragua," in *Radical Women in Latin America: Left and Right,* edited by Victoria González and Karen Kampwirth (University Park: Penn State University Press, 1997), 111–132.

20. Kampwirth, *Feminism and the Legacy,* 66–69.

21. See Karen Kampwirth, "Arnoldo Alemán Takes on the NGOs: Antifeminism and the New Populism in Nicaragua," *Latin American Politics and Society* 45, no. 2 (Summer 2003): 68–69.

22. Tracy Fitzsimmons, "A Monstrous Regiment of Women? State, Regime, and Women's Political Organizing in Latin America," *Latin American Research Review* 35, no. 2 (June 2000): 225.

23. For a list of women's movement participants, see Kampwirth, *Feminism and the Legacy,* 211, note 23.

24. Blandón, "Coalición Nacional"; Kampwirth, *Feminism and the Legacy,* 69–70; *La Boletina* 25 (March 1996): 27–28.

25. Kampwirth, "Arnoldo Alemán."

26. It is quite unusual for a sitting president to participate in a street demonstration; apparently the point of the demonstration was to illustrate his close ties to the Catholic Church (Sofía Montenegro, cited in Elvira Cuadra, Angel Saldomando, and Sofía Montenegro, "La Sentencia contra las mujeres: La agonía de la democracia," supplement to *Confidencial* 508, October 22–28, 2006). Another illustration of the president's close ties to the church was his declaration of March 25, 2000, and all subsequent years as the Dia Nacional del Niño por Nacer, a date that coincided with the Catholic feast of the Annunciation. In 2000, the new state holiday was celebrated by Catholic organizations in the national baseball stadium.

27. In the face of lobbying efforts by feminists, Article 165 was not overturned but was instead put off to be addressed in the subsequent legislative session. Until 2006, all proposals to overturn Article 165 were tabled. Indeed, in interviews I did a few weeks after the FSLN congressmen and women voted unanimously to overturn Article 165, a number of feminist activists told me that their FSLN contacts in the National Assembly had assured them over the years that although they were not willing to support most feminists in their desire to see abortion become more available, they also promised to protect therapeutic abortion by tabling (*engavetando,* literally "putting in a drawer") all proposals to eliminate Article 165.

28. Infopress Central America, "NGOs Under Attack," March 10, 2000, 2.

29. Sofía Montenegro, interview, August 7, 2001; on church-state relations under Alemán and Enrique Bolaños, his successor as president, see Paul Jeffrey, "La corrupción y la Iglesia en Nicaragua," *El Nuevo Diario,* March 31, 2005, www.elnuevodiario.com.ni.

30. The night watch, a program run by the neighborhood defense committees (CDS) in the early 1980s, was supposed to guard against the contras, but in Managua (where the contras were not active), it served to reduce street crime and burglaries. The program caused some household conflicts: many men opposed their wives carrying guns and being out all night.

31. Anonymous interview, April 1991.

32. See Karen Kampwirth, "Resisting the Feminist Threat: Antifeminist Politics in Post-Sandinista Nicaragua," *NWSA Journal* 18, no. 2 (Summer 2006): 94–95, note 4.

33. Elida de Solórzano, interview, January 31, 1991.

34. Asael Pérez, interview, December 5, 2002

35. Asael Pérez, interview, December 5, 2002

36. For a review of these studies, see Karen Kampwirth, "Women in the Armed Struggles in Nicaragua: Sandinistas and Contras Compared," in *Radical Women in Latin America: Left and Right,* edited byVictoria Gonzalez and Karen Kampwirth (University Park: Penn State University Press, 2001), 84, note 20.

37. Max Padilla, "La autonomia de la familia," speech to the World Congress of Families II, November 15, 1999, www.thefamily.com/.

38. Padilla, "La autonomia," p. 4.

39. Austin Ruse, "The UN's Assault on Faith, Family, and Country," www.iol .ie/~hlii/AustinRuse.html.

40. Catholic Family and Human Rights Institute, "Nicaraguan Delegate Fired for Pro-Family Views Briefs Policymakers," *Fax Archive* 4, no. 11 (2001): 1.

41. Until it was overturned on the eve of the 2006 election, Article 165 of the penal code was often interpreted to allow three exceptions to the ban on abortion: in case of a documented rape, when the pregnant woman's life was in danger, or when the fetus had severe birth defects. Danger to the pregnant woman or fetal abnormality was determined by a team of at least three doctors; see Lester Juarez Ordonez, "Demandan aborto para salvar niña embarazada," *El Nuevo Diario,* February 19, 2003, www.elnuevodiario.com.ni. The team of doctors that examined Rosa "determined that the little one would run very high risks if the pregnancy were interrupted or if it were continued"; see Elizabeth Romero, "Niña violada en peligro," *La Prensa,* February 19, 2003, www.laprensa.com.ni.

42. Envío, "The Names of the Rose," *Envío* (March 2003): 3.

43. Eloisa Ibarra, Valerie Imhof, and Luis Galeano, "MIFAMILIA quiere asumir a la nina," *El Nuevo Diario,* February 20, 2003, www.elnuevodiario.com.ni; and Romero, "Niña violada."

44. Mirna Velásquez Sevilla and Ary Pantoja, "Abortistas excomulgados," *La Prensa,* February 24, 2003, www.laprensa.com.ni.

45. www.redfeminista.org/EXCOMUNION.asp.

46. According to a CID-Gallup poll taken after Rosa had the abortion, 64 percent of Nicaraguans approved of the abortion, 27 percent said "it would have been better to leave her to have the baby," and 9 percent did not know or did not respond. For details, see JairoVillegas S., "Reaparece Rosa," *La Prensa,* March 16, 2003.

47. "Every year the Health Ministry records about 600 ectopic pregnancies (when the fetus is implanted outside the womb)," said Matilde Jirón, a doctor specializing in reproductive health. "You have to add about 400 molar pregnancies (when the placenta grows tumors). In both these cases, therapeutic abortion is

absolutely necessary to save the mother's life. Between 10 and 15 percent of pregnancies miscarry naturally, but many of the remainder come to us bleeding or with other problems associated with their pregnancies. To staunch the blood may affect the fetus. To leave the mother to bleed may kill both her and her child. Tell me, what are doctors to do?" (Nicaragua Network Hotline, "Topic 5: Reactions to National Assembly's Criminalizing Therapeutic Abortion," *Nica Net Hotline,* November 2, 2006, www.nicanet.org).

48. Ortega and Jaime Morales Carazo were historical enemies, and not only for having been on opposite sides of the Contra war: Morales's house was expropriated early in the revolution and given to Daniel Ortega, who to this day lives there (but who has since apparently paid for the house). Many other former contras and even members of the Somoza family's National Guard joined the Sandinista electoral coalition in 2006 (see, e.g., EFE, "Partido somocista se adhiere al FSLN," *El Nuevo Diario,* August 26, 2006; Ary Pantoja, "Más ex somocistas en FSLN," *El Nuevo Diario,* August 27, 2006; José Adán Silva, "Ortega insiste en perdón y olvido," *La Prensa,* September 4, 2006; Leonicio Vanegas, "'Tal vez Ortega nos cumple': Contras decepcionados de los liberales," *El Nuevo Diario,* September 2, 2006). Loyal Sandinistas often had difficulty justifying such alliances to themselves. When I was riding in a car with a Sandinista friend in June 2006, we passed one of the many billboards promoting "Jaime," and I asked what he thought. Miguel said something vaguely positive about him, and then I asked, "But isn't he a Contra?" He corrected me: "Oh no, he was part of the opposition, but he was never a Contra." But Morales Carazo's background was not hidden. It is quite possible that my friend was aware of it but found it painful to admit he planned to vote for a Contra. In his acceptance speech at the FSLN congress in May, Morales Carazo told the crowd how he had first met "Commander Ortega" when he had been "Chief Negotiator for the Contra" during the Sapoa negotiations in 1988. See Jaime Morales Carazo, "Intervención de Jaime Morales Carazo," www.fsln-nicaragua.com/.

49. Carlos, interview, December 2, 2006

50. Pedro, interview, November 26, 2006.

51. Quoted in Silvia González Siles, "Daniel Ortega ahora se compara con Cristo," *La Prensa,* October 31, 2006.

52. Julia Ríos, "Rosario Murillo, el poder tras el 'orteguismo,'" *El Nuevo Diario,* January 10, 2007. Editor's note: There is another version of the story that says the two renewed vows originally made in Costa Rica before the triumph of the revolution. Envío, "Nicaragua Briefs: Ortega and Murillo Tie Knot . . . Again?" *Envío* 290 (September 2005), www.envio.org.ni/.

53. Rosario Murillo, "Extracto de la entrevista ofrecida por Rosario Murillo, jefa de campaña del Frente Sandinista de Liberación Nacional, a la emisora *Nueva Radio Ya,*" August 21, 2006, www.izquierda.info/.

54. Giaconda Belli, "De la era de Acuario a la Inquisición: Candidatos sandinistas e Iglesia católica: El FSLN contra el derecho al aborto," www.socialismo-o-barbarie.org/.

55. Tina, personal communication, December 2, 2006.

56. In the years following 1990, the women's movement (nearly all of whose leaders were originally mobilized during the revolution) became increasingly alienated from the FSLN in general and from Daniel Ortega in particular. This was due to a number of factors, especially feminist attempts to break the control of the vanguardist

Sandinista party over their organizations and feminist responses to the allegations that Ortega sexually abused his stepdaughter Zoilámerica Narvaez from the time she was eleven years old (a conflict in which Rosario Murillo sided with her husband against her daughter). These tensions manifested themselves in an agreement signed in 2006 by one faction of the women's movement (calling itself the Movimiento Autónomo de Mujeres, or MAM) with the FSLN's rival, the MRS party.

57. The Sandinistas did not oppose therapeutic abortion, but they felt they had to vote against it for electoral reasons, to avoid the danger of the Catholic Church effectively vetoing the FSLN by campaigning against the party. One male Sandinista activist with contacts within the top leadership told me the same thing, the only difference being that he assumed the FSLN would find the votes to restore therapeutic abortion. This is evidence that the FSLN's sudden opposition to therapeutic abortion is an indication of cynicism rather than of a principled right-wing stand. From a different perspective, Delia Arellano, representative of the Alianza Liberal Nacional in the National Assembly and a long-term opponent of therapeutic abortion, made a similar point. She told me the FSLN would have never voted the way it did had the election not loomed near. She told me the vote had to happen during the campaign because, if not, "it would have come out the same way, no, no." I asked why the vote would have been "no" to the proposal to abolish therapeutic abortion and she answered: "Because the Sandinista Front is leftist" (interview, December 5, 2006).

58. Evelyn Flores, interview, November 29, 2006. The opponents of therapeutic abortion were able to take advantage of these images in their own propaganda. When I interviewed Reverend Roberto Rojas of Asamblea de Dios in his crowded office (on November 28, 2006), he gave me a four-page, notebook-paper-size flyer from the 3-foot-tall pile next to his desk. He told me those flyers were produced with help from the newspaper *La Prensa,* which covered printing costs (others told me later that these flyers were included with all copies of *La Prensa* over a period of many days). The cover of the flyer read, "Their business is coming to an end! That is why they lie. Don't let yourself be fooled! Abortion is murder." The cover was illustrated by four medical professionals whose pale eyes and European features were disguised by surgical masks. Behind them were images of floating cordobas, the national currency. On the inside two pages, debate points were presented, and there the words "therapeutic abortion" (as opposed to just abortion) were used. On the back cover, readers were asked, "Who are you going be believe? Those who ENRICH THEMSELVES from the bloody business of abortion? Those who lie, deceive, and manipulate?" Those questions were illustrated with images from the MAM march in favor of therapeutic abortion rights (including a person in a distorted witch mask wearing a pointed black hat, and three women in burkas holding large biological signs for women, along with the ominous doctors from the first page and the floating cordobas). The final question "Or a people who love and defend life?" was illustrated with a photo of crowds at the October march against abortion.

59. Ana María Pizarro, interview, December 1, 2006. She put AMNLAE, Ipas, IXCHEN, Movimiento Feminista, ISNIM Women's Center (Centro de Mujeres ISNIM), and Puntos de Encuentro on her list of women's organizations that took the minimalist position of defending therapeutic abortion but not abortion for social reasons.

60. Rafael Cabrera, interview, November 28, 2006.

61. One of the anti–therapeutic abortion activists I interviewed said that if a pregnant woman's life is in danger, the best thing would be to let the woman die,

noting that "God permits the things that are going to be" (Dr. José Bayardo Morales, *Iglesia Verbo,* interview, December 7, 2006). Yet most of those who admitted there could be cases when a woman's life was threatened by a pregnancy did not take that position. For them, the abolition of Article 165 (which permitted therapeutic abortion) was still a good thing since Article 134 of the new civil code allowed doctors to perform an abortion to save the woman's life (Article 134 permits doctors to commit acts that would otherwise be crimes if they are necessary to save a patient's life). But feminist lawyer Juanita Jiménez of the Network of Women Against Violence and the Autonomous Feminist Movement (Movimiento Autónomo Feminista) noted that Article 134 is not really a replacement for Article 165. For Article 134 requires that a doctor has the confidence that he or she will be able to prove in court, beyond a reasonable doubt, that the woman's life was in immediate danger. As she points out, "There are not many doctors who would have the nerve to risk a trial" (interview, December 6, 2006).

62. Joaquín Tórrez, "Un puente infantil de amistad EU-Nicaragua," *El Nuevo Diario,* December 9, 1998.

63. I asked Elizabeth de Rojas what she meant by "family values," and she explained that they included "respect for parents, the cohesion of the family unit, discipline, communication, being respectful" (interview, December 4, 2006).

64. On these organizations, see Kampwirth, "Resisting the Feminist Threat," 83–86. Others volunteered the same year, 1998, as the beginning of an evangelical-Catholic alliance against abortion, and also mentioned the key role played by Max Padilla from the Ministry of the Family; see Rafael Cabrera, interview, November 28, 2006, and Reverend Ricardo Hernández, interview, December 7, 2006. This alliance was very important for various reasons, including the fact that the evangelicals are a significant minority of Nicaraguans. According to Sara Miller Llana, "At the end of the 1970s, only 5 percent of Nicaraguans were evangelicals. Now they account for more than 20 percent—some say more than 30 percent—of the population"; see Llana, "Evangelicals Flex Growing Clout in Nicaragua's Election," *Christian Science Monitor,* November 2, 2006. According to the last census, 22 percent of Nicaraguans are evangelical; a 2007 CID-Gallup poll reported that 26 percent are evangelical; see Emiliano Chamorro, "Iglesia católica sufre bajas mientras evangélicos crecen," *La Prensa,* June 20, 2007. Nonetheless, evangelicals (which in Nicaraguan Spanish is a synonym for "Protestants") were divided over the issue of therapeutic abortion, with many evangelicals, especially those belonging to the Council of Protestant Churches of Nicaragua (Consejo de Iglesias Pro-Alianza Denominacional, or CEPAD), an alliance of thirty-three denominations, taking public positions in favor of protecting the right to therapeutic abortion; see Ramona López, CEPAD, interview, November 30, 2006; William González, Universidad Evangélica Nicaragüense Martin Luther King, interview, December 5, 2006; Tania Sirias, "Presidente de Universidad Evangélica y el aborto terapéutico: Fuera electorerismo y escuchar a mujeres," *El Nuevo Diario,* October 13, 2006.

65. I'm grateful to Marta Juarez and Amy Bank of Puntos de Encuentro for letting me listen to recordings of the interviews.

66. Elena, interview, December 2, 2006.

67. It is worth noting that in this invitation, Catholics were invited to a march against abortion, not against therapeutic abortion. In much of the material distributed in the campaign, either the word "therapeutic" was not included at all, or it was in small print.

68. Anonymous interviews, December 3, 2006. The interviewees' names have been changed to protect the privacy of the women.

69. CID-Gallup, "República de Nicaragua: Nicaragüenses conservadores frente al aborto terapéutico, Población mucho más anuentes en casos especiales," February 2007, www.euram.com.ni/.

70. Francesc Relea, "Aborto 'hipoteca' a Daniel Ortega," *El Nuevo Diario,* January 23, 2007.

71. Ada Julia Brenes, ed., *Movimiento de mujeres en Centroamérica* (Managua: Programa Regional La Corriente, 2007).

72. Quoted in Tania Sirias, "Nuevas Leyes la dejaron morir," *El Nuevo Diario,* February 7, 2007.

73. "Daniel Ortega Presidente: Del poder 'desde abajo' al gobierno." *Envío* 296–297

74. Quoted in Lourdes Arróliga, "FSLN, ALN, PLC alineados con Iglesia," *Confidencial* 507, October 15–21, 2006.

9

Poverty Politics

Rose J. Spalding

SOCIAL INJUSTICES AND REPRESSION OF DISSENTERS DURING the Somoza dictatorship fueled the Sandinista movement, and pursuit of the "logic of the majority" became the byword of the revolution. Yet the power to address poverty and promote human agency is often elusive. This chapter focuses on social programs and antipoverty initiatives in Nicaragua after the Somoza dictatorship and includes discussion of human development policy across three periods: the Sandinista Revolution (1979–1990), the market transition following the Sandinista defeat (1990–2006), and the neo-Sandinista period under the second Ortega administration (2007–2012). It concludes by noting that the postrevolutionary Sandinista government faced many of the same challenges that the Sandinista National Liberation Front (Frente Sandinista de Liberación Nacional, or FSLN) confronted in the 1980s—challenges that neither the Sandinista Revolution nor the subsequent neoliberal governments were able to surmount. The second Ortega government confronted a series of difficult, constrained decisions about how to address the problems of entrenched poverty and unmet basic needs. Central dilemmas involved prioritizing the neediest or responding to partisan pressures, building on or breaking with past policies, accommodating to or reducing dependence on traditional external funders, and working with or in opposition to civil society. The political constraints and economic parameters in the second Sandinista administration were quite different from those that shaped the early revolutionary period, although the discourse style and realignment strategies resonated across time. Comparative social policy analysis can help us dig beneath the rhetoric to clarify the levels of continuity and discontinuity between the revolutionary Sandinismo of the early 1980s and the neo-Sandinismo emerging in the second Ortega administration.

Sandinista Social Development Model
in the Revolutionary Period, 1979–1990

The FSLN-dominated government that emerged from the overthrow of Anastasio Somoza Debayle in 1979 employed an innovative approach to national development. The government's vision departed from a conventional social democratic model in the degree of direct state ownership and from more orthodox socialist systems in the extent of private participation in the national economy. Variously labeled a "mixed economy,"[1] a model driven by "state-centered accumulation,"[2] an economy in "transition to socialism,"[3] and a "semi-centralized economy,"[4] the Sandinista revolutionary model defied easy categorization.[5]

This economic model targeted resources to marginalized sectors but catalyzed external and internal opposition that undermined its redistributive impulse. During the revolutionary period, the Nicaraguan state acquired the assets of the Somoza family and a somewhat nebulous group of Somoza allies (Somocistas), thus claiming control of substantial agricultural land and a ream of industrial and commercial activities. The collapse of the banking system, following panicked asset stripping during the 1978–1979 insurrection, led to the creation of a network of state-owned banks under the Sandinista government. The new banking system modified credit distribution practices, improving access for small producers and domestic market crops.[6] The Sandinista government quickly assumed control over the export of major commodities, marginalizing traditional intermediaries and appropriating the returns to this sector.

With broad-based public support and control over the state apparatus, the revolutionary government introduced a series of social programs designed to address the needs of historically marginalized sectors. To deepen and complement structural reforms (agrarian reform, bank transformation, controls on export earnings), the government mobilized state and popular resources to better meet basic human needs (literacy and education, health services, nutrition).

The 1980 national literacy crusade was emblematic of this effort. Launched before the government reached its first anniversary, this campaign recruited around 85,000 volunteers to carry out a five-month intensive literacy program in both urban and rural areas.[7] Funded on a shoestring using volunteerism, donations, community fund-raising, and the sale of patriotic bonds, this campaign targeted that half of the population over the age of ten identified as illiterate. Plan architects, drawing on Paulo Freire's transformative conceptual framework, the successful Cuban literacy model, and the assistance of international advisers, placed *brigadistas* (volunteers in the literacy brigade) in homes and villages where illiteracy was concentrated, encouraging mutual learning and bonds of solidarity. This campaign reportedly reduced the national illiteracy rate by around 27 percentage points, winning the 1980 literacy achievement prize from the United Nations Educational, Scientific, and Cultural Organization.[8]

A follow-up project established the Collectives of Popular Education, drawing heavily on recently trained literates for staffing. By 1981, 17,000 "popular teachers," 70 percent of whom had just completed literacy instruction themselves, targeted 141,000 adults for continuing instruction through the fourth-grade level.[9] The government also expanded the traditional educational system, with increases registered at every level (see Table 9.1). Primary school enrollment, critical in terms of reducing extreme marginality, reportedly increased by 45 percent in the 1978–1983 period, accompanied by a 62 percent increase in the number of primary teachers. Total enrollment in the educational system rose a reported 90 percent in five years, increasing from 511,623 in 1978 to 970,104 in 1983. Education spending as a percentage of gross domestic product (GDP) doubled during this period, rising from 2.6 percent in 1978 to 5.2 percent in 1983.[10]

Committed to "the logic of the majority," the FSLN government also developed innovative policies to make basic health services more inclusive. The decentralized health care system of the Somoza regime had divided health coverage among several institutions, and none had much range outside Managua.[11] The result was a health care system that concentrated resources in urban areas and excluded the bulk of the population. The national

Table 9.1 Student Enrollment by Level and Year, 1978–1989

Year	Preschool	Primary	Secondary	Postsecondary	Special	Adult	Total
1978	9,000	369,640	98,874	23,291	355[a]	10,463	511,623
1979	18,292	411,315	110,276	28,759	355[a]	18,137	587,584
1980–							
1981	30,524	472,167	139,743	34,710	1,430	172,389	850,963
1982	38,534	509,240	139,957	33,838	1,591	170,410	893,570
1983	50,163	536,656	158,215	35,588	1,624	187,858	970,104
1984	60,557	534,317	161,845	34,552	1,484	143,360	936,115
1985	62,784	561,551	151,269	29,001	2,102	114,784	921,509
1986	72,569	556,684	167,079	26,775	2,057	120,851	946,015
1987	76,635	583,725	177,202	26,878	2,292	118,312	985,044
1988	74,227	599,957	172,108	25,478	2,269	83,797	957,736
1989	64,956	595,612	143,978	n.a.	n.a.	n.a.	n.a.

Source: Juan Bautista Arríen, Miguel De Castilla Urbina, and Rafael Lucio Gil, *La educación en Nicaragua entre siglos, dudas, y esperanzas* (Managua: UCA, 1998), 62.

Note: a. These numbers are estimates.

social security system, for example, covered only 8.8 percent of the population, and the public health system offered few services.[12]

After the overthrow of the Somoza government, public health resources were combined under the Ministry of Health and expanded to provide broader coverage. The number of medical consultations in the first half of 1980 reportedly increased 121 percent over first half of 1978.[13] As with the literacy crusade, volunteers mobilized for health campaigns; these brigades succeeded in eliminating new polio cases in 1982, and official infant mortality rates fell from 121 per 1,000 live births in 1978 to 90 per 1,000 in 1982.[14]

In addition to expanding health and education services, the Sandinista government developed new nutrition policies. A national food security program, which included highly controversial rationing and food distribution controls, was associated with improved caloric intake in the early 1980s. According to Peter Utting, per capita consumption of basic food products like rice and eggs increased substantially during this period. The annual average per capita consumption of kilocalories and protein grams rose from 2,053 and 52, respectively, in 1976–1978 to 2,232 and 56 in 1983, contributing to generally improved nutritional levels.[15] Overall, the Sandinista Revolution achieved greater social inclusion, particularly during the first half of its decade in power.

Reform sustainability, however, soon proved to be a problem. As domestic and external resources withered and the economy began to contract, social programs came under increasing pressure. The Reagan administration's interpretation of Sandinista Nicaragua as a Soviet and Cuban stronghold fueled a military opposition that crippled social reform. Defense spending, which absorbed 37 percent of government outlays in 1983, claimed over half the budget by 1985.[16] The growing Contra war redirected social assistance toward war injuries and population displacement and took a heavy toll on the regime's ability to provide basic services. Attacks on schools and health centers in the war zones caused over 500 schools to be abandoned.[17] The draft pulled teenage boys off the streets and out of school, leading to long-term human development losses. The scarce technical resource base of the country and the controversial nature of some of these policies further complicated the staffing of social programs, as lightly trained volunteers and unlicensed workers became key service providers.

Responding to war dislocations and the economic crisis, the Sandinista leadership made several policy adjustments. The heterodox 1988 Stabilization and Adjustment Plan tamped down the 33,000 percent hyperinflation rate by cutting costs and relaxing economic controls.[18] Price controls were lifted, and subsidies that had cushioned price increases were reduced. In spite of these efforts, macroeconomic disequilibrium and economic contraction continued. By 1989, GDP per capita approximated levels found in the 1940s.[19]

Unemployment, illiteracy, hunger, and disease made a comeback. Budgetary constraints limited the capacity of the government to meet people's basic needs, and cascading price increases eroded people's ability to provide for themselves. Tracing average food consumption across the decade, Utting estimates that by 1989, average per capita kilocaloric and protein consumption of the main food products had dropped to 1,591 and 37, respectively, amounts that were 14 and 26 percent below minimum recommended levels.[20]

Educational expansion slowed after 1983 and became more erratic (Table 9.1). Participation in adult education fell sharply, with enrollment levels in 1988 reaching less than half what they had been five years earlier. Postsecondary education enrollment dropped back toward prerevolutionary numbers by 1988, and secondary education also experienced several reversals. The budget for the education sector was cut 20 percent in 1989, and even primary and preschool enrollments had declined by the end of the decade.[21] The combined preschool, primary, and secondary enrollments, which had peaked in 1987 at 837,562, dropped 4 percent to 804,546 two years later.

Social spending in constant 1980 prices fell across the decade. Using 1981 spending as the benchmark (1981 = 100), Rossella Cominetti and Gonzalo Ruíz found that per capita social spending fell gradually to 73 in 1985, and then plummeted to 10 in 1989. The revolutionary economic model, which had allowed the Sandinista government to reduce certain kinds of poverty by addressing basic needs and human development priorities in the euphoric early years, had come under intense pressure by the end of the decade. As the Sandinista Revolution lost its ability to continue addressing social marginality, poverty levels rose again.[22] Electoral defeat soon followed.

Market Transition and Neoliberal Poverty Reduction Strategies, 1990–2006

For the next three administrations the development model shifted, as did the poverty reduction strategies. With guidance from the US Agency for International Development (USAID) and the International Monetary Fund (IMF), the postrevolutionary governments approved privatization, trade liberalization, and deregulation policies associated with neoliberal economic reform. Growth resumed after transition-era adjustments, and poverty levels gradually declined. The poverty rate stagnated, however, after a decade of transition, in spite of continued economic growth and the application of successive poverty reduction policies. Market-friendly economic reform in the 1990–2006 period proved unable, by itself, to resolve the problems of social marginality.

Postrevolutionary reform began quickly as the Chamorro government sharply reduced the size and role of the state through privatization and large-scale layoffs.[23] Renewed US aid supported the Occupational Conversion Plan introduced in 1991 to provide severance pay of up to $2,000 to state workers who would forfeit public employment. By the end of 1993, 25 percent of civilian state workers had left the public sector. According to a Government of Nicaragua overview of structural reforms in the 1990s, public employment (including the armed forces) dropped from 285,000 to 89,000 from 1990 to 1999.[24]

To revive the private sector, the government transferred resources to businesses, reestablished private banking, and reopened foreign trade. Between 1990 and 1995, 346 companies managed by the National Public Sector Corporations (Corporaciones Nacionales del Sector Público, or CORNAP), representing around 30 percent of Nicaragua's GDP, were removed from the state sector (privatized, returned, or liquidated).[25] State trade monopolies were eliminated in 1991–1992, and import tariffs were unilaterally reduced. Under new legislation, the free trade zone expanded. US market access, which had been provided to the region during the Reagan administration under the Caribbean Basin Initiative, now became available to Nicaragua.[26] Structural adjustment agreements were signed in June 1994 and March 1998, placing Nicaragua's economic policy under the guidance of the IMF.

Ending hyperinflation had a positive impact on general welfare, and the large-scale infusion of new external aid improved economic opportunities in urban areas. Nonetheless, the 1991–1993 reforms had detrimental consequences for several low-income sectors. In a revealing comment, the World Bank's initial assessment of Nicaragua's poverty programs under the Chamorro government noted that

> small-scale agriculture, where Nicaragua's poorest are concentrated, has lost, as the elimination of state market structures is only slowly being replaced in rural areas . . . the poorest consumers have lost, as the general subsidies on basic goods [have] been eliminated and commerce has been freed, allowing vastly greater product availability, but also higher prices . . . the unemployed and underemployed have lost, as employment guarantees are eliminated and rising real wages only benefit the employed.[27]

Between the war damage and economic crisis of the late 1980s and the dislocations of economic transition in the early 1990s, poverty generally worsened. Using the unsatisfied basic needs (UBN) methodology, which was standard at the time, the National Statistics and Census Institute (Instituto Nacional de Estadísticas y Censos, or INEC) calculated that 74.8 percent of the population was poor (had one or more basic needs unmet) in 1993, up from 69.4 percent in 1985.[28] Using the World Bank's $2 per day per capita standard, Mario J. Arana and Juan F. Rocha calculated that Nicaragua's total poverty rate rose from 42.8 percent in 1985 to 68.3 percent in 1993, reflecting substantial poverty increases during that critical eight-year period.[29]

As the postrevolutionary governments reestablished loan flows with international financial institutions, new poverty assessment methods were introduced. Living standards measurement surveys (LSMS), conducted in 1993, 1998, 2001, and 2005, charted income poverty trends across this thirteen-year postrevolutionary period.[30] Measuring poverty in terms of the ability of household income to cover basic consumption needs, the LSMS employed two categories: "poverty," in which income falls below levels required for both minimal food and nonfood consumption, and "extreme poverty," in which income is so low that even minimal food needs cannot be covered (see Table 9.2).[31] This minimalist definition produced a less-alarming profile, albeit one that still captured the wide reach of poverty in Nicaragua. In 1993, using this measurement methodology, INEC estimated that 50.3 percent of the population lived in poverty (as opposed to 74.8 percent according to the UBN method), and 19.4 percent lived in "extreme poverty." Income deprivation was particularly acute in the rural areas, where over three-fourths of the population was found to be poor, and over one-third were classified as extremely poor.

Defenders of the neoliberal economic model claimed that these Chamorro-era economic stabilization and adjustment programs provided a solid economic foundation and that healthy growth would lead to poverty

Table 9.2 Nicaragua Poverty Trends (percentage of population)

Year	Poverty, Extreme + Relative			Poverty, Extreme		
	National	Urban	Rural	National	Urban	Rural
1993	50.3	31.9	76.1	19.4	7.3	36.3
1998	47.9	30.5	68.5	17.3	7.6	28.9
2001	45.8	30.1	67.8	15.1	6.2	27.4
2005	48.3	30.9	70.3	17.2	6.7	30.5

Source: INIDE (Instituto Nacional de Información de Desarrollo), *Perfil y características de los pobres en Nicaragua 2005* (Managua: INIDE, 2007), 11.

abatement. In fact, poverty rates did decline during the 1990s as the transition was assimilated, although the problem remained generalized. According to the second LSMS, 47.9 percent of the population lived in poverty, and extreme poverty affected 17.3 percent in 1998—decreases of 2.4 and 2.1 percentage points, respectively (see Table 9.2).

Detailed World Bank studies of Nicaraguan poverty trends in the 1990s concluded that the drop was due largely to conjunctural developments (increased land use in the 1990s and reconstruction aid after Hurricane Mitch) that would not generate a sustained decline.[32] Economic crises in the 2001–2003 period, including commodity price shocks (declining coffee prices, rising oil prices) and the collapse of several major banks created new challenges. For the 2001–2005 period, LSMS data indicated that progress toward reducing the poverty rate slowed and perhaps even reversed. The Nicaraguan government statistics institute, the National Institute for Development Information (Instituto Nacional de Información de Desarrollo, or INIDE; previously the INEC), reported that poverty levels rose from 45.8 percent in 2001 to 48.3 percent in 2005, and the extreme poverty rate increased from 15.1 percent to 17.2 percent (see Table 9.2).[33]

Nicaragua's tenacious poverty rate had long been a concern to international funders. As international financial institutions became central actors shaping Nicaragua's economic policy, the postrevolutionary government's failure to raise the living standards of the poor was increasingly perceived as their failure as well. The widespread belief during the 1990s that freeing markets and promoting economic growth would reduce poverty was increasingly challenged by the high levels of poverty that persisted even after the successful completion of structural reform and economic reactivation. Postrevolutionary governments from Chamorro forward were urged to develop a more coherent and better-targeted poverty program.[34] The clear objectives and rigorous timeline embedded in the Millennium Development Goals (MDGs) increased the pressure for demonstrable results.

Continuing demands for debt relief for the world's poorest countries led to the construction of the IMF–World Bank heavily indebted poor countries (HIPC) initiative, in which debt payments were reduced in order to allow increased spending on poverty reduction. Attainment of HIPC relief was conditioned on the creation of an approved poverty reduction strategy. To meet this requirement, Nicaraguan government officials developed a series of "poverty reduction strategy plans" (PRSPs) beginning with the Strengthened Economic Growth and Poverty Reduction Strategy (Estrategia Reforzada de Crecimiento Económico y Reducción de Pobreza, or ERCERP), produced by the Alemán government in 2000, and followed by the Bolaños government's National Development Plan (Plan Nacional de

Desarrollo, or PND), presented in 2003. According to an assessment of Nicaragua's poverty reduction programs done by the IMF and the International Development Association (IDA), the first effort (which these lenders, using their internal discourse, labeled PRSP I) gave relatively more attention to increasing social services, which had remained underdeveloped through the 1990s.[35] The PND (PRSP II), in turn, put more emphasis on increased production and expanded infrastructure in "cluster" zones.[36]

Both plans received some level of civil society consultation, most notably through the National Council for Economic and Social Planning (Consejo Nacional de Planificación Económica Social, or CONPES) and the municipal-level mechanisms developed subsequently.[37] However, various studies of HIPC poverty reduction strategies in Nicaragua and elsewhere have called attention to problems in achieving local ownership. As with other externally imposed economic plans, including the structural adjustment program during the Alemán administration, the gap between formal commitments and actual compliance was wide. Geske Dijkstra, as well as David Booth, Arturo Grigsby, and Carlos Toranzo, found that the Nicaraguan poverty strategies failed to incorporate local civil society recommendations and did not reflect authentic authorship or commitment to reform on the part of the government.[38]

Social programming in Nicaragua during the postrevolutionary period tended to be highly fragmented, with both external donors and nongovernmental organizations (NGOs) following their own preferences. In 2001, the World Bank noted nearly 100 social safety net programs of different types, whose resources equaled almost 10 percent of GDP. Because of "the inability of the Government of Nicaragua to establish priorities and a strategy to guide donors and NGOs in the 1990s," these social programs were characterized by dispersion, duplication, inadequate targeting, significant gaps, inefficiencies, internal contradictions, and weak monitoring.[39]

The push toward more effective programming eventually led the Alemán administration to endorse a few programs with improved targeting and monitoring mechanisms. One of these, the Network of Social Protection (Red de Protección Social, or RPS), was a "conditional cash transfer" (CCT) program launched in 2000, with forceful backing and financing from the Inter-American Development Bank. This program, modeled on Mexico's Education, Health, and Nutrition Program (Programa de Educación, Salud y Alimentación, or PROGRESA, later renamed Oportunidades) and similar to the Family Allowance Program (Programa de Asignación Familiar, or PRAF) in Honduras and the School Grant (Bolsa Escola, predecessor to Family Grant, or Bolsa Família) Program in Brazil, provided a cash transfer to low-income families that met performance requirements for human development (especially childhood vaccinations and school attendance). Annual benefits totaling up to $240 per household were provided in return for regular school attendance (for households with children ages 7–13) and completion of health checkups.[40]

As elsewhere in Latin America, rigorous evaluations of the program (compared with a control group) concluded that this approach was effective in improving income and raising human capital, with very low "leakage" to nonpoor households. During the 2000–2002 period, participation in this program improved school enrollment by 13 percentage points, reduced child labor for those ages seven to thirteen by 5.6 percentage points, and reduced stunting in children under age five by 5.5 percentage points compared with outcomes in control districts.[41] The RPS used a poverty map to check the derailment of benefits toward those less needy; 81 percent of beneficiaries were found to be in the bottom 40 percent of household income. Based on initial positive results, the RPS pilot program was extended for three years in 2002, with benefits going to almost 30,000 households, estimated at 3 percent of the population.[42]

Critics, however, claimed this program was too expensive for a poor country and would ultimately be unsustainable.[43] As executive authority shifted from Alemán to the Bolaños administration (2002–2007), the overall contours of antipoverty programming changed. Determining that the country was off course economically because of unexpectedly low rates of economic growth and was, in any case, unlikely to meet the Millennium Development Goals, the Bolaños administration shifted away from an emphasis on social programs, which were viewed as "assistentialism," toward programs that focused on increased production in regions where growth opportunities were thought to be propitious.[44] Working with the idea of "clusters" that linked market forces and government incentives to promote targeted development, the new PND encouraged out-migration from economically depressed zones into population centers that were already expanding and demonstrating economic potential.

Controversy about the PND led to modifications in its operational version, and "poverty reduction spending" reportedly increased, rising from 10.4 percent of GDP in 2002 to 12.3 percent in 2004.[45] Many public sector projects, however, were not well targeted to assist the poor. Social spending directed to subsidizing universities, for example, was regressive.[46] Weak targeting was common even among projects officially classified as "poverty reducing." Critically analyzing seventy-nine programs in the Nicaraguan government's 2001–2005 poverty reduction portfolio, the World Bank found that the majority (55 percent) needed "reformulation" because of their insufficient ability to demonstrate poverty risk reduction.[47] Worse yet, fifteen percent of the projects, with a combined budget totaling 24 percent of the portfolio, were simply designated "not appropriate."[48] The Bank's diagnosis of the central government's 2005 budget noted that 55 percent of social spending and 47 percent of "poverty reduction spending" benefited the nonpoor. Carlos Lacayo's critical analysis of the structure of capital spending on poverty identified the emphasis on the transport sector as a particular concern. He concluded that the January 2004–September 2005 central government budget

> earmarks 38 percent of total Capital Spending on Poverty for the transport sector. This equals three key sectors together (Water, Sewerage and Sanitation; Education; and Health), plus part of the investment in human capital in the Protection, Assistance and Social Security sector. This investment represents almost 2.5 times more than that in the education sector, in a country in which the main problem of structural poverty is the education level, and where 75 percent of the labor force has 3 or fewer years of education.[49]

Weak targeting combined with modest resources to undermine the effectiveness of these antipoverty initiatives. With the obligation to maintain balanced accounts and accumulate large reserves in order to receive IMF approval and with legal loopholes and exemptions reducing tax revenue, postrevolutionary governments had very limited resources with which to work. Strong political alliances with nonpoor beneficiaries and heavy external pressure to honor poorly negotiated domestic bonds channeled scarce resources away from the poorest.[50] These administrations were unwilling and unable to redirect sufficient resources to strengthen the work on poverty abatement. Ironically, the period in which the Nicaraguan government was pressed hardest by international funders to formalize coherent poverty reduction strategies was the period in which the national poverty rate declined the least.

Postrevolutionary governments did achieve some notable social sector successes. Substantial progress was made, for example, toward reducing infant and child mortality rates, which dropped from 40 and 50 per 1,000 live births, respectively, in 1998 to 31 and 40 per 1,000 live births in 2001 (see Table 9.3). Child labor also reportedly decreased, falling from a labor force participation rate of 20 percent in 2001 for ten- to fourteen-year-olds to 14 percent in 2005.[51] Ninety-two percent of primary school students now had textbooks (rented, lent, or donated by the schools) in 2005. Almost 70 percent of preschool and primary students were in school feeding programs, up from only 15 percent in 2001; this program showed signs of progressivity, covering 77 percent of students from the "extremely poor" households.[52]

Table 9.3 Selected Nicaragua Social Indicators, 1993–2005, and MDGs for 2015

	1993	1998	2001	2005	2015 Goal	Will be achieved?
Illiteracy rate, 10 years and over (%)	21.5	18.8	18.7	18.4	10	Unlikely
Primary school enrollment (%)	75.6	79.6	83	84.1	100	Unlikely
Infant mortality (per 1,000 live births)	—	40	31	—	20	Possible
Child mortality, under 5 years (per 1,000 live births)	—	50	40	—	24	Possible
Chronic malnutrition, under 5 years (%)	23.7	19.7	17.8	17	7	Unlikely
Maternal mortality (per 100,000 births)	98	106	115	95.7 (2006 data)	22	Very unlikely
Access to drinking water (%)	68	71.7	70.3	71.5	90	Unlikely

Source: Compiled from World Bank, *Nicaragua Poverty Assessment,* vol. 1, Main Report, no. 39736-NI (Washington, DC: World Bank, May 30, 2008), 28, 29.

However, many of these improvements varied sharply by household wealth. The strongest 1998–2001 reductions in the prevalence of malnutrition (47 percent), for example, occurred in the richest 20 percent of households; only a modest 7 percent reduction took place in the poorest 20 percent.[53] Similar patterns were found in access to secure water supplies: access for the nonpoor increased from 90 percent in 1998 to 92 percent in 2005, whereas access for the poor and extremely poor dropped from 74 percent to 71 percent and 64.5 percent to 62 percent, respectively.[54] In spite of piecemeal improvements, overall social performance remained weak. Based on the 1990–2005 trajectory, the World Bank projected in 2008 that Nicaragua was unlikely to achieve most MDGs by 2015.[55]

The 2005 LSMS found other evidence of widespread service deprivation: 44 percent of households relied on untreated latrines or lacked formal sanitation facilities;[56] 20 percent of households discarded their solid waste in rivers and lakes; and 26 percent of households were not connected to the electrical grid, a figure that rose to 57 percent in rural areas, and frequent blackouts affected even those who were.

The official illiteracy rate barely moved between 1998 and 2005, remaining above 18 percent (see Table 9.3). Primary school enrollment crept up over the years but, at only 84 percent coverage of the relevant age group in 2005, was unlikely to reach the 2015 Millennium Development Goal of full coverage. The average educational level in 2005 was only 5.6 years, with the average for the extremely poor reaching only 2.7 years.[57] School desertion at the secondary level remained very high: Nicaragua ranked near the bottom in Latin America on secondary school completion. Structural poverty continued to be deeply engrained and widespread in Nicaragua, especially in the rural areas. The prevailing deficits reflected the social failings of the postrevolutionary governments; they would present a major challenge to the incoming FSLN officials.

Neo-Sandinismo: Social Programs Under the Second Sandinista Government, 2007–2012

The Sandinista leadership offered a complex set of messages, both in its behavior as the main "opposition" force during its sixteen years out of power and in its 2006 electoral campaign. Often aligning with the government in support of neoliberal economic policies, the FSLN retained a rhetorical commitment to redistributive social programs and attending to the needs of the less advantaged. The populist discourse of Daniel Ortega raised expectations that social policy would become more inclusive under the new Sandinista government. According to Sandinista leader Orlando Núñez, Nicaragua was spending $180 million each year for fifty-three programs and agencies to reduce poverty, without achieving meaningful results.[58] The challenge for the second Ortega administration was to construct an alternative.

The postrevolutionary Sandinista government's vision was outlined in a new development plan, the National Human Development Plan (Plan Nacional de Desarrollo Humano, or PNDH), which advanced an array of social initiatives, three of which were central to the poverty reduction strategy: improved access to basic social services, particularly education; a nutrition/rural production program called "Hambre Cero" (Zero Hunger); and several microcredit and loan projects designed for cooperatives and small and medium-size producers.

Basic Social Services

Education policy initiatives during the postrevolutionary phase had generally conformed to the decentralization model favored by international funders. A school "autonomy" process, launched under Chamorro, was designed to decrease central government control of the school system, increase parental involvement, and as part of that process, promote local fund-raising efforts to help finance decentralized education. By 1996, 31 percent of primary and 72 percent of secondary school students attended officially autonomous schools.[59] As this initiative developed, school committees and principals introduced a fee structure to collect revenues by charging parents for various activities and services. "Cost sharing" involved a 10 córdoba monthly fee for secondary school students. User fees were constitutionally prohibited for primary schools, but autonomous primary schools were encouraged to collect 5 córdobas monthly per student on a voluntary basis. The World Bank projected in 1995 that parental contributions would cover 7 and 20 percent, respectively, of primary and secondary school expenditures.[60]

These fees appeared modest but tended to proliferate over time and became burdensome for low-income families with several children. According to Marlene Valdivia, secretary-general of the Ministry of Education, school fees averaged around 20 córdobas by 2006 but could range from 10 to 100 córdobas for varied transactions (examinations, diplomas, report cards, etc.), depending on the school principal.[61] Primary school students were in theory exempt, but the line between voluntary and required contributions was not always clear at the local level. According to program critics, these fees contributed to Nicaragua's ongoing school desertion problem.[62] In 2005, 25 percent of school dropouts cited lack of money as the main reason for withdrawing.[63] Fees became one more barrier to education, along with the costs of transportation and clothing and the opportunity costs of lost income resulting from school attendance.

Ortega's 2006 campaign platform included a commitment to free education at both the primary and secondary levels and to an end to illiteracy.[64] The new administration quickly decreed the elimination of autonomous schools and school fees and then struggled to identify new funds to replace lost revenues.[65] Echoing the reforms associated with the Sandinista Revolution, Minister of Education Miguel De Castilla Urbina launched a new literacy campaign entitled "From Martí to Fidel" in honor of the Cuban literacy pedagogy adopted in Nicaragua in both the revolutionary and, to a lesser degree, postrevolutionary Sandinista periods. As vice minister of education from July 1979 to January 1984, De Castilla had worked in planning and education policy development during the first literacy crusade. Now named to head the ministry, De Castilla proclaimed a second literacy program targeted to an estimated 500,000 adults who were unable to read and write, and set the goal of raising their educational level to sixth grade over the next five years.[66]

A central obstacle to improved educational outcomes in Nicaragua had long been inadequate funding. Although the education sector received 14 percent of the central government budget in 2005 (not including the 6 percent for university education), the total revenues collected were so modest that per capita spending on public education in Nicaragua remained the lowest in Central America by some distance.[67]

In part to reassure external funders and local forces worried about the return of revolutionary turmoil, the Ortega government generally adhered to the 2007 budget framework proposed by the outgoing Bolaños administration.[68] The IEEPP comparison of the 2007 budget proposed by the Bolaños government and that introduced by Ortega found, however, that although the two budgets were similar in many respects, the Ortega budget increased the Ministry of Education allocation by 12 percent.[69] Over half (57 percent) of this increase was targeted to *gratuidad,* that is, reducing the overall cost of education to the family through increased public spending on school meals, books, and student school supplies.[70] The new government's Economic and Financial Program (Programa Económico-Financiero), 2007–2010, also projected an increase in 2010 antipoverty spending to 17.8 percent of GDP, over 4 percentage points higher than 2006.[71]

Zero Hunger

Malnutrition remained a serious and entrenched problem in Nicaragua.[72] The World Bank reported that 17 percent of Nicaraguan children under the age of five suffered from chronic malnutrition in 2005, only marginally lower than the 17.8 percent found in 2001 (see Table 9.3). In rural areas, 30.5 percent of the population lived in "extreme poverty," lacking the income needed to cover even basic food (see Table 9.2).

The Hambre Cero program (Zero Hunger, see also Chapter 10) was designed to both address nutritional needs and improve income-earning potential by capitalizing the rural poor. This program included three components: the Food Productivity Bond (Bono Productivo Alimentario, or BPA), which involved a transfer of farm animals (cows, pigs, chickens) and other productive supplies to small rural producers; a health and nutrition program for mothers and children in low-income communities; and the national feeding program for preschool and primary school students.[73]

The BPA initiative emerged from a pilot version begun in 1998 by the Center for Rural and Social Promotion, Research, and Development (Centro para la Promoción, la Investigación, y el Desarrollo Rural y Social, or CIPRES) under the leadership of Orlando Núñez, Sandinista intellectual and director of the agricultural ministry's research arm in the 1980s. That program, launched with international aid in the wake of Hurricane Mitch, provided 2,500 families a free transfer of agricultural goods, including high-value farm animals.[74]

After five years, CIPRES conducted an evaluation of the program, comparing food consumption patterns of program beneficiaries with those of a control group of families from the same departments. Striking improvements were found. For example, 85 percent of participating families reported that they consumed eggs that week, whereas only 41 percent of nonparticipating families did so; 58 percent of the former consumed milk, versus only 15 percent of the latter.[75] These results encouraged the civil society network Civil Coordinator (Coordinadora Civil) to call for an expansion of this program, a call that was taken up by the FSLN late in the 2006 campaign. The program quickly became a pro-poor centerpiece for the new Sandinista government.

The new BPA program distributed a basic food production package to needy rural families, thereby addressing nutritional needs and building productive capacity in the countryside. It was initially planned for a projected 15,000 families during the first year and was to expand to 75,000 families over five years.[76] As with the earlier CIPRES program, ownership of these productive capital goods was to be registered in the name of the woman of the household, both in the belief that women better attend to household food needs and to promote development with a gender focus.[77] Because participants were required to own or have access to land, they did not constitute the most deprived sector of society. However, various targeting guidelines were designed to focus benefits on the rural poor—for example, land ownership limitations and criteria that excluded those who owned farm animals or were already enrolled in a similar program. At the end of eighteen months, participants were required to contribute 20 percent of the value of the package (5,000 córdobas, or around US$270) into a revolving fund that they jointly managed. Criticized for excluding the most marginalized by the requirement of land access, program officials subsequently developed a modified version called "Bono de Patio" for families with less than one *manzana* (.7 hectares) of land.[78]

Recognizing that nutritional problems were not solely the result of inadequate access to food, the Zero Hunger program included a nutrition education and resources component for pregnant women and young children. Planned for 5,000 of the "poorest communities," this program was designed to promote breastfeeding, good health practices, increased nutrition monitoring, food fortification, and micronutrient distribution for this vulnerable population. This initiative, along with the third component of the Zero Hunger program, the school feeding program, built on well-established operations that had, under previous administrations, often been delivered by NGOs supported with external funding.

Microcredit and Small and Medium-Size Producers

Small and medium-size enterprises have long been the mainstay of economic life in Nicaragua. In 1998, 97.9 percent of business establishments (formal and informal) reportedly employed five or fewer workers.[79] In the countryside, according to the 2001 agricultural census, 96 percent of producers were classified as small and medium-size.[80]

In spite of their centrality to the national economy, the access of small and medium-size producers to credit and development support has been quite limited. Philosophical rejection of revolutionary statism and economic structuralism made successive postrevolutionary governments reluctant to pursue a developmental role, a position that their primary external funders reinforced. The tradition of nonrepayment of bank credit that had developed during the 1980s brought development banking into ill repute. The state-run Banco Nacional de Desarrollo, the traditional source of rural credit for small producers dating back to the Somoza era, had fallen into technical bankruptcy and been closed in 1997.[81]

The eleven private commercial banks and three financial institutions that emerged in the postrevolution period targeted large producers and projects, providing little support for other sectors. Tomás Rodríguez and Ligia Gómez found that only 14.5 percent of producers in the agriculture sector received formal credit in 1998, and the 9.7 percent of producers who ranked in the highest stratum (capital over $40,000) received 71 percent of this flow.[82]

NGO-led microfinance gradually expanded into this void, and several specialized nonprofit credit institutions emerged, capitalized by international donors. The Nicaraguan Association of Microfinance Institutions (Asociación Nicaragüense de Instituciones de Microfinanzas, or ASOMIF), created to coordinate and support this sector, included twenty members in 2006. Resources allocated by this sector expanded from US$45.4 million (101,463 clients) in 1999 to US$179 million (308,000 clients) in 2006.[83] Even this sector, however, covered only a modest portion of the country's small and medium-size producers. Informal credit distribution remained widespread, with interest rates that could triple those in the formal sector.[84]

As the neoliberal project wore on, a push emerged for the reestablishment of a state development bank, and the FSLN took up this campaign.[85] Under the new Sandinista government, the commitment to expanded public sector lending and rural credit deepened. In 2007, a small state bank, Banco Produzcamos, was approved by the legislature. Noting the high interest rates charged by many microfinance institutions and informal lenders, the administration also created a state-run microloan operation, Usura Cero (Zero Usury), focusing on market women. This program, opening originally in Managua, reported almost 20,000 clients in July 2008, with operations in fifteen *municipios* in the central and Pacific regions.[86]

Funding to expand credit access for small and medium-size producers, market women, and cooperatives was drawn from many sources, including major new contributions from the government of Hugo Chávez in Venezuela. Ortega and Chávez shared a discourse that denounced neoliberal globalization and Western imperialism, and they had long proclaimed their mutual admiration. The 2006 FSLN victory strengthened the bonds with Venezuela and led to the formalization of more extensive aid commitments.

Following Ortega's inauguration and Nicaragua's rapid integration into the Bolivarian Alternative for Latin America (Alternativa Bolivariana para las Américas, or ALBA) alliance, Chávez offered funding to support various social programs and productive projects. Significantly, Venezuela's concessionary oil sales allowed Nicaragua to pay only half of the cost of its petroleum imports, with the remainder classified as either a donation or long-term loan. Under this arrangement, Venezuela effectively transferred $69 million to Nicaragua in 2007: $34 million in donations to support Hambre Cero, Usura Cero, and other government initiatives, and the remainder as a subsidized loan to ALBA-CARUNA. Formerly a small microfinance institution established by a group of National Union of Farmers and Ranchers (Unión Nacional de Agricultores y Ganaderos, or UNAG) leaders in the 1990s, the National Rural Fund (Caja Rural Nacional, or CARUNA) was rebaptized with an ALBA label. ALBA-CARUNA expanded operations using low-cost Venezuelan loans to distribute subsidized credit to a network of small and medium-size producers and cooperatives. Total Venezuelan funding for Nicaragua in 2007, including donations, loans, and investments, was $185 million, representing 18 percent of total foreign aid.[87] By 2010, Venezuelan aid had increased to $511 million, equal to 43 percent of all foreign assistance.[88]

As distribution of social benefits got under way, concern mounted about the targeting mechanisms employed in programs like Hambre Cero, Usura Cero, and ALBA-CARUNA. Various analysts expressed fears that these resources would be used by the government to build a client base rather than to target poverty and strengthen citizen autonomy.[89] Ortega's statement that Usura Cero application materials would be distributed through the Councils of Citizens' Power (Consejos del Poder Ciudadano, or CPCs) intensified these questions, as did the role of CPC representatives in the selection of BPA beneficiaries.[90] The CPC network, which some commentators envisioned as a rebirth of the revolutionary-era Sandinista Defense Committees (Comités de

Defensa Sandinista), was criticized as a potential patronage mechanism that could be used to deploy state resources in the service of narrow partisan interests. Administration backtracking on an offer to use the existing NGO network to distribute Hambre Cero "bonos" and Ortega's inflammatory rhetoric about independent microfinance lenders fed deepening concern in the NGO and donor communities about the centralization of power and prospects for electoral manipulation.

Neo-Sandinista supporters defended the Ortega administration programs as an expression of state interest in the resource needs of the poor, particularly women and peasant producers, who had been marginalized under the neoliberal governments. Claiming that administrative costs in the NGO sector exceeded state resources, the Ortega administration placed these projects in the public sector and worked to rebuild state service delivery capacity. To counter criticism and improve transparency, government agencies such as the Ministry of Agriculture and Forestry (Ministerio Agropecuario y Forestal, or MAGFOR) built databases and posted information about beneficiaries on their websites. As criticism mounted, technical assistance in program monitoring and evaluation was sought from international funders.[91]

Comparisons, Challenges, and Conclusions

A review of antipoverty policy across these three periods helps to identify connections and disconnections between Sandinismo in its revolutionary and neo-Sandinista phases. This framework also highlights continuity and change between neo-Sandinismo and postrevolutionary neoliberalism under the three preceding administrations (see Table 9.4). When comparing first- and second-generation Sandinismo, not only do we find continuity in the occupant of the presidency and the party in power, but we also see parallels in their identification with the Sandino legacy, the use of inclusionary and anti-imperialist discourse, and modification of international alliance strategies, with Venezuela replacing the Cold War socialist countries as the main new funder.

In terms of social development policy, the resuscitated literacy campaign harks back to one of the revolution's major achievements. The renewed emphasis on improved credit access resonates with the "democratized credit" theme of the revolutionary period. The Hambre Cero commitment to strengthen the peasant economy was perhaps a late-learned lesson of the 1980s, when peasant defections fed the Contra war and the excessive emphasis on state farms was reconsidered. Like its revolutionary predecessor,

Table 9.4 A Comparison of the Neo-Sandinista Period with Previous Periods

	Continuities	Discontinuities
Sandinista Revolution period, 1979–1990	FSLN, Daniel Ortega Sandino iconography Anti-imperialism discourse Shifts in international alliance strategies Strengthened social programs (literacy, basic health and education, nutrition, credit access)	Weaker popular base Independent civil society Stronger Sandinista economic elite FSLN leadership schisms Stronger institutional constraints No Contra war Social and economic policy less redistributive
Postrevolutionary neoliberal period, 1990–2006	High, stagnant poverty Low education and production levels High dependence on external funding Social programs financed and monitored by external donors Fragmented government, dependent on pacts	Increased friction with the United States Increased Venezuelan aid Increased pro-poor policy expectations More rivalry with NGOs Some new/expanded social initiatives

the neo-Sandinista government highlighted those who were left behind, even as it attempted to reassure local and international elites about its intentions. Like many of the 1980s initiatives, the recent medley of social programs—the new literacy campaign, strengthened basic health and education programs, rural development, and credit initiatives—emphasized the pivotal role of the state in the direct transfer of development resources and pointed to weaknesses in the market model.

At the same time, major differences emerged between the revolutionary version of Sandinismo and the neo-Sandinista variant. At the time of the revolution, the FSLN had a sweeping popular mandate and broad control of the state apparatus. Liberation theology was in full flower, and Marxist frameworks still mobilized on the left. State ownership of productive resources like land and finance reinforced the leaders' considerable influence; opposition, at least initially, was scattered and paltry. Civil society in the early 1980s was weak, leaving ample space for the new government to build its own organizations. Other branches of government, although nominally independent, especially after the 1987 Constitution was approved, basically took direction from the FSLN leadership.

In contrast, the postrevolutionary Sandinista government, now en-sconced in the restricted world of electoral politics, lacked the political resources to pursue sweeping change, even if it were so inclined. Ortega began his second term with a comparatively well-organized opposition and a much weaker mandate. With only 38 percent of the presidential vote and a victory carved from Nicaragua's peculiar electoral rules, the FSLN had to continuously orchestrate alliances in order to govern.

During the 1990s, Nicaraguan civil society developed and became largely independent of FSLN control. A host of NGOs emerged during the postrevolutionary period; those staffed by displaced Sandinista activists labored alongside those opposed to the revolution. As the state continued to contract along key dimensions, these organizations absorbed some of its functions, mobilizing external funding to provide basic services. Many civil society organizations also learned to monitor and check political authorities. Over time, they developed a number of legal avenues to gain access to government officials at the municipal, departmental, and national levels. Although their success was always limited, leaders of these organizations developed considerable political capacity, often including an ability to cooperate across party lines.

Not only had the political landscape changed dramatically by 2006, but so had the economic base of the FSLN leadership. Whether through family connections, the appropriation of state property during the chaotic transition in 1990, or their own entrepreneurial activities during the era of market reform, key Sandinista leaders had acquired a stake in business, financial services, and international trade. The redistributive zeal of the early revolution was attenuated by the rise of this Sandinista business class. New class alliances, combined with the scars of defeat and memories of war, tended to de-radicalize second-generation Sandinismo, as did the departure of many of the party's intellectual leaders.

Although freed from the 1980s burden of war, the second Sandinista government was now more delimited by an established institutional order, layers of political opposition, the pronounced economic interests of its own business sector, and close external donor monitoring. Even with relatively unregulated Venezuelan aid, the Ortega government operated within sharp constraints. Social and economic policy focused less on redistribution and more on increasing specific resources for targeted populations.

In fact, the economic and political panorama faced by the neo-Sandinista government strongly resembled that which its immediate postrevolutionary predecessors confronted. Like the neoliberal administrations before it, the Ortega administration faced ongoing challenges associated with Nicaragua's low education and production levels and its high, stagnant poverty rates.

Even after years of neoliberal restructuring, the Nicaraguan state still depended heavily on external donors, with much of this aid conditioned on the achievement of specific macroeconomic and policy goals.

In addition to the narrow space for policy innovation, the challenges of governing a divided country persisted. Government through pacts with erstwhile rivals had become the modus operandi for the country's political leaders from Chamorro through Bolaños, and the second Sandinista government continued the tradition.

In other ways, however, the reelection of Ortega did represent a departure from politics as usual in Nicaragua. The cooperative relationship with the United States, particularly under the Chamorro and Bolaños administrations, was tested with the return to office of Daniel Ortega, and episodes of tension alternated with efforts to improve relations. Venezuela now emerged as an alliance rival and alternative source of aid.

Expectations about social reform rose, at least initially, in keeping with public promises and hope, putting greater pressure on the government to address basic needs. The commitment to stronger state capacity characteristic of the Ortega administration clashed with the greater decentralization found in previous administrations, particularly in the service delivery sector. As we have seen, the push to provide services through government agencies placed the neo-Sandinista government in conflict with NGOs, many of which had taken on planning and administrative functions during the period of state contraction and had developed considerable service capacity. Instead of viewing the independent NGOs as mechanisms to promote democratic development (facilitating participation and communication) and improve policy performance (providing knowledge of local communities, technical advice, and vigilant policy monitoring), the neo-Sandinista government tended to approach them as rivals. That conflict came at a cost.

In the end, the new Sandinista government entered office markedly different from its revolutionary predecessor. It did not launch major national campaigns to mobilize large sectors of society to remake the nation. It did not expropriate and redistribute land or other productive resources, nor did it assume control of the banking system and redirect the flow of national financial resources. No longer capable of redistributive measures, which, in any case, had failed to deliver the promised prosperity, the neo-Sandinista government opted for inclusionary policies that provided some measure of benefit to less-privileged sectors without directly challenging established elites.

The Ortega government's proposals for a new literacy campaign and greater educational achievements, programs to improve nutrition and working capital for small farmers, and expanded credit access for micro, small and medium-size businesses, with special attention to the needs of poor women in the countryside, could help meet basic human needs and promote human agency. The challenge is to integrate these programs into an inclusive and sustainable development process while avoiding the fault line of clientelism, in which citizens become supplicants and grateful followers instead of empowered actors demanding their due. Unless the second Sandinista government can meet this challenge, Nicaragua's failed legacy of antipoverty programs is likely to continue.

Notes

Research funding for this project was provided by the University Research Council of DePaul University.
1. Government of Nicaragua, Ministry of Planning (MIPLAN), *Programa económico de austeridad y eficiencia 81* (Managua: MIPLAN, 1981).
2. David F. Ruccio, "The State and Planning in Nicaragua," in *The Political Economy of Revolutionary Nicaragua,* edited by Rose J. Spalding (Boston: Allen and Unwin, 1987), 61–82.
3. See Richard R. Fagen, Carmen Diana Deere, and José Luis Coraggio, eds., *Transition and Development: Problems of Third World Socialism* (New York: Monthly Review Press, 1986); and Harry E. Vanden and Gary Prevost, *Democracy and Socialism in Sandinista Nicaragua* (Boulder, CO: Lynne Rienner, 1993).
4. David R. Dye, *Democracy Adrift: Caudillo Politics in Nicaragua* (Managua: PRODENI, 2004).
5. On internal debates over the economic model, see Alejandro Martínez Cuenca, *Nicaragua: Una década de retos* (Managua: Nueva Nicaragua, 1990).
6. Laura J. Enríquez and Rose J. Spalding, "Banking Systems and Revolutionary Change: The Politics of Agricultural Credit in Nicaragua," in *The Political Economy of Revolutionary Nicaragua,* edited by Rose J. Spalding (Boston: Allen and Unwin, 1987), 105–125; and Miguel Alemán, "Mercado financiero en Nicaragua: 1960–1990," in *Crédito para el Desarrollo Rural en Nicaragua,* edited by Johan Bastiaensen (Managua: Nitlapán-UCA, 2002), 49–53.
7. Sheryl Hirshon, with Judy Butler, *And Also Teach Them to Read* (Westport, CT: Lawrence Hill, 1983), 11; and Valerie Miller, *Between Struggle and Hope: The Nicaraguan Literacy Crusade* (Boulder, CO: Westview, 1985).
8. The official illiteracy rate registered in the 1971 census was 42.2 percent. Roughly 50 percent of the adult population was classified as illiterate in the 1980 census, but around 9 percent of the population was reported to have severe learning disabilities that prevented full participation in the literacy campaign. This segment was eliminated to calculate an "effective illiteracy rate" of around 40 percent. According to Miller's estimation, illiteracy was reduced from around 40 percent at the beginning of the campaign to 13 percent at the end. Dennis Gilbert notes that since the calculations at the end of the campaign excluded adults classified as "learning impaired," the actual final illiteracy rate was 23 percent. INEC (Instituto Nacional de Estadísticas y Censos), *VIII Censo de población y IV de vivienda: Resumen*

censal (Managua: INEC, 2006), 60; Miller, *Between Struggle and Hope,* 60; Dennis Gilbert, "The Society and Its Environment," in *Nicaragua: A Country Study,* 3rd ed., edited by Tim L. Merrill (Washington, DC: Library of Congress, 1994), 74.

9. Miguel De Castilla Urbina, "La educación como poder, crisis sin solución en la transición revolucionaria: El caso de Nicaragua, 1978–1981," in *Estado y clases sociales en Nicaragua,* edited by *Asociación Nicaragüense de Científicos Sociales* (Managua: CIERA, 1982), 247.

10. Juan Bautista Arríen, Miguel De Castilla Urbina, and Rafael Lucio Gil, *La educación en Nicaragua entre siglos, dudas, y esperanzas* (Managua: UCA, 1998), 99.

11. They included the Ministerio de Salud Pública, the Junta Nacional de Asistencia y Previsión Social, the Instituto Nicaragüense de Seguridad Social, nineteen local social assistance boards, and the Red Cross. Orlando Núñez, *El somocismo y el modelo capitalista agroexportador* (Managua: Depto. de Ciencias Sociales, UNAN, 1981), 108.

12. Núñez, *El somocismo,* 108.

13. Government of Nicaragua MIPLAN, *Programa económico,* 104.

14. Thomas W. Walker, *Nicaragua: Living in the Shadow of the Eagle* (Boulder, CO: Westview, 2003), 122.

15. Peter Utting, *Economic Adjustment Under the Sandinistas: Policy Reform, Food Security, and Livelihood in Nicaragua* (Geneva: UNRISD, 1991), 45.

16. Harvey Williams, "The Social Programs," in *Revolution and Counterrevolution in Nicaragua,* edited by Thomas W. Walker (Boulder, CO: Westview, 1991), 197.

17. Williams, "The Social Programs," 198.

18. Martínez Cuenca, *Nicaragua,* 129–144.

19. Roser Solá Montserrat, *Un siglo y medio de economía nicaragüense: Las raíces del presente* (Managua: Universidad Centroamericana, 2007), 173.

20. Utting, *Economic Adjustment,* 45.

21. Arríen, De Castilla Urbina, and Gil, *La educación en Nicaragua,* 63.

22. Rossella Cominetti and Gonzalo Ruíz, "Evolución del Gasto Público Social en América Latina: 1980–1995," LCSHD Paper Series (May 1997). Washington, DC: Department of Human Development, World Bank, www.wds.worldbank .org/, 122.

23. David Close, *Nicaragua: The Chamorro Years* (Boulder, CO: Lynne Rienner, 1999).

24. Government of Nicaragua, *A Strengthened Poverty Reduction Strategy: 2000,* povlibrary.worldbank.org/, 14.

25. Government of Nicaragua, *A Strengthened Poverty Reduction,* 74.

26. Although some changes took hold quickly, others generated more resistance, and the Chamorro government advanced only via negotiation. Facing active rebellion on land issues, for example, the government compromised on the dismantling of state farms, returning some land to former owners but giving 32 percent of the land to workers, 21 percent to former contras, and 17 percent to former soldiers as a reward for demobilization. Rose J. Spalding, *Capitalists and Revolution in Nicaragua: Opposition and Accommodation, 1979–1993* (Chapel Hill: University of North Carolina Press, 1994), 174–177.

27. World Bank, *Republic of Nicaragua Poverty Assessment,* vol. 1, report no. 14038-NI (Washington, DC: World Bank, 1995), 32.

28. Juan Bautista Arríen and Miguel De Castilla Urbina, *Educación y pobreza en Nicaragua* (Managua: Universidad Centroamericana, 2001), 83–85.

29. Mario J. Arana and Juan F. Rocha, "Efecto de las políticas macroeconómicas y sociales sobre la pobreza en el caso de Nicaragua," paper presented to the Seminarios Internacionales sobre Políticas Macroeconómicas y Pobreza, June 3–5 and October 30–November 2, 1997, www.iadb.org/, 16.

30. The international debate about how best to measure poverty has been lively and sustained. During the 1980s, the UBN methodology was widely used in Nicaragua and elsewhere. This method focuses on five basic need indicators: crowding (people per bedroom), services (water and sewage), housing quality (construction material for floor, walls, and roof), education (the number of children ages seven to fourteen not attending school), and economic dependence (household head completion of primary school and ratio of nonworking to working members of household). This method traditionally found high levels of poverty in Nicaragua. See INIDE (Instituto Nacional de Información de Desarrollo), *Perfil y características de los pobres en Nicaragua 2005* (Managua: INIDE, 2007), 32.

The World Bank rejected this measurement method in the early 1990s, noting the absence of consensus on what constitutes basic needs and the dependence of this definition on previous government investments in social services and infrastructure, with a consequent deemphasis on current income and consumption levels. The minimalist methodology adopted by the World Bank, which defines extreme poverty in terms of basic food consumption (see below), has been criticized by Araceli Damián and Julio Boltvinik as limiting this category to those living at subhuman levels of existence ("eating raw food on the floor with their hands"). Critics like welfare economist Amartya Sen have called for a redefinition using indicators that focus on the expansion of human "agency" and "capabilities" rather than household income. For discussion, see World Bank, *Republic of Nicaragua Poverty Assessment,* vols. 1–2, report no. 14038-NI, 5; Araceli Damián and Julio Boltvinik, "A Table to Eat On: The Meaning and Measurement of Poverty in Latin America," in *Latin America After Neoliberalism,* edited by Eric Hershberg and Fred Rosen (New York: New Press, 2006), 144–170; Amartya Sen, *Development as Freedom* (New York: Anchor, 1999).

31. The "extreme poverty" line was determined based on the annual per capita cost of a basic food basket that provided 2,187 kcal/day per capita in 1998 (C$2,489 or US$237); because of demographic changes, the number of calories was changed to 2,200 kcal/day in 2001 (C$2,691 or US$202); and, in the INIDE assessment, the number was 2,241 kcal/day (C$3,928 or US$235) in 2005. The "poverty" line was determined using the observed pattern of food/nonfood consumption of families whose food expenditures were C$2,489 in 1998, that is, 59 percent for food and 41 percent for nonfood, producing an overall poverty line of C$4,223 (US$401) per capita in 1998, C$5,157 (US$386) in 2001, and C$7,155 (US$428) in 2005. World Bank, *Nicaragua Poverty Assessment: Raising Welfare and Reducing Vulnerability,* Report no. 26128-NI (Washington, DC: World Bank, 2003), 2; Néstor Avendaño and Camilo Pacheco, "El perfil de la pobreza humana de Nicaragua en 2005," in *Nicaragua: Informe Económico,* GEA-COPADES, 129–146 (Managua: GEA and COPADES: 2007), 134.

32. World Bank, *Nicaragua Poverty Assessment: Raising Welfare and Reducing Vulnerability,* report no. 26128-NI (Washington, DC: World Bank, 2003), 6.

33. On the positive side, both the World Bank and INIDE sources reported that the gap between the actual earnings of the poor and the poverty/extreme poverty lines had shrunk between 2001 and 2005, as some earnings crept up and/or some consumer costs declined. This finding suggested that some progress in reducing poverty severity had been made during this period, although it was not large enough to translate into an overall reduction in the poverty rates. World Bank analysts also took comfort in 2005 LSMS data on crowding, access to potable water, housing quality, and school attendance, which registered some improvement over 2001. World Bank, *Nicaragua Poverty Assessment,* vol. 1, Main Report, no. 39736-NI, www.wds.worldbank.org/, ii; INIDE, *Perfil y características,* 13–17.

34. For example, see World Bank, *Republic of Nicaragua Poverty Assessment,* vol. 1, report no. 14038-NI, 63–68.

35. IMF-IDA (International Monetary Fund and International Development Association), *Nicaragua: Joint Staff Advisory Note on the Poverty Reduction Strategy Paper* (Washington, DC: IMF/IDA, 2005, 1), siteresources.worldbank.org/.

36. Republic of Nicaragua, *National Development Plan* (Managua: República de Nicaragua, 2005, 129), http://siteresources.worldbank.org/.

37. Government of Nicaragua, *Strengthened Poverty Reduction*), Annex 1, 50–64; República de Nicaragua, Consejo Nacional de Planificación Económica Social, *Informe 2003* (Managua: República de Nicaragua, 2004); CONPES (Consejo Nacional de Planificación Económica Social), *Consulta Municipal sobre la ERCERP: Sistematización de las memorias de trabajo en los once municipios* (Managua: CONPES/PAI, 2003).

38. Geske Dijkstra, "The PRSP Approach and the Illusion of Improved Aid Effectiveness: Lessons from Bolivia, Honduras, and Nicaragua," *Development Policy Review* 23, no. 4 (2005): 443–464; and David Booth, Arturo Grigsby, and Carlos Toranzo, "Politics and Poverty Reduction Strategies: Lessons from Latin American HIPCs," Overseas Development Institute, Working Paper 262 (February 2006).

39. World Bank, *Nicaragua: Poverty Reduction and Local Development Project* (Washington, DC: World Bank, 2001, 2), www.wds.worldbank.org/.

40. This program was introduced in six high-poverty zones (78–90 percent of total households in these areas were classified as poor), using either geographical targeting (where more than 55 percent of households were in extreme poverty) or household targeting (when less than 45 percent of households were in extreme poverty). ODI (Overseas Development Institute), "Red de Protección Social Nicaragua," Policy Brief no. 3 (February 2006), www.odi.org.uk/, 1–2.

41. John A. Maluccio and Rafael Flores, "Impact Evaluation of a Conditional Cash Transfer Program: The Nicaraguan Red de Protección Social," Research Report no. 141 (Washington, DC: International Food Policy Research Institute, 2005), www.ifpri.org/, x.

42. ODI, "Red de Protección Social Nicaragua," 1.

43. Ferdinando Regalia, "An Assessment of Poverty and Safety Nets in Nicaragua" (Washington, DC: IADB, 2000), www.iadb.org/.

44. Republic of Nicaragua, *National Development Plan;* and Mario De Franco, former Secretario de Coordinación y Estrategia de la Presidencia [Bolaños administration], author interview, July 20, 2007.

45. IMF-IDA, *Nicaragua: Joint Staff Advisory Note,* 5, 9, note 14.

46. World Bank, *Nicaragua Poverty Assessment,* vol. 1, Main Report, no. 39736-NI, www.wds.worldbank.org/, v–vi.

47. World Bank, *Nicaragua Poverty Assessment: Raising Welfare,* report no. 26128-NI, 41.

48. Questions were raised about spending that emphasized "institutional strengthening" in line ministries and projects that were "too large (housing programs transferring more than US$2,000), or if they require managerial or financial capabilities beyond those of the poor (for example, delivery of a herd of 25 cattle, or housing programs requiring access to credit)." At the same time, the resource flow was "inadequate" for "health, nutrition, and educational development of children zero–three, access to legal title for housing and property, and attention to personal risks, especially domestic violence." World Bank, *Nicaragua Poverty Assessment: Raising Welfare,* report no. 26128-NI, 41.

49. Carlos Lacayo, *Segundo proyecto de desarrollo rural municipal: Informe final* (Managua: Ministerio de Hacienda y Crédito Público, 2006), 9.

50. The prospect that HIPC debt relief would generate additional resources for social development and poverty abatement had raised new hope for more effective intervention. However, the rapid growth of the domestic debt burden siphoned off resources that might have gone to this effort. Research by Néstor Avendaño and Adolfo José Acevedo Vogl found that the obligation to pay off bonds issued to compensate depositors when Nicaraguan banks failed in 2001 and the maturation of bonds given in compensation for expropriated properties during the 1980s cut into the resources available for state social spending. This internal debt burden had quickly absorbed the resources freed by external debt relief. See Avendaño, *La Economía de Nicaragua: Evaluación 2005, Pronóstico 2006, y Prognosis 2007–2011* (Managua: COPADES, 2006); and Acevedo Vogl, Coordinadora Civil, author interview, July 12, 2007.

51. INIDE (Instituto Nacional de Información de Desarrollo), *Encuesta nacional de hogares sobre medición del nivel de vida 2005: Informe general* (Managua: INIDE, 2007), 64.

52. INIDE, *Encuesta nacional,* 17; INIDE, *Perfil y características,* 111.

53. World Bank, *Key Issues in Central America Health Reforms: Diagnosis and Strategic Implications,* vol. 2, report no. 36426-LAC (Washington, DC: World Bank, 2007), www.wds.worldbank.org/, 144.

54. World Bank, *Nicaragua Poverty Assessment,* vol. 1: Main Report, no. 39736-NI, www.wds.worldbank.org/, 66.

55. In addition to goals discussed in Table 9.3, the World Bank classified the 2015 achievement of MDGs for access to reproductive services and sanitation as "very unlikely." On the positive side, achievement of the MDG for extreme poverty reduction was categorized as "possible." World Bank, *Nicaragua Poverty Assessment,* vol 1, Main Report, no. 39736-NI, 29.

56. INIDE, *Perfil y características,* 86 (whether household had sanitation facilities), 87 (discarding solid waste in rivers), 89 (lack of access to electrical grid).

57. INIDE, *Perfil y características de los pobres,* 56, 87, 89.

58. Orlando Núñez, "'Hambre Cero': US$90 millones en tres años," *Confidencial* 516, December 17, 2006–January 7, 2007.

59. Arríen, De Castilla Urbina, and Gil, *La educación en Nicaragua,* 194.

60. World Bank, *Staff Appraisal Report, Nicaragua, Basic Education Project,* report no. 13705-NI (Washington, DC: World Bank, 1995), 12.

61. Marlene Valdivia, secretary-general of the Ministry of Education, Nicaragua Network delegation interview, July 17, 2007.

62. Programa de Observatorio de la Reforma de la Educación en Centroamérica, *América Central: La educación en el año 2002* (Managua: Universidad Centroamericana, 2003), 36.

63. INIDE, *Encuesta nacional,* 15.

64. Daniel Ortega, *Programa del gobierno de reconciliación y unidad nacional, 2006–2011,* Acto de Clausura del III Congreso FSLN, Sesión "Sandino, La Victoria," May 28, 2006, 56–58.

65. Marlene Valdivia, interview, July 17, 2007.

66. Government of Nicaragua, Ministry of Education (MINED), "Políticas educativas 2007–2011," 2007, www.mined.gob.ni/; and "Profesor Miguel de Castilla participa en el XV Congreso Nacional de UNEN," *Notas de Prensa,* July 18, 2007, www.mined.gob.ni/.

67. IEEPP (Instituto de Estudios Estratégicos y Políticas Públicas), "Cifras y perspectivas del gasto público 2007 en Salud y Educación," *Presupuesto Ciudadano* (June 2007): 6. The document noted (on p. 8) that Nicaraguan public education spending of $28 per capita compared unfavorably with Honduras ($45), Guatemala ($46), and El Salvador ($51). Nicaragua's per capita spending on secondary education, as a percentage of per capita GDP, remained one of the lowest in Latin America.

68. The Ortega 2007 budget included no increase in teacher salaries, and it committed the government to honor the heavy internal debt. IEEPP, "Cifras y perspectivas," 17.

69. IEEPP, "Cifras y perspectivas," 11–12.

70. IEEPP, "Cifras y perspectivas," 12, 16.

71. Gobierno de Unidad y Reconciliación Nacional, *Programa Económico-Financiero 2007–2010,* 2007, www.bcn.gob.ni/, 15.

72. CEPAL (Comisión Económica para América Latina y el Caribe), *Análisis del impacto social y económico de la desnutrición infantil en América Latina: Resultados del estudio en Centroamérica y República Dominicana: Panorama General* (Santiago, Chile: CEPAL and Programa Mundial de Alimentos, 2007), 12.

73. "Programa Hambre Cero: Combatir la Pobreza en Nicaragua y Alcanzar la Soberanía Alimentaria" (n.p., 2007).

74. CIPRES (Centro para la Promoción, la Investigación y el Desarrollo Rural y Social), "Programa Productivo Alimentario," *Cuadernos de CIPRES* 28, 3rd ed. (Managua: Ediciones Graphic Print, S.A., 2007), 8.

75. CIPRES, "Programa Productivo Alimentario," 57.

76. The full package included a pregnant cow, a pregnant pig, five hens and a rooster, fruit and forest trees, seeds, fertilizer and animal feed, a biodigestor stove (designed to reduce deforestation), construction materials, and other implements. This package was valued at $1,500 per household (plus $500 in technical training and assistance). "Programa Hambre Cero."

77. Orlando Núñez, "'Hambre Cero': US$90 millones en tres años," interview with Iván Olivares, *Confidencial* 516, December 17, 2006–January 7, 2007.

78. Brigitte McBain-Haas, with Martin Wolpold-Bosien, "The Right to Food and the Fight Against Hunger in Nicaragua: One Year of the Zero Hunger Program" (Heidelberg, Germany: FIAN International Secretariat, 2008), www.fian.org/.

79. Rick Van der Kamp, *PYMES, Competitividad y SDE en Nicaragua* (Managua: Nitlapán-UCA, 2006), 16.

80. CIPRES, "Programa Productivo Alimentario," 26.

81. Government of Nicaragua, *Strengthened Poverty Reduction,* 74.

82. Tomás Rodríguez and Ligia Gómez Rodríguez, "Mercado de crédito rural en Nicaragua," in *Crédito para el Desarrollo Rural en Nicaragua,* edited by John Baetiaensen (Managua: Nitlapán-UCA, 2002), 56–57.

83. Rodríguez and Gómez Rodríguez, "Mercado de crédito rural en Nicaragua," 72; ASOMIF (Asociación Nicaragüense de Instituciones de Microfinanzas), *Memoria Institucional 2006* (Managua: LITONIC, 2007), 6.

84. According to the World Bank, 45 out of every 100 loans in Nicaragua were provided by informal lenders and merchants, with interest rates that ran as high as 12 percent per month, around three times the rates charged by banks, cooperatives, and formal financial institutions. World Bank, *Nicaragua Poverty Assessment,* vol. 1, Main Report, no. 39736-NI, xiii.

85. Daniel Ortega, *Programa del gobierno,* 40–41.

86. Leonor Corea, Director, Usura Cero, author interview, July 31, 2008.

87. Half of the cost of Venezuelan petroleum imports would be paid at market rates and was due in ninety days. Twenty-five percent was reclassified as a private loan from the Venezuelan state petroleum company Petróleos de Venezuela, S.A. (PDVSA) to ALBA-CARUNA, to be repaid slowly at a heavily subsidized 2 percent interest rate. The remaining 25 percent was given to the Nicaraguan government as a donation. Banco Central de Nicaragua, *Informe de Cooperación Oficial Nicaragua 2007* (Managua: Banco Central de Nicaragua, 2008), www.bcn.gob.ni/, 12, 28.

88. In addition to funds for Zero Hunger and other agricultural production support, Venezuelan assistance in 2010 supported reduced rates for public transportation and small electricity users; wage subsidies for low-income workers in the public sector; financial assistance for the electrical industry; street repair following natural disasters; and the promotion of "fair trade" exports, particularly to Venezuela. See Banco Central de Nicaragua, *Informe de Cooperación Oficial Externa 2010* (Managua: Banco Central de Nicaragua, 2011), www.bcn.gob.ni/, 5, 14–15.

89. Paul Kester, "Informe Evaluativo (2007–2008) Programa Productivo Alimentario (PPA) 'Hambre Cero'" (February 2009), www.embajadaholanda-nic.com/; McBain-Haas, with Wolpold-Bosien, "The Right to Food"; DEPPA (División de Estudios, Publicaciones, Propuestas y Análisis) and FUNIDES (Fundación Nicaragüense para el Desarrollo Económico y Social), *Herramientas para fortalecer programas de protección social: Nicaragua. Incluye herramientas para diseñar, implementar, monitorear y evaluar Hambre Cero* (Managua: DEPPA-FUNIDES, 2007), 19–23.

90. Esteban Solís, "Consejos controlarán créditos," *El Nuevo Diario,* July 18, 2007.

91. See Inter-American Development Bank, *Nicaragua: Program to Support Agrifood Production,* NI-L1020 Loan Proposal, May 16, 2008, idbdocs.iadb.org/.

10

The Politics of Land Reform

Eduardo Baumeister

THIS CHAPTER HAS FOUR SECTIONS. IN THE FIRST SECTION, I DIS-
cuss agrarian structures in other countries in order to place Nicaragua in
comparative perspective, with reference to both the pre-1979 period and to
the era of agrarian reform in the 1980s. The second section treats the evolution of agricultural production from the end of the 1970s to the present.
In the third section, I analyze changes in the structure of Nicaraguan agriculture during two key periods: from 1979 to the end of the 1980s and then
through the 1990s. The outcome of these changes strengthened the position
of midsize farmers, as well as of a portion of smallholders, while collective
and state-owned agriculture effectively disappeared. The final section recounts the events of the recent past and asks how the return of the FSLN to
power in 2007 might affect the future of Nicaraguan agriculture.

Types of Agrarian Structures

At the end of the 1970s, rural Nicaragua possessed a set of characteristics
unique in Latin America. Its agro-export economy and very large rural population, although similar to what existed in the rest of Central America and
the Andean countries, was quite different from the midsize and large countries of Latin America, where since the 1950s the urban sector had become
increasingly important socially and economically. Further, Nicaragua's
agrarian structures also differed from the classic Latin American models.[1]

This chapter was translated by David Close.

For example, unlike in prerevolutionary Cuba, the Caribbean, and even some Central American states, there were few large plantations owned by foreign capital. Neither were there extensive *latifundias* (very large agricultural properties) that were abandoning precapitalist forms to enter both domestic and export markets, as was the case in countries like Bolivia, Chile, Peru, and Mexico, all of which attempted serious agrarian reforms in the twentieth century.[2] In a real sense, Nicaragua possessed a unique agrarian structure.

The term "agrarian structure" deserves elaboration. I use the term to indicate the relationships existing between or among models for organizing agricultural production and the homes that provide the labor for the producing units. It is conventional to speak of four classes of structures—plantations, cattle ranches, coffee estates, and midsize single-family farms—which are described below. None of them was as important in Nicaragua as in other Latin American countries.

The first class comprises foreign-owned plantations, such as the banana plantations in Costa Rica, Honduras, Guatemala, or Panama, or the large sugar plantations found in prerevolutionary Cuba or the Dominican Republic before, during, and after the Trujillo era. In Nicaragua there were only a few banana plantations during the twentieth century. This can be attributed to the conditions of political instability, often in the form of internal war and direct confrontations with the United States from the end of the nineteenth century to the 1930s.[3]

A second type of agricultural model is the cattle-ranching hacienda, which had semifeudal labor relations. Examples of this model existed in prerevolutionary Mexico, the mountainous regions of some Andean states, Paraguay, extensive parts of Brazil and Colombia, and the Bolivian lowlands, even after the revolution of 1952.

At the beginning of the 1970s, it was estimated that some 34 percent of Nicaraguan land was concentrated in large holdings of whatever type and accounted for about 30 percent of the wealth generated by the agricultural sector.[4] However, similar studies from the late 1950s and early 1960s showed cattle-ranching haciendas occupying higher percentages of the nation's land in Guatemala (40 percent), Ecuador (45 percent), Colombia (49.5 percent), and Peru (82.4 percent).[5] Equally significant are "medium multifamily" units, which employ from four to twelve workers and have characteristics of both haciendas that hire wage workers and more purely family farms. In the late 1950s and early 1960s, these units held 43 percent of Nicaragua's land,[6] but accounted for 31.5 percent in Guatemala, 19.3 percent in Ecuador, 5.7 percent in Peru, and 11.4 percent in Chile.[7]

The third model, the great coffee estate, common in Guatemala and El Salvador, was also relatively insignificant in Nicaragua. Falling into this class are coffee *fincas* producing over 1,000 *quintales* (hundredweight) of coffee annually, which generally means having some fifteen permanent salaried employees, at least seventy seasonal hands, and the administrative structures required to manage such an operation.[8] Such estates accounted for 66 percent of national coffee production in El Salvador, 75 percent in Guatemala, and only 30 percent in Nicaragua.[9]

Finally, although Nicaragua was not dominated by *latifundias,* it would be incorrect to see its agriculture as the preserve of independent peasants or yeomen. That would be true of Costa Rican coffee producers or many of the grain growers of the Argentine pampas. Neither did Nicaragua have the type of peasant economy found among the indigenous peoples of the highlands of Bolivia, Ecuador, or Guatemala.

Pre-1979 Nicaraguan Agrarian Structures

As the above suggests, in the decades leading to the revolutionary triumph of 1979, Nicaraguan agriculture was distinguished by the coexistence of various forms of agrarian structures, none of which dominated. The export side of this complex system was built on cattle, coffee, cotton, and sugar. Comparing Nicaragua's agriculture to what is found in its Central American neighbors casts further light on the country's singularity.

For example, cattle ranching in Nicaragua has always been characterized by its extensive use of land, 1 hectare (roughly 2.5 acres) of pasture per head, low levels of capital investment, and the presence of sectors dedicated to cattle breeding and dairy farming. One finds a large number of small-scale cattle operations using between 15 and 50 hectares, employing no more than four *campistos,* workers who receive both a salary and a small parcel of land (usually less than 2 hectares). Occasionally, the owner takes a part of the produce from these parcels as rent. Recently, however, the international market for beef has led to the emergence of a sector of large-scale operations dedicated to finishing cattle before sending them to market. Because these operations need better pastures, they are more capital-intensive and clearly commercial enterprises.

Unlike in El Salvador or Guatemala, where large coffee estates dominate, in Nicaragua coffee production has been centered in midsize farms of 20 to 50 hectares.[10] As with cattle ranching, coffee production is land-intensive, and per hectare yields are well below those of Costa Rica or El Salvador, with an average holding having fewer than ten permanent employees and producing from 200 to 500 *quintales* annually. These medium-size coffee *fincas* were particularly important in expansion of production in Matagalpa and Jinotega in the 1960s and 1970s. Although coffee estates existed in the departments of Managua and Carazo in the Pacific zone, as well as in the central and northern zones of Matagalpa, Jinotega, and Madriz, it was the midsize *fincas,* characteristic of the agricultural frontier, that produced the bulk of the country's coffee.

Conditions in cotton farming were different. This sector grew in the 1950s in response to increased worldwide demand for the product and was concentrated in a few areas of the northern Pacific region, in the departments of León and Chinandega. As elsewhere in Central America and in Peru, cotton was the preserve of midsize and large commercial farmers.

As already alluded to above, comparing the structure of Nicaraguan agriculture to what existed in other Latin American countries prior to 1979 shows the country's distinctiveness. Foremost among its distinguishing features is the weight of a sector of midsize capitalist farms, the medium multifamily sector mentioned earlier. They are not classic family farms, because they employ hired hands and may have other families living on the property. In general, there are no more than ten hired workers, who live either on the property or in surrounding towns. This class of farm was most common in the central region and on the agricultural frontier. Second, alongside these midsize holdings existed a large number of landless laborers who worked on both these holdings and on larger farms, some as permanent employees and others as seasonal help. Table 10.1 illustrates conditions in Nicaragua and its Central American neighbors.

With 50 percent of its agricultural production coming from midsize family holdings, Nicaragua led the region in the 1960s, and its numbers were dramatically different from those of El Salvador or Honduras.[11] Though not family farms in the North American sense, they were family businesses, where

Table 10.1 Percentages of Midsize Agrarian Holdings and Landless Peasants in Central America in the 1960s

Country	Percentage of Gross Agricultural Product from Medium-Size Farms	Percentage of Rural Families Without Land
Costa Rica	37	42
El Salvador	22	16
Guatemala	36	17
Honduras	12	26
Nicaragua	50	31

Sources: United Nations Food and Agriculture Organization–International Labour Organization (Organización Internacional del Trabajo) (FAO-OIT), *Tenencia de la tierra y desarrollo rural en Centroamérica* (San José, Costa Rica: EDUCA, 1976), 70, Annex C; Solon Barraclough and Arthur Domike, "La estructura agraria en siete países de América Latina," in *La lucha de clases en el campo,* edited by Ernest Feder (México, DF: Fondo de Cultura Economica, 1975), 69.

the owner or the owner's children were the frontline administrators. In addition, Nicaragua had the second-highest proportion of landless rural families, giving rise to a large sector of permanent or seasonal rural wage workers; in Nicaragua's agrarian reform in the 1980s, this sector drove the emphasis placed on state farms using landless laborers.[12] Further, in the cases of Honduras and Guatemala, the number of landless included those who had some access to rented or leased land, as would workers on large estates.[13]

In Nicaragua, these midsize capitalist farmers also had an important presence in export agriculture, unlike the rest of Central America, where larger units predominated. Table 10.2 shows that 58 percent of Nicaraguan coffee exports came from medium multifamily producers, whereas the figure for Guatemala was 19 percent, for El Salvador, 33 percent, and for Costa Rica, 38 percent. The pattern held in cotton production and with respect to permanently cultivated crops (coffee, cotton, sugarcane, bananas, and African palm) as a whole.[14]

The Influence of Somocismo and of the Traditional Elements of the Bourgeoisie

The foregoing analysis set out the structural traits of Nicarguan agriculture, which coexisted with other factors, notably high levels of concentration in the ownership of processing facilities, marketing, and the control of banks. This part of the story begins with the Somocista faction of the big property-owning classes, made up of the various branches of the Somoza family,

Table 10.2 Importance of Midsize Capitalists in Different Sectors of Central American Agriculture in the 1960s (percentage)

Country	Coffee Production	Cotton Production	Land Under Permanent Cultivation
Costa Rica	38	42	33
El Salvador	33	28	26
Guatemala	19	n.d.	n.d.
Nicaragua	58	60	52

Sources: Adapted from United Nations Food and Agriculture Organization–International Labour Organization (Organización Internacional del Trabajo) (FAO-OIT), *Tenencia de la tierra y desarrollo rural en Centroamérica* (San José, Costa Rica: EDUCA, 1976). Coffee holdings in Guatemala are estimated from Keith Griffin, *Concentración de tierras y pobreza rural* (México, DF: Fondo de Cultura Economica, 1983), and correspond to production in the country's west (the so-called Boca Costa, which accounts for 80 percent of national production), for holdings between 102 and 530 *manzanas*, for the 1965–1966 agricultural cycle. One *manzana* equals approximately 1.7 acres or 0.7 hectares.

politicians close to the dictatorship, and the top officers of the National Guard; many of them had *fincas* or other agro-industrial interests. When the Sandinista Revolution occurred, the Somozas and their closest collaborators controlled some 1,100 *fincas,* covering 1.1 million *manzanas* (770,000 hectares, or 1.8 million acres), about 15 percent of all land held by agrarian capitalists. Their interests were especially notable in tobacco, rice, sugar, and slaughterhouses for the export trade.

Another group was the opposition bourgeoisie, powerful economic forces not aligned with Somocismo, formed by established families from the cities of the Pacific (Matagalpa, Granada, León, Chinandega) who were active in business associations organized by the Superior Council of Private Enterprise (Consejo Superior de la Empresa Privada, or COSEP), the apex organization of Nicaraguan big business. At the moment of the Sandinista triumph, it was widely believed that the above two groups controlled Nicaraguan agriculture. Studies done after 1980, however, showed that although these two groups were indeed powerful, they coexisted with extensive intermediate strata that had significant weight in commerce and banking, if not an organized presence as an economic interest, something that became clear with the formation of the National Union of Farmers and Ranchers (Unión Nacional de Agricultores y Ganaderos, or UNAG) in 1981.[15]

A study done at the start of the 1970s indicated that financial groups, organized around private sector banks, controlled 68 percent of banking services by value, 38 percent of the country's commercial activity—with an especially strong presence in foreign trade—71 percent of the construction sector, but only 22 percent of agriculture.[16] This suggests that the lack of presence of midsize and small producers in politics and organized business groups led to an underestimation of their economic weight, which was in fact considerable.

Effects of Agrarian Structure on Agrarian Reform

Sandinista agrarian reform emphasized the following:

1. Transforming land distribution, emphasizing the transfer of land from large *fincas,* especially those that belonged to the Somozas and their allies, those with large bank debts, and those that did not exploit their holdings adequately. The lands were distributed to state farms and collective, socialist cooperatives.
2. Modernizing production techniques, promoting greater use of tractors and other machinery (which came principally as donations from Eastern bloc countries) and chemical fertilizers, and concentrating (with limited success) on some twenty major agro-industrial projects

(sugar mills; palm oil plantations; intensive cattle production; vegetables; coffee; and basic grains like rice, beans, and corn) centered
on state farms and collective cooperatives.
3. Dramatically extending the availability of financing through the state
development banking sector. This eventually covered 75 percent of
all agricultural lands.

Table 10.3 shows that agricultural output was lower in 1980, the year
after the revolutionary triumph of 1979, than it had been in 1978. This was
due to declining output during the insurrection in the first half of 1979, *fincas* being abandoned, and the startup problems of both the new state and its
agrarian reform plan. From then until 1984, although output did not regain
prerevolutionary levels, it did surpass those of 1980. In this period, more intensive productive techniques were used in the state sector and in a group
of cooperatives, located mostly in the Pacific zone of Nicaragua. Thereafter,
however, production fell, for reasons related to the counterrevolutionary insurgency that produced shortfalls of labor and other financial and material
resources. By 1990, agricultural output per rural inhabitant was 25 percent
lower than in 1980 and about half that of the late 1970s.
   Emphasizing collective agriculture (state farms and socialist cooperatives) left small-scale and midsize farmers behind, which had several consequences. First, it led these sectors to embrace anti-Sandinista politics,
especially in the country's central region. Election returns from 1990 through
2006 show that outside urban regions, support for the FSLN was weak in the
central and Atlantic zones, a direct and lingering consequence of agrarian reform policies. Second, the low priority accorded these small and medium-
size sectors resulted in a 13 percent decline in agricultural production in the

**Table 10.3 Changes in Agricultural Output and Rural Population in Nicaragua,
1978–2005**

Year	Gross Agricultural Product (in 1980 córdobas)	Rural Population (in millions)	GDP per Rural Inhabitant (in córdobas per capita)
1978	7,045	1.4	4.84
1980	4,827	1.5	3.16
1985	5,181	1.7	3.04
1990	4,495	1.8	2.42
2005	8,598	2.2	3.82

Sources: Gross agricultural product from Banco Central de Nicaragua (Central Bank of Nicaragua), *Statistical Yearbook, 2009* (Managua: Banco Central de Nicaragua, 2010), table 1-10,
www.bcn.gob.ni; rural population figures from Economic and Social Council of the United Nations, *World Urbanization Prospects: The 2005 Revision* (New York: United Nations, 2005), www
.un.org; the estimate for 1978 is from the author's calculations.

second half of the 1980s and a drop of 21 percent in the output per rural inhabitant (see Table 10.3). Obviously, these figures translated into economic hardship for peasant families, which in turn caused them to turn against the Sandinistas in the 1990 elections.

The Dynamics of Agricultural Production, 1978–2006

Analyzing the period from 1978 to 2006 gives the following aggregate results. Taking 1978 as the base (1978 = 100), agricultural production was 64 in 1990 and 122 in 2005. However, output per rural inhabitant was only 79 in 2005, or 21 percent below that of 1978 (see Table 10.3). In short, those nearly thirty years marked by drastic changes in agrarian structure and the extension of the agricultural frontier yielded very uneven growth in output and very low levels of productivity, whether measured by output per acre or per rural inhabitant.

Agricultural output grew by 4 percent per annum between 1990 and 2005, slightly below the 4.2 percent recorded annually from 1990 to 1998, yet still higher than the 1999–2005 figure. Growth remained unstable, and the increase in agricultural output trailed population growth. Several factors combined to explain these results. First, peace meant that former war zones returned to production, as land from former cooperatives went to individual, demobilized soldiers. There was also increased credit available for rehabilitating coffee *fincas,* as well as a general recovery in coffee production in Matagalpa, Jinotega, and other departments in the north and center of the country. Harvests since the late 1990s thus have been substantially above past levels.

A second element contributing to higher agricultural production has been the growth in sugarcane production. It occurs in large, agro-industrial plantations and uses workers who specialize in cutting sugarcane to bring in the harvest. As with coffee, harvests since the late 1990s have reached historic highs.

Production of basic grains is a third factor in play here. In 1989, 435,000 *manzanas* were sown with corn and beans; a figure that rose to 661,000 *manzanas* in 1999, according to Ministry of Agriculture statistics. The increase resulted from population growth, resettlement of war zones, and the opening of the Central American market, notably in El Salvador, for beans. Nicaragua became self-sufficient in the production of white corn and beans and exported its surplus to neighboring countries.

Fourth, the 1990s saw an important expansion of livestock farming, especially in the dairy sector, where cheese and other secondary products entered the Central American market (again, emphasizing El Salvador). Exports to the United States of "ethnic" dairy products have also expanded with the growth of the Central American immigrant community there. The

2001 census showed that Nicaragua had about 2.6 million head of cattle, dramatically above the 1.5 million counted in 1990 and even surpassing the herd of 2.5 million of the late 1970s (see Table 10.8).[17] Despite the aggregate growth, output per acre did not grow but remained at the level of the 1970s and 1980s. In fact, a reduced availability of credit for most sectors of agriculture suggests that output per unit of land may have fallen as the use of chemical fertilizers was reduced.[18]

Tables 10.4 and 10.5 examine the question of land distribution. Table 10.4 indicates that the number of argricultural holdings in Nicaragua grew by some 92 percent, while the area these holdings occupied increased by roughly 26 percent, between 1971 and 2001. The most striking changes are found in very large holdings of over 500 *manzanas,* whose 2001 numbers were 42 percent of what they were in 1971, and which occupied approximately 57 percent as much land as thirty years earlier. Similarly, the proportion of land held by farms of between 10 and 200 *manzanas* grew from 41.7 percent to 57.5 percent of all land under production.

These data are presented in greater detail in Table 10.5, which brings together the available data on the distribution of land among *fincas* of different sizes, including holdings created by the Sandinista agrarian reform, and shows how land distribution changed from 1963 to 2001. Two changes in particular stand out. The first is the reduction of the proportion of *fincas* with over 500 *manzanas* of land, which fell from 41.2 percent of the total in 1963 to just 16.5 percent in 2001. Even taking the last prerevolutionary year (1978) as the base, the proportion fell by roughly half. This sector held 2.9 million *manzanas* in 1978 but not quite 1.5 million in 2001. However,

Table 10.4 Land Tenancy in Nicaragua, 1971 and 2001

Size of Holding (*manzanas*)	1971		2001	
	Number of Holdings (%)	Area (%)	Number of Holdings (%)	Area (%)
1–10	44.2	2.9	47.4	4.3
10–50	31.4	13.3	33.0	20.5
50–200	18.7	28.4	16.3	37.0
200–500	3.7	21.0	2.6	18.4
>500	1.9	34.5	0.8	19.8
Total percentage	99.9	100.1	100.1	100
Total units	104,063	7,086,308	199,549	8,935,020

Sources: Estimates based on Instituto Nacional de Estadistica y Censo, *Segundo Censo Nacional Agropecuario* (Managua: Gobierno de la Republica de Nicaragua, Instituto Nacional de Estadisticas y Censos, 1971); Instituto Nacional de Estadistica y Censos, T*ercer Censo Nacional Agropecuario* (Managua: Gobierno de la Republica de Nicaragua, CENAGRO-INEC, 2002).

Table 10.5 Landholdings by Size and by Sector in Nicaragua, Selected Years, 1963–2001

	1963	1978	1988	2001
0–10 *manzanas*	3.5	2.1	3.1	4.5
10–50 *manzanas*	11.2	15.4	16.7	20.0
50–200 *manzanas*	26.5	30.1	28.4	36.6
200–500 *manzanas*	17.6	16.2	12.8	18.0
>500 *manzanas*	41.2	36.2	13.5	16.5
State sector	0	0	11.7	0.4
Collective tenancy	0	0	13.8	4.0
Total	100	100	100	100
Agricultural production (millions of córdobas)	87	104	189	218
Agricultural land (millions of *manzanas*)[a]	5.4	8.1	7.7	8.9
Median holding (*manzanas*)	62	78	41	41

Sources: 1963 data from Dirección General de Estadísticos y Censos, *Primer Censo Nacional Agropecaurio;* 1978, 1988, and 2001 data from CIERA (Centro de Investigaciones y Estudios de la Reforma Agraria), *Censo Agropecaurio. Fincas* in 1963 and 1971 are defined by criteria use in the manual recount of the 1971 census.

Note: a. Reduction in the land under cultivation in 1988 is explained by the abandonment of farms during the armed conflict of the 1980s.

the latter figure excludes state-owned or collectively held properties; counting them raises the proportion of holdings over 500 *manzanas* to 20.9 percent of the total.

The second point to note is the growth of holdings between 10 and 50 *manzanas,* on the one hand, and from 50 to 200, on the other.[19] The former held 11.2 percent of the land in 1963 but 20 percent in 2001; the latter sector grew from holding 26.5 to 36.6 percent of the land in this period. Much of this growth is explained by the redistribution of cooperatives and state-held lands in the early 1990s, but there were also land sales and the reopening of the agrarian frontier after the war. The growth of these small and midsize sectors brings with it a reduction in the size of the median *fincas;* from 62 *manzanas* in 1963, it grew to 78 in 1978, before falling to 41 in 1988, a size still maintained in 2001.

Agrarian Reform and Land Redistribution, 1979–2001

Since 1979, land has been redistributed in two ways. The FSLN's agrarian reform came first, concentrating land in state farms or collectively run cooperatives. The second began in the latter part of the 1980s but is principally associated with the early years of Violeta Barrios de Chamorro's govern-ment. It included the so-called economic and social *concertaciónes* (inter-sectoral agreements) of the early 1990s, the transition accords between the Sandinistas and the Chamorro administration, and the internal dynamics of the cooperative sector. This period saw the effective end of the state agri-cultural sector, a change that benefited the big property owners of old, de-mobilized soldiers and former counterrevolutionary fighters, and employees of the now-defunct state farms.[20]

We see the two above processes at work in Tables 10.6 and 10.7, which indicate the sectors that gained and lost land. To grasp the problems emerg-ing since 1979, it is useful to look at the 1980s (Table 10.6). Between 1979 and 1989, 2.1 million *manzanas* were shifted to different strata due to the "concentrating" effects of the agrarian reform, while another roughly 400,000 were abandoned due to the armed conflict and were thus effectively deducted from the total of agricultural land in war zones, mostly in the Atlantic inte-rior parts of Nicaragua.[21] It is important to note in Table 10.6 that 81.6 per-cent of the lands affected came from *fincas* of over 500 *manzanas* and that 91.7 percent of the land transferred went to the state sector or to collective forms of tenancy. These latter included credit and service co-ops and *surco muerto* co-ops—which combined collective land ownership with individu-ally cultivated plots—but the bulk of the land went to collectively organized co-ops, thus reflecting the main thrust of Sandinista agrarian reform.[22]

The End of the State Sector, 1988–2001

As early as the mid-1980s, a number of trends were forming that reached fruition after the 1990 elections.[23] The most important were the end of the

Table 10.6 Changes in Land Tenancy, 1978–1988

Size of Holding (*manzanas*)	Lost (%)	Gained (%)
0–10	0	3.6
10–50	0	4.7
50–200	6.2	0
200–500	12.2	
>500	81.6	
State sector		42.1
Collective tenancy		49.6
Total	100	100

Source: Eduardo Baumiester and Edgard Fernández, *Analisis de la tenencia de la tierra en Nicaragua* (Managua: MAGFOR, INEC, FAO, 2005).

state sector in agriculture and the distribution of land in co-ops to private owners. The social results of these changes were mixed.

Some of the lands went to large-scale farmers, generally via policies of the Chamorro government (1990–1996), while part remained in the hands of the former co-op members, who became private owners. Many of the latter also bought the rights of other ex-co-op members, and that, combined with the expansion of farms into new areas, meant that agricultural holdings expanded by at least a million *manzanas* between the late 1980s and 2001 (see Table 10.5). More recent estimates put land currently dedicated to agriculture at 9.7 million *manzanas,* some 1.7 million more than in 1980.[24]

Table 10.7 shows which sectors have gained and lost in this process of redistribution. Regarding lands taken from the reformed sector, 39 percent went to farms in the 50–200-*manzana* stratum, and 24.6 percent to those in the 200–500-*manzana* sector; thus holdings between 50 and 500 *manzanas* received nearly two-thirds of the redistributed lands. Similar results can be observed in other Latin American agrarian reforms; that is, the reduction of the stratum of traditional haciendas, the modernization of the remaining haciendas, and the strengthening of intermediate sectors.[25] It must also be noted that a relatively large proportion of the lands that were part of the agrarian reform—both state enterprises and co-ops—were taken out of production and thus were not registered in the census of 2001. Some were converted to urban uses (e.g., the expansion of Managua toward Masaya) or other commercial ends (such as shrimp farming in Chinandega, enterprise zones around Managua and other cities, and tourism along the Pacific Coast from Chinandega to the Costa Rican border).

In sum, we see two decades, the 1980s and 1990s, during which a substantial part of agricultural land was permanently redistributed. In some cases, the land went to collective (state or cooperative) ownership before

Table 10.7 Changes in Land Tenancy, 1988–2001

Size of Holding (*manzanas*)	Lost (%)	Gained (%)
0–10	0	6.6
10–50	0	15.6
50–200	0	39.0
200–500	0	24.6
>500		14.2
State sector	53.6	
Collective tennancy	46.4	
Total	100	100

Source: Eduardo Baumeister and Edgard Fernández, *Analisis de la tenencia de la tierra en Nicaragua* (Managua: MAGFOR, INEC, FAO, 2005).

then passing to new, rather different sectors of private owners. In other cases, the land went out of agricultural production and was put to new uses.

The Effects of Agrarian Reform on Agricultural Production

At this point, we must ask how these myriad changes have affected agricultural production. The first step is to go beyond the agrarian reform in considering changes in agricultural policy. The 1980s marked an attempt to redistribute land and to accelerate modernization by concentrating land in the state sector and in collective enterprises.[26] These goals were frustrated by internal political problems, among them the discontent of broad sectors of the rural population but, above all, the conflict with the United States. Production fell sharply, and by the end of the decade, it was well below what it had been ten years earlier (see Table 10.3). Nevertheless, some elements of rural life improved, due to greater literacy and enhanced public health.[27] From 1990 to the present, output has risen, but less quickly than before the revolution and with less use of machinery and other capital inputs, as well as with reduced access to credit. It is at best paradoxical that in the 1980s at least 44 percent of farmers, of all types and from all strata, had access to credit, whereas the Census of Agriculture (Censo Agropecuario) of 2001 shows that proportion reduced to 15 percent.[28]

A second change has been the complete privatization of the marketing of agricultural products, domestically and internationally, as well as imports of machinery, fertilizers, and so on. Imports of foods such as rice, yellow corn, vegetable oils, fats, fruits, and vegetables have also increased. According to the United Nations Food and Agriculture Organization (FAO) data, the value of these imports tripled from about $100 million in 1990 to around $300 million in 2004.[29] At the same time, agricultural exports also grew, albeit more slowly than imports, going from $242 million in 1990 to some $506 million in 2002, a twofold increase.[30]

Returning to Table 10.3, we see between 1990 and 2005 a significant recovery in the agricultural sector, which finally surpassed 1978 levels. However, output per person still lagged behind the 1970s. This same period also shows a combination of an agrarian structure in which small and medium-size producers have the greatest weight, an expanded agricultural frontier that brought more land into production, and the liberalization of domestic and foreign trade. The neoliberal onslaught, though, was not strong enough to overturn the most important agrarian changes. Unfortunately, neither were projects centered on small and midsize farmers and the Area of Peoples' Property (Area de Propriedad del Pueblo, or APP, public lands), imposed by UNAG and the Asociación de Trabajadores del Campo (Rural

Workers' Union, or ATC), especially successful. The overall result has been overlooked by analysts, rather like Nicaragua's overall political situation. In sum, the years since 1990 have seen no model dominate.

The Situation in Recent Years

Data from the 2001 Censo Agropecuario indicate that at least 218,000 farmers and ranchers have direct access to the land, meaning that a bit more than 60 percent of all rural homes have some access to land (see Table 10.8).[31] It further shows that 79 percent of those with agricultural occupations have access to land. They may be owners, leaseholders, wage workers, or those engaged in subsistence-level activities. This high proportion of rural families with access to land is a positive factor, and combined with the high proportion of small and medium-size agricultural producers, suggests that the latter control much of Nicaragua's land. Yet this high level of access to land must be set against the high levels of poverty encountered in rural Nicaragua.

World Bank estimates in 2003 (based on a per capita daily consumption of a market basket of goods worth $1.06) put 35.7 percent of Nicaragua's rural population among the nonpoor and 64.3 percent in poverty, of whom 24.7 percent live in extreme poverty.[32] Extreme poverty in Nicaragua means consuming no more $0.55 worth of goods per person per day. Having a quarter of the rural population in extreme poverty, two-fifths more living in

Table 10.8 Proportion of Agricultural Land Held, Cattle Owned, and Personnel Employed by Size of Holding in Nicaragua, 2001

Size of Holding (*manzanas*)	As a Percentage of All Farms	Area as Percentage of National Total	Full-time Workers per Holding[a]	Share of Cultivated Land (%)	Share of Land in Permanent Use (%)	Share of National Cattle Herd (%)
0–10	47.3	00.3	0.2	16.3	16.1	5.1
10–50	33.0	20.5	0.4	35.0	24.9	21.2
50–200	16.3	37.0	1.2	29.9	24.5	41.3
200–500	2.6	18.4	4.1	10.3	12.9	19.0
>500	0.8	19.8	11.3	8.5	21.6	13.4
Total[b]	100	100	0.6**	100	100	100
(N in thousands)	199	8,935	126	957	423	2,657

Source: Author's calculations based on Instituto Nacional de Estadistica y Censos, *Tercer Censo Nacional Agropecuario* (Managua: Gobierno de la Republica de Nicaragua, CENAGRO-INEC, 2002).

Notes: a. Mean number of employees per holding.

b. May not equal 100 due to rounding.

** mean number of workers per holding.

poverty, and only a little over a third not living in poverty should be inconsistent with the levels of access to land (even if to small parcels) found in Nicaragua because the basket of goods used to measure extreme poverty consists of the basic foodstuffs needed to feed a typical family. How can we explain this?

Several factors are at play. In the 1960s, 1970s, and 1980s, a very high proportion of rural earnings came from salaries earned by harvesting export crops. Now, however, migrant workers from El Salvador and Honduras come to Nicaragua due to local labor shortages.[33]

In the 1980s, alongside low levels of agricultural activity produced by the war and government policies, the productivity of agricultural labor fell (owing to a reduction in the working day and in the intensity of work done), and the model within which part of rural families' earning came from wages while part came from working their own parcels was maintained. From 1990 to the present, there has been a sharp fall in permanent salaried work in agriculture. In part, this has resulted from the disappearance of the state farms and cooperatives on the one hand, and, in the private sector, the effective disappearance of cotton production and significant cuts in the production of irrigated rice on the other. But agrarian wages, by themselves, do not guarantee the reproduction of the rural labor force, leaving rural workers in an even more precarious position than in the past.[34]

In fact, the minimum wage in agriculture as reported by the 2001 Censo Agropecuario was $1.65 daily.[35] If we suppose an average rural family to have six members and that two of them work full-time, 365 days a year, both generous assumptions, this converts to a family wage equal to $0.55 per person.[36] That, of course, leaves them in extreme poverty. Thus due both to shrinking demand for labor and low real wages, wage work has ceased to be an important part of the economic strategy of the rural population in recent years.

It is thus no surprise to see Nicaraguans going to Costa Rica and El Salvador as seasonal, migrant workers, where salaries, even for illegal immigrants, are higher than in Nicaragua.[37] Further, production of basic grains—rice, corn, and beans—that was supported by loans from state banks for some sectors of small farmers in the 1980s now presents a problem because credit is tighter.[38] Accordingly, a number of Nicaraguan farmers prefer to work in neighboring countries in order to cover their basic living costs and to partially finance their next year's planting. At the same time, there is an impressive push of small, medium-size, and large producers of both basic grains and livestock into the easternmost reaches of the departments of Jinotega, Matagalpa, Chontales, and Rio San Juan, as well as the more heavily populated parts of the two autonomous regions of the Atlantic Coast. This move to open new lands to cultivation, however, carries with it environmental risks, due to the nature of the soils in these regions, and it also causes conflict between the newcomers and the indigenous communities of the Caribbean Coast (see Chapter 7).

The sixteen years between Sandinista administrations produced paradoxical results for both agriculture and the rural population in general. First, despite neoliberal economic policies that reduced the state's role in providing credit, technical assistance, and domestic and foreign marketing, the agricultural sector grew, eclipsing pre-1979 levels. Small and midsize farmers, as well as agribusiness-level farmers, many of whom had returned to the country and to farming, contributed to the recovery and later expansion. They were particularly important in the central and Atlantic regions. The big losers were salaried laborers and semi-proletarians. First, the loss of jobs on state farms lowered their real incomes.[39] Furthermore, many of those working for state enterprises did not receive land after the breakup of the APP in 1990. A segment of those workers, many from the northern part of the Pacific zone, migrated in the 1990s. Some went to Costa Rica in search of better wages, others moved to the cities, and still others relocated to former combat zones or the agricultural frontier.

Unlike Honduras, Costa Rica, or Guatemala, Nicaragua did not create an important nontraditional agricultural export sector, such as fruits and vegetables for the global market. Growing these nontraditional crops demands both greater productivity per *manzana* and a greater availability of labor than the structural weaknesses of Nicaragua's traditional landholders, including its small farmers, permitted. Thus Nicaraguan agriculture from 1990 through the first decade of the twenty-first century remained focused on its traditional products. Meanwhile, the rest of Central America was reducing its production of grains and cattle and expanding the intensive cultivation of fruits and vegetables for export.

Nicaragua has also seen slower growth in its food-processing industries, which has led to increased food imports since 1990. Domestic firms have not been able to take advantage of this change, and firms from the rest of Central America, Mexico, and the United States have taken up the slack. Understandably, this has lowered Nicaragua's trade surplus in agricultural products.

The failure both to develop untraditional exports and to expand the food-processing sector must be considered in light of a series of factors found in contemporary Nicaragua. The country has not found a way to foster the more intensive agriculture that would generate higher earnings and wages throughout the sector, including for small farmers. Further, the state has not promoted medium- and long-term plans for the agricultural sector. Consequently, the country lacks the necessary infrastructure, sufficiently technically proficient owners and workers (human capital), and medium- and long-term agricultural credit facilities. These factors would have been enough to limit Nicaragua's capacity for agricultural innovation, but there was a further complication in the form of political instability, which has been present since the Chamorro administration and continues in the second Ortega government.

The FSLN Governs Again

It is the different social origins of the senior agricultural bureaucrats that most distinguishes the post-2006 FSLN government from that of the 1980s. In the earlier period, when Comandante Jaime Wheelock was minister of agriculture, the top thirty bureaucrats (vice ministers, regional heads of the Ministry of Agricultural Development and Agrarian Reform [Ministerio de Desarrollo Agropecuario y Reforma Agraria, or MIDINRA], and directors of state enterprises or major projects) were young professionals, mostly from old families from Nicaragua's Pacific zone, with experience in big business, who had been radicalized in private Catholic high schools in Managua and Granada. Their contemporary counterparts come from the National Union of Farmers and Ranchers, the co-ops, and nongovernmental organizations (NGOs). Many come from rural or small-town backgrounds and were activists or low-level bureaucrats in the 1980s. The principal exception is Álvaro Fiallos, president of both the Institute for Rural Development (Instituto de Desarrollo Rural, or IDR) and UNAG, who headed the cotton section of MIDINRA in the 1980s.[40] It is highly unusual in Nicaragua and in Central America generally for high government officials to come from the ranks of small and medium-size agricultural producers.

Nevertheless, it is too early to point to the effects of these bureaucrats' leadership, as projects geared to the needs of small and medium-size farmers have scarcely begun. The Development Bank (Banco de Fomento) that was approved toward the end of the Bolaños administration has yet to be put into operation by the Ortega government, while the Nicaraguan Basic Foodstuffs Enterprise (Empresa Nicaragüense de Alimentos Básicos, or ENABAS), the state enterprise charged with marketing basic grains (rice, corn, beans), has not been active.

The International Context

Since 2006, but especially since 2007, world prices for agricultural products have risen dramatically. This is especially true of foodstuffs: basic grains, meat, milk, and oil seeds. However, soaring petroleum prices have raised the price of agricultural inputs such as fuel, machinery, fertilizers, and pesticides. Both have important consequences for Nicaraguan agriculture.

Rising prices for basic grains could produce benefits for small and medium-size producers. Similar effects can be expected in livestock-related exports (meat, cattle on the hoof, and dairy products), coffee exports, and eventually sugarcane for ethanol and African palm oil for biodiesel. Moreover, increasing demand from within Central America, especially El Salvador, and the prospect of an expanding Venezuelan market should raise exports.

Thus the coming years could produce significant growth in the agricultural sector and rising incomes for all farmers.[41] This projection assumes some ability among farmers and ranchers to offset rising prices for petroleum-derived products, as well as for land sale prices and leases. Consequently, much depends on the institutional capacity of the state, the private sector, and especially the farmers' organizations to produce positive outcomes. This is especially the case with the least-favored sectors: the highly vulnerable rural families, notably those with no or insufficient land and those who live in regions subject to drought or in remote areas with poor access to markets.

What is clear is that President Daniel Ortega will find more economic success in rural areas than in the nation's cities. Urban Nicaragua faces significant economic problems. Increasing the number of formal sector jobs and raising incomes will be challenging, due to ever-higher costs for food, energy, transport, construction materials, and other everyday necessities. The country's economic engine continues to be agriculture.

Institutional Resources and Policies

Since 1990, the Nicaraguan state has decreased in both size and capacity to a point not seen since the Somoza era. Historic institutions like the Banco Nacional have disappeared, as has government marketing of basic grains, while the agricultural extension service is woefully understaffed. One result is that policies targeting the large number of small farmers have to be delivered in conjunction with NGOs, farmers' organizations, and the private banks. This, in turn, leads to the need to unify policy objectives and coordinate policy delivery.

One of the greatest dilemmas facing the FSLN in returning to power after sixteen years of uninterrupted neoliberal policy hegemony is how to provide policies that genuinely assist poor farmers (such as increasing their capital through long-term credits to be repaid by the recipients), yet avoid falling into opportunistic, populist redistributive programs. The latter is tempting, given the continual round of elections (municipal, regional, and national) found in Nicaragua and the FSLN's need to consolidate its support in rural areas, especially in the central region and on the Atlantic Coast. A further complication is the level of spending required to permit the small producers to overcome social deficits (health and education) and infrastructural problems (roads and electricity) and increase their productivity (tools, inputs, and animals).

During the 1980s and 1990s, the relative importance of small and medium-size farmers grew, but their productivity, income, and capitalization remained limited. A significant number of small producers control land, but it is poor quality. Nicaraguan agricultural policy can convert these small-scale producers into a dynamic element to the extent that it can give them access to loans and new technology. This sector has the potential to supply the domestic market and capture new export markets elsewhere in Central America.

One of the great contemporary dilemmas facing the government is finding the right balance between the market, with its multiple private actors (NGOs, co-ops, microfinance, and private firms of all sizes), and the public sector (the state and certain co-ops, like CARUNA or Nicaraoco-op) in providing inputs and credits, purchasing agricultural products, and transporting and processing those products.[42] Table 10.9 shows the contributions of the various sources of agricultural credit. The government and Venezuelan aid account for a bit over one-quarter of the total, with the remainder coming from a variety of sources. Similar patterns are found in other parts of the chain of agricultural production.

Hambre Cero and Rural Poverty

The Zero Hunger (Hambre Cero) program was inspired by data from Nicaragua's 2001 Census of Agriculture.[43] Out of almost 200,000 agricultural holdings in the country, fewer than 100,000 had any livestock at all. It was the smallest holdings that were most likely to be in this condition. Thus they could grow basic grains but did not have access to animal protein or milk. Furthermore, not having livestock impedes their access to capital,

Table 10.9 Sources of Agricultural Credit in Nicaragua, 2008

Sector	Financing Provided (%)
State	21.0
Commercial banks and regulated microfinance	67.5
Unregulated microfinance	6.7
Venezuelan cooperation	4.8
Total	100

Source: Compiled from Government of Nicaragua, Ministerio Agropecuario y Forestal (MAGFOR), *MAGFOR Plan, 2008* (Managua: MAGFOR, 2008), 11.

which in Nicaragua is correlated with building or increasing herds of farm animals, especially cattle.

For the 2010–2011 period, the government planned to deliver animals—a cow, a sow, and some chickens—to 75,000 women, representing roughly 20 percent of the rural poor, a group that includes 80 percent of the rural population. The program faces a structural limit because a significant number of the families involved may have problems securing enough feed for the animals, and they may also encounter difficulties in finding a bull to impregnate the cow.[44] Since only 50 to 60 percent of serviced cows actually become pregnant, there is a good chance that in any year many families in the Hambre Cero program will not have a cow produce a calf and will not have milk. And if the family is successful in breeding livestock every year and their herd gets bigger, they will have to expand their holdings to grow enough feed.

Implementing Hambre Cero is closely linked to the Councils of Citizens' Power (Consejos del Poder Ciudadano, or CPCs), which themselves are closely linked to the FSLN. This raises the possibility of partisan criteria being applied in the selection of beneficiaries. Hambre Cero does not aim at universal coverage, even of the rural poor who do not have livestock, and there are always marginal cases: a woman who may have too little land to support the animals or slightly too much land to qualify for the program.[45]

Finally, the program was conceived before the recent increase in the price of basic grains. Should prices for corn and beans remain high, poor farmers with little land could face a dilemma: grow grains and raise their incomes or set land aside for animals. Given the low level of productivity for cattle in Nicaragua, cultivating an extra *manzana* of land will bring better returns than adding an animal or two.

Conclusion: The Dilemma Facing the FSLN

The 1980s saw the strengthening of state and parastatal structures. There were the APP, as well as state-controlled credit, investments in agro-industry, and domestic and foreign commerce. Further, the agricultural bureaucracy expanded significantly. The revolutionary government bet on agro-industry and intensified production in the state sector, complemented by cooperatives that were worked collectively.

Now both the resources controlled by the state and the state's policy objectives are very different. Today there is greater reliance on conventional sources of development assistance, such as multinational aid from the Inter-American Development Bank, the World Bank, the European Union, and the Central American Bank for Economic Integration and bilateral aid from the United States and various European countries. Further, programs today focus on small and medium-size farmers organized in traditional credit and marketing co-ops, as well as on the rural poor with some land, the targets of Hambre Cero.

From these changes a dilemma arises that is reminiscent of some of the problems of the 1980s. On the one hand, the government keeps criticizing private enterprise, foreign assistance, and the NGOs. On the other hand, the government needs resources from these entities to further the development of agriculture in Nicaragua. One must note that Central America and Venezuela offer new markets that should produce opportunities to increase production, raise incomes, create jobs in the agricultural sector, and reduce rural poverty. It is evident that securing those good outcomes depends on getting better prices and having a strong demand for basic grains, milk and milk products, and beef. Even more, achieving those ends without affecting internal demand requires more money, better roads, more technical assistance, and an assured supply of agricultural inputs (improved seed, fertilizer, etc.). Neither the state nor the private sector in Nicaragua is meeting those needs to the extent that would be necessary to secure the objective of significant agricultural growth.

Taken together, the foregoing suggest a replay of the way Nicaraguan governments treated economic questions in the past: giving higher priority to the political objective of strengthening control over all parts of government, including at the local level, than to policies for economic growth. If this pattern persists, it will be difficult to treat agricultural questions effectively. Under such conditions, the Sandinista government's agricultural policy would likely take positions that juggle closer cooperation with the private sector, the rhetoric of anti-imperialism, attacks on the oligarchy, relations with donors, and attitudes toward what may be called "redistributive populism" that swing wildly from highly positive to terribly negative. And all this will happen in a country that depends greatly on agriculture and foreign resources to make its way in the world.

Notes

1. However, the Andean countries were principally mineral exporters, although Ecuador and Peru also had strong agro-export economies.

2. Plantations and haciendas are both very large holdings that differ in two respects. Modern plantations use large amounts of fixed capital (intensive mechanized farming, sophisticated irrigation systems, processing capacity, and large-scale transportation systems) and employ only wage labor, with a large permanent workforce. Haciendas use less fixed capital, land itself being the principal investment, and their workforce can combine permanent wage labor, seasonal workers, and tenants who get access to a parcel of land as part of their remuneration. One may also speak of "capitalized haciendas," a sort of midpoint between the two ideal types,

which invest heavily in machinery and purchase land to expand production. Examples of this latter case arose in the cotton and coffee sectors in Nicaragua and other Central American states.

3. At the peak of the expansion of banana plantations, in 1946, just after World War II, Costa Rica exported 9 million cases of bananas and Guatemala 15 million, but Nicaragua managed only 200,000; see Eduardo Baumeister, *Estructura y reforma agraria in Nicaragua, 1979–1989* (Managua: Ediciones CDR-ULA, 1998), 101.

4. The estimate is based on Interamerican Committee on Agricultural Development (Comité Intermericano de Desarrollo Agricola, CIDA) studies; and Eduardo Baumeister, *Estructura y reforma agraria in Nicaragua, 1979–1989* (Managua: Ediciones CDR-ULA, 1998), 111.

5. The figure for Peru includes lands held collectively in the mountains, which could be quite extensive. Fernando Eguren, personal communication.

6. Baumiester, *Estructura,* 177.

7. Rodolfo Stavenhagen, *Las clases sociales en las sociedades agrarias* (México City: Siglo 21, 1969), 89.

8. Editors' note: *Finca* is synonymous with "ranch" or "farm" in Nicaragua.

9. Baumeister, *Estructura,* 116.

10. However, coffee production can be combined with other activities, such as cattle ranching, on farms of up to 200 hectares.

11. CIDA identified four types of rural holdings: (1) subfamily, without enough land to meet the basic needs of one family as determined by local standards, and which provide 2 person-years of work; (2) family, with the land needed to meet a family's needs, by local standards, and yielding 2–3.9 person-years of work; (3) medium multifamily, which require 4–12 person-years of work and cannot be met by one family; and (4) general large multifamily, which employ over twelve permanent workers; see Solon Barraclough, *Notas sobre la tenenncia de la tierra* (Santiago: Icira, 1970), table 1. Data for Nicaragua come from the *Censo Agropecuario de 2001,* which indicated that subfamily farms needed 3.7 workers, of whom 3.5 were from the owner's family; family farms required 4.4 workers, 4 from the family; medium multifamily farms had 6.3 permanent workers, of whom 2.1 were hired; and large farms had 14.8 workers, 11.3 of whom were hired hands. Similar data for Honduras are in Eduardo Baumeister, ed., *Agro hondureño y su futuro* (Tegucigalpa: Editorial Guaymuras, 1996), table 12, p. 38.

12. Cristobal Kay, "Rural Poverty and Development Strategies in Latin America," *Journal of Agrarian Change* 6, no. 4 (October 2006): 48.

13. See Rafael Menjivar, "Los problemas de mundo rural," in *Centroamérica Hoy,* edited by Edelberto Torres Rivas (Mexico City: Siglo 21, 1975), 258–259.

14. Two factors that help explain the importance of the medium multifamily sector in Nicaragua are (1) the settlement of the agricultural frontier, moving from the Pacific toward the Atlantic Coast, which allowed peasants to achieve holdings requiring more capital investment, mainly in cattle and coffee; and (2) low population density, especially in the central and Atlantic regions, which meant less readily available labor and thus demanded more capital.

15. Editors' note: The National Union of Farmers and Ranchers (UNAG), was set up by the revolutionary government to represent nonpeasant landholders.

16. Eduardo Baumeister and Oscar Niera, "La conformación de una economía mixta: Estructura de clases y política estatal en la trasformación nicaragüense," in *La transición difícil: La autodeterminación de los pequeños países periféricos,*

edited by José Luis Corragio and Carmen Diana Deere (México, D.F: Siglo 21, 1987), 287.

17. The estimate of the herd in the late 1970s comes from Baumeister, *Estructura,* 200.

18. Data assembled from the 2001 *Censo Agropecuario* indicate that 15 percent of *fincas* had access to credit, 3.7 percent used tractors, 12 percent used organic fertilizers, and 43.6 percent used fertilizer of some kind.

19. The characteristics of these small and midsize holdings can be found in Table 10.8.

20. Orlando Núñez, ed., *La guerra y el campesinado en Nicaragua* (Managua: CIPRES, 1998).

21. Michael Lipton distinguishes between agrarian reforms that concentrate resources and those that redistribute them. See Michael Lipton, "Towards a Theory of Land Reform," in *Agrarian Reform and Agrarian Reformism,* edited by David Lehmann (London: Faber, 1974), 269–315.

22. Editors' note: Sandinista agrarian policy provided for three models of cooperatives: credit and service, where the peasants maintained ownership of the land; *sucro muerto* co-ops, so called because privately worked (not privately owned) plots were separated by an unsown furrow; and Sandinista Agricultural Co-ops, which were both collectively owned and collectively worked. There were also some co-ops that predated the revolution, which were usually called traditional cooperatives.

23. For the shift in Sandinista agrarian reform policy, see Ivan Gutiérrez, "Las políticas de tierras de la reforma agraria sandinistas," in *El debate sobre la reforma agraria en Nicaragua,* edited by Raul Ruben and Jan de Groot (Managua: Editorial Ciencias Sociales, 1989), 113–128.

24. Drawn from CIPRES (Centro para la Promoción, la Investigación, y el Desarrollo Rural y Social), *Los pequeños y medianos productores en Nicaragua* (Managua: CIPRES, 2006), xii.

25. William Thiessenhusen, ed., *Searching for Agrarian Reform in Latin America* (Boston: Unwin Hyman, 1989).

26. Rapid mechanization was also part of the policy. FAO figures show a doubling of the number of tractors imported between 1980 and 1984, as compared to 1978.

27. In 1979, illiteracy in rural areas stood at 73.7 percent among those 10 or older, according to INEC, *Informe preliminario del censo de analfabetas (21 de octubre a 15 de noviembre 1979).* The 1995 census showed a fall to 41.2 percent and that of 2005 showed a level of 37.8 percent; see INEC (Instituto Nacional de Estadísticas y Censos), *VIII Censo de población y IV de vivienda: Resumen censal* (Managua: INEC, 2006). It is generally accepted that toward the end of the 1980s illiteracy was below 1995 levels, although there are no data available.

28. Baumeister, *Estructura,* table 8.14, 188.

29. UN Food and Agriculture Organization (FAO), *FAOSTAT* (FAO, 2007), faostat.fao.org.

30. The 1990 figures are from FAOSTAT, and the 2005 figures come from the Banco Central de Nicaragua, *Estadísticas macroeconómicas,* www.bcn.gob.ni/.

31. Author's estimate based on calculations from the *Censo Agropecuario, 2001,* and INEC, *VIII Censo de población;* INEC, *Censo de población, 2005* (Managua: INEC, 2006).

32. World Bank, *Nicaragua: Reporte de Pobreza,* report no. 26128-NI (Washington, DC: World Bank, 2003), www.wds.worldbank.org/. The most commonly

used international benchmarks draw the poverty line at $2/day and the level for extreme poverty at $1/day.

33. The generally accepted estimates are that in December 1978 about 240,000 Nicaraguans worked to harvest export crops, but by December 2000 the number had dropped to 93,000.

34. In the 1971 Censo de Población, 46 percent of the agricultural workforce described itself as salaried. In 2005, the corresponding figure was 33 percent; see INEC, *VIII Censo de la poblacion;* and INEC, *Censo de población, 1971* (Managua: INEC, 1972). These figures indicate that increases in the economically active agricultural population were concentrated in the classes of smallholders and unpaid family labor, both of which connote low productivity.

35. Editors' note: These data are also available from the World Bank, *Agriculture in Nicaragua: Promoting Competitiveness and Stimulating Broad-Based Growth* (Washington, DC: World Bank, 2003), 44–45.

36. The figures are derived from data published by the Banco Central de Nicaragua, which peg the minimum agricultural salary at 667 córdobas per month and use an exchange rate of 13.44 córdobas per US dollar; www.bcn.gob.ni/.

37. The average daily wage for agricultural labor in 2003–2004 was $8.27 in Costa Rica, $2.47 in El Salvador, and $1.56 in Nicaragua. See Juan Diego Trejos, *Mercado de trabajo, ingresos laborales y pobreza en Nicaragua* (Geneva: Internacional Labor Organization, 2004).

38. CIERA (Centro de Investigaciones y Estudios de la Reforma Agraria), *Censo Agropecuario, 2001* (Managua: CIERA, 2001). Figures assembled from the 2001 *Censo Agropecuario* show about 15 percent of all farmers receiving loans; at the end of the 1980s, the figure was 44 percent. The latter percentage, of an estimated total of 189,000 farmers and ranchers, comes from CIERA, vol. 9, table 266, 198; compare INEC, *Encuesta socio-demográfica, 1985* (Managua: INEC, 1992), which counted 149,842 agricultural producers in 1985.

39. Particularly important was the loss of wages in kind, known as the AFA (arroz, frijoles, aceite; or rice, beans, oil), which was universally paid in the 1980s.

40. Fiallos was also a university professor who had studied abroad, a large-scale cotton grower from León, and a founding member of the Nicaraguan Union of Agricultural Producers (Unión de Productores Agropecuarios de Nicaragua, or UPANIC) in 1979, before the revolution.

41. Editors' note: Obviously the global economic crisis that began in the fall of 2008 could affect this forecast significantly.

42. Editors' note: CARUNA (Caja Rural Nacional, or National Rural Credit Union) is the body that administers development projects funded by the Bolivarian Alternative for Latin America (ALBA), an international alliance initiated by Venezuelan president Hugo Chávez, whose members are Bolivia, Cuba, Dominica, Ecuador, Nicaragua, and Venezuela. Nicaraoco-op is a processing and marketing cooperative formed by a consortium of Nicaraguan farmers' groups.

43. Formally called the Food Productivity Bond (Bono Productivo Alimentario, or BPA); see also Chapter 9.

44. Families receive a pregnant cow, but finding a bull the next year is their responsibility.

45. By definition, landless families are excluded from the program. This probably eliminates a quarter of the rural poor. At the other end, there is an effective upper limit of 10 *manzanas,* roughly 7 hectares or 17 acres.

11

The FSLN and International Solidarity

Hector Perla Jr.

BEGINNING WITH THE MONROE DOCTRINE, THE UNITED STATES has justified its policy toward Latin America using the discourse of liberty. However, in practice its policies have been quite different. This is particularly true for Central America, where the United States has historically exercised a great deal of political, economic, and military power. Yet, even within this region, Nicaragua stands out for the number of times it has been invaded and length of time that it has spent under direct US rule. More importantly, Nicaragua also stands out for the fierce resistance it has generated to oppose these occupations and domination. Starting with the resistance against the filibusterer William Walker, and continuing with Augusto César Sandino's resistance to the US invasion force in the 1930s, which earned him the title "General de Hombres Libres" (General of Free Men), Nicaragua's dogged resistance to US aggression has inspired a great many non-Nicaraguans to take up their cause.

Most recently, the triumph of the Sandinista Revolution in 1979 and the Sandinista National Liberation Front's (Frente Sandinista de Liberación Nacional's, or FSLN's) subsequent resistance to US efforts to oust them from power throughout the 1980s inspired thousands of individuals from all over the world to join them in their struggle for self-determination. Impressively, one of the most important constituencies to take up the Sandinista cause was a significant portion of the US public. In the United States, this movement became part of what was known as the Central American Peace and Solidarity Movement (CAPM).[1]

Even more impressively, according to Reagan administration officials and key congressional leaders of the time, the grassroots pressure on Congress and the constant bombarding of the public with information by this movement was the principal reason the administration's Central America policy was constrained.[2] What moved this collection of individuals and organizations to oppose their government's policy, and often even identify with the Sandinista cause? How did this movement become so effective at shaping opposition to Reagan's policy? These questions take on greater significance if we recall that the Reagan administration got its way on most of its foreign policy initiatives.

This chapter explores these two questions and is divided into five sections. In the first, I document the transnational origins of the movement. Next, I look at the CAPM's growth and spread around the country. The third section traces the strategies and objectives for which the movement mobilized. In the fourth section, I briefly explore the CAPM's decline in the postrevolutionary period. Finally, I conclude with an analysis of the movement's achievements.

Origins of the Central American
Peace and Solidarity Movement

How can we best understand the origins of this US-based solidarity movement with Nicaragua? To date, right-wing politicians and pundits have accused it and its leaders of being Sandinista front organizations or, alternatively, naïve dupes of astute communist manipulators.[3] However, serious scholarship on the movement has shown that this is far from accurate. Nevertheless, most social scientists that have studied the movement have erred too far on the other side, describing it as if it were solely a domestic movement.[4] As a result, they have completely neglected the purposive agency that Nicaraguans, both in their home country and in the United States, played in the rise and success of the movement. Largely, this has resulted from scholars trying to fit the CAPM discretely within a nation-state-centered paradigm. In contrast, to better understand the movement's origins and development, I utilize a transnational framework of analysis. By doing so, I am able to more accurately see the movement's origins as well as its relationship to revolutionary social forces in Nicaragua.[5] It also avoids the false dichotomy created by analysis that reifies the nation-state and allows us to see the CAPM as it really was: a transnational social movement with US and Central American citizens acting together synergistically.

The CAPM was a heterogeneous collection of groups ranging from nonprofits, campus-, church-, and community-based organizations, foundations, and ad hoc committees to national organizations and transnational advocacy networks. By 1986, they numbered over 2,000 formal organizations and were located throughout the United States.[6] What unified them was that they all challenged Reagan's Central America policy in at least one of four ways: (1) opposing and mobilizing opposition to Reagan's financing of the Nicaraguan contras and the Salvadoran and/or Guatemalan regimes; (2) providing material, monetary, technical, and personal aid to the people negatively affected by Reagan's policies and/or to the Reagan administration's opponents in the region; (3) challenging and refuting the administration's framing of the problems and US participation in Central American politics; and (4) providing sanctuary to Central American refugees as *political* refugees fleeing the human rights violations of the Reagan administration's Central American allies.[7]

History

The grassroots movement in opposition to US Nicaragua policy can be described as having two phases.[8] The first phase lasted from the early 1970s until the early 1980s. During the first phase of the movement's development, it was characterized by opposition to the Somoza dictatorship and support for the social forces organized to bring an end to the dictatorship, especially the FSLN. It was also characterized by the fact that the movement tried to get the US administration to isolate the dictator and, after the triumph of the revolution, tried to encourage amicable or at least working relations between the Sandinista Revolution and the US government. The second phase of the movement coincided with the ever-increasing hostility of the Reagan administration to the Nicaraguan revolutionary process, beginning with economic and political pressures and culminating in the Contra war. In response to the escalating aggression, ever-greater numbers of people began opposing US-Nicaraguan policy and support for the contras.

Phase 1

The roots of what came to be called the CAPM are found in the earliest Central American immigrants to the United States. In the Nicaraguan case, many of these early members of the Central American diaspora came to the United States fleeing the repressive Somoza regime. In the late 1970s and early 1980s, Nicaraguan exiles were mobilizing to generate awareness about the negative impact of US policy. Originally, they organized to protest the brutality of the Somoza regime and to oppose US support of the dictatorship. By the 1970s, many of these Nicaraguans were organized into various local Nicaraguan committees around the United States. Among the early organizations formed by the Nicaraguan immigrant community were Casa Nicaragua (various chapters), NICA (various chapters), Washington Area Nicaragua

Solidarity Organization, Committee in Solidarity with the People of Nicaragua, and Los Muchachos de DC.[9] These early Nicaraguan organizations had or established direct connections with the FSLN. An example of this was the "National Solidarity Week for Nicaragua and El Salvador" that took place in Washington, DC, during February 1980. The week-long activities were designed to educate the North American community and raise money for the Central American revolutionaries. It culminated with visits from two representatives of the Sandinista government, Noel González from the foreign ministry and Sayda Hernández from the Luisa Amanda Espinoza Association of Nicaraguan Women (Asociación de Mujeres Nicaragüenses, Luisia Amanda Espinosa, or AMNLAE).[10]

The role of these Central American immigrant-organizers was fundamental to the growth of the CAPM. As Nora Hamilton and Norma Chinchilla document, "The goals of anti-intervention and solidarity work, with its explicit challenge to US government policies, made it logically the focus of US citizens rather than recently arrived immigrants. But behind all of these campaigns . . . were the immigrants, with their access to information, their passion for the cause, and their optimism about the capacity of ordinary people to bring about change."[11] When the Sandinista Revolution triumphed in 1979, many of the most committed and experienced cadre returned to Nicaragua to participate in the building of the revolution and the new Nicaragua. Those that remained active in the United States worked to raise money and awareness for the FSLN literacy campaign and the revolution. They also began trying to get North Americans to travel to Nicaragua to observe, participate, and return to the United States to share with others what they had seen.

The first solidarity organization to incorporate North Americans at the national level was the National Network in Solidarity with the Nicaraguan People (later renamed the Nicaragua Network, or NicaNet). It was formed shortly before the triumph of the revolution. According to Katherine Hoyt, NicaNet national co-coordinator, not only was the organization's founding conference held in response to an appeal from the Nicaraguan social movement, but also a number of its founding member committees were made up of Nicaraguans living in the United States.[12] "In February 1979, the network was founded to support the popular struggle to overthrow the forty-three-year-old, US-supported Somoza family dictatorship, and after the July 19 victory, to support the efforts of the Sandinista Revolution to provide a better life for the nation's people."[13] By 1980, the Nicaragua Network had grown to incorporate about fifty member committees, eventually growing to over 200 committees across the United States. During this time, NicaNet's resources were used to facilitate support for Nicaragua among individuals connected to important institutions through delegations and meetings. The network's major projects included supporting Nicaragua's literacy campaign and organizing national speaking tours for Sandinista representatives.

Phase 2

The movement's second phase coincided with the hardening of US-Nicaraguan policy against the Sandinistas. Efforts had been under way in earnest since at least 1982 to organize, fund, and train a rebel force with the objective of overthrowing the FSLN government. While the contras, as this rebel force came to be called, could not directly defeat the Sandinista People's Army (Ejercito Popular Sandinista, or EPS), it could and did inflict significant suffering on the Nicaraguan people. In fact, that is exactly what it was designed to do, punish the Nicaraguan civilian population so that they would rebel against the revolutionary government and overthrow it.

In this context, a renewed cry went out from Nicaragua asking North Americans to come see for themselves what their government's policy was doing and to return home to tell others what they had seen. The FSLN leadership hoped that allowing US citizens to witness the effects of US policy would encourage them to return home to tell people about the negative impact of the Reagan administration's policy on the Nicaraguan people.[14] Sandinista efforts were extremely successful, with over 100,000 US citizens traveling to Nicaragua by 1986.[15] By the mid-1980s, Witness for Peace (WFP) and the Pledge of Resistance had become two of the largest nationwide organizations working to influence US policy toward Nicaragua. In both cases, mass organizations affiliated with the FSLN or religious organizations supportive of the revolution, such as AMNLAE, the Mothers of the Heroes and Martyrs, and the Evangelical Committee for Aid to Development (Comité Evangélico Pro-Ayuda al Desarrollo, or CEPAD), played a direct role in the creation and development of WFP and later the Pledge of Resistance.[16]

At the same time, the FSLN leadership hoped that by increasing US public opposition to US policy, these organizations' work would have a strong deterrent component. In particular, they hoped to build sufficient opposition to constrain the Reagan administration's ability to escalate the conflict. As Holly Sklar explains,

> An invasion of Nicaragua would also trigger mass protest in the United States like nothing this country has seen since the civil rights and Vietnam War–era peace movements. About 2,000 people were arrested in Pledge of Resistance protests following the imposition of the US trade embargo on Nicaragua in May 1985. . . . An estimated 100,000 people

demonstrated in Washington in the April 1987 National Mobilization for Peace and Justice in Central America . . . more than 500 people were arrested while attempting to block the gates at CIA headquarters. Tens of thousands of Americans demonstrated across the country in response to the March 1988 deployment of US troops to Honduras, providing only a glimmer of the protest that would meet a direct invasion of Nicaragua.[17]

By the mid-1980s, much of the public opposition to US–Central American policy was focused specifically on stopping Reagan's efforts in Nicaragua. In large part this can be attributed to the success of large national organizations such as Witness for Peace, NicaNet, and the Pledge of Resistance, which together mobilized well over 100,000 Americans to oppose US policy toward Central America. So what becomes clear is that the FSLN played vital roles in the creation and development of many of the CAPM's US-based movement organizations, including three of the four largest, the Nicaragua Network, Witness for Peace, and Pledge of Resistance. And as sociologist Christian Smith's study of the CAPM has documented, it was these national organizations that formed the backbone of the movement.[18]

The Growth and Spread of the Movement

How was the movement able to grow and spread so fast? There are several factors that facilitated the movement's dynamic growth. The first is the open, democratic nature of the political system implemented by the Sandinistas. This fact, combined with the brutal repression and violence by the contras, gave the Nicaraguan Revolution credibility and legitimacy among a large and important sector of the US populace. Second, the movement's growth was helped by the high level of media coverage, which, although not always accurate, kept the political situation and US involvement in Central America in the public eye and on people's minds. This in turn was in large part a function of President Reagan's obsession with very publicly and visibly "drawing the line against communism" in Central America. His commitment not only clearly signaled to the public both the significance of the conflict but also made it an important issue for the US left on which to challenge the administration. Finally, the movement was greatly facilitated by the direct people-to-people links established between Nicaraguan civil society organizations and North American solidarity, peace, religious, and human rights organizations. The geographic and cultural proximity of the two countries made travel and meaningful communication flows relatively fluid. These linkages also allowed the movement to thwart the administration's attempts to control the flow of information the US public received about the conflict and its Nicaragua policy.

Repression and Violence

The contras' propensity to commit human rights violations not only inflicted great harm on the Nicaraguan people but ironically also opened political opportunities for the solidarity movement transnationally. The Reagan administration became vulnerable to attacks about its commitment to human rights. In contrast, the Sandinista government was judged to be much less repressive, more open, and democratic, especially when compared to other Central American regimes (except Costa Rica) or to previous Nicaraguan regimes. These two factors combined to lend the Sandinistas more credibility and legitimacy not only among progressives but also with many liberal and even mainstream religious organizations. This latter credibility was particularly important because it allowed the solidarity movement to grow beyond just the traditional confines of US antiwar liberals to reach a broader mainstream audience. Indeed, by the middle of the decade solidarity organizations were operating in almost every state and generating significant amounts of grassroots pressure on Congress.

News Media Coverage

During the 1980s, the conflicts in Central America, and Nicaragua in particular, were among the most covered news stories in the US mainstream media (see Figure 11.1). Consequently, it was one of the areas of the world to which the US public was exposed the most. But the US public did not objectively observe the situation in Central America. Instead, it received information about what was happening in the region as competing frames from the Reagan administration and its Central American opponents, most often as filtered through the media.[19] As Charlotte Ryan explains in her study of grassroots activism, "Today, the media have become critical arenas for this struggle. . . . But gaining attention alone is not what a social movement wants; the real battle is over whose interpretation, whose framing of reality, gets the floor."[20] Accordingly, the Reagan administration launched a broad public diplomacy campaign designed to portray the Sandinista government as illegitimate, undemocratic, and repressive but, most importantly, as a communist proxy of the Soviet Union that posed a direct threat to US national security. At the same time, the administration's discourse sought to portray the contras as freedom fighters, going so far as to call them "the moral equivalent of our founding fathers."[21]

However, this framing was countered by Reagan's opponents and contradicted by the news stories from the region. Even though these stories did not often detail the gruesome atrocities by Reagan's allies, they did provide an alternative framing of the conflict and its origins. Specifically, much of

Figure 11.1 Coverage of Nicaragua in Mainstream US Press

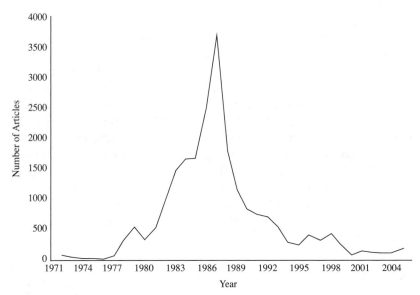

Sources: Based on coverage in five major US newspapers (as reported in a keyword search for "Nicaragua" on Lexis-Nexis): *New York Times, Los Angeles Times, USA Today, Miami Herald,* and *Washington Post.*

the US media coverage focused on the human suffering caused by the contras' efforts to overthrow the FSLN by punishing Nicaragua's civilian population, both through economic sabotage and military actions. Moreover, this type of coverage primarily focused on domestic Nicaraguan causes for the war between the Sandinista government and the counterrevolutionaries that were completely unrelated to Reagan's supposed "communist, Soviet threat." As a result, Reagan's continued support of the contras contrasted sharply with Americans' concern that the United States would be drawn into another Vietnam, thereby increasing the likelihood that the solidarity movement's critiques of Reagan's policy would receive attention and attract supporters to their cause.

Direct People-to-People Links

It must be emphasized that it was the FSLN and its supporters' cultivation of and credibility within this activist network that helped the solidarity movement grow.[22] As the Contra war intensified and fear of a US invasion increased in the wake of the invasion of Grenada (1983), the FSLN nurtured direct people-to-people links that would generate a grassroots movement of US citizens to oppose Reagan's policy. To foment this opposition, the Sandinistas established direct relations with many civil society organizations in the United States. They also sent many of their most effective cadres and supporters on speaking tours of the United States and encouraged delegations of US citizens to visit or work in the border region between Honduras and Nicaragua, where fighting with the contras was heaviest. This was done primarily through mass organizations affiliated with the FSLN or religious organizations supportive of the Sandinista Revolution, such as AMNLAE, the Mothers of the Heroes and Martyrs, the Institute for Social Justice–John XXIII, and CEPAD.

CAPM's Goals and Strategies

So what were the goals and strategies of the solidarity movement? In this section I present evidence that the Sandinistas and their supporters sought to create new mobilizing structures and utilize existing ones to (1) draw US citizens' attention to the suffering of Nicaraguans as a result of the Reagan administration's foreign policy, (2) promote a sustained social movement by US citizens against Reagan's Nicaragua policy and in support of the Sandinista Revolution, and (3) influence the US public's understanding of the Nicaraguan conflict by presenting an alternative frame that contested Reagan's version of the region's problems.

Draw US Citizens' Attention

Because the US public was generally ignorant of US foreign policy in Central America, the Sandinistas' ability to disseminate an alternative frame that would both reach and mobilize the US public more effectively than the administration's framing of the conflict was essential to their strategy of defeating US foreign policy. Thus, once the CAPM is understood as a transnational movement that the FSLN helped create, we can identify a previously unrecognized strategy by which an aggrieved population used transnational substate actors to constrain the foreign policy of a transgressing state by influencing its domestic politics. Specifically in the case of the CAPM, Central American activists and organizations sought support from US citizens and organizations to counter the Reagan administration's foreign policy toward Nicaragua.

I call this tactic the "signal flare strategy," because Central American activists and organizations sought to alert the US public to the negative impact of Reagan's foreign policy on the Nicaraguan people by communicating information directly to them. Much like a traditional signal flare is used to draw attention to a castaway's plight in the hope of attracting aid, so too the political signal flare strategy tried to draw attention to the plight of Nicaragua's aggrieved population. Whenever possible, it was done through the media, but more importantly in the Central American case, the FSLN set in motion a drive to actively communicate it through transnational substate actors (civil society and religious, social movement, and solidarity organizations). These transnational substate actors in turn disseminated this information to the general public, the media, and Congress. Once the negative impact of the Reagan administration's Central America policy was in the public domain, maintaining support for its policy became extremely difficult, eventually leading to limitations, constraints, and prohibitions on Reagan's policy.

There is perhaps no better example of the signal flare strategy's effectiveness than the Pledge of Resistance. The organization was born a week after the US invasion of Grenada in 1983, at a meeting of fifty-three Christian peace and justice activists "who were in close communication with alarmed Nicaraguan church leaders."[23] The fears of the Nicaraguan religious leaders—that the Grenada invasion was merely the prelude to Reagan's true goal, the invasion of Nicaragua—were transmitted directly to those North Americans present at the meeting. After seeing what the United States had done in Grenada and talking with Nicaraguan church leaders who asked them for solidarity in preventing a US invasion of Nicaragua, the North American activists launched the Pledge of Resistance.[24] Thus, it was born as a direct result of the plea for help from Nicaragua.[25] Within a little more than a year, the sentiment of those fifty-three activists had been turned into a pledge by nearly 50,000 US citizens to protest legally or through civil disobedience in case of a major US escalation in Central America. By the end of 1986, at least 80,000 Americans had signed the Pledge of Resistance.[26]

Similarly, Witness for Peace emerged from the 1983 experience of church people that traveled to Nicaragua to witness firsthand the effects of the Contra war. The delegation, coordinated through CEPAD, was led by a former Maryknoll nun who had been a missionary in Nicaragua during the 1960s and 1970s but had been asked by those she worked with to return to the United States to educate people and work to change US policy toward Nicaragua. The delegates were struck by the plight of the contra victims they met and motivated by the contras' refusal to attack while North Americans were present. Upon returning to Managua from the countryside, the delegates met and planned with religious leaders from CEPAD and various Sandinista commanders. Sixto Ulloa, responsible for CEPAD's international relations, then arranged for the group to meet with President Daniel Ortega, who enthusiastically encouraged and supported the idea of bringing ever-larger delegations of North Americans to Nicaragua's war zones. The FSLN leadership wanted US citizens to witness for themselves the effects of US policy but, more importantly, to encourage them to return to the United States to tell people that what they had seen was the result of Reagan administration policy.[27]

Promote Sustained Collective Action

A good example of how Nicaraguans used the signal flare strategy to promote sustained collective action in the United States was through the development of a dense network of communication with their North American allies. One of the Nicaraguan organizations most effective at mobilizing opposition to US foreign policy was called the Mothers of the Heroes and Martyrs. The organization, made up of mostly poor women who had lost children fighting the Somoza dictatorship or the contras, was started by the FSLN's women's organization AMNLAE in 1979. One of their most valuable traits was their ability to frame the costs of the war in starkly human terms. The mothers told the stories of their children's deaths to all who would listen, including international delegations visiting Nicaragua and on speaking tours across the United States. Their stories of maternal grief evoked poignant emotions that transcended national and cultural divides, allowing their framing of the Central American conflict to resonate with diverse international audiences. Visiting delegations' direct contact with the mothers was extremely effective at presenting the conflict in a way that challenged the Reagan administration's depiction of the contras as "freedom fighters."[28] As Christian Smith finds in his study of the CAPM, "Nothing so deeply disturbed and enraged so many Americans, sending them headlong into the struggle to defeat White House policy, as hearing flesh-and-blood men, women, and children tell heartrending stories of hunger, terror, disappearances, torture, executions, rape, and mass murder."[29]

At the same time, throughout the 1980s huge nationwide demonstrations were held to protest the Reagan administration's policy in Nicaragua. Not since Vietnam had an administration's foreign policy been so controversial. Church and student groups, peace activists, community organizations, foundations, and nongovernmental organizations proliferated, many of them with the express purpose of changing US policy toward Nicaragua. By mid-decade, thousands of CAPM organizations were operating throughout the country, bringing hundreds of thousands of US citizens into direct opposition with Reagan's foreign policy on a prolonged and consistent basis throughout his eight years in office.[30]

Meanwhile, the direct assistance—and US volunteers—sent to Nicaragua by various CAPM organizations were invaluable in helping the Sandinistas reduce the costs of further resistance to Reagan's coercive punishment. In August 1985, when Congress authorized $27 million in humanitarian aid to the contras, Quest for Peace launched a campaign to raise the same amount in humanitarian assistance for the Nicaraguan people. It reached that goal in a little over a year. In October 1986, after Congress approved $100 million in military aid for the contras, Quest for Peace repeated the campaign. By December 1987, they had successfully raised $59 million in physical aid and $41 million in contributed services. Other documented efforts include hundreds of thousands of dollars sent by the American Friends Service Committee and Oxfam, more than seventy sister-city projects providing direct aid, thousands of volunteers providing their time and skill in Nicaragua, and the "US Citizens Reparations Campaign," led by NicaNet, which was designed to compensate the Nicaraguan people for the damage caused by US government policies.[31]

Offer an Alternative Frame

The Reagan administration sought to portray his policy as a defensive response to Soviet aggression in the hemisphere. The role of the Central Americans' signal flare strategy was to challenge Reagan by offering an alternative frame around which opposition could grow. Thus, the growth and success of the solidarity movement was a function of its ability to generate an alternative frame that would both reach and resonate with the US public more effectively than the administration's framing of the conflict.

The ability of the Central American revolutionaries to create a signal flare was also facilitated by news reports of human rights violations by US regional allies, which allowed the CAPM to offer an alternative frame that resonated with the US public. Had Reagan's allies' atrocities not been so visible or frequent, the US public might have accepted his framing of the contras as "the moral equivalent of our founding fathers."

As Sandinista vice president Sergio Ramírez stated at a 1982 solidarity conference in Managua, "Our intellectuals should make contact with US writers, scientists, artists, and academics at once and urge them to protest any kind of intervention in Central America or the Caribbean."[32] The importance that the FSLN assigned to establishing these relationships and the creation of a solidarity movement is illustrated by the comments of Carlos Fernando Chamorro, then-editor of the Sandinista newspaper *Barricada,* who stated at another international conference, "Solidarity has a fundamental role to play in isolating the enemy, neutralizing other enemies, encouraging other forces, and directly supporting the struggles of the people. . . . We ask you to become a militia of solidarity with the people of Nicaragua, a militia for peace."[33]

Postrevolution Decline

Yet by the early 1990s, the Central American Peace and Solidarity Movement had begun to decline. The organizations primarily focused on Nicaragua solidarity were particularly hard hit because of several developments in Nicaragua. These events and allegations, and their subsequent effect on the solidarity movement, clearly illustrate how intertwined and interdependent the movement was with on-the-ground politics and actors in Nicaragua. The first major setback for the Nicaraguan solidarity movement was the electoral defeat of the FSLN in 1990. This was followed shortly thereafter by the allegations of corruption against long-time party leaders, known as *La Piñata*, and the sexual abuse allegations against Daniel Ortega. Lastly, Nicaraguan solidarity organizations were also deeply affected by the purge and/or defection of a large percentage of the Sandinistas' most internationally effective, well-known, and respected cadre.

This string of negative allegations and political developments took a heavy toll on international support for the FSLN, a once-credible and admired revolutionary movement. As a consequence, support for the solidarity movement associated with the Sandinista Revolution was also hit hard. To deal with these developments and the changes on the ground in Nicaragua, organizations like NicaNet, Witness for Peace, Quest for Peace, and Pledge of Resistance have had to make significant changes in how they operate or have ceased to exist.[34] Most significantly, these organizations are no longer single-issue organizations. In other words, most of them now do solidarity, justice, and anti-intervention work for other countries and causes. Witness for Peace is the organization that has gone the furthest in adopting this model. It currently has programs in several Latin American countries: Colombia, Mexico, Nicaragua, and Cuba. It is also leading delegations to Venezuela and Bolivia.[35] In this sense, the organization has continued educating the US public by organizing international delegations. Alternatively, Quest for Peace has been able to maintain its exclusive focus on Nicaragua. However, it has always been and continues to be part of a larger organization, the Quixote Center, which has several other programs.[36]

The Nicaragua Network has been able to keep its primary focus on Nicaragua, but at considerable expense and through substantial hardship. The organization no longer maintains a staff person in Nicaragua, and there are only two full-time staff people at the national office. It has been able to do this by collaborating with Nicaraguan organizations such as Kairos Training Association (Asociación Kairos para la Formación) to handle its in-country logistics, as well as working with incipient groups that are focused on hot topics and slightly broadening the vision and focus of its mission. For example, NicaNet has been extremely active in the 50 Years Is Enough Campaign, the Alliance for Social Justice, Mexico Solidarity Network, Chiapas Media Project, Answer Coalition, and the movement against the Central American Free Trade Agreement. As national co-coordinator Chuck Kaufman explained, "Today we do anti-globalization work, but we do it through the lens of Nicaragua and the struggle of the Nicaraguan people."[37]

Impressively, despite the setbacks the Nicaraguan solidarity movement has faced in the years since the end of the revolutionary government, the movement's national organizations continue to keep working tenaciously on many of the same issues that plagued Nicaragua during the 1980s and 1990s. Foremost among them are continued human rights violations, lack of economic justice (severe inequality and grinding poverty), limited rights for women, lingering rural underdevelopment, and violations of Nicaragua's political sovereignty through undue interference by the US embassy and administration officials to influence electoral outcomes.

Assessing the CAPM's Achievements

While losing significant strength since the electoral defeat of the Sandinistas, the movement itself made significant accomplishments throughout the 1980s. Unfortunately, they have often been overlooked or not adequately acknowledged by scholars. Often this has occurred because many of the scholars who have studied the movement had at one time been active in the movement and thus have been hit hard by the negative events of the last fifteen or so years in Nicaragua. As a result, they have not been able to take the theoretical distance to appreciate just how much the movement accomplished. Ironically, it has been scholars of US public opinion not necessarily active in the movement and even the movement's opponents, such as right-wing pundits and politicians, who have acknowledged just how formidable a social force the movement actually was.

I conclude by listing a few of the major accomplishments of the movement. While there are many more, smaller victories, I simply list the ones that I feel are the most important or symbolic of what a transnational grassroots movement for social justice can accomplish when people in the global South and North come together for a common purpose.

First, when US-Nicaragua policy is compared with other contemporaneous cases of the Reagan Doctrine, we can appreciate the degree to which the solidarity movement was in fact quite successful. Several points stand out and should be mentioned specifically. The most obvious is that the United States was not able to escalate its war in Central America or use the powerful weapons and resources at its disposal against the revolutionary movements. Most importantly, the United States never sent troops to invade Nicaragua. In fact, by all accounts to date from administration insiders, this option was off the table.[38] All the evidence shows that the solidarity movement played an important role in making this so.

Second, and even more impressively, US-Nicaragua policy is the only example of the Reagan Doctrine in which the president did not get all the funds he requested from Congress. In the other cases, he was often given more than he asked for. Conversely, in the Nicaraguan case, the administration almost always got less than it asked for, and for a brief point in time, aid to the contras was outlawed. All these outcomes are major accomplishments in a US foreign policy formation system that is thoroughly skewed in favor of the executive branch. The movement helped overcome the structural incentives that usually impede Congress from taking strong stances against US foreign policy involving the use of force for fear of negative electoral consequences. By making this a priority issue and guaranteeing that people would know whether their congressperson was voting the right way on US-Nicaragua policy, the movement provided the necessary environment to guarantee that Congress would make a stand.

Third, Reagan's policy in Nicaragua was defeated. The contras were never able to militarily overthrow the FSLN government as the mujahideen did the Soviets in Afghanistan. In the end, the FSLN was voted out of power through the democratic process that it had inaugurated. This is the very same democratic process that the Reagan administration sought so desperately to undermine, delegitimize, and destroy throughout his presidency. Lastly, despite Reagan and his successors' best efforts, Sandinismo and the FSLN specifically continue to be a formidable political force in Nicaragua.

Notes

1. The CAPM also included solidarity and peace groups that focused primarily on El Salvador and Guatemala. However, in this chapter I deal only with the Nicaraguan side of the CAPM. When I refer to the CAPM, I am referring to that part of the movement that was primarily focused on Nicaragua work.

2. For a discussion of how public opinion constrained the Reagan administration's ability to implement his Central American policy, see Richard Sobel, *The Im-*

pact of Public Opinion on US Foreign Policy Since Vietnam (New York: Oxford University Press: 2001); and Richard Sobel, ed., *Public Opinion in US Foreign Policy: The Controversy over Contra Aid* (Lanham, MD: Rowman and Littlefield, 1993), especially chapters 6 and 12.

3. See David Hoffman, "Reagan Has a Texas-Sized Sales Job; Public Skeptical of Contra Aid," *Washington Post,* March 16, 1986, A20; Ronald Reagan, *Speaking My Mind* (New York: Simon and Schuster, 1989), 145. See also Elliot Abrams and J. Edward Fox, "Public Opinion and Reagan Policy: Administration Commentaries," in *Public Opinion in US Foreign Policy: The Controversy over Contra Aid,* edited by Richard Sobel (Lanham, MD: Rowman and Littlefield, 1993), 105–119, which also contains comments by Otto Reich; and Chapter 12 in the same work.

4. Christian Smith, *Resisting Reagan* (Chicago: University of Chicago Press, 1996); and Sharon Erickson-Nepstad, *Convictions of the Soul* (New York: Oxford University Press, 2004).

5. This includes FSLN cadre and mass organizations, as well as allied or supportive Nicaraguan civil society organizations, including some in the United States.

6. Smith, *Resisting Reagan,* 387.

7. The contras were the US-organized, -trained, and -financed rebel group that sought to overthrow the FSLN government during the 1980s. Their name derives from the shortened version of the Spanish word *contrarevolucionarios,* meaning "counterrevolutionaries."

8. Part of the reason that academics have seen the movement as purely a US domestic movement is that most social movement scholars who have studied the CAPM have focused only on the second phase of the movement.

9. Nora Hamilton and Norma Stoltz Chinchilla, *Seeking Community in a Global City: Guatemalans and Salvadorans in Los Angeles* (Philadelphia: Temple University Press, 2001), 129–130; Katherine Hoyt, "February 1979–February 2004: Nicaragua Network Celebrates 25 Years of Solidarity," *Nicaragua Monitor,* December 2003–January 2004.

10. Judith Valente, "D.C.-Area Hispanics Collect Funds to Spread Revolutionary Information," *Washington Post,* February 25, 1980, A20.

11. Hamilton and Chinchilla, *Seeking Community,* 129–130.

12. Hoyt, "February 1979–February 2004."

13. NicaNet: The Nicaragua Network, www.nicanet.org/#about.

14. Ed Griffin-Nolan, *Witness for Peace* (Louisville, KY: Westminster/John Knox Press, 1991), 27–28.

15. Smith, *Resisting Reagan,* 158.

16. Griffin-Nolan, *Witness for Peace,* p. 28.

17. Holly Sklar, *Washington's War on Nicaragua* (Boston: South End Press, 1988), 354.

18. Smith, *Resisting Reagan,* 60.

19. A full exploration of the role of the media and, specifically, the frame contestation that took place is beyond the scope of this chapter. For a comprehensive study, including content and frame analysis of mainstream US media coverage of the Central American conflict, see Hector Perla Jr., "Days of Decision: Media Framing and Opposition to the Use of Force in US Foreign Policy," paper presented at the 2004 Midwest Political Science Association annual meeting, March 16–March 21, Chicago.

20. Charlotte Ryan, *Prime Time Activism* (Boston: South End Press, 1991), 53.

21. Lou Cannon, "Reagan Says US Owes 'Contras' Help; Conservative Gathering Hears Emotionally Charged Speech," *Washington Post,* March 2, 1985, A1.

22. For a detailed account of the fundamental role played by the FSLN in the creation and growth of the CAPM, see Hector Perla Jr., "Challenging Reagan: The Rise of the Transnational Central American Peace and Solidarity Movement," presented at the 2004 Midwest Political Science Association Annual Conference, March 16–March 21, Chicago.

23. Smith, *Resisting Reagan,* 78–80.

24. Smith, *Resisting Reagan,* 78–80.

25. For a slightly different account of its founding, see Ken Butigan, "Pledge of Resistance," September 19, 2006, paceebene.org/.

26. Roger Peace, *A Just and Lasting Peace* (Chicago: Noble Press, 1991), 88.

27. Griffin-Nolan, *Witness for Peace,* 27–28.

28. Lorraine Bayard de Volo, "Global and Local Framing of Maternal Identity: Obligation and the Mothers of Matagalpa, Nicaragua," in *Globalizations and Social Movements: Culture, Power, and the Transnational Public Sphere,* edited by John A. Guidry, Michael D. Kennedy, and Mayer N. Zald (Ann Arbor: University of Michigan Press, 2000), 127–145.

29. Smith, *Resisting Reagan,* 151.

30. Smith, *Resisting Reagan,* 387–388.

31. Peace, *A Just and Lasting Peace,* 87–90; James McGinnis, *Solidarity with the People of Nicaragua* (Maryknoll, NY: Orbis Books, 1985), 136.

32. Sergio Ramírez, "US Working People Can Stop Intervention," in *Nicaragua: The Sandinista People's Revolution, Speeches by Sandinista Leaders,* edited by Bruce Marcus (New York: Pathfinder Press, 1985), 7.

33. Carlos Fernando Chamorro, "Without Solidarity It Is Difficult to Talk About Revolution," *Nicaragua: The Sandinista People's Revolution, Speeches by Sandinista Leaders,* edited by Bruce Marcus (New York: Pathfinder Press, 1985), 14–17.

34. The one organization that no longer exists is the Pledge of Resistance. It has been reincarnated in the sense that there now exists an organization called the Iraq Pledge of Resistance, which is modeled on the successful version applied in Central America. But as far as I can tell, it is not the same organization and does not do any work with regard to Nicaragua.

35. See the Witness for Peace website, www.witnessforpeace.org/.

36. For more on the Quixote Center, see quest.quixote.org.

37. Author's interview with Chuck Kaufman, Managua, Nicaragua, June 23, 2006.

38. Abrams and Fox, "Public Opinion and Reagan Policy: Administration Commentaries," 116.

12

The Nicaraguan Exception?

Salvador Martí i Puig and David Close

EVERY COUNTRY'S POLITICS ARE UNIQUE, BUT SOME ARE PARticularly striking. Since 1979, Nicaragua has been one of the exceptional cases. Its revolutionary government was exceptionally pluralistic, and its turn to electoral democracy in 1984 and acceptance of electoral defeat in 1990 were unprecedented among Marxist-oriented revolutionary states. Since then, the continued significance of the Sandinista National Liberation Front (Frente Sandinista de Liberación Nacional, or FSLN) and its conclusion of a power-sharing agreement with the Liberals while in opposition, along with Daniel Ortega's return to the presidency after sixteen years absence, all help set Nicaragua apart.[1] In this conclusion, we examine more closely the variety of factors that have combined to give Nicaragua its singular politics since 1979 and what the country's politics are like now.

Nicaragua, Nicaragüita: A Country and a Revolution

Nicaragua appeared on the world's political radar with the Sandinista Revolution. This was a "different" revolution, marked by the breadth of the revolutionary coalition, which encompassed all who opposed the Somozas' dictatorship, from the church to libertarians; its lack of dogmatism; and the Sandinistas' collegial leadership. It was also a revolution that inspired great international solidarity, especially after becoming the target of the Reagan administration and the contras whom Washington so openly supported. Hundreds of thousands of people took David's side against Goliath. Writers, entertainers, poets, politicians, professors, and anyone with a thirst for justice backed the Nicaraguan experiment. And those who backed Nicaragua's struggle also supported wars of national liberation in neighboring El Salvador and Guatemala.

It was impossible for people committed to progressive causes to ignore the Sandinista Revolution. The success of a revolution in a poor nation confronting the United States and the neoliberal economic wave of the 1980s made it the lodestar of the Western left. But it was not ideology alone that drew people. The revolution was not just "counterhegemonic" or socialist but also about trying to end poverty and exclusion in a part of the world marked by inequality and underdevelopment.

It is said that in the heat of battle, you acquire the stature of your enemy. Here the opponent was truly colossal. Combating underdevelopment, inequality, and injustice was a task as complicated as it was massive. And the Nicaraguan Revolution faced it while confronting domestic and international obstacles.

Internally, there was an agrarian economy featuring a modern agro-export sector and subsistence sector little changed over the centuries.[2] Further, the economy was not especially diversified, added little value to the goods it produced, had a poorly educated labor force, and did not inspire much confidence among investors. International factors, such as a changing international market, poor prices for the primary products Nicaragua exported, and a financial blockade added to the country's woes. And there was the counterrevolutionary war, too.

Then, after barely ten years, the revolutionary government fell when Nicaragua's citizens rejected it at the polls. They did so in part because they had come to disavow the revolution's objectives and methods, but perhaps more due to the failure of the Sandinista state to face up to the terrible challenges posed by economic collapse and continuing war. Nicaragua's population was exhausted.

Unfortunately, the new political order did little to address the demands of ordinary Nicaraguans, the poor majority who were the focus of Sandinista policies. Although there was no growth in the economy from 1990 through 1993, from 1994 to 2007 the annual increase in gross domestic product (GDP) ranged from 3 to 7 percent.[3] These are respectable numbers, and they are associated with some decline in poverty. In 2000, 69 percent of Nicaraguans lived in poverty ($2 per capita per day), and 42 percent lived in extreme poverty ($1 a day).[4] By 2006, the figure for those living in poverty had fallen to 45 percent, whereas those living in indigence constituted some 30 percent of the population.[5] Nevertheless, the three right-of-center governments in office between 1990 and 2006 never made poverty reduction a priority. Rather, they concentrated on trying to generate economic growth and then waiting for the benefits to trickle down. Only the Sandinistas seemed cognizant of the ravages of poverty in Nicaragua, yet Daniel Ortega's return to the presidency in 2006 did not make it clear that things might change.

In his first three presidential campaigns (1984, 1990, and 1996), Ortega was an aggressive man of the left, forcefully calling for greater equality and the redistribution of wealth and power in society. His race in 2001 was strikingly different. Reconciliation was the theme, designed to calm those who feared that an Ortega presidency would mean a return to the 1980s. Tough issues were avoided, and policies were only treated in the most general terms. Moreover, the private sector, including its fairly substantial Sandinista wing, was very neoliberal in its view of the state's role in the economy. Thus it was a surprise when Daniel rediscovered state intervention in the 2006 campaign. Some of this activity was aimed at business—credits, subsidies, and debt forgiveness—but there was something for the poor Sandinista voter, too.

This new policy direction first became clear in Ortega's inauguration with the announcement of a *giro social,* a social policy that would have two foci. One was poverty alleviation and comprised three programs: Zero Hunger (Hambre Cero), Zero Usury (Usura Cero), and Zero Unemployment (Desempleo Cero).[6] Eduardo Baumeister's analysis of Hambre Cero in Chapter 10 notes that program's strengths and weaknesses, including the apparent misapplication of the policy to make it correspond better to partisan objectives. In this, Ortega and the FSLN join an extremely long line of governments for whom short-run, attend-to-the-base reasoning can produce suboptimal policy performance.

The second focus of the *giro social* was to eliminate all user fees for public primary and secondary schools, as well as for medical services received in public clinics and hospitals. However, no extra money was budgeted for these ends. Further, by prohibiting education and health workers to charge for their services, the government provoked strikes in both sectors during its first months in office.[7] There is, though, another problem. As Rose Spalding observes in Chapter 9, the administration's poverty reduction initiatives, broadly defined, appear well conceived, but, as with Hambre Cero, it is not clear that Ortega and the FSLN administer these programs in ways that maximize democratic development instead of partisan goals.

These sorts of contradictions were typical of Ortega's return to office. He declared that his heart is with the left, but that because he is responsible, his head is with the right. At the same time that the president committed his administration to follow the same economic policies that conservative administrations had followed since 1990, including participation in the Central American–Dominican Republic Free Trade Agreement (CAFTA-DR), he was also delivering fiercely anticapitalist and anti-imperialist blasts in

international affairs.[8] Nevertheless, although he continued the right's policies, Daniel Ortega did not do especially well with them. Growth slowed
slightly (4.2 to 3.9 percent), corn and bean production fell (8.7 and 4.2 percent, respectively), and while inflation rose by 10.7 percent overall, the price
of a basic market basket of goods soared 24.8 percent.[9]

President Ortega also began leaving his mark beyond the economic
sphere. The campaign had proclaimed "El Pueblo Presidente" ("the people
are the president"). To move this from rhetoric to reality, Ortega and his
wife Rosario Murillo, who was his campaign manager and then became the
functional equivalent of the minister of the presidency, had for some time
bruited the Councils of Citizens' Power (Consejos de Poder Ciudadano, or
CPC). They are presented as civil society organizations, but in practice they
work more like a party-controlled mass organization, meaning that they
work from the top down and are more apt to mobilize their members than
encourage them toward independent political participation.[10] Data from mid-
2008 showed very low levels of participation: a CID-Gallup poll showed
that only 2.5 percent of those interviewed in Managua belonged to a CPC,
with the figure dropping to 1.8 percent outside the capital. In June Murillo
declared, "We have made it clear from the beginning that the FSLN Political Secretaries are the Delegates of Citizens' Power in the departments.
. . . It seems to me that we're assuming citizens' power is something apart
from the FSLN. And that can't be! . . . We have to recognize that without
the Sandinista Front there is no citizens' power."[11]

Finally, there is the question of Ortega's foreign policy. This is arguably
where he has been most successful. He has forged close links with Hugo
Chávez and Evo Morales, Mahmoud Ahmadinejad and Muammar Gadhafi
(of Venezuela, Bolivia, Iran, and Libya, respectively) while maintaining
correct relations with Washington, though less so after 2009. Further, Ortega
retained diplomatic ties with Taiwan, while Oscar Arias, the centrist president of Costa Rica, embraced Beijing.

If aligning Nicaragua with ideologically like-minded states—Cuba,
Ecuador, Bolivia, Venezuela, Iran, and Libya—let Ortega reinforce the
FSLN's self-image as a revolutionary party, the decision also has a pragmatic
side. These states do not demand as rigorous an accounting of how their aid
is spent as do donors from North America or the European Union (EU). Similarly, choosing Taipei over Beijing can be seen as a practical choice because Taiwan appeared more ready to finance key projects.[12] Finally, Hugo
Chávez is more than Ortega's greatest political ally, for he serves Nicaraguan interests very well by promising massive aid, estimated at over $5 bil-
lion; unfortunately, given the lack of transparency of both the Nicaraguan
and Venezuelan governments, those figures are difficult to confirm.[13] What

is known is that total Venezuelan assistance to Nicaragua—donations and loans to both the public and private sectors—totalled $283.4 million in the first half of 2009.[14]

In 2009, Daniel Ortega aligned Nicaragua with Venezuela in its response to the coup in Honduras that ousted Manuel Zelaya, a latecomer to the Bolivarian Alliance (which currently inlcudes Venezuela, Bolivia, Ecuador, and Nicaragua) but the only one to actually fall from power. Both Ortega and Chávez took a maximalist position, demanding the immediate restitution of the status quo ante, disdaining efforts by Costa Rican president Oscar Arias to negotiate a settlement that would have seen the return of Zelaya to office but with his freedom of action significantly curtailed. In the end, neither position prospered. The leader of the Honduran coup, Roberto Micheletti, simply stonewalled almost all the world's leaders, including President Barack Obama, and carried the day.[15]

However, none of the above international maneuvering has changed Nicaragua's status as a vulnerable, economically dependent country that has been incapable of finding a path to sustained, equitable, and inclusive development since attaining independence in 1821. In the 1980s, the revolutionary government sought that path. In the first decade of the twenty-first century, there is some evidence that Daniel Ortega's second presidency may be doing the same, but success remains elusive. In the short term, then, it appears that little will change in Nicaragua. The rich and powerful will stay that way; the poor and the powerless, too. Only those who do what the poor in Nicaragua have always done to get ahead—hitch their wagon to a powerful patron and see their loyalty pay off—have a chance to do well. Is that what the Sandinista Revolution was about?

Chapiollo Politics:
Nicaragua's Emerging Model of Governance

Like everywhere else in the world, Nicaragua has developed its own model of governance—how governing is carried out and how state and society interact. We use a Nicaraguan word, *chapiollo* (native-born), to describe this well-institutionalized way of doing politics.[16] This shorthand description of the Nicaraguan political regime tells us three things: (1) what makes a ruler legitimate, (2) what instruments a legitimate ruler may use to govern, and (3) in whose interest a legitimate ruler governs. That is, it tells what must be done to get to govern, how the winners are expected to govern, and to whom they are accountable. We can now take a closer look at *chapiollo* politics as practiced in the second Ortega administration.

Who Gets to Govern?

In a hereditary monarchy, the ruler comes from the royal family. In a Marxist state, the ruler comes from the revolutionary vanguard. Rulers in contemporary, constitutional democracies have won free elections. Tyrants govern because they impose themselves by main force.

In 2011 in Nicaragua, the right to rule comes from elections. The 2006 elections were unprecedented for producing a fight among three substantial parties—the FSLN, the Constitutionalist Liberal Party (Partido Liberal Constitutionalista, or PLC), and the Nicaraguan Liberal Alliance (Alianza Liberal Nicaragüense, or ALN)—along with a fourth, smaller party, the Sandinista Renewal Movement (Movimiento Renovador Sandinista, or MRS). What produced this deviation from the Sandinista versus anti-Sandinista straight fights since 1990 were splits in the FSLN and PLC that reflected both programmatic and personal differences related to the Pact the two parties forged in 2000. However, we cannot forget that one goal of the Pact was to limit electoral competition, thus ensuring that only the FSLN and PLC could run successfully.

Nor should we overlook the Pact's distribution of key government posts between the partners, a practice that has politicized even normally nonpartisan offices like the Supreme Court (described in Chapter 5), the Controller's Office, and the Electoral Authority. The Pact thus extends the right to participate in governing to electoral losers. Although this is standard in coalition governments, where parties in the cabinet share responsibility for an administration's fate, Nicaragua's case is distinct. First, the Pact partner can remain the government's fiercest critic. Second, formally being an ally, as with the National Convergence (Convergencia Nacional), the parties that ran with the FSLN in the the United Nicaragua Will Triumph Alliance (Alianza Unida Nicaragua Triunfa) in 2006 need not net a notable presence in government.[17] However, Nicaragua has a strong spoils system in politics that both the PLC and FSLN embrace wholeheartedly, as was seen when the newly elected Ortega administration swept the bureaucracy with a partisan broom.[18]

In short, to the victors and their friends go both the spoils of office and control over government. This is hardly unique, and, more importantly, it is a deeply rooted tradition in Nicaraguan politics. It is, in fact, one of the elements of the resigned pragmatism that Andrés Pérez Baltodano examines in Chapter 4. We would do well to see it as an informal institution: "socially shared rules, usually unwritten, that are created, communicated, and enforced outside officially sanctioned channels."[19] Personal rule and government-opposition pacts are also longstanding political norms in Nicaragua that fall into the category of informal institutions.

The lineup of political actors in 2011 offers a glimpse of how these informal institutions work. Not only do the Sandinistas hold the presidency and a plurality of seats in the National Assembly, but for the government's first two years, it was able to fashion a legislative majority thanks to the Pact with the PLC. Ironically, PLC leader Arnoldo Alemán Lacayo's status as a convicted felon guarantees this majority. As Elena Martínez Barahona makes clear in Chapter 5, the judiciary is one of the plums of the Pact, but it is effectively controlled by the FSLN. Thus Sandinista judges could give Alemán a very flexible regime of house arrest, or a restrictive one, or even order him back to jail, depending on what was needed to get the PLC to vote with the government. Although the former president has been a free man since January 2009, he continues in his role as Pact partner, but with some changes.

All this leaves Nicaragua with a peculiar party system. There is one plurality party, now the Sandinistas; two parties that would dominate were they to unite, the PLC and the ALN; and the Sandinista dissidents in MRS, who often vote against the FSLN. Together the Pact's parties have 63 of 92 seats, more than enough to amend the constitution, which would require 56 votes in consecutive legislatures, should they so wish. That this has not happened may be due to Alemán's reluctance to give Ortega the right to immediate reelection, perhaps suspecting that it would lead to the Liberals' permanent exclusion from the presidency. Events in 2009 should have strengthened the former president's suspicions: a Supreme Court decision rendered only by Sandinista justices (Chapter 6) declared that constitutional prohibitions on consecutive terms and a lifetime two-term limit for the president would not apply to the Sandinista leader.[20]

In January 2010, Daniel Ortega changed the rules again by issuing a decree (3-2010) extending the appointments of twenty-seven individuals, among them Supreme Court justices, Supreme Electoral Council (Consejo Supremo Electoral, or CSE) magistrates, comptrollers, the human rights ombudsperson, and the superintendent of banks as well as the directors of that institution. All these appointments were to expire in the first half of 2010, and all had to be elected or ratified by the National Assembly.[21] Legislative attempts to overturn the decree were blocked by the Supreme Court. In April, because the National Assembly building was blockaded by Sandinista protesters, legislators convened a session at a Holiday Inn and met at the headquarters of ALN leader Eduardo Montealgre, where they were attacked by armed Sandinistas.[22] We return to the growing role of coercion as a governing instrument below.

Then there is the executive. Like so many of its predecessors in Nicaragua and the rest of Latin America, the present Ortega administration is hyperpresidential. In this it resembles the Alemán government (1996–2001), as well as most governments in the nation's history, except the Chamorro and Bolaños administrations. What distinguishes the Ortega government from Alemán's is the role assumed by Rosario Murillo, Ortega's wife. We noted above that Murillo is effectively Ortega's minister of the presidency and in her own right the coordinator of the Communications and Citizenship Council (Consejo de Comunicación y Ciudadanía) of the Presidency of the Republic, an executive organization in the office of the president, which, among other things, controls the government's advertising budget, a useful tool in any government.

Ortega is not the first president to put a close family member in a position of responsibility: President Violeta Barrios de Chamorro named her son-in-law Antonio Lacayo her minister of the presidency. However, since that time the constitution was amended to make such appointments illegal. The Ortegas get around this provision by not giving Murillo a salary. Nevertheless, in a country that ended forty-three years of family dictatorship in 1979, appointing a presidential spouse to an important government post must dredge up unpleasant memories. But what is really hard to understand is how it could be done by one of the leaders of the FSLN insurgency that brought down the Somozas. It looks like the answer to who governs is increasingly the Ortegas, through the FSLN.

How Shall They Govern?

How shall the ruler rule? The question has a two-part answer. One focuses on governing instruments. It asks how a government makes and implements its policies. Is governance closed, partisan, and exclusionary or open and accommodating? And if the former, what happens to those outside the circle of partisan loyalists? Are they simply denied government patronage, or are they pressured into silence? The question is relevant because Nicaraguan history offers too many examples of coercive politics.

In Chapter 3, David Close noted that violence was no longer a central oppositional instrument in Nicaragua. However, that does not mean that political violence has disappeared from Nicaragua. Since 1990 there have been numerous violent confrontations between university students and government over the question of funding, and bus and taxi owners have clashed violently with every administration since 1990 (including Ortega's) over issues such as fuel prices. Further, seeing violence set aside need not mean that government cannot harass its opponents through bureaucratic means. We need look back no further than the Alemán administration to see that done.[23] And since 2008, the FSLN has adopted the tactics of its Pact partner.

Two examples stand out. First, in June 2008 two minor parties, the MRS, which has representatives in the National Assembly, and the Conservative

Party (Partido Conservador de Nicaragua, or PCN), which does not, lost their party status, meaning they could not contest the November 2008 municipal elections.[24] The two parties lost official status for allegedly failing to meet regulations regarding the registration of candidates and reporting changes in party structures. The CSE, which is responsible for determining party status, is a partisan body, dominated by the FSLN and its Pact partner, the PLC. The highly partisan character of the CSE casts doubt on its actions. As a result, even if the alleged violations are well founded, it is likely that the CSE's actions would be met with skepticism. Add to this Martínez Barahona's findings regarding partisan influence in the judiciary, and criticisms of the Ortega administration claiming that it uses state institutions to advance the president's objectives take on a higher degree of plausibility.

The second example involves charges by the government in October 2008 that a research center (Centro de Investigaciones de la Comunicación, or CINCO) and two nongovernmental organizations (NGOs), one foreign (Oxfam UK) and one domestic (Movimiento Autónomo de Mujeres, or MAM), were engaged in money laundering.[25] The domestic organizations were critical of the government, and Oxfam UK gave some money to the MAM. These charges, which were eventually dropped, formed part of a larger movement by the Ortega administration against civil society generally, which it depicted as being composed of rightist organizations working against the government.[26] This echoes stances taken by Arnoldo Alemán of the PLC when he was president.[27] In both cases, there is sufficient evidence to argue that the administration was seeking to silence critical voices in civil society.

Much more dramatic has been the escalating use of coercion by the administration to secure its political ends. In addition to the violence used by the Sandinistas to defend Decree 3-2010, noted above, there was also the force mobilized by the government to bully members of the opposition protesting what they saw as the fraudulent results of the 2008 municipal elections, an issue we treat below. The reappearance of regime violence is an unsettling throwback to the days of the Somozas and suggests that the Ortega government believes that violence and intimidation will do more to secure its ends than ordinary political bargaining or even the Pact. By May 2010, things had reached the point at which the newsweekly *Confidencial* published an article claiming that the Ortega administration was offering Nicaraguans a choice between seeing the president reelected or facing political and social chaos brought about by FSLN supporters.[28]

On reflection, we must conclude that the governing style of the second Ortega government is less pluralistic and accepting of legitimate criticism and competition than was the first. It has fallen into the pattern of exclusionary, pacted, spoils-system politics that has long marked Nicaraguan public life. Moreover, the similarities between the Alemán and Ortega governments in their treatment of civil society indicate that both wished to concentrate power within the structures of the parties they dominated. And by 2010, Ortega was going beyond anything Alemán had done in his use of force and coercion.

The second part of the answer to how the ruler shall rule simply asks about policies formulated and applied. What, that is, is the Ortega administration doing?

On two fronts, the FSLN government is clearly doing more and doing it better than the three conservative administrations that preceded it. First, as Miguel González and Dolores Figueroa note in Chapter 7, Ortega's is the first government that has taken up the cause of the Atlantic Coast since the FSLN left office in 1990. Second, the new Ortega government, representing what Spalding calls neo-Sandinismo in Chapter 9, has put social policy close to the top of the agenda for the first time in sixteen years. Antipoverty measures figure prominently in this mix, the best known of them being the Hambre Cero program that Baumeister discusses in some detail in Chapter 10 (see also Chapter 9).

However, deciding to address poverty directly does not mean that the FSLN abandoned orthodox economics. Like both the Chilean Concertación, the center-left alliance that governed between 1989 and 2010, and Luiz Inácio Lula da Silva's administration in Brazil (2003–2011), the Sandinistas have maintained the market while starting to rebuild a welfare state. In fact, the Ortega administration has maintained good relations with the International Monetary Fund (IMF).

It is notable that the FSLN appears to have borrowed many of its innovative social policies from Lula's Brazil. This implies a lack of policy capacity in the FSLN, scarcely surprising in a party out of office for sixteen years, not to mention differences in resources the Brazilian state commands compared to the Nicaraguan. It may, though, also reflect President Ortega's lack of interest in matters of policy and administration. Like Arnoldo Alemán, his Pact partner, Ortega's political skills run more to partisan matters and overall strategy. Some evidence of this is found in the Councils of Citizens' Power.

Although the CPCs' lineage doubtless reaches back to the Sandinista Defense Committees (Comités de Defensa Sandinistas, or CDSs) of the revolutionary 1980s, looking at them in action suggests they also have a lot in common with the political machines found in US cities at the turn of the twentieth century. Like those boss-run machines, the CPCs channel political activity up through the party and also distribute material benefits from government to citizens.[29] This provides incentives for participation while giving government control over the products of citizen action. Of course, in the United States boss politics gave rise to the Progressive Era reforms, which eventually put an end to old-time bossism. Ortega's relations with civil society indicate that he is not comfortable with independent political actors, which may explain why the CPCs reportedly have been involved in harassing the FSLN's political opponents.[30]

Politics is always rough-and-tumble, and no government makes life easy for its opponents, who are unlikely to get funds and whose requests will be held to the most exacting standards or be the pretext for a thorough investigation. However, the current Sandinista administration took this a step further than most by targeting the embassies and ambassadors of major aid donors, notably those from the EU, whom the president accused of being in league with the civil society organizations his administration charged with money laundering.[31]

The argument had three parts. First, in August 2008, Swedish ambassador Eva Zetterberg publicly voiced concerns about "authoritarian signals" from the government following the suspension of the official party status of the MRS and Conservatives. In return, the ambassador was branded a "devil."[32] Then in October, at the Seventeenth Inter-American Summit (Cumbre Iberoamericana), the Ortega administration charged "certain ambassadors" from countries of the European Union with "lending themselves to the political maneuvers of opposition parties to destabilize and overthrow the Ortega government."[33]

Second, there is the government's claim, described earlier, that Oxfam UK was engaged in money laundering with the research center CINCO and the women's group MAM. For some time, at least since the Alemán administration (1996–2001), NGOs like Oxfam UK have been administering a portion of official development aid. This reflects the donors' skepticism about the government's ability to apply the aid as the donors wish, which can be read as opposition to the government in Managua. The third piece of the argument was that because both the foreign governments and the NGOs are critics of the government, they are deemed to be aligned with the FSLN's opposition and working to bring down the government.

Frankly, the Ortega administration's position seems exaggerated. However, there is an interesting question here. If the EU countries and the foreign NGOs do withdraw their assistance, what will Nicaragua do? It is a poor country, and its antipoverty programs are costly. The answer lies in Ortega's foreign policy.

As noted above, Daniel Ortega's greatest policy success may have been in foreign affairs. This assertion merits greater attention, principally because it reveals how the first and second Ortega governments have engaged the world. Normally, when we think of foreign policy, what comes to mind is a government's international relations: how it plays the great diplomatic game of high politics, where the stakes are peace or war. Some governments take a pragmatic view, looking for how best to secure their aims for their nation in the anarchic international system. Others are more ideologically inclined, allowing the pursuit of abstract principles to guide them in world affairs. Although some commentators might deny small countries a role in international politics, both Ortega administrations have played the great game, even if as minor participants.

Revolutionary Nicaragua was building socialism and was a full partner in the staunchly anti-imperialist Non-Aligned Movement (NAM). It also maintained close ties with other revolutionary movements, notably El Salvador's FMLN (Frente Faribundo Martí para la Liberación Nacional, or Faribundo Marti National Liberation Front). Nevertheless, its international relations were determinedly pluralistic. The Sandinistas spoke of diversifying dependency, seeking the development assistance it needed from a wide variety of donors. To a significant extent it succeeded, establishing good relations not just with social democratic Europe but also with Canada's Conservative government. Yet the value of these links was measured less in aid received than in having liberal democratic allies who could try to deflect Washington's efforts to oust the Sandinistas. Obviously, these efforts did not succeed, which partly explains why the Sandinistas had to resort to a mainstay of Nicaraguan foreign relations since 1909 and find a powerful patron. Although this role had always been filled before by the United States, in this instance it was the Soviet Union, indeed the entire Soviet bloc, which provided the revolutionary government with at least some of the materiel it needed to fight the US-funded counterrevolutionaries, the Contra.

This first Sandinista government's foreign policy was thus both ideological and pragmatic.[34] It was unquestionably a pragmatic policy aimed at keeping the Sandinista state alive. But precisely because the Sandinista state had a strong ideological identity (its vision of the good society and how to attain it), it allied with like-minded states in the NAM and the socialist bloc. This ideological commitment allowed the Reagan administration to justify its pressures against Managua with Cold War arguments. The revolutionary government had little choice but to try to buy time to save its project. In the end, the FSLN never did say "Uncle!" as President Ronald Reagan demanded. It was the Nicaraguan people who did so in the 1990 elections. Thus the Sandinistas learned a lesson that all democratic governments learn sooner or later: foreign policy cannot long run contrary to the will of the people.

In his second term, Daniel Ortega is just as pragmatic and ideological as he was two decades earlier. However, he is less pluralistic, partly because the international situation has changed radically since the 1980s and partly because he has a patron whose support lets him be more selective in his foreign relations. Dealing first with the former, since September 11, 2001, the War on Terror has defined Washington's foreign policy objectives. As a result, a self-declared anti-imperialist government is now an annoyance, not a danger as it was during the Cold War, unless it is manifestly linked to terrorist groups. This state of affairs gives Ortega more freedom to pursue his preferred foreign policy objectives without having to trim his ideological sails. It may explain why the first ambassador named to the United States in Ortega's second term was the pro-US Arturo Cruz Sequiera; that is, it was done to stay below Washington's radar. Moreover, dealing with ideologically like-minded states has also brought substantial material benefits, so ideology and pragmatism go together. This is certainly true of Nicaragua's relations with Hugo Chávez's Venezuela, the country's new special friend and de facto protector.[35]

We need to look at this current blend of pragmatism and ideology in more detail. Ortega has managed to preserve correct relations with Washington, though they are more difficult in 2011 than they were in 2007; has chosen to deal with Taiwan, not the People's Republic of China; and has made Nicaragua a key player in an alliance of like-minded states opposed to the neoliberal economic model. Managua's main international partners are Venezuela, Iran, Libya, Bolivia, Ecuador, and Cuba; recently, Russia and Belarus have joined the list. More importantly here, Venezuela and to a considerably lesser extent Iran and Libya have become important providers of economic assistance to Nicaragua.

This matters for two reasons. One is obviously that these states can substitute for the meddlesome donors of the European Union and North America. Although developed capitalist democracies like Spain and Canada demand a rendering of accounts for aid received, not least because their aid agencies are responsible to their respective parliaments, it appears that these new sources of money and materiel do not, or at least they do not demand the same rigorous accounting. The other reason is that they deliver significant sums. One estimate suggests that the money available from just one of several cooperation agreements with Venezuela "almost equals the total western foreign aid that Nicaragua gets in a year."[36] As a result, Daniel Ortega can seriously contemplate reducing the profile of donors from the EU and North America, and relying on his new, more understanding and forgiving partners.

Yet approaching his third year in office, Ortega appeared to lose his touch in foreign affairs. The immediate cause was that the European Union responded to the problematic municipal elections of 2008, discussed below, by suspending aid payments of about $40 million and the United States suspended Millennium Challenge Account payments of $64 million to Nicaragua for the same reason. As a result, Nicaragua faced a significant budget shortfall for 2009.[37] Although Hugo Chávez promised to cover the deficit, Nicaraguan papers reported in April 2009 that a supposed donation of power-generating plants shortly before the 2006 election was in fact a loan, complete with 6 percent interest. This led to questions about whether new assistance from Caracas might also take the form of a loan.[38] And Ortega's musings about the benefits of a single-party state while on a visit to Cuba in April 2009 further tarnished his image in Western capitals and put other Nicaraguan parties on high alert.[39]

There is little doubt that the Nicaraguan president's relations with Hugo Chávez facilitate Nicaragua's less pluralistic and frankly more confrontational foreign policy. Nicaragua now can get by with reduced assistance from the developed liberal democracies. Thus it can avoid having to comply with their conditions and can put an end to listening to their lectures on good governmental behavior. Indeed, the only conditions Ortega's second government seems willing to meet are the IMF's, as they affect only economic policies. That is one benefit of having a patron who is both open-handed and uncritical, something that might not have applied quite so fully to the Soviet bloc states in the 1980s. Put differently, because both Chávez and Ortega practice a highly personal diplomacy, it may be that Ortega gets a better deal with fewer strings than he would from a state with a more institutionalized diplomacy.[40]

In short, the turn away from the pluralistic approach apparent in Nicaragua's foreign policy since 2007 should be attributed to the context in which those relations now take place: having Washington less concerned with Central America and having Hugo Chávez's Venezuela become Nicaragua's main foreign supporter. Although there is no doubt that Daniel Ortega enjoys the freedom these changed conditions offer him, his foreign policy continues to reflect a balance of pragmatic and ideological drivers. It is our impression, however, that Ortega's personal foreign policy profile is more prominent in his second administration than it was in his first. If this is confirmed, it would be consistent with the general pattern of concentration of power in the president's hands.

The picture that emerges shows the Ortega administration governing with highly partisan instruments. Like many Nicaraguan leaders before him, Ortega shows minimal confidence in governmental machinery that cannot be turned fully to his ends and those of his party. This too is an informal political institution in Nicaragua, a norm of governing whose violation is thought to significantly complicate the business of ruling, if not make it impossible. It is spoils-system politics, and to work well it needs a government with significant capacity to act as it sees fit. As a result, governmental account-ability is necessarily limited.

To Whom Is the Government Accountable?

Divine right monarchs were accountable only to God. Marxist revolutionary vanguards are judged by history. Constitutional democrats are responsible to the citizens through elections and the several branches of government between elections. Moreover, they are always accountable before the law. In present-day Nicaragua, things are less straightforward.

First, there are the voters. Political power only comes through electoral victory in today's Nicaragua, so a sufficient part of the electorate must be kept happy to ensure success at the polls. However, in Nicaragua those re-sponsible for running elections and counting the votes, the CSE, are chosen by the National Assembly to reflect the FSLN-PLC Pact, leaving open the possibility that elections are not administered fairly and their results need not reflect the people's expressed preferences.

Although all general elections and most municipal and regional elec-tions since 1990 have been fairly run (as Shelley McConnell makes clear in Chapter 6), the partisan element present in electoral administration is cause for concern. Voters impose vertical accountability on governments: gov-ernments answer to voters. Horizontal accountability comes from within the state: the constitution, legislature, courts, and other levels of government. And the media operate as both vertical and horizontal checks, depending on who uses the information they present. There have been times since 1990 when instruments of horizontal accountability and the media have worked well to countervail the force of the executive in Nicaragua. In the second Or-tega administration this is less the case, as the president controls the legis-lature, the courts, the electoral authority, and the controller's office—the nation's auditor. Along with his wife, he also dominates the Sandinista party. The media still function, but there are Sandinista TV and radio stations to ensure the government's message gets out, and government harassment of the media is reaching worrying proportions.[41]

Increasingly it appeared that Daniel Ortega and his administration were accountable to the voters of Nicaragua but to no one else. The Ortega sys-tem is a nearly perfect match for the electoral caudillismo practiced a decade earlier by Arnoldo Alemán.[42] The most obvious difference between the two presidencies is that Alemán's was defended by the right and criticized by the left, whereas in Ortega's case the critics and the defenders switched sides.

However, in the municipal election of November 2008, Nicaragua may have turned away from accountability to the electorate. As the only midterm elections held nationally in Nicaragua, the votes in 146 cities and towns are a crucial test of strength for a president and the governing party. Matching or improving the totals from the general election show that the president is still popular, improving his or her ability to bargain with other parties in the National Assembly.

The results of the 2008 contest were curious. First, the FSLN won in a landslide, taking 105 mayoralties and council majorities (72 percent) to 37 for the Liberals (25 percent) and 4 (3 percent) for other parties. Although the winners took office in January 2009, the CSE has published neither final results for all municipalities nor the votes won by each party. Earlier results, apparently based on counting roughly 90 percent of the ballots in all constituencies, showed the FSLN leading the PLC by about 3.5 percent, but without taking votes for other parties into account and with a turnout of some 45 percent.[43] If third parties took a percentage of the vote paralleling the percentage of towns they won (2.74), and the FSLN and PLC maintained the same proportion of the vote that was published the day after the election—both assumptions are admittedly unverifiable—the Sandinistas would have taken just over half the vote (about 50.2 percent—6 points better than their previous best since 1984) and the Liberals around 46.8 percent. Turning a 3.4 percent edge in votes into a 47 percent margin in mayoralties and councils won is plausible, if unusual. Similarly, the FSLN could have won half the vote thanks to good organization and mobilization of its supporters, especially with more than half the electorate staying home. However, the result is certainly one that those who did not vote Sandinista would want to have explained very clearly. And the CSE's failure to publish a final official tally only bred suspicion.

It was against the above background that the PLC claimed to be the victim of fraud, alleging that the CSE had simply not counted votes from many polls won by the party and that where results were recorded, they did not match those on the official tallies signed by the party scrutineers present at the counts in each poll. The Liberals made their case most strongly in Managua, where they claimed that the CSE-approved results, which gave the FSLN 51 percent of the vote, ignored about a third of the returns. Had those been counted, the PLC asserted that it would have won the capital.[44]

If the mechanics of the vote were problematic, the Sandinistas' response to the charges of fraud was truly troubling. Harkening back to its days as a revolutionary movement, the FSLN mobilized its supporters to take to the streets to confront its opponents, the majority of whom—though not all—appeared to be engaged in peaceful protest. Carrying clubs and sometimes machetes while clad in party T-shirts, the Sandinista followers blocked access to CSE offices, denying opposition officials the chance to present formal complaints. In one case, a team of masked operatives, carrying AK-47s and again wearing the distinctive party T-shirt, attacked and burned an opposition radio station in León, Nicaragua's second-largest city. While some might say that this was just loyal Sandinistas defending their triumph against the rightist parties that governed from 1990 to 2006, a cold-eyed skeptic would see a patronage-based machine mobilizing its clients to save a fraudulent win.

To account for the FSLN's behavior in this election, one could point to the informal institutions operating in Nicaraguan politics, namely boss-run, caudillo governments and near-hegemonic governing parties. Alternatively, one could recall that Daniel Ortega and most of his close confidants hail from a Leninist vanguard party, whose operational code is not terribly different from the historic Nicaraguan norm, though its justification for its actions is distinct. Finally, one can switch the focus from structures to agents and ask about President Ortega's personal views on power, its possession, and exercise—a topic worthy of a study of its own. The most likely conclusion is that the outcome was overdetermined, as many variables pointed in the same direction.

In any event, the question of to whom the Ortega government is accountable does not appear to admit of an easy, clear answer. Yes, it needs at least a plurality of Nicaraguans' votes to win. However, the administration's control of the nation's electoral machinery and its courts suggests that a result can be manufactured if it does not emerge naturally, and the administration has shown itself ready to resort to force to defend its gains. The evidence available points toward a government that is increasingly accountable only to itself.

The Nicaraguan Exception?

When the Sandinistas came to power, they were not like other revolutionary movements. Their plural leadership both condemned and precluded caudillismo and the cult of personality so often developed by revolutionary leaders. In addition, although all revolutions are coalitions of classes and interests, the Sandinista Revolution made pluralism one of its vital principles, certainly outstripping the Somozas' dictatorship in this regard. The FSLN then put this pluralism into practice by abandoning Leninist dogma and putting the right to govern on the line in free, competitive elections. And when they lost their second try at elections, the Sandinistas left office, admittedly only after some lame-duck jiggery-pokery with *La Piñata,* and learned the arts of opposition.

It was on crossing to the minority side of the aisle that the FSLN's exceptionalism started to fade. The party failed to take advantage of opportunities to break with its past and inter the verticalism that had carried over from its days as an armed insurgent movement. Before long, the party split along predictable lines: social democrats (pluralists) versus unreconstructed revolutionaries (monists). In the end, the verticalists, backing Ortega, won. However, in winning they not only completed the Sandinistas' transition from movement to party but also adopted the ways of caudillismo, as Daniel Ortega became what in African politics would be called Nicaragua's Big Man. Thus the Frente Sandinista de Liberación Nacional turned into a Nicaraguan political party much like any other.

Part of this Nicaraguanization of the Sandinistas is attributable to path dependency. Nicaragua has seen presidents centralize power and abuse their opponents before. Indeed, this is a too-familiar part of Latin American history more generally. However, the Sandinista Revolution was about leaving that path. Whether it was losing power that ended the FSLN's experiment in innovation or whether Daniel Ortega would have proceeded in the same direction even had he won in 1990 is unknowable.

What distinguishes the FSLN and its leader from the rest of the country's political spectrum is that they alone recognize the need to address Nicaragua's crushing poverty. It might be asked, though, if in 2011 the allegiance to neoliberal economics shown by most anti-Sandinista parties is not becoming a spent force and that in the future other political formations will make redistributive policies the keystone of their politics. Perhaps Daniel Ortega foresees such a thing, and it is to forestall this eventuality that he seeks to arrogate power to himself and his party. This is what Pérez Baltodano in Chapter 4 labeled "resigned pragmatism," taking power for the sake of having power. We are not convinced, however, that it is what revolutionary Sandinismo would have done in 1979 when it took power from the Somozas. It may be yet more evidence of the Nicaraguanization of the FSLN and more proof that Nicaragua is not the exceptional political system it was when "los muchachos sandinistas" began the work of revolutionary transformation.

Notes

1. Ortega shares this distinction with Peru's Alan García and Costa Rica's Oscar Arias, both of whom also recaptured their countries' presidencies in 2006 after sixteen years out of office.

2. See, however, Eduardo Baumeister's comments in Chapter 10 of this volume.

3. Banco Central de Nicaragua, *Producción Bruto a precios constantes, 1960–1999,* www.bcn.gob.ni/; and *Anuario de Estadisticas Economicas, 2001–2007,* www.bcn.gob.ni/.

4. United Nations Economic Commission on Latin America and the Caribbean (ECLAC), *Social Panorama of Latin America, 2005,* www.eclac.org/, 70–71.

5. The poverty figure is from UNICEF, *At a Glance: Nicaragua,* www.unicef.org/. The indigence data come from ECLAC, *Combating Hunger and Poverty,* www.eclac.org/. It should be noted that the organizations use slightly different criteria in defining poverty and indigence.

6. Hambre Cero got the most publicity. It originally had three parts: a Bono Productivo (Productive Bonus), a school lunch program, and a program to address chronic infant malnutrition. Details regarding the program and its associated policies are found in Chapters 9 and 10. Projected to reach 75,000 families, the initiative began with a $150 million price tag. Its first director was the sociologist Orlando Nuñez, who had been the director of an FSLN-related NGO, Centro para la Promoción, la Investigación, y el Desarrollo Rural y Social (CIPRES). However, he soon left this post to become a presidential adviser. As a result, Hambre Cero declined in importance. Usura Cero aims to give small, low-interest loans to small-scale urban merchants. This program has been deemed successful, but some argue that it lacks transparency; see Ludwin Loásiga López and Luis Núñez Salmerón, "Usura Cero, 'Exitoso' Pero Nada Transparente," *La Prensa,* October 9, 2008, www.laprensa.com.ni/.

7. There were three important strikes in 2007. In the doctors' strike, the Sandinista health workers' union, FETSALUD (La Central de Trabajadores de la Salud, or Federation of Health Workers), did not back the strikers, who asked that government live up to its side of their contract. The teachers went out for a month looking for more money. They reached a shaky deal with the Ministry of Finance and the Social Security Institute. The third strike was waged by former banana workers whose health had been damaged by the pesticide Nemagon, used extensively in banana plantations. These workers sought free health care and damages for harm suffered.

8. See Envío, "With Water, Water Everywhere, Who's on the President's Ark?" *Envío* (November 2007), www.envio.org.ni/.

9. Carlos F. Chamorro, "FUNIDES advierte sobre tendencia económica 2008," *Confidencial* 562, November 25–December 1, 2007, www.confidencial.com.ni/.

10. Envío, "How Many Conflicts Will the New 'Direct Democracy' Trigger?" *Envío* (December 2007), www.envio.org.ni/.

11. Envío, "Murrillo Acquires Even More Power," *Envío* (July 2008), www.envio.org.ni/.

12. One of the megaprojects backed by the Ortega administration is the Dry Canal: a rail line following the Rio San Juan to link the Pacific and Atlantic coasts that would compete with the Panama Canal. Since a Hong Kong firm, Hutchinson Whampoa, won contracts to upgrade facilities in Panama, there was speculation that Beijing would not assist the Nicaraguan project. However, Taiwan would be keen to finance a competitor to the Panama Canal.

13. Tim Rogers, "Ortega Balances Venezuelan Aid, IMF," *Nica Times,* April 27–May 3, 2007, www.nicatimes.net.

14. See, however, Banco Central de Nicaragua, *Informe de Cooperación Oficial Externa, Primer Semestre, 2009* (Managua: Banco Central de Nicaragua, 2009), 15–16.

15. Special issues of *Nueva Sociedad* 226 (March–April 2010) and *NACLA: Report on the Americas* 43, no. 1 (March–April, 2010) focus on the Honduran coup and its aftermath.

16. *Chapiollo* also conveys the notion of being homespun, thus of being from among the people, a son or daughter of the soil.

17. Lourdes Arroliga, "Convergencia casi nula en gobierno FSLN," *Confidencial* 545, July 29–August 4, 2007, www.confidencial.com.ni/.

18. Rafael Lara, "7 mil 500, despedidos en solo año y medio," *El Nuevo Diario,* April 30, 2008, www.elnuevodiario.com.ni/.

19. Gretchen Helmke and Steven Levitsky, "Introduction," in *Informal Institutions and Democracy: Lessons from Latin America,* edited by Gretchen Helmke and Steven Levitsky, (Baltimore: Johns Hopkins University Press, 2006), 5.

20. When Arnoldo Alemán had corruption charges dismissed against him in January, a Sandinista justice absented herself and was replaced by a Liberal, which gave the panel hearing the former president's appeal a Liberal majority and ensured that charges against him would be dropped. For details, see Eduardo Cruz and Yader Luna, "Ortega y Alemán, 'dando y dando'," *La Prensa,* January 17, 2009, archivo .laprensa.com.ni/.

21. Envío, "Chaos All Around," *Envío* 344 (March 2010), www.envio.org.ni/.

22. Carlos Salinas Maldonado, "Crisis política desemboca en violencia," *Confidencial,* April 20, 2010, www.confidencial.com.ni/.

23. See, generally, David Close and Kalowatie Deonandan, eds., *Undoing Democracy: The Politics of Electoral Caudillismo* (Lanham, MD: Lexington Books, 2004).

24. Envío, "Where Are We After 29 Years, and After 290 Hours?" *Envío* 324 (July 2008), www.envio.org.ni/.

25. Rory Carroll, "Oxfam Targeted as Nicaragua Attacks 'Trojan Horse' NGOs," *Guardian,* October 14, 2008, www.guardian.co.uk/. The formal basis for the charge was that MAM was not properly incorporated and should not have received funds administered by Oxfam. In that case, it is interesting that the charge was money laundering, which in Nicaraguan usage is associated with drug dealing, and not some lesser offense.

26. Elizabeth Romero, "Fiscalía no acusará a Cinco," *La Prensa,* January 23, 2009, www.laprensa.com.ni/.

27. Karen Kampwirth, "Alemán's War on the NGO Community: Antifeminism and the New Populism in Nicaragua," *Latin American Politics and Society* 45, no. 2 (Fall 2003): 133–158.

28. Carlos Salinas Maldonado, "Orden FSLN reelección o caos," *Confidencial* 679, April 25–May 1, 2010, 1–2.

29. See James Morley, "Nicaraguan Councils Stir Fear of Dictatorship," *New York Times,* May 4, 2008, www.nytimes.com/; Envío, "The Path Taking Us There," *Envío* 325 (August 2008), www.envio.org.ni/; and Envío, "Criticism Isn't Synonymous with Hatred," *Envío* 326 (September 2008), www.envio.org.ni/.

30. Blake Schmidt, "International Groups Decry Persecution," *Nica Times,* October 31, 2008, www.nicatimes.nt/.

31. José Adán Silva, "Cayó como bomba en Unión Europea," *El Nuevo Diario,* October 31, 2008, www.elnuevodiario.com.ni/.

32. Nicaragua Network, "Two Foreign Interventions Draw Angry Responses from Government," *NicaNet,* August 19, 2008, www.nicanet.org/.

33. Silva, "Cayó como bomba en Unión Europea."

34. This theme is expanded in David Close, "Nicaragua's Pragmatic Ideologues," in *Latin American Foreign Policies Between Pragmatism and Ideology,* edited by Gian Luca Gardini and Peter Lambert (London: Palgrave, 2011), 197–212.

35. Venezuela is clearly not a great power; indeed, it cannot yet begin to challenge Brazil's status as the dominant Latin American power. That Venezuela can assume a role always held previously by a great power suggests to us that the War on Terror has created opportunities for ambitious minor international actors to expand their theaters of operation without worrying too much about vexing the regional hegemon.

36. Ricardo Castillo Argüello, "La economía política de los petrodólares," *Confidencial* 606, October 19–25, 2008, 1, 13–14.

37. Tim Rogers, "Ortega Defiant After US, Europe Yank Aid," *Christian Science Monitor,* December 5, 2008, www.csmonitor.com/.

38. ACAN-EFE (Agencia Centroamericana de Noticias-EFE), "Piden a Chávez donar plantas eléctricas," *La Prensa* (April 23, 2009), www.laprensa.com.ni/.

39. Leyla Jarquín and Malltide Córdoba, "Partido Único Alarma," *El Nuevo Diario,* April 23, 2009, www.elnuevodiario.com.ni/.

40. Were Managua to establish diplomatic relations with Beijing, the People's Republic of China could be an exception to that rule, because it has shown substantial forbearance in its dealings with Omar al-Bashir of Sudan and Robert Mugabe of Zimbabwe.

41. "Reporters Without Borders Writes to President Daniel Ortega About Poor State of Public Freedoms," October 21, 2008, www.rsf.org/.

42. Close and Deonandan, *Undoing Democracy.*

43. These data come from an Associated Press dispatch, "Oposición rechaza resultados de elección en Nicaragua," published in *El Universo* of Guayaquil, Ecuador, November 10, 2008, www.eluniverso.com/. The CSE page from which the data in this article were taken no longer exists.

44. The clearest statement of the opposition's position comes from the domestic election observer organization, Ethics and Transparency (Etica y Transparencia), "Looking at the Ruins of a Defiled Electoral Process," *Envío* 332 (March 2009), www.envio.org.ni/. The government's case is made in Government of Nicaragua, Ministerio de Relaciones Exteriores de la República de Nicaragua (Nicaragan Ministry of Foreign Relations), *Libro Blanco: La realidad del proceso electoral municipal del 2008 en Nicaragua* (Managua: Ministerio de Relaciones Exteriores de la República de Nicaragua, 2009), www.cancelleria.gob.ni/. This publication presents no electoral results.

Bibliography

ACAN-EFE (Agencia Centroamericana de Noticias-EFE.). "Piden a Chávez donar plantas eléctricas." *La Prensa,* April 23, 2009. www.laprensa.com.ni/.

"Accords of the Meeting of the Registered Parties." English translation in the appendix to Jose Luís Coraggio, *Nicaragua: Revolution and Democracy.* Boston: Allen and Unwin, 1985, 100–104.

Acevedo Vogl, Adolfo José. "HIPC Relief: Where Are You?" 2005. quest/quixote .org/.

Acosta, María Luisa. *Régimen legal de la autonomía de las regiones de la Costa Caribe nicaragüense.* Managua: Editarte, 2004.

Aguilera, Amparo. "Hambre Cero busca fondos." *El Nuevo Diario,* July 10, 2007.

Aguirre, Erik. "De lucha ideologica a poder contranatura." *El Nuevo Diario,* April 4, 2007. www.elnuevodiario.com.ni.

Alaniz, Luis. "Pobreza Nacional." *FUNIDES.* www.funides.org.

Alcántara, Manuel. *Sistemas políticos de América Latina.* Vol. 2. Madrid: Tecnos, 1999.

Alcántara, Manuel, Mercedes García Montero, and Francisco Sánchez López. *El poder legislativo en América Latina a través de sus normas.* Salamanca: Ediciones Universidad de Salamanca, 2005.

Alegría, Claribel, and Mark Flakoll. *Nicaragua: La revolución sandinista. Una crónica política, 1855–1979.* México: Ediciones Era, 1982.

Alemán, Miguel. "Mercado financiero en Nicaragua: 1960–1990." In *Crédito para el Desarrollo Rural en Nicaragua,* edited by Johan Bastiaensen, 49–53. Managua: NITLAPAN-UCA, 2002.

Alvarado, Daysi, Alejandro Bravo, and Carlos Fernando López. *Agenda municipal de los partidos políticos de Nicaragua.* Managua: AMUNIC, 2004.

Alvarez Montalván, Emilio. *Cultura política nicaragüense.* Managua: Hispamer, 2000.

Ameringer, Charles. *The Democratic Left in Exile: The Antidictatorial Struggle in the Caribbean, 1945–1959.* Miami: University of Miami Press, 1974.

AMUNIC (Asociación de Municípios de Nicaragua). "Municipios destacados en el primer evento de mediación del Sistema de Reconocimiento al Desempeño Municipal." *Acta* SIDREM, December 13, 2006.

————. *Transferencias Municipales*. Managua: AMUNIC, 2001.

Anaya, James, and Claudio Grossman. "The Case of *Awas Tingni v. Nicaragua:* A New Step in the International Law of Indigenous Peoples."*Arizona Journal of International and Comparative Law* 19 (2002): 1–15.

Anderson, Leslie E., and Lawrence Dodd. "Comportamiento electoral y democracia en Nicaragua." *América Latina Hoy* 30 (2002): 205–230.

————. *Learning Democracy: Citizen Engagement and Electoral Choice in Nicaragua, 1990–2001*. Chicago: University of Chicago Press, 2005.

Angus Reid Consultants. *Online Polls*. www.angus-reid.com.

Antonio, Margarita. "Who Do the Coast Lands Belong to and Who Will Get Them?" *Envío* 329 (December 2008). www.envio.org.ni/.

Arana, Mario J., and Juan F. Rocha. "Efecto de las políticas macroeconómicas y sociales sobre la pobreza en el caso de Nicaragua." Paper presented to the Seminarios Internacionales sobre Políticas Macroeconómicas y Pobreza, June 3–5 and October 30–November 2, 1997. www.iadb.org/.

Arauz, Rita. "Coming Out as a Lesbian Is What Brought Me to Social Consciousness." In *Sandino's Daughters Revisited: Feminism in Nicaragua,* edited by Margaret Randall, 265–285. New Brunswick, NJ: Rutgers University Press, 1994.

Arce, Bayardo. "Gobernadores en unidad nacional." *El Nuevo Diario,* June 25, 2006. www.elnuevodiario.com.ni.

Arríen, Juan Bautista, and Miguel De Castilla Urbina. *Educación y pobreza en Nicaragua*. Managua: Universidad Centroamericana, 2001.

Arríen, Juan Bautista, Miguel De Castilla Urbina, and Rafael Lucio Gil. *La educación en Nicaragua entre siglos, dudas, y esperanzas*. Managua: Universidad Centroamericana, 1998.

Arríen, Juan Bautista, Xabier Gorrostiaga, Carlos Tunnermann Bernheim, Rafael Lucio Gil, and Miguel de Castilla Urbina. *Nicaragua: La educación en los noventa*. Managua: Universidad Centroamericana, 1997.

Arróliga, Lourdes. "Bancada en la Corte." *Confidencial,* June 15–21, 2003

————. "Convergencia casi nula en gobierno FSLN." *Confidencial* 545, July 29–August 4, 2007. www.confidencial.com.ni/.

————. "CSJ: Luz verde al pluripartidismo." *Confidencial* 317, November 24–30. www.confidencial.com.ni/.

————. "FSLN, ALN, PLC alineados con Iglesia." *Confidencial* 507, October 2006, 15–21. www.confidencial.com.ni/.

————. "La ruta de la fraude en Managua." *Confidencial* 610, November 16–22, 2008. www.confidencial.com.ni/.

————. "Partidización en elección CSJ." *Confidencial* 529, April 1–7, 2007. www .confidencial.com.ni/.

————. "Sigue Pacto PLC-FSLN en la justicia." *Confidencial* 430, March 20–April 2, 2005. www.confidencial.com.ni/.

Asamblea Nacional de Nicaragua. *Constitución Política de Nicaragua*. Managua: Editorial Jurídica Asamblea Nacional de Nicaragua, 2003.

————. *Estatuto de Autonomía de las Dos Regiones de la Costa Atlántica de Nicaragua*. Managua: *La Gaceta Diario Oficial,* no. 238, 30 de Octubre 1987.

————. *Ley de Régimen de Propiedad Comunal de los Pueblos Indígenas y Comunidades Étnicas de las Regiones Autónomas de la Costa Atlántica de Nicaragua y de los Ríos Bocay, Coco, Indio y Maíz.* Managua: *La Gaceta Diario Oficial,* no. 16, January 23, 2003.

———. *Reglamento a la Ley 28,* Decreto 3584. Managua: *La Gaceta Diario Oficial,* 2003.

ASOMIF (Asociación Nicaragüense de Instituciones de Microfinanzas). *Memoria Institucional 2006.* Managua: LITONIC, 2007.

Assies, Willem, Gemma van der Har, and Andre Hoekema, eds. *The Challenge of Diversity: Indigenous Peoples and Reform of the State in Latin America.* Amsterdam: Thela Thesis, 2000.

Avendaño, Néstor. *La economía de Nicaragua: Evaluación 2005, pronóstico 2006, y prognosis 2007–2011.* Managua: COPADE, 2006.

———. *La economía y la pobreza de Nicaragua, 2002–2006.* Managua: 3H Comercial, S.A., 2007.

———. "Nicaragua: Debt Relief/HIPC vs. Poverty." quest.quixote.org/.

———. "Notas sobre la tercera visita del FMI a Nicaragua durante el período 26 de junio al 6 de julio de 2007." *Nicaragua: Informe Económico* (June 5–July 6, 2007): 116–128.

Avendaño, Néstor, and Camilo Pacheco. "El perfil de la pobreza humana de Nicaragua en 2005." In *Nicaragua: Informe Económico* (July 2007): 129–146.

Babb, Florence. *After Revolution: Mapping Gender and Cultural Politics in Neoliberal Nicaragua.* Austin: University of Texas Press, 2001.

———. "Out in Nicaragua: Local and Transnational Desires After the Revolution." *Cultural Anthropology* 18, no. 3 (2003): 304–328.

Banco Central de Nicaragua. *Producción bruto a precios constantes, 1960–1999.* www.bcn.gob.ni/.

———. *Anuario de Estadisticas Economicas, 2001–2007.* www.bcn.gob.ni/.

———. *Estadísticas macroeconómicas.* www.bcn.gob.ni/.

———. *Informe Anual, 2001.* Managua: Banco Central de Nicaragua, 2001.

———. *Informe de Cooperación Oficial Nicaragua 2007.* Managua: Banco Central de Nicaragua, 2008. www.bcn.gob.ni/.

———. *Informe de Cooperación Oficial Externa, primer semestre, 2009.* Managua: Banco Central de Nicaragua, 2009.

———. *Informe de Cooperación Oficial Externa 2010.* Managua: Banco Central de Nicaragua, 2011. www.bcn.gob.ni/.

———. *Statistical Yearbook, 2009.* Managua: Banco Central de Nicaragua, 2010. www.bcn.gob.ni/.

Baracco, Luciano. *Nicaragua: The Imagining of a Nation from Nineteenth-Century Liberals to Twentieth-Century Sandinistas.* New York: Algora Publishers, 2005.

Barbarena, Edgardo. "Dos para vos . . . dos para mí." *El Nuevo Diario,* March 21, 2000. archivo.elnuevodiario.com.ni/.

Barnes, William A. "Rereading the Nicaraguan Pre-election Polls in the Light of the Election Results." In *The 1990 Elections in Nicaragua and Their Aftermath,* edited by Vanessa Castro and Gary Prevost, 41–99. Lanham, MD: Rowman and Littlefield, 1992.

Barómetro legislativo. "¿Qué alternativa solucionará el problema del crédito para los pequeños y medianos productores?" No. 3 (June 2007): 3–4.

Barraclough, Solon. *Notas sobre la tenenncia de la tierra.* Santiago: Icira, 1970.

Barraclough, Solon, and Arthur Domike. "La estructura agraria en siete países de América Latina." In *La lucha de clases en el campo,* edited by Ernest Feder. México, DF: Fondo de Cultura Economica, 1975.

Bastiaensen, Johan de. *Crédito para el desarrollo rural en Nicaragua.* Managua: NITLAPAN-UCA, 2002.

Baumeister, Eduardo. *Estructura y reforma agraria in Nicaragua, 1979–1989.* Managua: Ediciones CDR-ULA, 1998.

———. *Nicaragua: Public Strategies and Rural Poverty in the Nineties.* San José, Costa Rica: RUTA, 2004.

———, ed. *Agro hondureño y su futuro.* Tegucigalpa: Editorial Guaymuras, 1996.

Baumeister, Eduardo, and Edgard Fernández. *Análisis de la tenencia de la tierra en Nicaragua partir del censo agropecuario 2001.* Managua: Ministerio de Agricultura, Ganadería, y Forestal (MAGFOR), Instituto Nicaragüense de Estadísticos y Censos (INEC), and United Nations Food and Agriculture Organization (FAO), 2005.

Baumeister, Eduardo, and Oscar Niera. "La conformación de una economía mixta: Estructura de clases y política estatal en la transformación nicaragüense." In *La transición difícil: La autodeterminación de los pequeños países periféricos,* edited by Jose Luis Coraggio and Carmen Diana Deere, 286–306. Mexico City: Siglo 21, 1986.

Bayard de Volo, Lorraine. "Global and Local Framing of Maternal Identity: Obligation and the Mothers of Matagalpa, Nicaragua." In *Globalizations and Social Movements: Culture, Power, and the Transnational Public Sphere,* edited by John A. Guidry, Michael D. Kennedy, and Mayer N. Zald, 127–145. Ann Arbor: University of Michigan Press, 2000.

———. *Mothers of Heroes and Martyrs: Gender Identity Politics in Nicaragua, 1979–1999.* Baltimore: Johns Hopkins University Press, 2001.

Belli, Giaconda. "De la era de Acuario a la Inquisición: Candidatos sandinistas e Iglesia católica: El FSLN contra el derecho al aborto." www.socialismo-o-barbarie.org/.

Bendaña, Alejandro. "The Rise and Fall of the FSLN." *NACLA Report on the Americas* 37, no. 6 (May–June 2004): 21–26.

Blandón, María Teresa. "The Coalición Nacional de Mujeres: An Alliance of Left-Wing Women, Right-Wing Women and Radical Feminists in Nicaragua." In *Radical Women in Latin America: Left and Right,* edited by Victoria González and Karen Kampwirth, 111–132. University Park: Penn State University Press, 2001.

———, ed. *Movimiento de mujeres en Centroamérica.* Managua: Programa Regional La Corriente, 1997.

Bodán, Oliver. "Arrancan cabildeos en CSJ." *Confidencial* 205, August 20–26, 2000. www.confidencial.com.ni/.

———. "Complejo reacomodo en la CSJ." *Confidencial* 185, March 26–April 1, 2000. www.confidencial.com.ni/.

———. "Hay indicios de dictadura." *Confidencial 168,* November 14–20, 1999. www.confidencial.com.ni/.

———. "Sala Constitucional pone 'manos arriba' al Contralor." *Confidencial* 120, November 22–28, 1998. www.confidencial.com.ni.

———. "Temor por retroceso en CSJ." *Confidencial* 151, June 18–24, 1999. www.confidencial.com.ni/.

Bodan, Oliver, and Lourdes Arróliga. "Circo político en las cortes." *Confidencial* 448, July 31–August 6, 2005. www.confidencial.com.ni/.

Bolt González, Mary. *Sencillamente diferentes: La autoestima de las mujeres lesbianas en los sectores urbanos de Nicaragua.* Managua: Centro Editorial de la Mujer (CEM), 1996.

Booth, David, Arturo Grigsby, and Carlos Toranzo. *Politics and Poverty Reduction Strategies: Lessons from Latin American HIPCs.* London: Overseas Development Institute, Working Paper 262, 1996.

Booth, John. *The End and the Beginning: The Nicaraguan Revolution.* Boulder, CO: Westview, 1985.

———. "The Somoza Regime in Nicaragua." In *Sultanistic Regimes,* edited by H. E. Chelabi and Juan Linz, 132–152. Baltimore: Johns Hopkins University Press, 1998.

Borge, Tomás. *La paciente impaciencia.* Managua: Vanguardia, 1989.

Bou, Marc. 2004. *El sistema de justicia en América Latina: Entre las reformas y la inercia institucional.* Institut Internacional de Governabilitat de Catalunya. www.iigov.org/.

Bravo, Alejandro. *Merecido Tributo.* Managua: ANE-CNE, 1995, 28–29.

Brenes, Ada Julia, ed. *Movimiento de mujeres en Centroamérica.* Managua: Programa Regional La Corriente, 2007.

Brenes, Ada Julia, Ivania Lovo, Olga Luz Restrepo, Sylvia Saakes, and Flor de María Zúniga, eds. *La mujer nicaragüense en los años 80.* Managua: Ediciones Nicarao, 1991.

Brenes, María Haydee. "Plantón de mujeres ante Corte Suprema." *El Nuevo Diario,* May 18, 2007.

Breslauer, George, Harry Kreisler, and Benjamin Ward. *Beyond the Cold War: Conflict and Cooperation in the Third World.* Berkeley: University of California Press, 1991.

Buitrago, Edgardo. "La intervención norteamericana y la política nicaragüense durante el período conservador (1910–1929)." In *Historia de Violencia en Nicaragua,* edited by Elisa Arévalo C. et al. Managua: UPOLI, 1997.

Burbank, Stephen B., and Barry Friedman, eds. *Judicial Independence at the Crossroads: An Interdisciplinary Approach.* Thousand Oaks, CA: Sage, 2002.

Butigan, Ken. "Pledge of Resistance." Pace e Bene. September 19, 2006. paceebene .org/.

Cabezas, Omar. *Fire from the Mountain: The Making of a Sandinista.* Translated by Kathleen Weaver. New York: Crown, 1985.

———. *La montaña es algo más que una inmensa estepa verde.* Managua: Nueva Nicaragua, 1982.

Campbell, Maia S. "The Rights of Indigenous Peoples to Political Participation and the Case of *YATAMA v. Nicaragua.*" *Arizona Journal of International and Comparative Law* 24, no. 2 (2007): 499–540.

Cannon, Lou. "Reagan Says US Owes 'Contras' Help; Conservative Gathering Hears Emotionally Charged Speech." *Washington Post,* March 2, 1985, A1.

Cardenal, Ernesto. "El FSLN está secuestrado." *Envío* 154 (November 1994). www .envio.org.ni/.

———. *La revolución perdida.* Managua: ANAMA, 2003.

———. "Sandinistas, no voten por el falso Sandinismo." *El Nuevo Diario,* October 26, 2006. www.elnuevodiario.com.ni.

Carroll, Rory. "Oxfam Targeted as Nicaragua Attacks 'Trojan Horse' NGOs." *Guardian*, October 14, 2008. www.guardian.co.uk/.
Carter Center. *Observing Nicaragua's Elections, 1989–90.* Atlanta: Carter Center, 1990.
———. *Observing the 1996 Nicaragua Elections.* Atlanta: Carter Center, 1997.
———. *Observing the 2001 Nicaragua Elections.* Atlanta: Carter Center, March 2002.
———. *Observing the 2006 Nicaragua Elections.* Atlanta: Carter Center, May 2007.
Cáseres, Sinforiano. "Rural Development Can't Be Resolved in Secret." *Envío* 310 (May 2007): 10–17.
Castillo Argüello, Ricardo. "La economía política de los petrodólares." *Confidencial* 606, October 19–25, 2008.
Catholic Family and Human Rights Institute. "Nicaraguan Delegate Fired for Pro-Family Views Briefs Policymakers." *Fax Archive* 4, no. 11 (2001): 1.
Centro Nicaragüense de Derechos Humanos (CENIDH). *Derechos Humanos en Nicaragua, 2003.* Managua: CENIDH, 2003.
———. *Derechos Humanos en Nicaragua, 2004.* Managua: CENIDH, 2004.
CEPAL (Comisión Económica para America Látina y el Caribe de las Naciones Unidas). *Análisis del impacto social y económico de la desnutrición infantil en América Latina: Resultados del estudio en Centroamérica y República Dominicana: Panorama General.* Santiago, Chile: CEPAL and Programa Mundial de Alimentos, 2007.
Chamorro, Carlos Fernando. "Elección política en la Suprema." *Confidencial* 156, August 22–28, 1999. www.confidencial.com.ni/.
———. "FUNIDES advierte sobre tendencia económica 2008." *Confidencial* 562, November 25–December 1, 2007. www.confidencial.com.ni/.
———. "La elección del 20 de octubre y el nuevo escenario político." *Pensamiento Propio* 2 (July–December 1996): 39–50.
———. "Without Solidarity It Is Difficult to Talk About Revolution." In *Nicaragua: The Sandinista People's Revolution, Speeches by Sandinista Leaders,* edited by Bruce Marcus, 14–17. New York: Pathfinder Press, 1985.
Chamorro, Emiliano. "Iglesia católica sufre bajas mientras evangélicos crecen." *La Prensa,* June 20, 2007.
Chamorro, Xiomara. "Así nació la crisis." *La Prensa,* November 28, 2003. www.laprensa.com.ni/.
Chelabi, H. E., and Juan José Linz. *Sultanistic Regimes.* Baltimore: John Hopkins University Press, 1997.
Chinchilla, Norma. "Nationalism, Feminism, and Revolution in Central America." In *Feminist Nationalism,* edited by Lois West, 201–219. New York: Routledge, 1997.
Christian, Shirley. *Nicaragua: Revolución en la família.* Barcelona: Planeta, 1986.
CID-Gallup. "República de Nicaragua: Nicaragüenses conservadores frente al aborto terapéutico, Población mucho mas anuentes en casos especiales." February 2007. www.euram.com.ni/.
CIDCA (Centro de Investigación y Documentación sobre la Costa Atlántica). *Demografía Costeña: Notas sobre la historia demográfica y población actual de los grupos étnicos de la Costa Atlántica Nicaragüense.* Managua: CIDCA, 1982.

————. Development Study Unit. *Ethnic Group and the Nation State: The Case of the Atlantic Coast of Nicaragua.* Stockholm: University of Stockholm, Department of Social Anthropology, 1987.

CIERA (Centro de Investigaciones y Estudios de la Reforma Agraria). *Censo Agropecuario, 2001.* Managua: CIERA, 2001.

CIPRES (Centro para la Promoción, la Investigación, y el Desarrollo Rural y Social). *Los pequeños y medianos productores en Nicaragua.* Managua: CIPRES, 2006.

————. "Programa Productivo Alimentario." *Cuadernos de CIPRES* no. 28. 3rd ed. Managua: Ediciones Graphic Print, S.A., 2007.

————. *Soberanía alimentaria y desarrollo agroindustrial: Pequeños y medianos productores agropecuarios.* Managua: CIPRES, 2006.

Close, David. *Nicaragua: Politics, Economics, and Society.* London: Pinter, 1988.

————. *Nicaragua: The Chamorro Years.* Boulder, CO: Lynne Rienner, 1999.

————. "Political Parties and Democracy in Nicaragua: Not Yet, Maybe Someday." Edinburgh, Scotland: ECPR, Workshop Papers, 2003.

————. "President Bolaños Runs a Reverse." In *Undoing Democracy: The Politics of Electoral Caudillismo,* edited by David Close and Kalowatie Deonandan, 167–182. Lanham, MD: Lexington Books, 2004.

————. "Undoing Democracy in Nicaragua." In *Undoing Democracy: The Politics of Electoral Caudillismo,* edited by David Close and Kalowatie Deonandan, 1–16. Lanham, MD; Lexington Books, 2004.

————. "Nicaragua's Pragmatic Ideologues." In *Latin American Foreign Policies Between Pragmatism and Ideology,* edited by Gian Luca Gardini and Peter Lambert, 197–212. London: Palgrave, 2011.

Close, David, and Kalowatie Deonandan, eds. *Undoing Democracy: The Politics of Electoral Caudillismo.* Lanham, MD: Lexington Books, 2004.

Close, David, and Gary Prevost. "Introduction: Transitioning from Revolutionary Movements to Political Parties and Making the Revolution 'Stick.'" In *From Revolutionary Movements to Political Parties,* edited by Kalowatie Deonandan, David Close, and Gary Prevost, 1–16. New York: Palgrave Macmillan, 2007.

Collinson, Helen, ed. *Women and Revolution in Nicaragua.* London: Zed Books, 1990.

Cominetti, Rossella, and Gonzalo Ruíz. "Evolución del Gasto Público Social en América Latina: 1980–1995." LCSHD Paper Series. Washington, DC: Department of Human Development, World Bank, May 1997. www.wds.world bank.org/.

CONADETI (Comisión Nacional de Demarcación y Titulación). *Informe técnico y financiero para el traspaso ordenado y transparente del proceso de demarcación de los pueblos indígenas y las comunidades étnicas de la Costa Atlántica de Nicaragua y de los Ríos Bocay, Coco, Indio y Maíz, Junio 2006–Junio 2008.* Bluefields, Nicaragua: CONADETI, 2008.

Conferencia Episcopal de Nicaragua. *Exhortación en ocasión de las elecciones generales de 2001.* Managua, August 15, 2001.

Consejo Nacional de Planificación Económica Social (CONPES). *Consulta Municipal sobre la ERCERP: Sistematización de las memorias de trabajo en los once municipios.* Managua: CONPES/PAI, 2003.

————. *Informe 2003*. Managua: República de Nicaragua, 2004.

Coraggio, José Luis. *Nicaragua: Revolution and Democracy*. Boston: Allen and Unwin, 1985.

Coronel Kautz, Ricardo. "Política y ética en Nicaragua." *El Nuevo Diario*, September 23, 2005. elnuevodiario.com.ni.

Crick, Bernard. *In Defence of Politics*. London: Weidenfield and Nicholson, 1963.

Criquillón, Ana. "The Nicaraguan Women's Movement: Feminist Reflections from Within." In *The New Politics of Survival: Grassroots Movements in Central America*, edited by Minor Sinclair, 209–237. New York: Monthly Review Press, 1995.

Crowley, Eduardo. *Dictators Never Die*. London: G. Hurst, 1979.

Cruz, Arturo, Jr. *Nicaragua's Conservative Republic, 1858–1893*. London and Oxford: Palgrave, in association with St. Antony's, 2002.

Cruz, Consuelo. *Political Culture and Institutional Development in Costa Rica and Nicaragua: World-Making in the Tropics*. Cambridge: Cambridge University Press, 2005.

Cruz, Eduardo, and Yader Luna. "Ortega y Alemán, 'dando y dando.'" *La Prensa*, January 17, 2009. archivo.laprensa.com.ni/.

Cuadra, Elvia, Angel Saldomando, and Sofía Montenegro. "La sentencia contra las mujeres: La agonía de la democracia." Supplement to *Confidencial* 508, October 22–28, 2006, 1–4.

Cuadra, Scarlet. "Electorado femenino por la revolución." *Barricada*, January 13, 1990, 3.

Cumbre de ALBA. "Acuerdo Energético entre Venezuela y Nicaragua." April 29, 2007. www.alternativaboliviariana.org/.

Dahl, Robert A., ed. *Political Oppositions in Western Democracies*. New Haven, CT: Yale University Press, 1966.

Dalton, Roque. *Las historias prohibidas del Pulgarcito*. La Habana: Casa de las Américas, 1974.

Damián, Araceli, and Julio Boltvinik. "A Table to Eat On: The Meaning and Measurement of Poverty in Latin America." In *Latin America After Neoliberalism*, edited by Eric Hershberg and Fred Rosen, 144–170. New York: New Press, 2006.

Debray, Régis. *Revolución en la revolución*. Havana: Casa de las Américas, 1967.

De Castilla Urbina, Miguel. "La educación como poder, crisis sin solución en la transición revolucionaria: El caso de Nicaragua, 1978–1981." In *Estado y clases sociales en Nicaragua*, edited by Asociación Nicaragüense de Científicos Sociales (ANICS), 195–252. Managua: CIERA, 1982.

"Declaration of the Delegation That at the Petition of a Group of Churches of Holland Attended the Elections Celebrated in Nicaragua November 4, 1984." Managua, 1984.

Dennis, Phillip. "Higher Education on the Miskitu Coast." *Texas Techsan Magazine* (March–April 2000): 20–21.

Deonandan, Kalowatie, David Close, and Gary Prevost, eds. *From Revolutionary Movements to Political Parties*. New York: Palgrave Macmillan, 2007.

DEPPA (División de Estudios, Publicaciones, Propuestas y Análisis) and FUNIDES (Fundación Nicaragüense para el Desarrollo Económico y Social). *Herramientas para fortalecer programas de protección social: Nicaragua, incluye herramientas para diseñar, implementar, monitorear y evaluar Hambre Cero*. Managua: FUNIDES, 2007. www.funides.org/.

Díaz Lacayo, Aldo. *El Frente Sandinista después de la derrota electoral.* Caracas: Centauro, 1994.

———. "These Elections Are Devoid of Ideology." *Envío* 241 (August 2001). www.envio.org.ni/.

Díaz Polanco, Héctor. *Indigenous Peoples in Latin America: The Quest for Self-Determination.* Boulder, CO: Westview, 1997.

Diedrich, Bernard. *Somoza.* New York: E. P. Dutton, 1981.

Dijkstra, Geske. "The PRSP Approach and the Illusion of Improved Aid Effectiveness: Lessons from Bolivia, Honduras, and Nicaragua." *Development Policy Review* 23 (2005): 443–464.

Dirección General de Estadístícas y Censos. *Primer Censo Nacional Agropecaurio.* Managua: DGEC, 1963.

Diskin, Martin. "Ethnic Discourse and the Challenge to Anthropology: The Nicaraguan Case." In *Nation States and Indians in Latin America,* edited by Urban Grez and Joel Sherzer, 156–180. Austin: University of Texas Press, 1991.

Duverger, Maurice. *Political Parties.* Translated by Barbara and Robert North. 3rd ed. London: Methuen, 1964.

Dye, David. *Democracy Adrift: Caudillo Politics in Nicaragua.* Managua: PRODENI, 2004.

———. *La democracia a la deriva: La política caudillista de Nicaragua.* Cambridge, MA: Hemisphere Initiatives, 2004.

Dye, David, Jack Spence, and George Vickers. *Patchwork Democracy: Nicaraguan Politics Ten Years After the Fall.* Cambridge, MA: Hemisphere Initatives, 2000.

———. *Retazos de democracia: La política nicaragüense diez años después de la derrota.* Cambridge, MA: Hemisphere Initiatives, 2000.

Economic and Social Council of the United Nations. *World Urbanization Prospects: The 2005 Revision.* New York: United Nations, 2005. www.un.org.

———. "Partido somocista se adhiere al FSLN." *El Nuevo Diario,* August 26, 2006.

El Nuevo Diario. "Desnutrición campea en Nicaragua." June 17, 2002. www .elnueveodiario.com.ni.

"Dos para vos . . . dos para mí." March 21, 2000. archivo.elnuevodiario.com.ni/.

———. "Fallo infame." October 7, 2004. archivo.elnuevodiario.com.ni/.

———. "Jerez sabía y se lucraba." December 9, 2003. archivo.elnuevodiario.com .ni/.

———. "Lavan a corruptos." July 21, 2004. archivo.elnuevodiario.com.ni/.

———. "Sentencia TAM cortó rabo y oreja." December 13, 2007. www.elnuevodiario .com.ni/.

El Universo (Guayaquil, Ecuador). "Oposición rechaza resultados de elección en Nicaragua." November 10, 2008. www.eluniverso.com/.

Enríquez, Laura J., and Rose Spalding. "Banking Systems and Revolutionary Change: The Politics of Agricultural Credit in Nicaragua." In *The Political Economy of Revolutionary Nicaragua,* edited by Rose Spalding, 105–125. Boston: Allen and Unwin, 1987.

Envío. "Asamblea Nacional: Primeros Pasos de un Nuevo Modelo Constitucional." *Envío* 47 (May 1985). www.envio.org.ni/.

———. "Chaos All Around." *Envío* 344 (March 2010). www.envio.org.ni/.

———. "¿Cómo votó Nicaragua?" *Envío* 102 (April 1990). www.envio.org.ni/.

———. "Criticism Isn't Synonymous with Hatred." *Envío* 326 (September 2008). www.envio.org.ni/.

———. "Daniel Ortega Presidente: Del poder 'desde abajo' al gobierno." *Envío* 296–297 (November–December 2006): 3–5. www.envio.org.ni/.

———. "Dilemas en la lucha contra el cáncer." *Envío* 240 (March 2002). www .envio.org.ni/.

———. "Election Data." *Envío* 104 (March 1990). www.envio.org.ni/.

———. "En la Asamblea Nacional: ¿Pacto con el PLC o alianza con ALN?" *Envío* 296–297 (November–December 2006): 45–57. www.envio.org.ni/.

———. "FSLN Discussion Papers." *Envío* 109 (August 1990). www.envio.org.ni/.

———. "How Many Conflicts Will the New 'Direct Democracy' Trigger?" *Envío* (December 2007). www.envio.org.ni/.

———. "How Nicaraguans Voted." *Envío* 185 (December 1996). www.envio.org.ni/.

———. "Los 33 días que conmovieron a Nicaragua: El nuevo escenario nacional." *Envío* 176 (November 1996). www.envio.org.ni/.

———. "Murrillo Acquires Even More Power." *Envío* (July 2008). www.envio.org.ni/.

———. "The Names of the Rose." *Envío* (March 2003): 3. www.envio.org.ni/.

———. "The 'New Era' Begins Amid Check Scams and Blank Checks." *Envío* 246 (January–February 2002). www.envio.org.ni/.

———. "Nicaragua Briefs: Ortega and Murillo Tie Knot . . . Again?" *Envío* 290 (September 2005). www.envio.org.ni/.

———. "Nicaragua comienza la cuenta regresiva." *Envío* 173 (August 1996). www .envio.org.ni/.

———. "Nicaragua's Municipal Elections: The Good, the Bad, the Uncertain." *Envío* 232 (November 2000). www.envio.org.ni/.

———. "Nicaragua's 1984 Elections—A History Worth the Retelling." *Envío* 102 (January 1990). www.envio.org.ni/.

———. "Nicaragua: 100 Days in Babel." *Envío* 309 (April 2007). www.envio.org.ni/.

———. "The Path Taking Us There." *Envío* 325 (August 2008). www.envio.org.ni/.

———. "Political Agreement (Unofficial Translation)." *Envío* 98 (September 1989). www.envio.org.ni/.

———. "Riding the Wind with the Sails Full." *Envío* 340 (November 2009). www.envio.org.ni/.

———. "The Twelve Days That Shook Nicaragua." *Envío* 269 (December 2003). www.envio.org.ni/.

———. "2004 Municipal Elections: FSLN-Convergence Victory in Numbers." *Envío* 280 (November 2004). www.envio.org.ni/.

———. "Update." *Envío* 21 (March 1983). www.envio.org.ni/.

———. "Where Are We After 29 Years, and After 290 Hours?" *Envío* 324 (July 2008). www.envio.org.ni/.

———. "With Water, Water Everywhere, Who's on the President's Ark?" *Envío* (November 2007). www.envio.org.ni/.

Erickson-Nepstad, Sharon. *Convictions of the Soul*. New York: Oxford University Press, 2004.

Escorcia, Jorge Flavio. *Municipalidad y Autonomía en Nicaragua*. León: Editorial Universitaria UNAN-León, 1999.

Esgueva, Antonio. *Las Constituciones Políticas y sus Reformas en la Historia de Nicaragua*. Vols 1–2. Managua: Editorial el Parlamento, 1994.

Etica y Transparencia. "Looking at the Ruins of a Defiled Electoral Process." *Envío* 332. www.envio.org.ni/.

Fagen, Richard R., Carmen Diana Deere, and José Luis Coraggio, eds. *Transition and Development: Problems of Third World Socialism*. New York: Monthly Review Press, 1986.

FAO-OIT (United Nations Food and Agriculture Organization and the International Labour Organization, *Tenencia de la tierra y desarrollo rural en Centroamérica*. San Jose, CR: EDUCA, 1976.

Feder, Ernest, ed. *La lucha de clases en el campo*. Mexico City: Fondo de Cultura Económica, 1975.

Fitzsimmons, Tracy. "A Monstrous Regiment of Women? State, Regime, and Women's Political Organizing in Latin America." *Latin American Research Review* 35 (2000): 216–229.

Flynn, Patricia. "Women Challenge the Myth." In *Revolution in Central America*, edited by John Althoff, 414–422. Boulder, CO: Westview, 1983.

Fruhling, Pierre, Miguel González, and Hans Petter Buvollen. *Ethnicidad y nación: El desarrollo de la autonomía de la Costa Atlántica de Nicaragua (1987–2007)*. Guatemala City: F y G Editores, 2007.

FSLN (Frente Sandinista de Liberación Nacional). *El papel de las Organizaciones de Masas en el proceso revolucionario*. Managua: SNPEP-FSLN, 1980.

———. "El programa de gobierno del FSLN." *Visión Sandinista* 54, August 1–7, 2001.

———. *Estatutos 2002 FSLN*. www.fsln-Nicaragua.com.

———. *Habla la Vanguardia. Discursos de la Dirección Nacional del Frente Sandinista*. Managua: DPEP-FSLN, 1982.

———. *Programa del Frente Sandinista de Liberación Nacional*. Managua: DPEP-FSLN, 1981 [1969].

———. *The 72-Hour Document: The Sandinista Blueprint for Constructing Communism in Nicaragua*. Washington, DC: US Department of State, 1979.

———. "Un programa para el siglo XX!" *Visión Sandinista* (February 2002).

FSLN-YATAMA. *Acuerdos YATAMA-FSLN. Plan de Gobierno de la Unidad Nicaragua Triunfa para la Costa Caribe*. Bilwi-Bluefields: FSLN and YATAMA, 2006.

Galeano, Eduardo. "El estadio y el palco." *El Nuevo Diario,* November 2, 2000. www.elnuevodiario.com.ni.

García Palacios, Omar. *La contraloría general de la república y el control externo en el estado democrático nicaragüense*. Managua: Editorial Universidad Centroamericana, 2006.

Gilbert, Dennis. *Sandinistas: The Party and the Revolution*. Oxford: Basil Blackwell, 1989.

———. "The Society and Its Environment." In *Nicaragua: A Country Study,* 3rd ed, edited by Tim Merrill. Washington, DC: Library of Congress, 1994. lcweb2 .loc.gov/frd/cs/nitoc.html.

Ginsburg, Tom. *Judicial Review in New Democracies: Constitutional Courts in Asian Cases*. Cambridge, UK: Cambridge University Press, 2003.

Gobat, Michel. *Confronting the American Dream: Nicaragua Under US Imperial Rule*. Durham, NC: Duke University Press, 2005.

Gómez Nadal, Paco. "Crisis en Nicaragua tras el arresto del principal rival político del presidente." Madrid, *El Pais,* November 24, 1999. www.elpais.com/.

González, Miguel. "Territorial Autonomy in Mesoamerica: With or Without State Consent. The Case of the Zapatista Autonomous Territories in Chiapas, Mexico, and of the Autonomous Regions in Nicaragua." Paper prepared for delivery at the workshop on Social Movements and Globalization: Resistance or Engagement, University Consortium on the Global South, York University, Toronto, April 20, 2004.

González, Miguel, Dolores Figueroa, and Arelly Barbeyto. "Genero, etnia, y partidos en las elecciones regionales de la Costa Caribe: Retos de la diversidad." *Wani: Revista del Caribe Nicaragüense,* no. 44 (2006): 16.

González, Miguel, Edward Jackson, and Yuri Zapata. "Análisis de la Economía y los Sistemas Políticos de la Costa Caribe." *Wani: Revista del Caribe Nicaragüense,* no. 31 (2001): 6–29.

González, Miguel, and Yuri Zapata. "Miskitu Politics: Fragmentation or Accommodation?" Paper prepared for delivery at the annual meeting of the American Anthropological Association, New Orleans, November 20–24, 2002.

González, Secundino. "La democracia en Nicaragua: Un balance pesimista." In *Centroamérica después de la crisis,* edited by Joan Botella and Joseph María Sanahuja. Barcelona: Institut de Ciencies Politiques i Socials, 1998.

Gonzalez Perez, Miguel. *Gobiernos Pluriétnicos: La conformación de regiones autónomas en la Costa Atlántica—Caribe de Nicaragua.* México: URACCAN y Plaza y Valdés, 1997.

González-Rivera, Victoria. "Somocista Women, Right-Wing Politics, and Feminism in Nicaragua, 1936–1979." In *Radical Women in Latin America: Left and Right,* edited by Victoria González-Rivera and Karen Kampwirth , 41–78. University Park: Penn State University Press, 2001.

González Siles, Silvia. "Daniel Ortega ahora se compara con Cristo." *La Prensa,* October 31, 2006. archivo.laprensa.com.ni/.

Gordon, Edmund T. *Disparate Diasporas: Identity and Politics in an African Nicaraguan Community.* Austin: University of Texas Press, 1998.

Gordon, Edmund T., Galio Gurdian, and Charles Hale. "Rights, Resources, and the Social Memory of Struggle: Reflections on a Study of Indigenous and Black Community Land Rights on Nicaragua's Atlantic Coast." *Human Organization* 62 (2003): 369–381.

Gould, Jeffrey. *To Die in This Way: Nicaraguan Indians and the Myth of Mestizaje, 1880–1995.* Durham, NC: Duke University Press, 1998.

Government of National Unity and Reconciliation. *Programa Económico Financiero.* 2007. www.bcn.gob.ni/.

Government of Nicaragua. *Incontrolables desafíos, una sola voluntad.* www.presidencia.gob.ni.

———. *Ley Electoral 2000.* www.bcn.gob.ni/.

———. "Nicaragua: Medium Term Development Strategy, 1992–1996." Document presented to the Grupo Consultivo, Washington, DC, March 26, 1992.

———. *A Strengthened Poverty Reduction Strategy: 2000.* povlibrary.worldbank.org/.

———. *A Strengthened Growth and Poverty Reduction Strategy: Third Progress Report.* Managua: Presidencia de la República, Secretaría Técnica, 2005.

Government of Nicaragua, Council of State. *Ley Electoral.* Managua: Gazeta Diario Oficial, 1984.

———. "Los sistemas electorales." Paper presented at the Seminar on Electoral Material and Political Systems, Managua, 1983.

Government of Nicaragua, JGRN (Governing Junta of National Reconstruction). "Decree 1472." July 1984.

———. "Decree 1496." August 1984.

Government of Nicaragua, Ministry of Agriculture and Forestry (MAGFOR). *MAGFOR Plan 2008.* Managua: MAGFOR, 2008.

———. "Mas de 2000 familias campesinas con bono." *Boletín Informativo MAGFOR/PPP* 25, 2007. www.magfor.gob.ni.

Government of Nicaragua, Ministry of Education (MINED). "Políticas educativas 2007–2011." 2007. www.mined.gob.ni/.

———. "Profesor Miguel de Castilla participa en el XV Congreso Nacional de UNEN." *Notas de Prensa,* July 18, 2007. www.mined.gob.ni/.

Government of Nicaragua, Ministry of Foreign Relations. *Libro Blanco: La realidad del proceso electoral municipal del 2008 en Nicaragua.* Managua: Ministerio de Relaciones Exteriores de la República de Nicaragua, 2009. www.cancelleria.gob.ni/.

———. *Libro blanco: La realidad del proceso electoral municipal del 2008 en Nicaragua.* Managua: MINEX, 2009. www.cancelleria.gob.ni/.

Government of Nicaragua, Ministry of Planning (MIPLAN). *Programa económico de austeridad y eficiencia 81.* Managua: MIPLAN, 1981.

Government of Nicaragua, Ministry of Natural Resources and the Environment (MARENA). *Informe del Estado Ambiental de Nicaragua.* Managua: MARENA, 2001.

Government of Nicaragua, Office of the President of the Republic, Technical Secretariat. *Nicaragua: Informe gasto en pobreza Enero–Junio 2006.* Managua: Presidencia de la República, 2006.

Government of Nicaragua, Supreme Electoral Council. *Electoral Results, 2006.* www.cse.gob.ni/intro.php.

———. *Ley Electoral.* Managua: *La Gaceta Diario Official,* January 24, 2000. www.cse.gob.ni/

———. *Electoral Law.* January 2000. www.cse.gob.ni/.

———. *Ley Marco para la estabilidad y gobernabilidad del país.* October 20, 2005, Political Database of the Americas. pdba.georgetown.edu/.

———. *Reforma parcial de la constitución política de la República de Nicaragua.* February 18, 2005, Political Database of the Americas. pdba.georgetown.edu/.

Grandin, Greg. *Empire's Workshop.* New York: Metropolitan Books, 2006.

Grigsby, Arturo. "New Government, New Economy?" *Envío* 248 (January–February 2002). www.envio.org.ni/.

Grigsby, William. "Todavia es tiempo para que el FSLN gire a la izquierda." *Sin Fronteras,* September 1, 2005. www.nicaraguita.org.

———. "2004 Elections: FSLN-Convergence Victories in Numbers." *Envío* 280 (November 2004). www.envio.org.ni/.

Griffin, Keith. *Concentración de tierras y pobreza rural.* México, DF: Fondo de Cultura Economica, 1983.

Griffin-Nolan, Ed. *Witness for Peace.* Louisville, KY: Westminster/John Knox Press, 1991.

Grinevald, Colette, and Maricela Kauffmann. "Toponimia del Territorio en la Lengua y Cultura Rama." In *The Rama: Struggling for Land and Culture,* edited by Miguel González et al. Managua: URACCAN and University of Tromso, Norway, 2006.

Grupo Empresarial de Análisis (GEA) and Consultores para el Desarrollo Empresarial, (COPADES). *Nicaragua: Informe Económico.* Managua: July 2007.

Guedán, Manuel. "Como ven nuestra política exterior?" *Confidencial* 527, March 18–24, 2007. www.confidencial.com.ni.

Guevara, Ernesto. *Guerrilla Warfare.* Melbourne: Ocean, 2006.

Gutiérrez, Ivan. "La política de tierras de la Reforma Agraria Sandinista." In *El debate sobre la reforma agraria en Nicaragua,* edited by Raul Ruben and Jan P. de Groot, 113–128. Managua: Editorial Ciencias Sociales, 1989.

Hale, Charles. *Resistance and Contradiction: Mískitu Indians and the Nicaraguan State, 1894–1987.* Stanford: Stanford University Press, 1994.

———. "Rethinking Indigenous Politics in the Era of the 'Indio Permitido.'" *NACLA Report on the Americas* 38 (September–October 2004): 16–20.

———. "Wan Tasbaya Dukiara: Nociones contenciosas de los derechos sobre la tierra en la historia Miskita." *Wani: Revista del Caribe Nicaragüense,* no. 12 (June 1992): 1–19.

Hamilton, Nora, and Norma Stoltz Chinchilla. *Seeking Community in a Global City: Guatemalans and Salvadorans in Los Angeles.* Philadelphia: Temple University Press, 2001.

Hart, Celia. "Las elecciones rosas de Nicaragua." *Argenpress,* November 16, 2006. www.argenpress.info.

Helmke, Gretchen, and Steven Levitsky. "Introduction." In *Informal Institutions and Democracy: Lessons from Latin America,* edited by Gretchen Helmke and Steven Levitsky. Baltimore: Johns Hopkins University Press, 2006.

Hirshon, Sheryl, with Judy Butler. *And Also Teach Them to Read.* Westport, CT: Lawrence Hill, 1983.

Hodgson, Peter C. "Providence." In *A New Handbook of Christian Theology,* edited by Donald W. Musser and Joseph L. Price. Cambridge, UK: Lutterworth Press, 1992, 394–397.

Hoffman, David. "Reagan Has a Texas-Sized Sales Job; Public Skeptical of Contra Aid." *Washington Post,* March 16, 1986.

Hooker, Juliet. "Beloved Enemies": Race and Official Mestizo Nationalism in Nicaragua." *Latin American Research Review* 40, no. 3 (October 2005): 14–39.

Horton, Lynn. *Peasants in Arms: War and Peace in the Mountains of Nicaragua, 1979–1994.* Athens: Ohio University Press, 1998.

Hoyt, Katherine. "February 1979–February 2004: Nicaragua Network Celebrates 25 Years of Solidarity." *Nicaragua Monitor,* December 2003–January 2004.

———. *The Many Faces of Sandinista Democracy.* Athens: Center for International Studies, Ohio University, 1997.

———. "Parties and Pacts in Contemporary Nicaragua." Paper presented to the congress of the Latin American Studies Association, Washington, DC, 2001.

Ibarra, Eloisa. "Suprema da largas a recursos contra las reformas del pacto." *El Nuevo Diario,* April 26, 2000. archivo.elnuevodiario.com.ni/.

———. "¿Visión clasista para rechazar la politización?" *El Nuevo Diario,* August 23, 2004. archivo.elnuevodiario.com.ni/.

Ibarra, Eloisa, Valerie Imhof, and Luis Galeano. "MIFAMILIA quiere asumir a la nina." *El Nuevo Diario,* February 20, 2003. www.elnuevodiario.com.ni.

IDEA. "Public Banks Revisited." Vol. 7 (May–June 2005): 1–2.

IEEPP (Instituto de Estudios Estratégicos y Políticas Públicas). "Cifras y perspectivas del gasto público 2007 en Salud y Educación." *Presupuesto Ciudadano,* no. 2 (June 2007).

IMF-IDA (International Monetary Fund and International Development Association). *Nicaragua: Joint Staff Advisory Note on the Poverty Reduction Strategy Paper.* 2005. siteresources.worldbank.org/.

INEC (Instituto Nacional de Estadísticas y Censos). *Segundo Censo Nacional Agropecuario.* Managua: Instituto Nacional de Estadísticas y Censos, 1971.

———. *Tercer Censo Nacional Agropecuario.* Managua: CENAGRO-INEC, 2002.

———. *Censo de población, 1971.* Managua: INEC, 1972.

———. *Censo de población, 2005.* Managua: INEC, 2006.

———. *Censos nacionales.* Managua: INEC, 1995.

———. *VIII Censo de población y IV de vivienda: Resumen censal.* Managua: INEC, 2006. www.inec.gob.ni.

———. *Encuesta nacional de hogares sobre medicion del nivel de vida.* Managua: INEC, 2001.

———. *Encuesta socio-demografica, 1985.* Managua: INEC, 1992.

———. *Informe preliminar del censo de analfabetas, 21 de octubre a 15 de noviembre 1979.* Managua: INEC, 1980.

———. *Tercer Censo Agropecuario.* Managua: INEC, 2002.

INIDE (Instituto Nacional de Información de Desarrollo). *Encuesta nacional de hogares sobre medición del nivel de vida, 2005: Informe general.* Managua: INIDE, 2007.

———. *Perfil y características de los pobres en Nicaragua, 2005.* Managua: INIDE, 2007.

Instituto de Estudios Nicaragüenses (IEN). *FSLN: De vanguardismo al acuerdo nacional.* Managua: IEN/Fundación Friedrich Ebert, 1993.

Inter-American Court of Human Rights. *Case of Yatama v. Nicaragua, Judgment of June 23, 2005.* Case no. 12.388. www.corteidh.or.cr/.

Inter-American Development Bank. *Nicaragua: Program to Support Agrifood Production.* NI-L1020 Loan Proposal, May 16, 2008. idbdocs.iadb.org/.

International Human Rights Law Group/Washington Office on Latin America. *A Political Opening in Nicaragua: Report on the Nicaraguan Elections of November 4, 1984.* Washington, DC: Washington Office on Latin America, December 11, 1984.

Invernizzi, Gabriele, Francisco Pisani, and Jesús Ceberio. *Sandinistas: Entrevistas con Humberto Ortega Saavedra, Jaime Wheelock, y Bayardo Arce Castaño.* Managua: Vanguardia, 1986.

Ionescu, Ghita, and Isobel Madariaga. *Opposition.* Harmondsworth, UK: Penguin Books, 1972.

IPADE (Instituto para el Desarrollo y la Democracia). *Elecciones municipales 2008/2009: Informe final.* www.ipade.org.ni/.

———. *Encuesta cultura política, actitud hacia las elecciones y los regímenes de autonomía municipal y regional.* Managua: IPADE, 2001.

———. *Encuesta cultura política y actitudes hacia las elecciones y el régimen de autonomía en las regiones autónomas.* Managua: IPADE, 1997.

———. *Encuesta cultura política y valores democráticos.* Managua: IPADE, 2007.

————. *Informe final preliminar: Elecciones municipales RAAN 2009.* www.ipade .org.ni/.

————. "IPADE brinda informe final de Observación de las Elecciones Regionales 2010." March, 18, 2010. www.ipade.org.ni/.

IPADE (Instituto para el Desarrollo y la Democracia) and CASC (Centro de Analisis Socio-Cultural). *Percepciones interregionales en el pacifico y el atlántico nicaragüenses.* Unpublished manuscript, 2004.

Irish Inter-Party Parliamentary Delegation. "Report of the Irish Inter-Party Parliamentary Delegation on the Elections in Nicaragua." Dublin, November 21, 1984.

Iseas, Rafael. *Acto de inauguración del banco de desarrollo económico y social de Venezuela en Nicaragua.* June 21, 2007. www.presidencia.gob.ni/.

Jarquín, Leyla, and Malltide Córdoba. "Partido Único Alarma." *El Nuevo Diario,* April 23, 2009. www.elnuevodiario.com.ni/.

Jaua, Elías. *Recibimiento a los miembros de la Comisión Mixta de Venezuela, 4 de marzo 2007.* www.presidencia.gob.ni/.

Jeffrey, Paul. "La corrupción y la Iglesia en Nicaragua." *El Nuevo Diario,* March 31, 2005. www.elnuevodiario.com.ni/.

Johnson, Kenneth F., and Paul Paris. "Nicaragua." In *Political Forces in Latin America,* edited by Ben G. Burnett and Kenneth F. Johnson, 115–133. Belmont, CA: Wadsworth, 1970.

Juárez Ordonez, Lester. "PLC cede en la reelección." *La Prensa,* October 25, 2007. www.laprensa.com.ni/.

————. "Demandan aborto para salvar niña embarazada." *El Nuevo Diario,* February 19, 2003. www.elnuevodiario.com.ni.

Kampwirth, Karen. "Arnoldo Alemán Takes On the NGOs: Antifeminism and the New Populism in Nicaragua." *Latin American Politics and Society* 45, no. 2 (Fall 2003): 133–158.

————. *Feminism and the Legacy of Revolution: Nicaragua, El Salvador, Chiapas.* Athens: Ohio University Press, 2004.

————. "Legislating Personal Politics in Sandinista Nicaragua, 1979–1992." *Women's Studies International Forum* 21, no. 1 (1998): 48–54.

————. "The Mother of the Nicaraguans: Doña Violeta and the UNO's Gender Agenda." *Latin American Perspectives* 23, no. 1 (1996): 67–88.

————. "'The Movement Came to Fill an Emptiness': Lesbian Feminists Talk About Life in Post-Sandinista Nicaragua." *Sojourner: The Women's Forum* 20, no. 4 (December 1994): 15–17.

————. "Resisting the Feminist Threat: Antifeminist Politics in Post-Sandinista Nicaragua." *NWSA Journal* (Journal of the National Women's Studies Association) 18, no. 2 (2006): 73–100.

————. "Social Policy." In *Nicaragua Without Illusions,* edited by Thomas W. Walker, 115–130. Wilmington, DE: Scholarly Resources Books, 1997.

————. "Women in the Armed Struggles in Nicaragua: Sandinistas and Contras Compared." In *Radical Women in Latin America: Left and Right,* edited by Victoria Gonzalez-Rivera and Karen Kampwirth. University Park: Penn State University Press, 2001.

Karl, Terry Lynn. "Central America at the End of the Cold War." In *Beyond the Cold War: Conflict and Cooperation in the Third World,* edited by George W. Breslauer, 222–251. Berkeley: University of California, International and Area Studies, 1991.

————. "Electoralism." In *International Encyclopedia of Elections,* edited by Richard Rose, 95–96. Washington, DC: CQ Press, 2000.

Kay, Cristobal. "Rural Poverty and Development Strategies in Latin America." *Journal of Agrarian Change* 6, no. 4 (October 2006): 455–508.

Kirkpatrick, Jeane J. "Dictatorships and Double Standards." *Commentary* (November 1979). www.commentarymagazine.com/.

Klare, Michael, and Peter Kornbluth, eds. *Low-Intensity Warfare: Counterinsurgency, Proinsurgency, and Antiterrorism in the Eighties.* New York: Pantheon Books, 1988.

La Agencia EFE. "Aumentan los evangélicos y agnósticos." *El Nuevo Diaro,* December 5, 2006.

Lacayo, Antonio. *La difícil transición nicaragüense.* Managua: Fundación UNO, 2005.

Lacayo, Carlos. *A Case Study of CAFTA-Nicaragua and the Potential Use of the Lessons of Nicaragua's Cash Transfers Project to Support the Losers in the Free Trade Agreements of the Central American Region: Final Report.* London: Department for International Development, DFID-Nicaragua. Unpublished report, 2006.

————. "Poverty and Social Protection Net." Washington, DC: Inter-American Development Bank, 2004. www.iadb.org/.

————. *Segundo proyecto de desarrollo rural municipal: Informe final.* Managua: Ministerio de Hacienda y Crédito Público, 2006.

La Nación, San José, Costa Rica. "Eligen a cuatro magistrados más para la CSJ." March 21, 2000.

La Prensa. "De la votación en plancha y otros demonios." April 3, 2007. www.laprensa.com.ni/.

————. "Ortega ofrece condonación y subsidio," July 20, 2006. www.laprensa.com.ni.

————. "Restituyen convivencia familiar a Alemán: Otra vez tiene Nicaragua por cárcel." January 11, 2008. www.laprensa.com.ni.

Lara, Rafael. "7 mil 500, despedidos en solo año y medio." *El Nuevo Diario,* April 30, 2008. www.elnuevodiario.com.ni/.

Latin American Studies Association (LASA). *The 1990 Electoral Process in Nicaragua.* Pittsburgh: LASA, 1990.

Latinobarómetro. "A Decade of Measurements." 2004. www.latinobarometro.org.

"Law of Political Parties." In *Nicaragua Under Siege,* edited by Marlene Dixon, 174–182. San Francisco: Synthesis Publications, 1985.

Lawson, Stephanie. "Conceptual Issues in the Comparative Study of Regime Change and Democratization." *Comparative Politics* 25 (1993): 183–295.

LeoGrande, William M. "Political Parties and Postrevolutionary Politics in Nicaragua." In *Political Parties and Democracy in Central America,* edited by Louis Goodman, William M. LeoGrande, and Johanna M. Forman, 187–202. Boulder, CO: Westview, 1992.

León, Sergio. "Gobierno quitara los cayos de los nuevos dueños." *La Prensa,* May 5, 2008. www.laprensa.com.ni/.

Linares, Sebastian. "La independencia judicial: Conceptualización y medición." *Política y Gobierno* 11 (2004): 73–136.

Linz, Juan. "Totalitarian and Authoritarian Regimes." In *Handbook of Political Science,* edited by Fred Greenstein and Nelson Polsby, vol. 3: 175–411. Reading, MA: Addison-Wesley Publishing, 1975.

Linz, Juan, and Alfred Stepan, eds. *Problems in Democratic Transition and Consolidation: Southern Europe, South America, and Post-Communist Europe.* Baltimore: Johns Hopkins University Press, 1996.

Lipset, Seymour Martin. *The First New Nation.* New York: Anchor Books, 1967.

Lipton, Michael. "Towards a Theory of Land Reform." In *Agrarian Reform and Agrarian Reformism,* edited by David Lehmann, 269–315. London: Faber, 1974.

Loásiga López, Ludwin. "FSLN: Ley Marco es negociable." *La Prensa,* December 14, 2006. www.laprensa.com.ni.

———. "Los liberales desilusionan a Estados Unidos." *La Prensa,* September 29, 2005. www.laprensa.com.ni.

———. "Otro intento para liberar a Alemán." *La Prensa,* September 14, 2004. www.laprensa.com.ni/.

———. "PLC celebra round judicial a favor de Arnoldo Alemán y reiteran que en Nicaragua justicia es de Ortega." *La Prensa,* May 27, 2006. www.laprensa.com.ni/.

Loásiga López, Ludwin, and Luis Núñez Salmerón. "Usura Cero, 'Exitoso' Pero Nada Transparente." *La Prensa,* October 9, 2008. www.laprensa.com.ni/.

Loásiga Mayorga, Jorge, and Mirna Velasquez Sevilla. "'Limpian' a Byron Jerez." *La Prensa,* March 19, 2005. www.laprensa.com.ni/.

López, Isidro. "Los más ricos de Centro América quieren gobernar Nicaragua. Recelo por participación abierta de la familia Pellas en la política." *Tiempos del Mundo,* February 24, 2000. www.tdm.com.ni.

López Castellanos, Nayar. *La ruptura del Frente Sandinista.* México: Plaza y Valdés, 1996.

López Pintor, Rafael, and Dieter Nohlen. *Elecciones de apertura: El caso de Nicaragua 1990.* San José: IIDH-CAPEL, 1993.

Magalhães, P. C. *The Limits to Judicialization: Legislative Politics and Constitutional Review in the Iberian Democracies.* PhD diss., Ohio State University, 2003.

Maier, Elizabeth. *Nicaragua: La mujer en la Revolución.* México, DF: Ediciones de Cultura Popular, 1980.

Maluccio, John A., and Rafael Flores. *Impact Evaluation of a Conditional Cash Transfer Program: The Nicaraguan Red de Protección Social.* Research Report 141. Washington, DC: International Food Policy Research Institute, 2005.

Martí i Puig, Salvador. "El FSLN d'organització político-mililtar a l'oposició parlamentària." BA honors' thesis in political science, Universidad Autónoma de Barcelona, 1992.

———. "La izquierda centroamericana: ¿Renacimiento o debacle?" In *América Central: Las democracias incierta,* edited by Ana Sofía Cardenal and Salvador Martí i Puig, 65–108. Madrid: Tecnos, 1998.

———. *Nicaragua, 1977–1996: La revolución enredada.* Madrid: Libros de la Catarata, 1997.

———. "Nicaragua postrevolucionaria: El laberinto sandinista y la difícil consolidación democrática." *Afers Internacionals* 34–35 (December 1996): 149–169.

———. *The Origins of the Peasant-Contra Rebellion in Nicaragua, 1979–1987.* London: ILAS, 2000.

———. *Tiranías, rebeliones, y democracia: Itinerarios políticos comparados en Centroamérica.* Barcelona: Edicions Bellaterra, 2004.

Martí i Puig, Salvador, and Carlos Figueroa Ibarra. *La izquierda revolucionaria en Centroamérica: De la lucha armada a la participación electoral.* Madrid: Libros de la Catarata, 2006.

Martí i Puig, Salvador, and Salvador Santiuste. "El FSLN: De guerrilla victoriosa a oposición negociadora." In *La izquierda revolucionaria en Centroamérica: De la lucha armada a la participación electoral,* edited by Salvador Martí i Puig and Carlos Figueroa Ibarra, 53–90. Madrid: Libros de la Catarata, 2006.

Martínez, Moisés, and Carlos Salinas. "Canal interoceánico seguirá esperando." *La Prensa,* December 6, 2008. www.laprensa.com.ni/.

Martínez Barahona, Elena. "Exploring Parliamentary Opposition in Contemporary Central America." Diploma Research Project in Social Science Data Analysis, University of Essex, 2004.

———. "Seeking the Political Role of the Third Government Branch: A Comparative Approach to High Courts in Central America." PhD diss., European University Institute, Florence, Italy, 2007.

Martínez Cuenca, Alejandro. *Nicaragua: Una década de retos.* Managua: Nueva Nicaragua, 1990.

McBain-Haas, Brigitte, with Martin Wolpold-Bosien. "The Right to Food and the Fight Against Hunger in Nicaragua: One Year of the Zero Hunger Program." Heidelberg, Germany: FIAN International Secretariat, 2008. www.fian.org/.

McConnell, Shelley A. "Can the Inter-American Democratic Charter Work? Nicaragua's 2004–05 Constitutional Crisis." Paper presented at the forty-eighth annual convention of the International Studies Association, Chicago, Illinois, March 2007.

———. "From Bullets to Ballots: Nicaragua's Revolutionary Transition to Democracy." PhD diss., Stanford University, 1998.

———. "Nicaragua's Turning Point." *Current History* 106, no. 697 (February 2007): 83–88.

McGinnis, James. *Solidarity with the People of Nicaragua.* Maryknoll, NY: Orbis Books, 1985.

Menjivar, Rafael. "Los problemas de mundo rural." In *Centroamérica Hoy,* edited by Edelberto Torres Rivas, 258–279. Mexico City: Siglo 21, 1975.

Mercado, Evaristo, Lestel Wilson, and Miguel González. *YATAMA: La lucha por una verdadera autonomía en la Moskitia nicaragüense.* Managua: URACCAN, 2005.

Miller, Valerie. *Between Struggle and Hope: The Nicaraguan Literacy Crusade.* Boulder, CO: Westview, 1985.

Miller Llana, Sara. "Evangelicals Flex Growing Clout in Nicaragua's Election." *Christian Science Monitor,* November 2, 2006.

Millett, Richard. *Guardians of the Dynasty.* Maryknoll, NY: Orbis Books, 1977.

Miranda, Bonifacio. *El Parlamentarismo Sui Generis.* Managua: Fondo Conjunto de Donantes para la Anticorrupción FAC II, 2006.

Monjárrez, Luís. *Breve análisis sobre la crisis de poder en el seno del gobierno de Nicaragua (diferendo en la coalición UNO-Poder Ejecutivo-Poder Legislativo.* León: Facultad de Ciencias Jurídicas and Sociales de León-UNAN, mímeo, 1992.

Montenegro, Sofia. "El retorno de Daniel Ortega." *Pueblos,* March 16, 2007. www.revista.pueblos.org.

Montenegro, Sofía, Elvira Cuadra Lira, Ángel Saldomando, and Yálani Zamora. *La gobernabilidad al servicio de las reformas.* Managua: CINCO, 2005.

Morales Carazo, Jaime. 2006. "Intervención de Jaime Morales Carazo." Congreso del FSLN, 28 de mayo 2006. www.fsln-nicaragua.com/.

Morley, James. "Nicaraguan Councils Stir Fear of Dictatorship." *New York Times,* May 4, 2008. www.nytimes.com/.

Murguialday, Clara. *Nicaragua, Revolución y Feminismo (1977–1989).* Madrid: Editorial Revolución, 1990.

Murillo, Rosario. "Es la hora de la luz." *Visión Sandinista,* July 25–31, 2001.

———. "Extracto de la entrevista ofrecida por Rosario Murillo, jefa de campaña del Frente Sandinista de Liberación Nacional, a la emisora *Nueva Radio Ya.*" August 21, 2006. www.izquierda.info/.

———. "Sin sorpresas en la vida de Pedro: Todo sobre sus navajas." *Con amor Nicaragua: Articulos,* no. 47, March 3–4, 2005. www.conamornicaragua.org.ni.

Nicaragua Hoy. "FSLN 'revisará estrategias' para seguir en el poder." August 27, 2009. www.nicaraguahoy.info/.

Nicaragua Network. "Ambassador Trivelli Tries Again for Right-Wing Unity While Momentum Shifts to the FSLN." *Nicaragua News Hotline,* September 5, 2006. www.nicanet.org/.

———. *List of Interventions by the United States Government in Nicaragua's Democratic Process.* Washington, DC: Nicaragua Network, 2006.

———. "Managua Criminal Appeals Court Sends Former President Arnoldo Alemán Back to House Arrest." *Nica Net Hotline,* December 18, 2007. www.nicanet.org.

———. "Topic 5: Reactions to National Assembly's Criminalizing Therapeutic Abortion." *Nica Net Hotline,* November 2, 2006. www.nicanet.org/.

———. "Two Foreign Interventions Draw Angry Responses from Government." *NicaNet,* August 19, 2008. www.nicanet.org/.

Núñez, Orlando. *El somocismo y el modelo capitalista agroexportador.* Managua: Departamento De Ciencias Sociales, UNAN, 1981.

———. "'Hambre Cero': US$90 millones en tres años." Interview with Iván Olivares. *Confidencial* 516, December 17, 2006–January 7, 2007, 1.

———, ed. *La guerra en Nicaragua.* Managua: CIPRES-NORAD, 1991.

———. *La guerra y el campesinado en Nicaragua.* Managua: CIPRES, 1998.

———. "Plan anti pobreza: US$1,500 en especie." Interview with Carlos F. Chamorro. *Confidencial* 520, January 28–February 3, 2007, 1.

Nuñez de Escorcia, Vilma. *Independencia del poder judicial.* 5th ed. Managua: Editorial Ciencias Sociales, 1990.

Obregón, Raúl. Interview. *Esta Semana.* Managua, Nicaragua, May 4, 2006. www.estasemana.ibw.com.ni/.

Observation Mission of the Official Delegation of the European Parliament. "The Presidential and Legislative Elections That Took Place in Nicaragua November 4, 1984." Managua, 1984.

ODI (Overseas Development Institute). "Red de Protección Social Nicaragua." Policy Brief no. 3 (February 2006). www.odi.org.uk/.

O'Donnell, Guillermo. "Illusions About Consolidation." *Journal of Democracy* 7, no. 2 (April 1996): 34–51.

Olivares, Ivan, and Lourdes Arróliga. "Un precedente en la justicia." *Confidencial* 342, June 8–14, 2003. www.confidencial.com.ni/.

Oquist, Paul. "Sociopolitical Dynamics in the 1990 Nicaraguan Election." In *The 1990 Elections in Nicaragua and Their Aftermath,* edited by Vanesa Castro and Gary Prevost, 1–40. Lanham, MD: Rowman and Littlefield, 1993.

Ortega, Daniel. "A vencer la pobreza." *Visión Sandinista,* December 22, 2001.
———. "Defender nuestro derecho a la rebelión." *Barricada Internacional* 339 (July 1991): 22–27.
———. "Escucha Hermana: La Canción de Alegría." July 17, 2007. www.presidencia .gob.ni/.
———. *Programa del gobierno de reconciliación y unidad nacional, 2006–2011.* Acto de Clausura del III Congreso FSLN, Sesión "Sandino, La Victoria." May 28, 2006.
Ortega, Daniel, and Agustin Jarquín. "Carta a los nicaragüenses: ¡Por los ideales más altos!" *Visión Sandinista,* August 22–28, 2001.
Ortega, Humberto. *Nicaragua: Revolución y democracia.* México: Organización Editorial Mexicana, 1991.
Ortega Hegg, Manuel. "Conceptualización de la Autonomía de la Costa Atlántica." Ponencia, *Fourth Simposio Internacional de Autonomía de la Costa Caribe de Nicaragua,* Managua, September 9, 2004.
———. *Los resultados electorales del 2006 en Nicaragua.* Fundacion Heinrich Boll, America Latina. boell-latinoamerica.org/.
Ortiz, Eduardo. *Comentarios sobre la Constitución Sandinista.* San José: Lehmann Editores, 1987.
Padilla, Max. "La autonomía de la familia." Speech to the World Congress of Families II, November 15, 1999. www.thefamily.com/.
Palacios Paiz, Marvin. "Elección de nuevos magistrados: Un sainete más del pacto." *El Nuevo Diario,* March 31, 2007. impreso.elnuevodiario.com.ni/.
Panebianco, Angelo. *Modelos de Partido.* Madrid: Alianza Editorial, 1995.
Pantoja, Ary. "Más ex somocistas en FSLN." *El Nuevo Diario,* August 27, 2006. www.elnuevodiario.com.ni.
Pastor, Robert A. *Condemned to Repetition: The United States and Nicaragua.* Princeton, NJ: Princeton University Press, 1988.
———. "Nicaragua's Choice: The Making of a Free Election." *Journal of Democracy* 1, no. 3 (Summer 1990): 13–25.
Peace, Roger. *A Just and Lasting Peace.* Chicago: Noble Press, 1991.
Pérez Baltodano, Andrés. "El veneno del antisemitismo." *Confidencial* 428, March 6–12, 2005. www.confidencial.com.ni.
———. *Entre el estado conquistador y el estado nación: Providencialismo, pensamiento político, y estructuras de poder en el desarrollo histórico de Nicaragua.* Managua: Fundacion Friederich Ebert en Nicaragua, 2003.
———. "The FSLN After the Debacle: The Struggle for the Definition of Sandinismo." *Journal of Interamerican Studies and World Affairs* 34 (1992): 111–139.
———. "Unholy Alliance: Church and State in Nicaragua, 1996–2002." In *Undoing Democracy: The Politics of Electoral Caudillismo,* edited by David Close and Kalowatie Deonandan, 87–102. Lanham, MD: Lexington Books, 2004.
Perkins, Doug. "Structure and Choice: The Role of Organizations, Patronage, and the Media in Party Formation." *Party Politics* 2 (1996): 355–375.
Perla, Hector, Jr. "Challenging Reagan: The Rise of the Transnational Central American Peace and Solidarity Movement." Paper presented at the 2004 annual meeting of the Midwest Political Science Association, March 16–March 21, Chicago.
———. "Days of Decision: Media Framing and Opposition to the Use of Force in US Foreign Policy." Paper presented at the 2004 annual meeting of the Midwest Political Science Association, March 16–March 21, Chicago.

Petrie Bejarano, Henry. "Ortega huérfano de estrategias." *El Nuevo Diario,* April 11, 2007. www.elnuevodiario.com.ni.

Pineda, Baron. *Shipwrecked Identities: Navigating Race on Nicaragua's Moskito Coast.* New Brunswick, NJ: Rutgers University Press, 2006.

PNUD (Programa de las Naciones Unidas para el Desarrollo). *El Desarrollo Humano en Nicaragua: Equidad para superar la vulnerabilidad.* Managua: PNUD, 2000.

———. *El Desarrollo Humano en Nicaragua 2002: Las Condiciones de la Esperanza.* Managua: PNUD, 2002.

———. *Informe de Desarrollo Humano 2005 de la Costa Caribe Nicaragua.* Managua: PNUD, 2005.

———. *Nicaragua: Evaluación de los resultados de desarrollo.* New York: PNUD, 2007.

Political Database of the Americas. *Nicaraguan Electoral Results.* pdba.george town.edu/Elecdata/Nica/nica.html.

———. *1996 Nicaraguan Presidential Election.* pdba.georgetown.edu/.

———. *Republic of Nicaragua, Electoral Results.* November 5, 2006, pdba.george town.edu/.

Prevost, Gary. "The FSLN." In *Nicaragua Without Illusions: Regime Transition and Structural Adjustment in the 1990s,* edited by Thomas W. Walker, 149–164. Wilmington, DE: Scholarly Resources, 1997.

———. "The FSLN in Opposition." In *The 1990 Elections in Nicaragua and Their Aftermath,* edited by Vanesa Castro and Gary Prevost, 109–122. Lanham, MD: Rowman and Littlefield, 1992.

Programa de Observatorio de la Reforma de la Educación en Centroamérica. *América Central: La educación en el año 2002.* Managua: Universidad Centroamericana, 2003.

"Programa Hambre Cero: Combatir la Pobreza en Nicaragua y Alcanzar la Soberanía Alimentaria." Unpublished paper, 2007.

Proyecto de Investigación Elites Parlamentarias Iberoamericanas. Instituto Interuniversitario de Estudios de Iberoamérica y Portugal, Universidad de Salamanca y Centro de Investigaciones Sociológicas (CIS), Agencia Española de Cooperación Internacional, 2002.

Proyecto Política de Justicia y Calidad de la Democracia en Centro América. Universidad de Salamanca, Comisión Interuniversitaria de Ciencia y Tecnología. CICYT (SEC 20001-1779), 2004.

Rama and Kriol Territorial Government. *Indigenas Rama y comunidades Kriol de la RAAS demandan a Presidente Ortega.* Press release, Bluefields, Nicaragua, December 3, 2008.

Ramírez, Sergio. *Adiós, muchachos: Una memoria de la revolución sandinista.* México: Aguilar, 1999.

———. "US Working People Can Stop Intervention." In *Nicaragua: The Sandinista People's Revolution: Speeches by Sandinista Leaders,* edited by Marcus Bruce, 1–7. New York: Pathfinder Press, 1985.

Randall, Margaret. "To Change Our Own Reality and Our World: A Conversation with Lesbians in Nicaragua." *Signs* 18 (1993): 907–924.

Reagan, Ronald. *Speaking My Mind.* New York: Simon and Schuster, 1989.

Regalia, Ferdinando. "An Assessment of Poverty and Safety Nets in Nicaragua." Washington, DC: Inter-American Development Bank, May 17, 2000. www .iadb.org/.

Reif, Linda L. "Women in Latin American Guerrilla Movements: A Comparative Perspective." *Comparative Politics* 18, no. 2 (January 1986): 147–169.

Relea, Francesc. "Aborto 'hipoteca' a Daniel Ortega." *El Nuevo Diario,* January 23, 2003.

"Reporters Without Borders Writes to President Daniel Ortega About Poor State of Public Freedoms." October 21, 2008. www.rsf.org/.

Republic of Nicaragua. *National Development Plan: 2005.* siteresources.worldbank .org/.

"Resultado de las elecciones para Presidente y Vicepresidente de la Republica y representantes ante la Asamblea Nacional, 4 de noviembre de 1984." *Monexico: Revista del Consejo de Estado* 8 (January 1985): 1–20.

Ríos, Julia. "Rosario Murillo, el poder tras el 'orteguismo.'" *El Nuevo Diario,* January 10, 2007.

Ríos-Figueroa, Julio. "Institutional Models of Judicial Independence in Latin America." Paper presented at the Twenty-Sixth Meeting of the Latin American Studies Association (LASA). Puerto Rico, March 15–18, 2006.

Rizo, Mario. "Citizenship and Identity in the Autonomous Regions of the Caribbean Coast of Nicaragua." In *Contributions to the First Human Development Report of the Autonomous Regions.* Managua: CIDCA-UCA, 2004.

Robinson, William I. *A Faustian Bargain: US Intervention in the Nicaraguan Elections and American Foreign Policy in the Post–Cold War Era.* Boulder, CO: Westview, 1992.

Rocha, José Luis. "La Mara 19 tras las huellas de las pandillas políticas." *Envío* 321 (December 2009). www.envio.org.ni/.

———. "PLC: The Resounding Winner." *Envío* 244 (November 2001). www.envio .org.ni/.

Rodríguez, Tomás, and Ligia Gómez. "Mercado de crédito rural en Nicaragua." In *Crédito para el desarrollo rural en Nicaragua,* edited by Johan Bastiaensen, 55–58. Managua: Nitlapán-UCA, FLACSO, 2002.

Rogers, Tim. "Ortega Balances Venezuelan Aid, IMF." *Nica Times,* April 27–May 3, 2007. www.nicatimes.net.

———. "Ortega Defiant After US, Europe Yank Aid." *Christian Science Monitor,* December 5, 2008. www.csmonitor.com/.

———. "Why Nicaragua's Capital Is in Flames." *Time,* November 14, 2008. www .time.com.

Romero, Elizabeth. "Fiscalia no acusará a Cinco." *La Prensa,* January 23, 2009. www.laprensa.com.ni/.

———. "Niña violada en peligro." *La Prensa,* February 19, 2003. www.laprensa .com.ni.

Rosenberg, Tina. "The Many Stories of Carlos Fernando Chamorro." *New York Times Magazine,* March 22, 2009. www.nytimes.com.

Roux, Theunis. "Legitimating Transformation: Political Resource Allocation in the South African Constitutional Court." In *Democratization and the Judiciary: The Accountability Function of Courts in New Democracies,* edited by Siri

Gloppen, Roberto Gargarella, and Elin Skaar, 92–111. London: Frank Cass, 2004.

Ruccio, David F. "The State and Planning in Nicaragua." In *The Political Economy of Revolutionary Nicaragua,* edited by Rose Spalding, 61–82. Boston: Allen and Unwin, 1987.

Ruse, Austin. "The UN's Assault on Faith, Family, and Country." www.iol.ie/~hlii/AustinRuse.html.

Ryan, Charlotte. *Prime Time Activism.* Boston: South End Press, 1991.

Ryan, Phil. *The Fall and Rise of the Market in Sandinista Nicaragua.* Montreal: McGill-Queen's University Press, 1995.

Salinas Maldonado, Carlos. "Crisis política desemboca en violencia." *Confidencial,* April 20, 2010. www.confidencial.com.ni/.

———. "Orden FSLN reelección o caos." *Confidencial* 679, April 25–May 1, 2010, 1–2.

Sandoval, Consuelo. "Otro intento para liberar a Alemán." *La Prensa,* September 14, 2004. www.laprensa.com.ni/.

Santiuste Cué, Salvador. "La incompleta transformación del FSLN." *América Latina Hoy* 27 (2001): 75–98.

Schedler, Andreas, Larry Diamond, and Marc F. Plattner. *The Self-Restraining State: Power and Accountability in New Democracies.* Boulder, CO: Lynne Rienner, 1999.

Schmidt, Blake. "International Groups Decry Persecution." *Nica Times,* October 31, 2008. www.nicatimes.nt/.

———. "US-Nicaragua Relations Chill as Ortega Faces Domestic Tests." *World Politics Review,* September 19, 2008. www.worldpoliticsreview.com/.

Schmitter, Philippe C. Remarks to the forum "Democratic Deficits: Addressing Challenges to Sustainability and Consolidation Around the World," September 18, 2007. Reported in *Noticias* (Washington, DC: Woodrow Wilson International Center for Scholars, Spring 2008).

Seligson, Mitchell, Luis Serra Vázquez, and Pablo López Ruíz. *The Political Culture of Democracy in Nicaragua.* Nashville, TN: Latin American Public Opinion Project (LAPOP), Vanderbilt University, 2004. sitemason.vanderbilt.edu/.

Sen, Amartya. *Development as Freedom.* New York: Anchor, 1999.

Serra, Luís. "Organizaciones populares: Entre las bases y el poder." *Pensamiento Propio* 56 (March 1988): 41–45.

Serrano, Alejandro. *Estado de derecho y derechos humanos.* Managua: Hispamer, 2004.

———. *La transformación judicial en Nicaragua (y otros ensayos).* Managua: Ediciones Jurídicas, 1988.

Sieder, Rachel, Line Schjolden, and Alan Angell, eds. *The Judicialization of Politics in Latin America.* New York: Palgrave, 2005.

Silva, José Adán. "Cayó como bomba en Unión Europea." *El Nuevo Diario,* October 31, 2008. www.elnuevodiario.com.ni/.

———. "Ortega insiste en perdón y olvido." *La Prensa,* September 4, 2006.

Sirias, Tania. "Mujeres al piso y 'chanchos' quemados: 'Acción inhumana y vuelta a Estado parroquial,' gritan frente a Asamblea." *El Nuevo Diario,* October 27, 2006.

———. "'Nuevas Leyes' la dejaron morir." *El Nuevo Diario,* February 7, 2007.

————. "Presidente de Universidad Evangélica y el aborto terapéutico: Fuera electorerismo y escuchar a mujeres." *El Nuevo Diario,* October 13, 2006.

Sistema de las Naciones Unidas, Nicaragua. *Objetivos de desarrollo del milenio, Nicaragua 2006.* Managua: Sistema de las Naciones Unidas, 2007.

Sklar, Holly. "Washington's Trying to Buy Nicaragua's Elections Again." *Z Magazine* 12 (December 1989): 49–64.

————. *Washington's War on Nicaragua.* Boston: South End Press, 1988.

Smith, Christian. *Resisting Reagan.* Chicago: University of Chicago Press, 1996.

Sobel, Richard. *The Impact of Public Opinion on US Foreign Policy Since Vietnam.* New York: Oxford University Press, 2001.

————, ed. *Public Opinion in US Foreign Policy.* Lanham, MD: Rowman and Littlefield, 1999.

Sobrado, Carlos, and Juan Roche. "Annex 3: Technical Document About Two Aspects Related to Defining the Extreme Poverty Line Based on the Nicaragua 2005 Living Standards Measurement Survey (LSMS)." In *Nicaragua Poverty Assessment,* World Bank, Vol. 1: Main Report, no. 39736-NI (Washington, DC: World Bank, May 30, 2008).

Solá Montserrat, Roser. *Un siglo y medio de economía nicaragüense: Las raíces del presente.* Managua: Universidad Centroamericana, 2007.

Solaún, Mauricio. *U.S. Intervention and Regime Change in Nicaragua.* Lincoln: University of Nebraska Press, 2005.

Solís, Esteban. "Consejos controlarán créditos." *El Nuevo Diario,* July 18, 2007.

Solís, Luis Guillermo, and Richard Wilson. *Political Transition and the Administration of Justice in Nicaragua.* Miami: Florida International University, Center for the Administration of Justice, 1991.

Sollis, Peter. "The Atlantic Coast of Nicaragua: Development and Autonomy." *Journal of Latin American Studies* 21 (1989): 481–520.

Spalding, Rose J. *Capitalists and Revolution in Nicaragua: Opposition and Accommodation, 1979–1993.* Chapel Hill: University of North Carolina Press, 1994.

————. "From Low-Intensity Warfare to Low-Intensity Peace: The Nicaraguan Peace Process." In *Comparative Peace Processes in Latin America,* edited by Cynthia J. Arnson, 31–64. Stanford: Stanford University Press and Woodrow Wilson Center Press, 1999.

————, ed. *The Political Economy of Revolutionary Nicaragua.* Boston: Allen and Unwin, 1987.

Stavenhagen, Rodolfo. *Las clases sociales en las sociedades agrarias.* México: Siglo 21, 1969.

Stephens, Beth. "Changes in the Laws Governing the Parent-Child Relationship in Post-revolutionary Nicaragua." *Hastings International and Comparative Law Review* 12 (1988): 137–171.

————. "A Developing Legal System Grapples with an Ancient Problem: Rape in Nicaragua." *Women's Rights Law Reporter* 17, no. 1 (1990): 69–88.

Stone Sweet, Alec. *Governing with Judges.* New York: Oxford University Press, 2000.

Tate, C. Neal, and Torbjorn Vallinder. *The Global Expansion of Judicial Power.* New York: New York University Press, 1995.

Téllez, Dora Maria. "A New Option for the Left." *Envío* 224 (March 2000). www.envio.org.ni/.

Thayer, Millie. "Identity, Revolution, and Democracy: Lesbian Movements in Central America." *Social Problems* 44 (1997): 386–407.

Thiessenhusen, William, ed. *Searching for Agrarian Reform in Latin America.* Boston: Unwin Hyman, 1989.

Tilly, Charles. *From Mobilization to Revolution.* New York: Random House, 1978.

Torres Lazo, Agustin. *La saga de los Somoza: Historia de un magnicidio.* Managua: Hispamer, 2001.

Tórrez, Joaquín. "Un puente infantil de amistad EU-Nicaragua." *El Nuevo Diario,* December 9, 1998.

Trejos, Juan Diego. *Mercado de trabajo, ingresos laborales y pobreza en Nicaragua.* Geneva: International Labor Organization, 2004.

Trucchi, Giorgio. "Nicaragua: 17 Years of Governing from Below." *La Rel.* www .rel-uita.org/.

Tunnerman, Carlos. "Una sentencia eminentemente política." *El Nuevo Diario,* December 12, 2007. impreso.elnuevodiario.com.ni/.

United Nations. *Report of the Seventh Congress on the Prevention of Crime and Treatment of Offenders, 1985.* New York: United Nations, 1985.

United Nations Children's Fund (UNICEF). *At a Glance: Nicaragua.* www.unicef .org/.

———. *Plan Nacional de Educación 2001–2015.* Managua: UNICEF, 2001.

United Nations Development Programme. *Democracy in Latin America: Toward a Citizens' Democracy.* Buenos Aires: Aguilar, Altea, Taurus, Alfaguara, 2005.

———. *Human Development Report, 2006.* New York: Oxford University Press, 2006.

———. *Human Development Report, 2007.* New York: Oxford University Press, 2007.

———. *Human Development Report, 2008.* New York: Oxford University Press, 2008.

United Nations Food and Agriculture Organization–International Labour Organization (Organización Internacional del Trabajo) (FAO-OIT). *Tenencia de la tierra y desarrollo rural en Centroamérica.* San José, Costa Rica: EDUCA, 1976.

United Nations Observer Mission to Verify the Elections in Nicaragua. *The Situation in Central America: Threats to International Peace and Security Initiatives.* A/44/917. New York: General Assembly of the United Nations, 1990.

Uriarte, M. J. "Fisk: Olvídense de Alemán." *La Prensa,* November 17, 2004. www.laprensa.com.ni.

Utting, Peter. *Economic Adjustment Under the Sandinistas: Policy Reform, Food Security, and Livelihood in Nicaragua.* Geneva: UNRISD, 1991.

Valdivia, Marlene. Interview, Nicaragua Network delegation, July 1, 2007.

Valente, Judith. "D.C.-Area Hispanics Collect Funds to Spread Revolutionary Information." *Washington Post,* February 25, 1980, A20.

Van Cott, Donna Lee. "Constitutional Reform in the Andes: Redefining Indigenous-State Relations." In *Multiculturalism in Latin America: Indigenous Rights, Diversity, and Democracy,* edited by Rachel Seider, 45–73. Basingstoke, UK: Palgrave Macmillan, 2002.

Vanden, Harry E., and Gary Prevost. *Democracy and Socialism in Sandinista Nicaragua.* Boulder, CO: Lynne Rienner, 1993.

Van der Kamp, Rick. *PYMES, Competitividad y SDE en Nicaragua.* Managua: NIT-LAPAN-UCA, 2006.

Vanegas, Leoncio. "'Tal vez Ortega nos cumple': Contras decepcionados de los liberales." *El Nuevo Diario,* September 22, 2006.

Vargas, Oscar René. "¿Dónde está la izquierda?" *El Semanario,* January 17–23, 1997.

Velasquez Sevilla, Mirna. "Jerez declarado inocente." *La Prensa,* October 7, 2004. www.laprensa.com.ni/.

———. "'Limpian' a Byron Jerez." *La Prensa,* March 19, 2005.

———. "Mayoría rechaza sentencia de CSJ." *La Prensa,* September 5, 2005. www.laprensa.com.ni/.

Velázquez Sevilla, Mirna, and Carolos Martínez Moran. "Magistrados 'pactan' por narcodolares." *La Prensa,* December 14, 2005. www.laprensa.com.ni/.

Velásquez Sevilla, Mirna, and Ary Pantoja. "Abortistas excomulgados." *La Prensa,* February 24, 2003. www.laprensa.com.ni.

Verner, Joel. "The Independence of Supreme Courts in Latin America: A Review of the Literature." *Journal of Latin American Studies* 16 (1984): 463–506.

Vértice. "La caída de Arnoldo Alemán." October 14–21, 2004. www.elsalvador.com/.

Vida Humana Internacional (VHI). "Grupos Provida de Centroamérica Felicitan a Bush." *Boletín Electrónico de Vida Humana Internacional (VHI)* 5, no. 15 (March 26, 2002). www.vidahumana.org/.

Vilas, Carlos M. "Asuntos de familia: Clases, linaje, y política en la Nicaragua contemporánea" [Family Affairs: Class, Lineage, and Politics in Contemporary Nicaragua]. *Polémica* 18 (1992): 6–30.

———. "Family Affairs: Class, Lineage, and Politics in Contemporary Nicaragua," *Journal of Latin American Studies* 24 (1992): 309–341.

———. *Between Earthquakes and Volcanoes.* New York: Monthly Review Press, 1995.

———. "El debate interno sandinista." Mímeo. México, DF: CIIH-UNAM, 1991.

———. "Especulaciones sobre una sorpresa: Las elecciones en Nicaragua." *Revista de Ciencias Sociales Desarrollo Económico* 118 (1990): 255–276.

———. "La democratización en los escenarios revolucionarios." In *América Central: Las democracias inciertas,* edited by Ana Sofía Cardenal and Salvador Martí i Puig, 281–330. Madrid: Tecnos, 1998.

———. *Perfiles de la Revolución sandinista.* La Habana: Ediciones Casa de las Américas, 1984.

Villegas S., Jairo. "Reaparece Rosa." *La Prensa,* March 16, 2003.

Von Muhlenbrock, Gisela. *Nicaragua: Amendments to the Electoral Law.* Washington, DC: Hispanic Law Division, Law Library, Library of Congress, April 1989.

Walker, Thomas. *Nicaragua: Living in the Shadow of the Eagle.* Boulder, CO: Westview, 2003.

Walter, Knut. *The Regime of Anastasio Somoza, 1936–1956.* Chapel Hill: University of North Carolina Press, 1993.

Wani: Revista del Caribe Nicaragüense. "En la Costa ¿La frustración mediatizará la democracia? Entrevista con Brooklyn Rivera." No. 9 (1991): 52–56.

Weber, Max. *Economy and Society: An Outline of Interpretive Sociology.* Edited by Gunther Roth and Claus Wittich. Berkeley: University of California Press, 1978.

Weller, Marc, and Stefan Wolff. *Autonomy, Self-Governance, and Conflict Resolution: Innovative Approaches to Institutional Design in Divided Societies.* New York: Routledge, 2005.

Wessel, Lois. "Reproductive Rights in Nicaragua: From the Sandinistas to the Government of Violeta Chamorro." *Feminist Studies* 17 (1991): 537–549.

Wheelock, Jaime. *El gran desafío.* Managua: Editorial Nueva Nicaragua, 1984.

Wickham-Crowley, Timothy P. *Guerrillas and Revolution in Latin America: A Comparative Study of Insurgents and Regimes Since 1956.* Princeton, NJ: Princeton University Press, 1992.

Williams, Harvey. "The Social Programs." In *Revolution and Counterrevolution in Nicaragua,* edited by Thomas W. Walker, 187–212, Boulder, CO: Westview, 1991.

Wolf, Daniel. "Falling Off the Bandwagon: Speculations on Electoral Politics and the Scope Available to Loyal Oppositions in Nicaragua." Paper presented to the Latin American Studies Association, New Orleans, LA, March 18, 1988.

Woodrow Wilson International Center. "Democratic Deficits: Addressing Challenges to Sutainability and Consolidation Around the World." *Noticias* (Spring 2008): 26.

World Bank. *Agriculture in Nicaragua: Promoting Competitiveness and Stimulating Broad-Based Growth.* Washington, DC: World Bank, 2003.

———. *Evaluación de la Pobreza en Nicaragua: Informe Principal.* Informe no. 39736-NI. Washington, DC: World Bank, 2007.

———. *Key Issues in Central America Health Reforms. Diagnosis and Implications.* Vols. 1–2. Report no. 36426-LAC. Washington, DC: World Bank, 2007.

———. *Nicaragua Poverty Assessment.* Vol. 1: Main Report, no. 39736-NI. Washington, DC: World Bank, May 30, 2008.

———. *Nicaragua Poverty Assessment: Raising Welfare and Reducing Vulnerability.* Report no. 26128-NI. Washington, DC: World Bank, 2003.

———. *Nicaragua: Poverty Reduction and Local Development Project.* Washington, DC: World Bank, 2001. www.wds.worldbank.org/.

———. *Nicaragua: Reporte de pobreza.* Report no. 26128-NI. Washington, DC: World Bank, 2003. www.wds.worldbank.org/.

———. *Republic of Nicaragua Poverty Assessment.* Vols. 1–2. Report no. 14038-NI. Washington, DC: World Bank, 1995.

———. *Staff Appraisal Report, Nicaragua, Basic Education Project.* Report no. 13705-NI. Washington, DC: World Bank, 1995.

Zamora, Augusto. *El futuro de Nicaragua.* Managua: Fondo Editorial Cira, 1995.

Zimmerman, Matilde. *Carlos Fonseca and the Nicaraguan Revolution.* Durham, NC: Duke University Press, 2000.

Contributors

Eduardo Baumeister has been an analyst and consultant on agricultural issues in Nicaragua for over thirty years. His current work focuses on poverty and the effects of the economic crisis on the rural poor in Nicaragua and throughout Latin America.

David Close is professor of political science at the Memorial University of Newfoundland, St. John's, NL, Canada. His latest book is *Latin American Politics: An Introduction*.

Dolores Figueroa is an analyst and consultant on development issues. Her work focuses on the role of indigenous women in society, human rights, and women's rights, and her published work has centered on the Caribbean Coast of Nicaragua.

Miguel González teaches in the International Development Studies Program at York University. He is the coauthor (with Haus Petter Buvollen) of *Etnicidad y Nación . . . El Desarrollo de la Autonomía de la Costa Atlántica de Nicaragua, 1987–2007* and coeditor (with Sven Hentoft, Arja Koskinen, and Oiala López) of *The Rama: Struggling for Land and Culture*.

Karen Kampwirth is professor of political science and chair of the Latin American Studies program at Knox College. She has published numerous books and journal articles on Latin American politics, including the edited volume, *Gender and Populism in Latin America: Passionate Politics*.

Salvador Martí i Puig is professor of political science at the University ode Salamanca, Spain. His research interests include indigenous politics in

337

Latin America and social movements. He is the author of *Tiranías, rebeliones y democracia: Itinerarios políticos comparados en Centroamérica* and editor of *Pueblos Indígenas en América Latina: Política y Derechos.*

Elena Martínez Barahona is professor of political science at the University of Salamanca, Spain. Her work focuses on the judiciary in Latin America, and she is the author of *Seeking the Political Role of the Third Governmental Branch: A Comparative Approach to High Courts in Central America.*

Shelley A. McConnell is assistant professor of political science at St. Lawrence University. Formerly she was associate director for Latin America with the Carter Center in Atlanta. She has written extensively about electoral institutions and processes in Nicaragua and Latin America.

Andrés Pérez Baltodano is professor of political science at the University of Western Ontario. His most recent book is *La subversión ética de nuestra realidad: Crisis y renovación del pensamiento crítico latinoamericano.*

Hector Perla Jr. is assistant professor of Latin American and Latino studies at the University of California, Santa Cruz. His research focuses on international relations, especially asymmetrical conflicts, and Central American politics. His publications have appeared in the *Latin American Research Review* and *Latin American Perspectives,* among others.

Rose J. Spalding is professor of political science at DePaul University. Her research interests are political economy and economic and social policy, with a special focus on Nicaragua. She is the author of numerous books, book chapters, and articles on revolutionary and postrevolutionary Nicaragua, including *Capitalists and Revolution in Nicaragua* and *The Political Economy of Revolutionary Nicaragua.*

Index

Violence: and Caribbean coast, 165–167; credibility of Sandinista Revolution enhanced by violence of the contras, 274–275; disappearance of state violence, 58, 63(n31); elections and the reduction in political utility of violence, 60–61; and elections of 1990, 133; FSLN's peaceful opposition during years out of power, 51; and municipal elections of 2008, 63(n31), 302–303; and politics of opposition, 50–51, 294–295; resurgence of violence, harassment, and coercive tactics under second FSLN government, 294–297, 306(n25)

Walker, William, 2
War on Terror, 299, 307(n35)
Washington Area Nicaragua Solidarity Organization, 271–272
Washington Consensus, 68
Water supplies, 226, 266(table)
Weber, Max, 51–52
Wheelock, Jaime, 3, 27, 42(n14), 261
Witness for Peace (WFP), 273, 274, 278, 281
Women. *See* Feminist movement; Zero Hunger program; Zero Usury program

Women's and Children's Police Stations, 191–192
Women's Legal Office, 186
Women's rights, 41(n5)
World Bank, 68, 222, 239(n30), 264

Xochiquetzal Foundation, 186, 189, 190

YATAMA (Miskitu Indian party), 141, 145; ethnic and party representation on RAAN and RAAS regional councils, 176(table); and first FSLN government, 167; FSLN-YATAMA alliance, 161–162, 172–174, 177, 181; and land demarcation bill, 177

Zamora, Francis, 206
Zapata, Roxana, 103–104
Zelaya, Manuel, 291
Zelaya, Rosa Maria, 114(n7), 136–137
Zeledón, Benjamin, 41(n2)
Zero Hunger program, 39, 233, 263–264, 289, 305(n6); described, 229–230, 242(n76)
Zero Unemployment program, 39, 289
Zero Usury program, 39, 232, 289
Zetterberg, Eva, 297

About the Book

HOW HAS THE SANDINISTA NATIONAL LIBERATION FRONT (Frente Sandinista de Liberación Nacional, or FSLN) affected Nicaragua and its politics since the Sandinista Revolution of 1979? Addressing this question, the authors offer a comprehensive assessment, discussing the country's political institutions and public policy, its political culture, and its leadership, as well as the FSLN as a political party. Their focus is on contemporary issues, but they also carefully sketch Nicaragua's history since 1979 to show the evolution of both the FSLN and the nation.

DAVID CLOSE is professor of political science at the Memorial University of Newfoundland. His previous publications on Nicaragua include *Nicaragua: Politics, Economics, and Society* and *Nicaragua: The Chamorro Years*. SALVADOR MARTÍ I PUIG is professor of political science at the University of Salamanca. His most recent book is *Etnicidad, autonomía, y gobernabilidad en América Latina*, and he is also author of, among other works, *Revolution enredada: Nicaragua, 1977–1996*. SHELLEY A. MCCONNELL is assistant professor of political science at St. Lawrence University. Previously, she served as senior research associate director of the Americas Program at the Carter Center.